Contemporary Issues in Criminological Theory and Research: The Role of Social Institutions

Edited by:

Richard Rosenfeld
Kenna Quinet
Crystal Garcia

WADSWORTH
CENGAGE Learning

ISBN-13: 978-1-111-77181-2
ISBN-10: 1-111-77181-2

Wadsworth
20 Davis Drive
Belmont, CA 94002-3098
USA

Cengage Learning is a leading provider of customized learning solutions with office locations around the globe, including Singapore, the United Kingdom, Australia, Mexico, Brazil, and Japan. Locate your local office at:
www.cengage.com/global

Cengage Learning products are represented in Canada by Nelson Education, Ltd.

To learn more about Wadsworth, visit

www.cengage.com/wadsworth

Purchase any of our products at your local college store or at our preferred online store
www.cengagebrain.com

Printed in the United States of America
1 2 3 4 5 6 7 14 13 12 11 10

CONTENTS

INSTITUTIONAL ANALYSIS IN CRIMINOLOGY: AN OVERVIEW OF THE CURRENT VOLUME

FAMILY 11

EDUCATION 49

i

POLITY

ACKNOWLEDGMENTS

The editors would like to thank the five Presidential Panel social institution area chairs: Ron Akers (religion), Shawn Bushway (economy), David Farrington (family), Allison Payne (education), and Thomas Stucky (polity). The editors would also like to thank Tami Barreto and the Indiana University Public Policy Institute for editorial support. Tami Barreto is an associate with the Indiana University Public Policy Institute providing editing and technical review services for faculty and policy analysts. The IU Public Policy Institute (www.policyinstitute.iu.edu) is a collaborative, multidisciplinary research institute within the Indiana University School of Public and Environmental Affairs. The Institute serves as an umbrella organization for research centers affiliated with SPEA, including the Center for Urban Policy and the Environment and the Center for Criminal Justice Research. The Institute also supports the Office of International Community Development and the Indiana Advisory Commission on Intergovernmental Relations (IACIR).

The Center for Criminal Justice Research within PPI works with public safety agencies and social services organizations to provide impartial applied research on criminal justice and public safety issues. CCJR provides analysis, evaluation, and assistance to criminal justice agencies; and community information and education on public safety questions.

Special thanks from the American Society of Criminology and the editors of this volume to the Cengage Learning/Wadsworth team, especially Carolyn Henderson Meier. Owing to the generosity of Cengage Learning/Wadsworth, this volume was provided free of charge to ASC 2010 conference attendees and is available, along with the 2009 volume, for course adoption. We appreciate Cengage Learning/Wadsworth's continued support of the ASC and the excellence in scholarship that it represents. For suggestions on how to use *Contemporary Issues in Criminological Theory and Research: The Role of Social Institutions* in your courses, please see the Teaching Tips column in the ASC newsletter, *The Criminologist*, due out in early 2011.

EDITORS

Richard Rosenfeld is Curators Professor of Criminology and Criminal Justice at the University of Missouri-St. Louis and the 2009-2010 President of the American Society of Criminology. He is an ASC Fellow and has served on the National Academy of Science's Committee on Law and Justice. Professor Rosenfeld has written widely on violent crime, crime statistics, and crime control policy. His current research focuses on explaining changes in crime rates over time.

Kenna Quinet is an Associate Professor of Criminal Justice, Law and Public Safety in the School of Public and Environmental Affairs at Indiana University Purdue University Indianapolis and a Faculty Fellow of the Indiana University Public Policy Institute, Center for Criminal Justice Research, Indiana University. Her primary research interests are homicide, missing persons, unidentified dead, and unclaimed dead. Kenna was co-chair of the 2010 Program Committee for the American Society of Criminology's annual conference in San Francisco.

Crystal A. Garcia is an Associate Professor of Criminal Justice, Law and Public Safety in the School of Public and Environmental Affairs at Indiana University Purdue University Indianapolis. Crystal's primary research and teaching interests include juvenile justice and crime policy, gender-specific programming, the death penalty, reentry, and community corrections. She is currently leading a statewide effort to collect and analyze disproportionate minority contact data in Indiana. Crystal was co-chair of the 2010 Program Committee for the American Society of Criminology's annual conference in San Francisco.

CONTRIBUTORS

Gordon Bazemore is a Professor and Director of the School of Criminology and Criminal Justice at Florida Atlantic University.

Michael L. Benson is a Professor in the School of Criminal Justice at the University of Cincinnati and Director of the School's Distance Learning Program.

Ricky N. Bluthenthal is a Professor of Preventive Medicine at the Institute for Prevention Research and the Keck School of Medicine at the University of Southern California.

Shawn Bushway is an Associate Professor in the School of Criminal Justice and Rockefeller College of Public Affairs & Policy at the University at Albany.

Todd Clear is a Professor and Dean of the School of Criminal Justice, Rutgers University.

Philip J. Cook is the ITT/Sanford Professor of Public Policy, and Professor of Economics and Sociology, at Duke University.

Hilary Cremin is a Senior Lecturer at the University of Cambridge Faculty of Education. She has been researching conflict resolution in schools for over 20 years.

Francis T. Cullen is Distinguished Research Professor of Criminal Justice and Sociology at the University of Cincinnati and a Past President of the American Society of Criminology.

Marie Gottschalk is a Professor in the Department of Political Science at the University of Pennsylvania.

Robert T. Greenbaum is an Associate Professor in the John Glenn School of Public Affairs at The Ohio State University.

Peter W. Greenwood is the Executive Director of the Association for Advancement of Evidence Based Practice.

Ben Grunwald is a doctoral student in the Department of Criminology at the University of Pennsylvania.

Gina Penly Hall is a doctoral student in the School of Criminal Justice at the University at Albany.

Mark S. Hamm is a Professor of Criminology at Indiana State University.

Cyndy Caravelis Hughes is an Assistant Professor at Western Carolina University in the Department of Criminology and Criminal Justice.

Sung Joon Jang is an Associate Professor of Sociology and Research Fellow in the Program on Prosocial Behavior of the Institute for Studies of Religion at Baylor University.

Byron R. Johnson is Distinguished Professor of the Social Sciences and director of the Institute for Studies of Religion at Baylor University.

Aaron Kupchik is an Associate Professor in the Department of Sociology and Criminal Justice at the University of Delaware.

Michael Levi is Professor of Criminology at Cardiff School of Social Sciences, Cardiff University, Wales, UK. He currently also holds an Economic and Social Research Council Professorial Fellowship.

Alan J. Lizotte is a Professor and Dean of the School of Criminal Justice at the University at Albany.

Jens Ludwig is the McCormick Foundation Professor of Social Service Administration, Law, and Public Policy, Director of the University of Chicago Crime Lab, and Co-Director of the National Bureau of Economic Research Working Group on the Economics of Crime.

John M. MacDonald is Associate Professor and Undergraduate Chair of Criminology at the University of Pennsylvania.

Brenda Morrison is an Assistant Professor at the School of Criminology, Simon Fraser University, where she is a Co-Director of the Centre for Restorative Justice.

Daniel S. Nagin is the Teresa and H. John Heinz III University Professor of Public Policy and Statistics at the Heinz College of Carnegie Mellon University.

Alex R. Piquero is a Professor in the College of Criminology and Criminal Justice at Florida State University; Adjunct Professor Key Centre for Ethics, Law, Justice, and Governance, Griffith University Australia; and Co-Editor of the Journal of Quantitative Criminology.

Peter Reuter is a Professor of Public Policy and Criminology at the University of Maryland.

Mara Schiff is an Associate Professor in the School of Criminology and Criminal Justice at Florida Atlantic University.

Jonathan Simon is the Adrian A. Kragen Professor of Law at UC Berkeley.

Robert Stokes is an Associate Professor of Sociology and Coordinator of the Environmental Policy Program in the Department of Culture and Communication at Drexel University.

Michael Tonry is Professor of Law and Public Policy, University of Minnesota Law School, and senior fellow, Netherlands Institute for the Study of Crime and Law Enforcement, Amsterdam.

Jeffrey T. Ulmer is an Associate Professor of Sociology and Crime, Law, and Justice, Penn State University.

Kelly Welch is an Assistant Professor in the Department of Sociology and Criminal Justice at Villanova University, where she focuses on race and crime, sociology of punishment, criminological theory, and social justice.

Brandon C. Welsh is an Associate Professor in the School of Criminology and Criminal Justice at Northeastern University and Senior Research Fellow at the Netherlands Institute for the Study of Crime and Law Enforcement, Amsterdam.

Margaret A. Zahn is a Professor of Sociology at North Carolina State University, Past President of the American Society of Criminology, former dean of Social Sciences at North Carolina State and a former division director at the National Institute of Justice.

Institutional Analysis in Criminology: An Overview of the Current Volume

Richard Rosenfeld

The chapters in this volume were originally presented in Presidential Panels at the 2010 meeting of the American Society of Criminology. Each of the panels directed attention to a major social institution – the family, education, religion, the economy, and the political system – and featured a lead paper and commentaries on the paper written by subject experts. Although far from exhaustive, the volume offers a broad range of theoretical perspectives and research findings, encompassing five major social institutions that should provoke productive discussion and future inquiry on the institutional underpinnings of crime and criminal justice.

Family

The volume leads off with a chapter by Welsh and Piquero that considers the effectiveness of family interventions in preventing antisocial and criminal behavior in children and adolescents. The authors make a strong case for the effectiveness of particular programs and call for greater investment in proven interventions. The commentaries by Ludwig and Greenwood generally endorse the authors' conclusions but raise important questions concerning the presumed greater effectiveness of early interventions that occur before serious antisocial behavior is manifested as opposed to interventions that target delinquent and criminal behavior after they emerge later in the life course. Earlier, they say, is not always or necessarily better, especially when interventions are evaluated on the basis of their cost effectiveness.

The Welsh and Piquero essay also raises a question that the discussants do not take up. The authors argue that effective family interventions can lead to "a safer, more sustainable society." In other words, they maintain that effective *micro-level* programs for families and children can help to reduce the crime rate, a *macro-level* property of groups and societies. That may be true for certain types of crime, but need not be true for other types of crime, particularly those with a strong market orientation such as drug dealing (see the chapter by Bushway and Reuter in this volume). Many crimes have both a supply and demand component. The programs Welsh and Piquero review, including the most effective ones, address the supply side of crime. That is, they would reduce the number of children and adolescents who engage in criminal behavior. But do they affect the demand side, that is, the market for the goods and services that criminals provide?

The demand for illegal goods is widespread in most modern societies, both developed and developing. If you doubt that, ask yourself if you know anyone who has every illegally downloaded music or movies from the Internet. Where the market for crime is strong, as Bushway and Reuter point out, reducing the existing supply of criminal entrepreneurs should increase the price of illegal goods. But that, in turn, should lead more criminal entrepreneurs to enter the market, attracted by the higher returns to crime. For many types of crime, then, effective programs that reduce the supply of criminals may not lead to reductions in the rate of crime, which is established by a dynamic interplay of supply and demand factors.

Institutional analysis, in this case a market analysis, leads to a number of questions regarding the possibilities and limits of early intervention programs with respect to reducing overall levels of crime. What other types of crime, in addition to drug dealing, have both a supply and demand side? Could not effective early interventions reduce *both* the supply of offenders and the demand for crime? Behaviors that are technically against the law, such as underage drinking, driving over the speed limit, and illegally downloading products from the Internet are engaged in by a broad segment of the population. Are most people who commit these crimes products of poor parenting or family dysfunction? How much of a reduction in such crimes should we expect to observe if the most effective early intervention programs were widely implemented?

EDUCATION

One of the principles of the institutional analysis of crime is to consider how the relationships among different institutions influence prevailing levels of crime and strategies of crime control. Social institutions are mutually interdependent and should not be examined in isolation from one another. Under certain conditions, however, institutional interdependence becomes *imbalance*, such that one institution dominates others by devaluing their central functions, forcing them to accommodate to the schedules and routines of the dominant institution, and penetrating them with the imagery and terms of discourse of the dominant institution. Steven Messner and I have applied the concept of institutional imbalance to crime in the United States. We argue that the institutional dominance of the economy weakens the social control and support functions of other institutions, thereby contributing to high rates of crime (Messner & Rosenfeld, 2007).

A similar approach is taken in the chapters on crime and education in the current volume. But here the contention is that the disciplinary regimes of American schools are being recast in the norms, practices, and even the terminology of the criminal justice system. Welch argues that, as in criminal justice, race is a significant cross-cutting dimension of school disciplinary systems, with more punitive sanctions applied to black students than to whites, even controlling for the seriousness of their infractions. In his response to Welch's chapter, Kupchik maintains that racial bias in the schools need not result from the prejudices of individual teachers and administrators. Rather, it is the expected outcome of broader patterns of *social reproduction* – the maintenance of social inequalities – in which the schools play a vital preparatory role. Kupchik's argument implies that modern education and criminal justice are cut from the same institutional cloth. Both are disciplinary institutions that prepare persons for the rigors of life in regimented, stratified societies that exact a high price from those unable or unwilling to fit in (cf. Foucault, 1977).

But education is not just social discipline by other means. At its best, education is liberating. Education introduces students to the life of the mind, to distant or imaginary worlds, to transcendent standards of judgment, truth, and beauty. In a democratic society, education promises personal transformation and social mobility. What kind of disciplinary system befits such an institution? According to Bazemore and Schiff, the first purpose of school discipline should be to repair the harm done to the victim and the community when an important rule is broken. The second purpose is to encourage responsible behavior by all members of the school community. Just discipline in the schools should be *restorative* and not simply punitive. The animating idea behind restorative justice is to mend the social bonds that are broken when rules are violated, including the bond between the rule-breaker and the community.

Interestingly, restorative-justice models first emerged in the criminal and juvenile justice systems and only recently have been tried in schools. They are not easy to implement in either context because they cut against the grain of existing punitive disciplinary principles and procedures. As Bazemore and Schiff indicate, if restorative justice is applied unequally – reserved for students of privilege who violate minor rules and denied to disadvantaged students and those who engage in serious misconduct – it can reproduce the very injustices it is intended to alleviate. Remaking the disciplinary system cannot be accomplished in isolation from transforming the social system of the school. That is the basis for the authors' recommendation to introduce restorative justice practices as part of "whole school" and "communal school" transformations that treat students and adults alike as responsible agents with a voice in setting the rules and procedures for handling violations. That is a tall order, especially when the external constraints on school operations are considered, as Cremin points out. But the chapters on education in this volume are an exemplar of institutional analysis in action and remind us that situating existing organizational practices such as school discipline in broader institutional context has important implications for social change as well as social reproduction.

RELIGION

If institutional analysis is underdeveloped in contemporary criminology (see Rosenfeld, 2010), it is wholly missing in the case of religion. Even analysts, like Messner and Rosenfeld (2007), who preach for greater attention to the role of social institutions in the study of crime manage to overlook religion.[1] Cullen discusses several reasons why religion is criminology's blind spot, which makes all the more remarkable the sheer volume of research that has been devoted to the connection between criminal behavior and religious involvement and belief. Johnson and Jang's chapter provides impressive evidence for religion's role in influencing individual behavior and shaping moral communities. They call attention to a related blind spot in criminology, how our obsession with crime hinders the study of *pro-social* individual behaviors and social processes. Religion, they argue, not only reduces bad behavior, it promotes good behavior.

A key question for future research on religion and crime, at both the micro and macro levels, is whether the religious factor is "unique," to use Ulmer's term, or whether the influence of religion on delinquency and crime is reducible to other determinants of strong attachment to parents and school, resistance to negative peer influences, and cohesive local communities. Is religion just one factor among many that may help to strengthen social bonds, promote pro-social learning, and create a sense of community, or does it have effects that are all its own? If so, what are the special characteristics of religious belief and practice that distinguish their influence from those of the family, education, the economy, and the political system? As Cullen suggests, these are fundamentally criminological questions and one does not have to be a believer or member of a faith community to endorse his call for a criminology of religion.

Religion is in the crime and justice news these days, but not for promoting pro-social behavior. Hamm takes on the difficult and contentious issue of how inmates are radicalized by exposure to religious extremism in prisons, with some going on to commit acts of violence in the name of religion once released. He does not suggest that all or most inmates are vulnerable to prison radicalization, nor that religion is the exclusive source of radicalization and subsequent violence. But he does highlight the influence of Islamist ideologies and recruitment efforts on prison radicalization. Not surprisingly, his chapter prompted constructive criticism from the two discussants.

In their responses, both Clear and Zahn suggest that Hamm exaggerates the threat of radical Islam in American prisons, noting the small number of cases resulting in terrorist violence. But Clear draws an important distinction between physical and "symbolic" violence. In light of the September 11, 2001, terrorist attacks and subsequent attention to Islamic terrorism in the United States, even small numbers of terrorist acts committed in the name of Islam carry heavy symbolic freight and prompt the question of how to respond to rare but serious violence. Clear advises that sheer suppression of prison radicalization may feed the very conditions of alienation and anger that make prisoners vulnerable to violent ideologies in the first place. Zahn points out that, even in Hamm's data, the threat from radical Christian groups in American prisons, such as Christian Identity, rivals or exceeds that of Muslim organizations.

These criticisms underscore the importance of a fundamental criminological insight: violence is *socially constructed*. The perceived threat of violence has as much or more to do with the meanings we attach to violent acts, groups, or doctrines as with the physical harm produced. In that sense all violence is symbolic, whether promoted under the banner of religion, politics, self defense, or honor. The social meanings of violence are not inherent in the act or threat itself. They are affixed to violence by interested parties, including offenders, victims, the groups that advocate on their behalf, agents of social control, and those who seek to understand the causes and consequences of violence and to formulate effective responses.

The prisons are filled with people who have committed violence for non-ideological reasons and will do so again when they are released. They far outnumber those whose violent acts or threats are inspired by membership in extremist groups or devotion to a cause. Criminologists devote considerable attention to explaining the apolitical violence of common criminals but are only just beginning to grapple with the rare, ideologically-charged violence that Hamm has studied. It will be a long while before settled answers emerge to the question of whether different kinds of explanations or social responses are needed for terrorist and non-terrorist violence. That is not surprising because these are among the most difficult theoretical and public policy questions we face today.[2]

ECONOMY

Unlike religion, the economy has always figured prominently in criminological theory and research. Two lines of research exist on the relationship between economic conditions and crime. One is *cross-sectional* in orientation because it investigates the relationship between crime rates and conditions such as poverty and unemployment *across* multiple units (e.g., neighborhoods, cities, nations) observed at a single point in time. The other is *longitudinal* in focus because it examines the relationship between changes in crime and economic conditions *within* social units over time. The results of cross-sectional research are very consistent: high crime rates are associated with high levels of economic deprivation. By contrast, the results of longitudinal research are decidedly mixed: some studies find that crime rates rise with increases in unemployment and other indicators of economic adversity, others find that crime rates fall under the same conditions, and still others find no relationship between changes in crime rates and the economy. The chapters in this volume by MacDonald and colleagues and by Levi reflect the divergent methods and results of the two research traditions on the economy and crime.

MacDonald reports the results of a cross-sectional study of the impact of Business Improvement Districts (BIDs) on adolescent violent crime rates in Los Angeles neighborhoods. The study finds little effect of the BIDs on crime. At the same time, however, it reaffirms the basic results of prior cross-sectional research, to wit, crime rates are higher in more disadvantaged communities. In their reaction essay, Hall and Lizotte question whether any causal inferences can be drawn from the MacDonald study because it did not examine changes in neighborhood crime rates before and after the BIDs were introduced. Greenbaum makes the same point in his reaction paper. What the discussants are saying, in effect, is that establishing the presence (or absence) of cause-effect relationships requires longitudinal data and research methods.

Hall and Lizotte also fault MacDonald and his colleagues for not carrying their cross-sectional analysis a step further by investigating the association between BIDs and adolescent violence under differing neighborhood conditions. For example, the study finds that cohesive neighborhoods in which residents help each other out have lower crime rates than those with less "collective efficacy" (see Sampson, Raudenbush, & Earls, 1997). Is it possible, they wonder, that BIDs are associated with crime rates only in those communities with high levels of collective efficacy? This is an important question, but addressing it with cross-sectional data would still leave open the issue of whether BIDs have a causal influence on adolescent violent crime rates.

Establishing whether one variable does or does not "cause" another is an ages-old philosophical problem that will not be resolved in social science research with longitudinal data and methods of analysis. Greater use of experimental methods that randomly allocate some subjects to a "treatment" condition and others to a "control" condition can increase confidence in the causal nature of research results, but genuine experiments are difficult to perform outside of the laboratory in the real world where the investigator has limited control over research conditions.

Still, longitudinal analysis can alleviate one aspect of the causal puzzle, the question of time order. At least two necessary conditions must be met for establishing that X causes Y: X and Y are associated with one another (such as the association between crime and economic deprivation), and X occurs before and not after Y occurs. Cross-sectional data can meet the condition of association but not the condition of time order between X and Y. Longitudinal data can meet both conditions. That is, data measured over multiple time points can be used to establish whether X and Y vary together and whether changes in X precede or at least do not follow changes in Y. If only the longitudinal analysis of crime were this straightforward.

Levi asks whether rates of fraud – intentional deception for unlawful personal gain – change over time in relation to changing economic conditions. Does fraud increase, as we might expect, when the economy turns down and more people are desperate to find ways of replacing lost income? In his reaction essay, Cook analyzes the longitudinal relationship between fraud rates and the business cycle in the United States. He finds that fraud does increase during economic recessions.

But Levi suggests that the relationship between fraud and economic conditions is quite complex. First, criminal fraud, in all of its manifestations, is not well-measured in the crime data of most nations, so it is difficult to tell whether fraud of various types is moving up or down over time. Second, deteriorating economic conditions do not always or necessarily produce increases in fraud; they may have just the opposite effect. Crime is a product of both criminal *motivations* (the felt need or desire to commit a crime) and criminal *opportunities* (the ease of carrying out the crime). Economic downturns may increase the motivation to engage in criminal behavior but reduce criminal opportunities (Cantor & Land, 1985). But, as Benson argues in his reaction essay, criminal motivations also may run high during periods of economic growth and prosperity if the belief spreads that "the sky's the limit" and "anything goes." Benson also discusses a third precondition for criminal behavior: possessing the requisite knowledge of how to commit the crime. The latter is an especially important element in the commission of crimes involving complex financial transactions, such as those Levi highlights. These are fundamental *theoretical* issues regarding the push-and-pull relationships between economic conditions and crime of all types. They will not be resolved by better data or research methods alone. As these insightful essays clearly reveal, we have a long way to go in building the theories required to explain the multifaceted connections between the economy and crime.

POLITY

The chief output of the political system is public policy. The volume of Presidential papers from last year's meeting of the American Society of Criminology deals directly with crime and justice policy (Frost, Freilich, & Clear, 2009). The current volume is concerned mainly with how social institutions of particular types are implicated in the genesis of crime. The two volumes go hand in hand. Criminal justice policies should be grounded in high-quality theory and research on the institutional origins of crime. But they also should be informed by equally good thinking and evidence regarding the institutional opportunities for and impediments to effective policies to reduce crime and enhance justice. It is fitting, therefore, to close the current volume with essays on punishment policy.

Crime control and the maintenance of internal order are functions of the political systems of modern societies. When crime rates rise and order is threatened, the political system responds, and very often the response is to increase punishment. As crime rates rose in the United States during the 1970s and 1980s, both federal and state officials responded with a series of sentencing and confinement policies that resulted in the dramatic expansion of the prison population. The United States now imprisons a far greater proportion of its population than does any other developed nation, which has led many analysts to characterize the current period in the history of American criminal justice as the era of "mass incarceration."

In their chapters in this volume Nagin and Gottschalk address the promise and prospects, respectively, of reducing mass incarceration. Nagin suggests that targeted policing strategies of proven effectiveness hold the promise of reducing crime *and* incarceration. Gottschalk discusses the prospects of reversing the imprisonment boom during the current economic crisis and concludes that tight public budgets are not sufficient to produce significant reforms in current sentencing policies. In their reaction essays, the discussants generally endorse Nagin and Gottshalk's analyses; they differ mainly on points of emphasis. Bushway and Reuter question whether drug and other market-oriented crimes can be reduced by more effective policing as long as consumer demand for illegal goods remains strong. Simon is somewhat more optimistic than Gottschalk that current resource constraints can set the stage for significant policy reform. Tonry takes issue with some aspects of Nagin's deterrence argument, but suggests that the essential issue is not what criminological research says about more or less effective ways of deterring crime, but, echoing Gottschalk, how politicians will respond. They will like Nagin's conclusion of less crime through better policing, according to Tonry, but not his prescription for getting there: shifting resources from prisons to the police.

These essays highlight both the opportunities for more effective crime-control policies and the institutional impediments to getting them enacted. The opportunities, in Nagin's view, come in the form of advances in policing and in the science base for valid evaluation of the impact of policing on crime. The recent economic crisis could also present an opportunity for reopening constructive public debate on the wisdom and efficacy of current sentencing and imprisonment policies. But, as Gottschalk advises, research evidence and informed debate alone do not change public policy. They must be brought into the policy process by an engaged citizenry that demands public action. To a significant degree, that is how the sentencing reforms that led to mass incarceration were enacted. Those reforms were not simply foisted on a naive public easily duped by cynical politicians. The so-called get-tough criminal justice policies reflected the angry and fearful mood of the times. It is a safe bet, however, that the politicians who responded and in some cases exploited that mood never envisioned that their policies would result in mass incarceration. As Tonry (1995) has argued, the policies of mass incarceration were policies of neglect. The public officials who supported them did not ask what impact they might have on prison populations or racial disparities in imprisonment or public budgets ten or twenty years in the future. They responded myopically to the problems of the day. We live with the consequences.

Elected officials still have distressingly short time horizons, but these times are different. Crime rates have returned to levels not seen since the 1960s. The economic crisis has aroused public anger and fear but not about street crime. Flat crime rates and strained budgets provide an opening for policies that would reduce the costs of mass incarceration. Whether an engaged public will demand more cost-effective crime control policy remains to be seen. But one thing is certain: if crime rates begin to rise again, as a consequence of continued economic stagnation or for other reasons, all bets are off.

REFERENCES

Cantor, D. & Land, K. (1985). Unemployment and crime rates in the Post-World War II United States: A theoretical and empirical analysis. *American Sociological Review 50*, 317-332.

Forst, B. (2009). *Terrorism, crime, and public policy.* New York, NY: Cambridge University Press.

Foucault, M. (1977). *Discipline and punish.* New York, NY: Random House.

Frost, N., Freilich, J., & Clear, T. (2009). *Contemporary issues in criminal justice policy.* Belmont, CA: Wadsworth.

Messner, S. & Rosenfeld, R. (2007). *Crime and the American dream.* Belmont, CA: Wadsworth.

Rosenfeld, R. (2010). Crime and social institutions. *Criminologist 35*, 1, 3-4.

Rosenfeld, R. & Messner, S. (2010). The intellectual origins of institutional-anomie theory. In F. Cullen, C. Lero Jonson, A. Myer, & F. Adler (eds.), *The origins of American criminology: Advances in criminological theory*, Volume 16. New Brunswick, NJ: Transaction Publishers.

Sampson, R., Raudenbush, S., & Earls, F. (1997). Neighborhoods and violent crime: A multilevel study of collective efficacy. *Science 277*, 918–924.

Tonry, M. (1995). *Malign neglect: Race, crime and punishment in America.* New York, NY: Oxford University Press.

ENDNOTES

[1] This is a truly remarkable omission given that Rosenfeld's dissertation advisor was a prominent sociologist of religion who held that crime and religion were two sides of the same coin (see Rosenfeld & Messner, 2010).

[2] See Forst (2009) for an excellent introduction to these issues.

FAMILY

Investing Where It Counts: Preventing Delinquency and Crime with Early Family-Based Programs

Brandon C. Welsh
Alex R. Piquero

Abstract

A policy of early prevention of delinquency and later offending should begin with a focus on the family domain. After decades of rigorous research in the United States and across the Western world – using prospective longitudinal studies – a great deal is known about early risk factors for offending. Some studies point to family factors as the most important, including poor child rearing, poor parental supervision, and inconsistent or harsh discipline. There is also an emerging evidence base on the effectiveness of early family-based programs designed to address these risk factors. Systematic reviews and meta-analyses incorporating the highest quality studies have shown that a number of program models are effective in preventing delinquency and later offending, including nurse home visits and parent management training. Results from our systematic review indicate that early family/parent training is an effective intervention for reducing behavior problems among young children. These programs also produce a wide range of other important benefits for families, including improved school readiness and school performance on the part of children and greater employment and educational opportunities for parents. There is also some evidence that these programs can pay back program costs and produce substantial monetary benefits for society.

Intervening in the early years of the life course to prevent delinquency and later criminal offending is an important component of crime policy at local, state, and national levels. Indeed, it is fair to say that support for early prevention in the United States has never been stronger. Robust bodies of research exist on many fronts, including public opinion (Cullen, Vose, Jonson, & Unnever, 2007; Nagin, Piquero, Scott, & Steinberg, 2006), evidence-based programs (Farrington & Welsh, 2007; Greenwood, 2006), and benefit-cost analyses (Aos, Miller, & Drake, 2006; Duncan, Ludwig, & Magnuson, 2007). This support is not limited to one field of study. As noted by Knudsen, Heckman, Cameron, and Shonkoff (2006, p. 10155), findings of neuroscience, behavioral research, and economics show a "striking convergence on a set of common principles that account for the potent effects of early environment on the capacity of human skill development," which affirms the need for greater investments in disadvantaged children in the early years of life (see also Heckman, 2006).

So where do we begin? We contend that a policy of early prevention of delinquency and later offending should begin with a focus on the social institution of the family. We are not the first to suggest this (see, e.g., Tolan, 2002). This approach does not preclude a focus on the individual child to improve cognitive competencies and skill formation or a focus on the community to improve access to social and economic opportunities. Rather, a focus on the family domain is a starting point and a way of recognizing the profound influence of family on healthy and positive child development.

In this paper we set out the case for this approach. We begin with an overview of the most important early family factors that predict offending. This is followed by a review of the scientific evidence on the effectiveness of early family-based prevention programs. The final part offers some conclusions and discusses implications for policy and research.

EARLY FAMILY RISK FACTORS

The link between the family and crime has been long-standing (Hirschi, 1995) and can easily be considered one of the "facts" of crime. Individual-level focused studies have documented strong relationships between family functioning—especially the supervision and monitoring of children's activities—and delinquency (Loeber & Stouthamer-Loeber, 1986). Two recent summaries of these studies are notable. Wasserman and Seracini (2001) identified three parenting practices that are important for predicting children's conduct problems: (1) parent-child conflict; (2) lack of monitoring; and (3) lack of positive involvement. Farrington (2010) identified six family factors that predict antisocial, delinquent, and criminal behavior: (1) criminal and antisocial parents and siblings; (2) large family size; (3) child-rearing methods (poor supervision, inconsistent discipline, parental coldness, and rejection, low parental involvement with the child); (4) abuse (physical or sexual) and neglect; (5) parental conflict and disrupted families; and (6) other parental features (especially young parents, substance abuse, stress, or depression of parents).

Of these risk factors, two emerge as the strongest. First, we consider the risk factor associated with criminal/antisocial parents, which has produced the oft-replicated finding that offending tends to be concentrated in certain families and transmitted across generations (Farrington, Jolliffe, Loeber, Stouthamer-Loeber, & Kalb, 2001; Thornberry, Freeman-Gallant, Lizotte, Krohn, & Smith, 2003). Farrington and Welsh (2007, pp. 58-60) have put forth several possible explanations to account for this strong pattern of results. First, the intergenerational transmission of offending is part of a larger cycle of antisocial behavior that is due to a shared set of risk factors that repeat themselves over time. Second, assortative mating patterns, such that offenders cohabit with or marry other offenders, sets that stage for a strong social learning and ineffective socialization system. A third explanation focuses on direct and mutual influences of family members on one another, such as younger siblings mimicking the behavior of older siblings. Fourth, criminal parents may disproportionately have delinquent children because of official criminal justice bias against known criminal families, who also tend to be known to official agencies because of other social problems. Lastly, the effect of a criminal parent on offspring antisocial behavior is mediated by environmental and/or genetic mechanisms, which is described in further detail below.

The second strongest risk factor for offspring delinquency concerns poor child-rearing methods, and includes poor parental supervision and inconsistent or harsh discipline (Derzon, 2010; Patterson, 1982). Studies indicate that parents who do not know the whereabouts of their children and parents who do not supervise them from an early age tend to have delinquent children, that harsh/punitive discipline is strongly linked to a child's delinquency, and that erratic/inconsistent discipline also predicts a child's misbehavior. Additionally, psychologists have focused more on parenting styles than parenting practices, including authoritarian, authoritative, and permissive, and have found that authoritarian styles characterized by controlling parents who are especially punitive (Chang, Schwartz, Dodge, & McBride-Chang, 2003; Stormshack, Bierman, McMahon, & Lengua, 2000) and hostile (Williams et al., 2010) tend to be linked to conduct problems and delinquency.

More generally, of these two child-rearing risk factors, poor parental supervision is usually the strongest and most replicable predictor of offending. To the extent that parents fail to monitor their child's behavior, fail to recognize their deviance, inadequately/adversely punish their deviance, and fail to use consistent and contingent rewards and penalties, effective prosocial socialization processes become compromised such that children will find it difficult to adopt strong self-control (Gottfredson & Hirschi, 1990). Failure in developing strong self-control will lead to poor self-regulation skills that segue into problems in behavior, school performance, and employment prospects.

At the same that there is good and consistent evidence regarding family risk factors for criminal offending that operates directly to crime and indirectly through the development of offspring self-control, it needs to be emphasized that families do not exist in isolation from their social environments. Thus, while there is much shared relation among the various familial risk factors, they also tend to be related to the contexts in which families find themselves in (poor housing, disadvantaged neighborhoods, problematic schools, and so forth) (Piquero & Lawton, 2002). As such, it is important to consider how familial factors are implicated in a more general causal process as there may be sequential and/or moderating effects.

With regard to sequential effects, it may be that socioeconomic and neighborhood factors influence family factors which in turn influence individual factors, which in turn influence offending. Disadvantaged neighborhoods are likely to have few resources that are promotive and supportive of effective parenting, have high residential turnover, and lack community sources of social control and collective efficacy. As a result, nuclear families have little opportunity and few resources that can help them become effective parents and effectively socialize their children. This "hampered parenting effect" thus leads to problems in monitoring and socialization such that their children do not adopt the prosocial characteristics and decision-making strategies that are associated with successful self-control and educational attainment, two critical factors that relate strongly to gainful employment prospects.

With regard to moderating effects, it may be that family factors relate to effective socialization and, in turn, delinquency/offending in different ways across gender, age, race/ethnicity, and neighborhood location. For example, it may be that males and minorities – both of whom are over-represented in (serious) criminal activity and exhibit lower self-control – are more susceptible to familial risk factors. Males and minorities, for example, may be supervised less than females and may be subject to more inconsistent disciplinary practices, both of which hamper socialization efforts and, in turn, produce self-control deficiencies. Thus, these groups may have more (i.e., a higher average) of the familial risk factors than their counterparts and consequently exhibit greater offending. Also, research has started to show that neighborhoods play a role in influencing child behavior via familial socialization practices (Leventhal & Brooks-Gunn, 2000), and that these effects are strongest in the first decade of life and wane over time. For example, studies are finding that while offspring self-control is strongly influenced by familial characteristics, there is some non-negligible neighborhood effects such that poor self-controlled children are disproportionately found in the poorest of neighborhoods, which also tend to have the most familial disadvantage and compromised familial supervision and socialization practices (Pratt, Turner, & Piquero, 2004; Gibson, Sullivan, Jones, & Piquero, 2010). Although these effects are not as strong as those exhibited by individual and familial risk factors, they do exert a non-trivial effect on family development and socialization.

A few studies that examined the interplay between communities and families on delinquency are worth highlighting. Piquero and Lawton (2002) used data from the Baltimore site of the National Collaborative Perinatal Project to examine the contribution of individual (through low birth weight), familial (through family adversity), and neighborhood (through disadvantage) to life-course-persistent styles of criminal offending and found that individual risk was exacerbated in disadvantaged familial and neighborhood contexts to relate to chronic styles of offending in adulthood. In a longitudinal study examining the interrelations among collective efficacy, authoritative parenting, delinquent peer association, and delinquency of a large sample of African-Americans, Simons, Simons, Burt, Brody, & Cutrona (2005) integrated community- and family-level processes and found: an association between increases in collective efficacy within a community and increases in authoritative parenting; that authoritative parenting and collective efficacy reduced delinquent peer affiliation and delinquency; and that the protective effect of authoritative parenting was even stronger in communities characterized by high collective efficacy. Although these two studies are important efforts linking individual, familial, and neighborhood contexts, sorting out these (and other) mediating/moderating effects regarding the family-crime relationship is important theoretically, difficult methodologically and statistically, yet paramount for designing and implementing policy efforts.

To be sure, research on familial risk factors tends to be focused on studying the childhood phase of the life-course, where researchers have been concerned with how these risk factors affect the socialization process and, in turn, delinquency and offending. However, familial factors are also relevant during adolescence and adulthood phases of the life-course, and in turn relate to antisocial and criminal activity therein. Although it is true that adolescence is a time where individuals shift from family- to peer-oriented contexts and activities, it does not negate the potential and continual influence of familial factors for predicting delinquency. Recently, Hoeve et al. (2007) conducted a cross-national comparison of the United States and the Netherlands on the long-term effects of parenting and familial factors on male young adult delinquency and found that while previously identified family factors such as socioeconomic status, supervision, punishment, and attachment were unrelated to delinquency in young adulthood, the lack of orderly and structured activities within the family during adolescence was a strong predictor of delinquency in young adulthood, even after controlling for prior aggression and demographic variables.

In adulthood, the most commonly assessed familial factor is marriage. A consistent set of studies, using different samples from different locations, report that marriage serves to reduce criminal activity among males (Horney, Osgood, & Marshall, 1995; King, Massoglia, & MacMillan, 2007; Laub & Sampson, 2003; Piquero, Brame, Mazerolle, & Haapanen, 2002; Sampson & Laub, 1993; Theobold & Farrington, 2009). The effect appears both within (where some studies have focused on men who were followed up before and after marriage, and otherwise have used propensity score matching to match married and unmarried men on their prior probability of getting married) and between (comparing married to unmarried males) individuals. Further probing of the marriage effect also finds that good quality marriages, especially those that have a history of investment in the marriage, also serve to reduce criminal activity and aid in the desistance process. Interestingly, it is worth noting that it is marriage per se and not involvement in some other relationship (i.e., girlfriend) where this marriage effect is observed (Horney et al., 1995; Piquero et al., 2002). But the positive marriage effect does not appear in the small set of studies that have investigated this question among females. Additionally, to the extent that children can be considered a family factor the empirical record is not very strong or clear in establishing any preventive effect on criminal activity.

THE EVIDENCE ON EFFECTIVENESS

Broadly speaking, family-based prevention programs have developed along two major fields of study: psychology and public health. When delivered by psychologists, these programs are often classified into parent management training, functional family therapy, or family preservation (Wasserman & Miller, 1998). Typically, they attempt to change the social contingencies in the family environment so that children are rewarded in some way for appropriate or prosocial behaviors and punished in some way for inappropriate or antisocial behaviors. Family-based programs delivered by health professionals such as nurses are typically less behavioral, mainly providing advice and guidance to parents or general parent education. Home visiting with new parents is one of the more popular forms of this type of family intervention (Olds, Sadler, & Kitzman, 2007).

Within these fields of study, there is an emerging evidence base on the effectiveness of early family-based programs designed to address some of the most important familial risk factors for delinquency. Systematic reviews and meta-analyses (which involves the statistical or quantitative analysis of the results of prior research studies and is reported as an effect size) incorporating the highest quality studies have shown that a number of program models are effective in preventing delinquency and later offending, including nurse home visits and parent management training (PMT).

Two recent reviews capture the broad-scale effectiveness of family-based prevention programs. Manning, Homel, & Smith (2010) carried out a meta-analysis of the effects of early developmental prevention programs for children up to age 5 years on delinquency and other outcomes in adolescence. Eleven high-quality studies were included that covered a variety of program modalities: structured preschool, center-based developmental day care, home visitation, family support services, and parental education (improvement of core parenting skills). Results show significant effects across a number of important domain outcomes, including educational success (mean effect size = 0.53), delinquency/deviance (0.48), cognitive development (0.34), involvement in the justice system (0.24), and family well-being (0.18). Program duration and intensity were associated with larger effect sizes, but not multi-component programs.

We (Piquero, Farrington, Welsh, Tremblay, & Jennings, 2009) carried out a systematic review and meta-analysis of the effects of early family/parent training programs for children up to age 5 years on antisocial behavior and delinquency. The review, which included 55 randomized controlled experiments, investigated the full range of these programs, including home visits, parent education plus daycare, and PMT. Results indicate that early family/parent training is an effective intervention for reducing antisocial behavior and delinquency, with a mean effect size of 0.35. These programs also produce a wide range of other important benefits for families, including improved school readiness and school performance on the part of children and greater employment and educational opportunities for parents. Significant differences were not detected across program type (traditional parent training versus home visiting) or outcome source (parent, teacher, or direct observer reports).

PARENT EDUCATION

Home visiting with new parents, especially mothers, is a common method of delivering the family-based intervention known as general parent education. Home visits focus on educating parents to improve the life chances of children from a very young age, often at birth and sometimes in the final trimester of pregnancy. Some of the main goals include the prevention of preterm or low weight births, the promotion of healthy child development or school readiness, and the prevention of child abuse and neglect (Gomby, Culross, & Behrman, 1999, p. 4). Home visits very often also serve to improve parental well being, linking parents to community resources to help with employment, education, or addiction recovery. Home visitors are usually nurses or other health professionals with a diverse array of skills in working with families.

Farrington and Welsh (2007) carried out a meta-analysis that included four home visitation programs (all randomized controlled experiments). It was found that this form of early intervention was effective in preventing antisocial behavior and delinquency, corresponding to a significant 12 percentage point differential (e.g., from 50 percent in a control group to 38% percent in an experimental group).

Bilukha et al. (2005) carried out a systematic review on the effects of home visitation on violence. Four studies were included that reported the effects of home visitation programs on violence by the visited children. Mixed results were found for effects on criminal violence (in adolescence) and child externalizing behavior across the four programs: two reported desirable but nonsignificant effects; one reported a significant desirable effect; and one reported mixed results. The review also assessed, using these four and many other studies, the effectiveness of early childhood home visitation on parental violence, intimate partner violence, and child maltreatment. For the first two outcomes, there was insufficient evidence to make a determination of effectiveness. Strong evidence of effectiveness was found for home visiting programs in preventing child abuse and neglect.

The best known home visiting program, and the only one with a direct measure of delinquency, is the Nurse-Family Partnership (NFP) initially carried out in Elmira, New York, by David Olds (see Olds et al., 2007). Four hundred first time mothers were randomly assigned to receive home visits from nurses during pregnancy, or to receive visits both during pregnancy and during the first two years of life, or to a control group who received no visits. Each visit lasted just over one hour and the mothers were visited on average every two weeks. The home visitors gave advice about prenatal and postnatal care of the child, about infant development, and about the importance of proper nutrition and avoiding smoking and drinking during pregnancy.

The results of the experiment showed that postnatal home visits caused a significant decrease in recorded child physical abuse and neglect during the first two years of life, especially by poor, unmarried, teenage mothers (Olds, Henderson, Chamberlin, & Tatelbaum, 1986), and in a 15-year follow-up, significantly fewer experimental compared to control group mothers were identified as perpetrators of child abuse and neglect (Olds et al., 1997). At the age of 15, children of the higher risk mothers who received home visits incurred significantly fewer arrests than controls (Olds et al., 1998). In the latest follow-up at age 19, compared to their control counterparts, girls of the full sample of mothers had incurred significantly fewer arrests and convictions and girls of the higher risk mothers had significantly fewer children of their own and less Medicaid use; few program effects were observed for the boys (Eckenrode et al., 2010). Several benefit-cost analyses (of the 15-year follow-up) show that the benefits of NFP outweigh its costs for the higher risk mothers. Greenwood et al. (2001) measured benefits to the government or taxpayer (welfare, education, employment, and criminal justice) not benefits to crime victims consequent upon reduced crimes. Aos, Lieb, Mayfield, Miller, and Pennucci (2004) measured a somewhat different range of benefits to the government (education, public assistance, substance abuse, teen pregnancy, child abuse and neglect, and criminal justice), as well as tangible benefits to crime victims. Both reported that benefits were about 3-4 times every dollar spent on the program.

PARENT MANAGEMENT TRAINING (PMT)

Patterson (1982) developed behavioral PMT. His careful observations of parent-child interaction showed that parents of antisocial children were deficient in their methods of child rearing. These parents failed to tell their children how they were expected to behave, failed to monitor their behavior to ensure that it was desirable, and failed to enforce rules promptly and unambiguously with appropriate rewards and penalties. The parents of antisocial children used more punishment (such as scolding, shouting, or threatening), but failed to make it contingent on the child's behavior.

Patterson attempted to train these parents in effective child rearing methods, namely, noticing what a child is doing, monitoring behavior over long periods, clearly stating house rules, making rewards and punishments contingent on behavior, and negotiating disagreements so that conflicts and crises did not escalate. His treatment was shown to be effective in reducing child stealing and antisocial behavior over short periods in small-scale studies (Patterson, Chamberlain, & Reid, 1982; Patterson, Reid, & Dishion, 1992).

Serketich and Dumas (1996) carried out a meta-analysis of 26 controlled studies of behavioral parent training (also called PMT) with young children up to age 10. Most were based on small numbers (average total sample size was 29), and most were randomized experiments. They concluded that PMT was effective in reducing child antisocial behavior, especially for (relatively) older children.

Farrington and Welsh (2007; see also Farrington & Welsh, 2003) carried out a meta-analysis that included 10 high quality evaluations of PMT programs and found that this type of early intervention produced a significant 20 percentage point reduction in antisocial behavior and delinquency (e.g., from 50 percent in a control group to 30 percent in an experimental group). Each of the 10 programs aimed to teach parents to use rewards and punishments consistently and contingently in child rearing. The programs were usually delivered in guided group meetings of parents, including role-playing and modeling exercises, and 3 of the programs were delivered by videotape. Just 1 of the 10 programs combined PMT with another intervention (skills training).

One example of an effective PMT program is Guiding Good Choices (Mason, Kosterman, Hawkins, Haggerty, & Spoth, 2003). This is a brief (5 weeks) universal program for parents of children aged 10-14. Among its many components, it helps parents to develop skills for establishing and communicating clear behavioral expectations, monitoring their children's behavior, and consistently enforcing family rules, as well as providing training in skills to manage and reduce family conflict. In a 3.5 year follow-up of a randomized experiment involving parents of 429 11-year-olds, adolescents whose parents were assigned to Guiding Good Choices had significantly lower rates of delinquent behavior and substance use than controls. A benefit-cost analysis found that for every dollar spent on the program, more than $11 were saved to society in the form of reduced costs to the justice system and crime victims (Aos et al., 2004).

CONCLUSIONS

There is much research and consistency in findings with respect to family factors that predict offending. Some of the most important include poor child rearing, poor parental supervision, and inconsistent or harsh discipline. There is also an emerging evidence base on the effectiveness of early family-based programs designed to address these risk factors, including nurse home visits and parent management training. These programs can assist parents and families in preventing antisocial and delinquent behavior by providing them with the tools necessary to engage in effective child rearing. These programs also produce a wide range of other important benefits for families, including improved school readiness and school performance on the part of children and greater employment and educational opportunities for parents. There is also some evidence that these programs can pay back program costs and produce substantial monetary benefits for society. Taken together, these developments signal the importance of the family domain and the need for this approach to play a central role in early prevention policy. They also capture the power of prevention and reiterate its importance as a key component of crime policy at local, state, and national levels.

Making further investments in early family-based prevention calls attention to several key policy and research issues. Family programs sometimes involve other interventions targeted on other domains (e.g., individual, community, school). One the hand, this can make it difficult to establish that it is the family intervention that caused the observed effects. On the other hand, there is no reason to believe that this would compromise the effectiveness of the family intervention. There is ample evidence of effective family-based prevention programs that take this approach (e.g., Lally, Mangione, & Honig, 1988; Mason et al., 2003). We were surprised by Manning et al.'s (2010) finding that multi-modal programs are not more effective than single modal ones, but their finding was not restricted to delinquency outcomes. It has been a consistent finding in the early prevention literature that comprehensive programs are more effective in preventing delinquency and later offending (Tremblay & Craig, 1995; Wasserman & Miller, 1998).

It is also important to be mindful of the threat of attenuation of program effects upon wider dissemination of programs. It is a widely held view that desirable effects on delinquency and other outcomes from early prevention trials will attenuate once they are "scaled-up" or "rolled-out" for wider public use (Dodge, 2001). This, of course, goes well beyond family-based prevention programs, but it is crucial to address because many of the programs employ small samples and have been evaluated under laboratory-like conditions, what may be termed efficacy trials. Attending to key factors such as population heterogeneity, fidelity to the model, and implementation context will help to mitigate this and may even enhance program effects (Welsh, Sullivan, & Olds, 2010).

We could benefit from further empirical work on: the genetic/biological link regarding family factors and delinquency (Raine, Brennan, & Farrington, 1997); sorting out the precise causal mechanisms that link family factors to antisocial behavior (Farrington, 2010); exploring moderating and interaction effects of family-based programs (Farrington & Welsh, 2007); and studying how antisocial children provoke differential parental socialization efforts (Lytton, 1990; Moffitt, 1993). It would also be desirable to know more about the economic efficiency of early family-based prevention programs. Future experiments on family-based interventions should include benefit-cost analyses that are both methodologically rigorous and comprehensive in their coverage of program costs and benefits.

Whether it is thinking about a higher-skilled, more productive labor force or a safer, more sustainable society in the years to come, Knudsen et al. (2006, p. 10161) remind us of where society needs to invest: "Prevention is more effective and less costly than remediation, and earlier is far better than later." Starting with a focus on the family will help make this happen.

REFERENCES

Aos, S., Lieb, R., Mayfield, J., Miller, M., & Pennucci, A. (2004). *Benefits and costs of prevention and early intervention programs for youth.* Olympia, WA: Washington State Institute for Public Policy.

Aos, S., Miller, M., & Drake, E. (2006). *Evidence-based public policy options to reduce future prison construction, criminal justice costs, and crime rates.* Olympia, WA: Washington State Institute for Public Policy.

Bilukha, O., Hahn, R., Crosby, A., Fullilove, M., Liberman, A., Moscicki, E., Snyder, S., Tuma, F., Corso, P., Schofield, A., & Briss, P. (2005). The effectiveness of early childhood home visitation in preventing violence: A systematic review. *American Journal of Preventive Medicine, 28*(2S1), 11-39.

Chang, L., Schwartz, D., Dodge, K., & McBride-Chang, C. (2003). Harsh parenting in relation to child emotion regulation and aggression. *Journal of Family Psychology, 17,* 598-606.

Cullen, F., Vose, B., Jonson, C., & Unnever, J. (2007). Public support for early intervention: Is child saving a 'habit of the heart'? *Victims and Offenders, 2,* 108-124.

Derzon, J. (2010). The correspondence of family features with problem, aggressive, criminal, and violent behavior: A meta-analysis. *Journal of Experimental Criminology, 6,* in press.

Dodge, K. (2001). The science of youth violence prevention: Progressing from developmental epidemiology to efficacy to effectiveness to public policy. *American Journal of Preventive Medicine, 20*(1S), 63-70.

Duncan, G., Ludwig, J., & Magnuson, K. (2007). Reducing poverty through preschool interventions. *The Future of Children, 17*(2), 143-160.

Eckenrode, J., Campa, M., Luckey, D., Henderson, C., Cole, R., Kitzman, H., Anson, E., Sidora-Arcoleo, K., Powers, J., & Olds, D. (2010). Long-term effects of prenatal and infancy nurse home visitation on the life course of youths: 19-year follow-up a randomized trial. *Archives of Pediatrics and Adolescent Medicine, 164,* 9-15.

Farrington, D. (2010). Families and crime. In J. Wilson & J. Petersilia (eds.), *Crime: Public policies for crime control,* 3rd ed. New York, NY: Oxford University Press, in press.

Farrington, D., Jolliffe, D., Loeber, R., Stouthamer-Loeber, M., & Kalb, L. (2001). The concentration of offenders in families, and family criminality in the prediction of boys' delinquency. *Journal of Adolescence, 24,* 579-596.

Farrington, D. & Welsh, B. (2003). Family-based prevention of offending: A meta-analysis. *Australian and New Zealand Journal of Criminology, 36,* 127-151.

Farrington, D. & Welsh, B. (2007). *Saving children from a life of crime: Early risk factors and effective interventions.* New York, NY: Oxford University Press.

Gibson, C., Sullivan, C., Jones, S., & Piquero, A. (2010). Assessing neighborhood influences on children's self-control. *Journal of Research in Crime and Delinquency, 47*, 31-62.

Gomby, D., Culross, P., & Behrman, R. (1999). Home visiting: Recent program evaluations—analysis and recommendations. *The Future of Children, 9*(1), 4-26.

Gottfredson, M., & Hirschi, T. (1990). *A general theory of crime.* Stanford, CA: Stanford University Press.

Greenwood, P. (2006). *Changing lives: Delinquency prevention as crime-control policy.* Chicago, IL: University of Chicago Press.

Greenwood, P., Karoly, L., Everingham, S., Houbé, J., Kilburn, M., Rydell, C., Sanders, M., & Chiesa, J. (2001). Estimating the costs and benefits of early childhood interventions: Nurse home visits and the Perry Preschool. In B. Welsh, D. Farrington, & L. Sherman (Eds.), *Costs and benefits of preventing crime* (pp. 123-148). Boulder, CO: Westview Press.

Heckman, J. (2006). Skill formation and the economics of investing in disadvantaged children. *Science, 312*, 1900-1902.

Hirschi, T. (1995). The family. In J. Wilson & J. Petersilia (eds.), *Crime.* Oakland, CA: Institute for Contemporary Studies Press.

Hoeve, M., Smeenk, W., Loeber, R., Stouthamer-Loeber, M., van der Laan, P., Gerris, J., & Dubas, J. (2007). Long-term effects of parenting and family characteristics on delinquency of male young adults. *European Journal of Criminology, 4*, 161-194.

Horney, J., Osgood, D., & Marshall, I. (1995). Criminal careers in the short-term: Intra-individual variability in crime and its relation to local life circumstances. *American Sociological Review, 60*, 655-673.

King, R., Massoglia, M., & MacMillan, R. (2007). The context of marriage and crime: Gender, the propensity to marry, and offending in early adulthood. *Criminology, 45*, 33-65.

Knudsen, E., Heckman, J., Cameron, J., & Shonkoff, J. (2006). Economic, neurobiological, and behavior perspectives on building America's future workforce. *Proceedings of the National Academy of Sciences, 103*, 10155-10162.

Lally, J., Mangione, P., & Honig, A. (1988). The Syracuse University Family Development Research Program: Long-range impact of an early intervention with low-income children and their families. In D. R. Powell (ed.), *Parent education as early childhood intervention* (pp. 79-104). Norwood, NJ: Ablex.

Laub, J., & Sampson, R. (2003). *Shared beginnings, divergent lives: Delinquent boys to age 70.* Cambridge, MA: Harvard University Press.

Leventhal, T., & Brooks-Gunn, J. (2000). The neighborhoods they live in: The effects of neighborhood residence on child and adolescent outcomes. *Psychological Bulletin, 126*, 309-337.

Loeber, R. & Stouthamer-Loeber, M. (1986). Family factors as correlates and predictors of juvenile conduct problems and delinquency. In M. Tonry

& N. Morris (eds.), *Crime and justice: A review of research*, vol. 7 (pp. 29-149). Chicago, IL: University of Chicago Press.

Lytton, H. (1990). Child and parent effects in boys' conduct disorder: A reinterpretation. *Developmental Psychology, 26*, 683-697.

Manning, M., Homel, R., & Smith, C. (2010). A meta-analysis of the effects of early developmental prevention programs in at-risk populations on non-health outcomes in adolescence. *Children and Youth Services Review, 32*, 506-519.

Mason, W., Kosterman, R., Hawkins, J., Haggerty, K., & Spoth, R. (2003). Reducing adolescents' growth in substance use and delinquency: Randomized trial effects of a parent-training prevention intervention. *Prevention Science, 4*, 203-212.

Moffitt, T. (1993). Adolescence-limited and life-course-persistent antisocial behavior: A developmental taxonomy. *Psychological Review, 100*, 674-701.

Nagin, D., Piquero, A., Scott, E., & Steinberg, L. (2006). Public preferences for rehabilitation versus incarceration of juvenile offenders: Evidence from a contingent valuation survey. *Criminology and Public Policy, 5*, 627-652.

Olds, D., Eckenrode, J., Henderson, C., Kitzman, H., Powers, J., Cole, R., Sidora, K., Morris, P., Pettitt, L., & Luckey, D. (1997). Long-term effects of home visitation on maternal life course and child abuse and neglect: Fifteen-year follow-up of a randomized trial. *Journal of the American Medical Association, 278*, 637-643.

Olds, D., Henderson, C., Chamberlin, R., & Tatelbaum, R. (1986). Preventing child abuse and neglect: A randomized trial of nurse home visitation. *Pediatrics, 78*, 65-78.

Olds, D., Henderson, C., Cole, R., Eckenrode, J., Kitzman, H., Luckey, D., Pettitt, L. M., Sidora, K., Morris, P., & Powers, J. (1998). Long-term effects of nurse home visitation on children's criminal and antisocial behavior: 15-year follow-up of a randomized controlled trial. *Journal of the American Medical Association, 280*, 1238-1244.

Olds, D., Sadler, L., & Kitzman, H. (2007). Programs for parents of infants and toddlers: Recent evidence from randomized trials. *Journal of Child Psychology and Psychiatry, 48*, 355-391.

Patterson, G. (1982). *Coercive family process*. Eugene, OR: Castalia.

Patterson, G., Chamberlain, P., & Reid, J. (1982). A comparative evaluation of a parent training program. *Behavior Therapy, 13*, 638-650.

Patterson, G., Reid, J., & Dishion, T. (1992). *Antisocial boys*. Eugene, OR: Castalia.

Piquero, A., Brame, R., Mazerolle, P., & Haapanen, R. (2002). Crime in emerging adulthood. *Criminology, 40*, 137-169.

Piquero, A., Farrington, D., Welsh, B., Tremblay, R., & Jennings, W. (2009). Effects of early family/parent training programs on antisocial behavior and delinquency. *Journal of Experimental Criminology, 5*, 83-120.

Piquero, A., & Lawton, B. (2002). Individual risk for crime is exacerbated in poor familial and neighborhood contexts: The contribution of low birth weight, family adversity, and neighborhood disadvantage to life-course-persistent offending. In R. Stettersten & T. Owens (eds.), *Advances in life-course research: New frontiers in socialization*, vol. 7 (pp. 263-298). London: JAI Press.

Pratt, T., Turner, M., & Piquero, A. R. (2004). Parental socialization and community context: A longitudinal analysis of the structural sources of social control. *Journal of Research in Crime and Delinquency, 41*, 219-243.

Raine, A., Brennan, P., & Farrington, D. (1997). Biosocial bases of violence: Conceptual and theoretical issues. In A. Raine, P. A. Brennan, D. Farrington, & S. Mednick (eds.), *Biosocial bases of violence*. New York, NY: Plenum.

Sampson, R. & Laub, J. (1993). *Crime in the making: Pathways and turning points through life*. Cambridge, MA: Harvard University Press.

Serketich, W. & Dumas, J. (1996). The effectiveness of behavioral parent training to modify antisocial behavior in children: A meta-analysis. *Behavior Therapy, 27*, 171-186.

Simons, R., Simons, L., Burt, C., Brody, G., & Cutrona, C. (2005). Collective efficacy, authoritative parenting, and delinquency: A longitudinal test of a model integrating community- and family-level processes. *Criminology, 43*, 989-1030.

Stormschak, E., Bierman, K., McMahon, R., & Lengua, L. (2000). Parenting practices and child disruptive behavior problems in early elementary school. *Journal of Clinical Child and Adolescent Psychology, 29*, 17-29.

Theobald, D., & Farrington, D. (2009). Effects of getting married on offending: Results from a prospective longitudinal survey of males. *European Journal of Criminology, 6*, 496-516.

Thornberry, T., Freeman-Gallant, A., Lizotte, A., Krohn, M., & Smith, C. (2003). Linked lives: The intergenerational transmission of antisocial behavior. *Journal of Abnormal Child Psychology, 31*, 171-184.

Tolan, P. (2002). Crime prevention: Focus on youth. In J. Wilson & J. Petersilia (eds.), *Crime: Public policies for crime control*, 2nd ed. (pp. 109-127). Oakland, CA: Institute for Contemporary Studies Press.

Tremblay, R. & Craig, W. (1995). Developmental crime prevention. In M. Tonry & D. Farrington (Eds.), *Building a safer society: Strategic approaches to crime prevention* (pp. 151-236). Chicago, IL: University of Chicago Press.

Wasserman, G., & Miller, L. (1998). The prevention of serious and violent juvenile offending. In R. Loeber & D. Farrington (eds.), *Serious and violent juvenile offenders: Risk factors and successful interventions* (pp. 197-247). Thousand Oaks, CA: Sage.

Wasserman, G., & Seracini, A. (2001). Family risk factors and interventions. In R. Loeber & D. Farrington (Eds.), *Child delinquents: Development, intervention and service needs* (pp. 165-189). Thousand Oaks, CA: Sage.

Welsh, B., Sullivan, C., & Olds, D. (2010). When early crime prevention goes to scale: A new look at the evidence. *Prevention Science, 11*, 115-125.

Williams, L., Degnan, K., Perez-Edgar, K., Henderson, H., Rubin, K., Pine, D., Steinberg, L., & Fox, N. (2010). Impact of behavioral inhibition and parenting style on internalizing and externalizing problems from childhood through adolescence. *Journal of Abnormal Child Psychology*, forthcoming.

Authors' Note: We are grateful to David Farrington for helpful comments.

Cost-Effective Crime Prevention

Jens Ludwig[*]

Introduction

Brandon Welsh and Alex Piquero argue that we should be devoting additional resources to early prevention programs that work with the families of disadvantaged children, which they suggest can help reduce delinquency, and might even be cost effective – that is, these programs may generate benefits to society that outweigh program costs. Their paper concludes with a more general endorsement of early intervention, including a quote from a paper in the *Proceedings of the National Academy of Sciences* by Eric Knudsen and co-authors (2006, p. 10161): "Prevention is more effective and less costly than remediation, and earlier is far better than later."

It is hard not to be sympathetic with their basic argument. The incarceration rate is currently so high in the United States that it certainly seems plausible that diverting a few billion dollars on the margin from prisons to social programs might represent a budget-neutral way to reduce delinquency and crime. This is not a new idea. Concern about the limits of mass incarceration go back at least to 1820s Paris, when what was viewed as the "apparent failure of French penal strategies" prompted calls to focus more attention on the "root causes" of crime such as poverty and income inequality (Beirne, 1987, p. 1143).

In what follows I would like to elaborate on four points that are either briefly touched on or implied by Welsh and Piquero's very interesting paper:

1. How strong is the empirical evidence in support of the interventions that Welsh and Piquero are promoting?
2. Is it really the case that programs that focus on working with families dominate programs that focus on providing services directly to children?
3. Is it always necessarily true that "prevention is more effective and less costly than remediation, and earlier is far better than later"?
4. If early childhood intervention is such a good idea, why aren't we already doing lots more of it?

Empirical Support for the Recommended Interventions

The value of the Welsh and Piquero recommendation to invest additional resources in early family-focused interventions hinges on the internal and external validity of the empirical studies of previous programs along these lines. Welsh and Piquero's review is more transparent than most about the internal validity of the research studies on which they are relying, in the sense that they are clear about the degree to which they are referring to evidence from a collection of experiments or instead to a set of studies that mix together findings from experimental and non-experimental research designs. At the same time lingering concerns about the external validity of the available studies adds an element of uncertainty to what exactly would happen in practice if policymakers followed Welsh and Piquero's recommendations.

While I greatly value Welsh and Piquero's emphasis on being transparent about the types of studies they are drawing on to support each of their key factual claims, many other meta-analyses pool together the results from true randomized experiments with the results of different non-experimental studies of varying quality. This practice strikes me as potentially problematic. The key practical challenge is to think about how much weight to give to non-experimental studies compared to randomized experiments. For example, a recent meta-analysis by Drake, Aos, and Miller (2009) follows the "University of Maryland" rule from Sherman et al. (1998, Chapter 2) and sorts studies into different categories: randomized experiments, "rigorous quasi-experimental research design(s) with a program and matched comparison group," and other non-experimental studies that employ multivariate statistical techniques to adjust for observable differences between program and control groups. To allow for the effect that non-experimental studies might overstate program impacts, they discount the effect sizes of quasi-experimental studies by 25 percent and discount the results of regular multivariate studies by 50 percent.

My concern with this type of meta-analytic approach is that we basically have no idea whether these discount factors for non-experimental findings are correct, and the relevant discount factors might vary across applications depending on the underlying processes through which people or places select (or are selected) into receiving some sort of program or policy. And, in fact, previous research raises the possibility that in some applications non-experimental studies may not even get the sign of the effect right (i.e., whether the program is helpful vs. harmful), much less come within a 25 percent or 50 percent band of the program's true impact.

Consider, for example, the area of education research. Going back at least to the famous Coleman Report of 1966, hundreds of studies have found little association between children's test scores and different measures of school resources. Yet the one large-scale randomized experiment conducted in this area found meaningfully large gains in student achievement from reducing class sizes during the early elementary school grades (see Hanushek, 2003, vs. Krueger, 2003). The two types of research evidence can be reconciled by the possibility that much education spending is compensatory – that is, extra resources may be devoted to populations that are at elevated risk for school failure due to student- and family-background characteristics that are unmeasured (or not well measured) in our social science datasets. In this case observational studies may understate the causal effects of extra resources on student outcomes.

Another example comes from the large non-experimental literature suggesting neighborhood environments seem to have powerful influences on people's criminal behavior and other outcomes (see for example Sampson, Morenoff, & Gannon-Rowley, 2002). Yet the one randomized experiment that has been carried out that moves families into less distressed areas, HUD's Moving to Opportunity (MTO) demonstration, finds a more complicated pattern of impacts (Kling, Ludwig, & Katz, 2005; Sanbonmatsu, Kling, Duncan, & Brooks-Gunn, 2006; Kling, Liebman, & Katz, 2007; Ludwig & Kling, 2007). Applying different non-experimental estimation methods to the MTO data, even with its rich set of baseline covariates on families, can often generate estimates of "neighborhood effects" on people's criminal or other behavior that is of the wrong sign compared to what is implied by the randomized experiment. Indeed a large empirical literature in economics and statistics going back to LaLonde (1986) shows that non-experimental studies across a variety of social policy applications can often get the sign of the true effect wrong (much less the magnitude). Moreover standard specification tests may not provide a reliable guide for determining when our non-experimental estimation methods are working well.

It is true that some meta-analyses find that quasi-experimental studies in some applications can have mean effect sizes that are not so far different from the mean effect sizes found with the randomized experimental evaluations of the particular intervention strategy of interest (see for example Lipsey, 2009). Depending on the application, it can be a little hard to know what to make of this because in some cases a detailed reading of the randomized experimental studies reveals that they also have some important methodological defects. But the larger problem is that knowing that some non-experimental methods can generate unbiased estimates in some applications is not so helpful without some systematic ability to determine when selection bias is, or is not, likely to be a serious problem.

I do not mean to sound dogmatic on this issue. I do believe that some carefully-done non-experimental designs, particularly difference-in-difference and regression discontinuity studies, are capable of generating unbiased estimates of causal relationships in selected applications (see Angrist & Pischke, 2009, for an extended discussion, and for examples, see Ludwig & Cook, 2000, and Ludwig & Miller, 2007). But determining whether a non-experimental study (and a randomized experiment for that matter) has adequately identified a causal effect requires a very careful reading of the original study and the researcher's own individual judgment.

Lumping experimental and non-experimental studies together into a meta-analysis in some ways obscures more than it clarifies.

While I appreciate Welsh and Piquero's clarity about which claims about program impacts come from randomized experiments vs. a mix of studies of varying quality, as they note in the conclusion to their essay, there are inevitably some remaining questions about the external validity of the available research findings. Many of these points are discussed in more detail in the nice paper by Welsh, Sullivan, and Olds (2010).

The fact that meta-analyses pool together results from multiple experiments need not mean that the average effect from those experiments represents the impact the program would achieve if taken to large scale. For example my University of Chicago colleague James Heckman has noted the potential problem of "randomization bias" – the type of person who is willing to sign up for a randomized experiment might be different (and respond differently to some intervention) than the sort of person who is not inclined to participate in an experiment in which there is some chance that they essentially receive a sugar pill placebo. This is important if program impacts are heterogeneous across the population (see also Angrist & Pischke, 2009). A nice empirical application that demonstrates the importance of treatment heterogeneity in practice is Evans and Garthwaite (2010), which might not be familiar to criminology readers.

There are also well-known concerns about the availability of the key inputs necessary to take programs to scale, and the possibility that some of these inputs might be in short supply (which could either greatly increase program costs or force program administrators to rely on lower-quality inputs). A sobering example of the practical importance of this sort of scale-up problem comes from Jepsen and Rivkin's (2009) study of reducing classroom sizes in elementary schools. The famous Tennessee STAR experiment found that reducing class sizes holding teacher quality constant (by randomly assigning teachers to large vs. small classrooms) can improve test scores for children, particularly disadvantaged, minority children. Yet when the state of California enacted large-scale across-the-board class size reductions, the state was forced to do so much new hiring that teacher quality seemed to decline. Worst of all, declines in teacher quality seemed to be most pronounced in the most disadvantaged schools, since they had the misfortune of losing some of their best teachers to newly-opened teaching slots in the most affluent schools in the state.

At the end of the day, I am inclined to agree with Welsh and Piquero that the evidence base for the effectiveness (and cost-effectiveness) of early family-focused interventions is at least as strong as what we have in almost any other area of crime prevention, and indeed far stronger than what we have to support the vast majority of crime-prevention dollars that are currently being spent nationwide in the U.S. Nevertheless, it does still seem important for policymakers to keep in mind that there is some uncertainty about what could exactly be accomplished from taking these intervention approaches to large-scale, both because of concerns about scale-up with the programs themselves and because of concerns about treatment heterogeneity across people.

DOES WORKING WITH FAMILIES DOMINATE WORKING WITH KIDS?

Welsh and Piquero note that working with families does not preclude also funding interventions that provide services directly to children, although in their conclusion they talk about the "importance of the family domain and the need for this approach to play a central role in early prevention policy." In a world of scarce resources, their paper effectively reads like an argument for prioritizing government funds for early family-oriented prevention programs over those that focus on working directly with children. This argument rests presumably in part on the fact that many meta-analyses suggest family-oriented programs have larger effect sizes than those that work with children.

But just because some intervention is more effective than another (in the sense of generating a larger effect size) does not mean that it is more cost effective. While we might have clear theoretical reasons to suspect that family-oriented early interventions might be more effective than those that focus on working just with children, theory is more ambiguous about which type of intervention would be more cost effective, given the difference in costs between the two types of approaches. The basic issue is that for a given level of resources we may often be able to work with children directly in a much more intensive way compared to what we can do in working with parents.

Suppose that we have, say, 30 poor children we would like to help, and we have $75,000 to hire a full-time staff member to provide therapeutic services to these children over a 50-week period. One possibility is to run a center-based program that works just with children and enrolls them for, say, 6 hours per day, so that for our $75,000 investment we are able to provide each poor child with $50 \times 5 \times 6 = 1,500$ contact-hours per year. Now consider the alternative of a family-based program. Most family-based programs, and certainly those involving home visitation, require working with one family at a time, which costs us some economies of scale. Based on my wife's experiences as a preschool special education teacher in Northern Virginia, carrying out home visits seems to involve a great deal of time for coordinating schedules and traveling (even in places with less horrible traffic than in the DC suburbs). Let us suppose a very efficient person was able to carry out three home visits per day, and that each home visit lasted two hours. This means that $75,000 would be able to provide each child with one two-hour home visit every two weeks, or a total of $25 \times 2 = 50$ contact-hours per year.

In my simple example, each hour of home visitation time needs to be 30 times as productive as each hour of classroom time with the child in order for the home visitation-type program to generate larger crime reductions for given spending. To maximize the social good that can be accomplished for given funding, we should be rank-ordering programs on the basis of some comparison of benefits to costs, such as the benefit-cost ratio (for more see Duncan & Magnuson, 2007, Ludwig & Phillips 2007).

Whether family-oriented early interventions dominate child-focused early interventions is an empirical question. My sense is that the existing research literature has not yet provided definitive evidence about which approach generates larger benefit-cost ratios. Since I am not as expert as Welsh and Piquero in this area, it is certainly possible that I am wrong, and that perhaps there is stronger evidence about benefit-cost ratios than what I have seen myself. But I suppose my main point is a more general one: We should be clear that we do not want to judge programs simply on the basis of their effect sizes – since the programs will differ with respect to their costs, as well as their benefits.

IS PREVENTION ALWAYS BETTER THAN REMEDIATION?

Many people have gravitated towards the idea that early intervention dominates later intervention, based in part on arguments about the relatively greater developmental plasticity of people during the earliest years of life, the possibility that there might be "sensitive" or "critical" periods for developing certain key cognitive or socio-emotional and behavioral skills, and the possibility that early skills help lay the foundation that make children more effective learners over the course of their subsequent schooling careers (see for example Shonkoff & Phillips, 2000, Knudsen et al., 2006). Yet the sweeping claim that "prevention is more effective and less costly than remediation, and earlier is far better than later" need not be true, and certainly need not be true in all cases.

One reason is that despite the appeal of conceptual arguments that early human capital investments increase the productivity of later investments – "learning begets learning" – in practice, fade out of social program impacts is far from uncommon. Consider for example the well-known Fast Track intervention, which served a disadvantaged population and provided parent-management training, child social-cognitive skills training, reading tutoring, home visiting, and mentoring over a 10-year period, with the most intensive services coming early during the intervention period. Follow-ups through 9th grade find little lasting gains in children's impacts except among the subset of youth initially at highest risk (Dodge, 2007).

This also raises the general question of how to forecast long-term program benefits from short-term impacts. In the area of medicine, we can forecast the impact of, say, Lipitor on long-term risk of cardiovascular disease by estimating the short-term impact on blood cholesterol levels, which is what medical researchers call a "surrogate clinical endpoint" that has been reliably shown to predict later disease risk. Whether similar surrogate endpoints exist in the social policy area remains unclear. For example with Head Start, previous studies of program participants from the

1970s-1990s find short-term impacts of around one-quarter standard deviation that for minority children seem to fade gradually through around age 10, and yet the program still seems to have long-term benefits on key life outcomes such as years of school completed (Currie & Thomas, 1995; Garces, Thomas, & Currie, 2002; Ludwig & Miller, 2007; Deming, 2009). On this basis, several years ago Deborah Phillips and I concluded that the recent federal government-funded experimental study of Head Start, which found impacts at the end of preschool equal to one-quarter of a standard deviation, provided encouraging evidence about the program's prospects for improving the long-term life chances for current cohorts of participating children (Ludwig & Phillips, 2007). So we were quite surprised to see that in the latest follow-up the Head Start experiment finds almost no detectable treatment-control differences in outcomes by the end of first grade. Whether this reflects treatment "fade out" or control group "catch up" remains unclear, but in either case highlights the difficulty of forecasting long-term benefits in the area of social policy from short-term impacts. The main point is that in a world in which treatment-control differences in outcomes may attenuate over time, it is not obvious that the largest changes in delinquency come from intervening in early childhood vs. adolescence.

A different issue is that while early prevention may have the advantage of greater developmental plasticity relative to later remediation programs, in some applications remediation programs have the advantage of being able to target resources more efficiently. To continue my stylized example from above, suppose we have 30 preschoolers whose future delinquency we would like to reduce, and $75,000 available to try to accomplish that end. Suppose that the administrators of some early childhood program try to prioritize enrollment slots for young children who, based on their family background characteristics and early life outcomes, are predicted to be at elevated risk for future delinquency. A very effective targeting program might be able to identify a pool of young children whose risk of engaging in delinquency during adolescence was, say, 50 percent. This would represent a very successful risk-prediction method (particularly if, for political and constitutional reasons, the program had to enroll girls as well as boys), but it also means that half of the children we enroll in our early childhood program would not have offended even absent the program. Our early childhood program winds up providing $2,500 worth of intervention services ($75,000/30) to each child that would eventually engage in delinquency.

Now consider instead a remediation program that provided intensive services to children later in life course, during adolescence, after they had engaged in delinquency. In this case we would be able to focus our $75,000 in resources on the 15 children who essentially self-identify as being delinquents with probability=1 (by actually engaging in delinquency during adolescence). Remediation enables us to more efficiently target resources and provide each of the children who would go on to engage in delinquency with $5,000 worth of services.

There are also some complications for this prevention vs. remediation calculus that are worth considering. One drawback to the remediation strategy is that the remediation strategy waits for the social harm to occur from delinquency before intervening to try to prevent additional social harm. The magnitude of this cost will depend a lot on our ability to identify the highest-risk adolescents at the very start of their criminal careers as they start to engage in the least costly offenses, rather than have to wait until they self-identify as very high risk by engaging in very socially costly behaviors.

Working in the other direction is the fact that if policymakers are focused on preventing delinquency, then one problem with early childhood interventions is that there is some delay before the benefits are realized. Suppose that some early childhood prevention program works with children who are five years old, and that every act of delinquency occurs at age 15. If we decided to serve our target sample of 30 five-year-olds through a wait-and-see remediation program during adolescence, rather than with an early childhood prevention program, we could take the $75,000 we had set aside for the early childhood program and put that into some sort of interest-bearing asset for 10 years. Even with a conservative investment strategy that earned just 3 percent per year, by the time our set of program children reached age 15 we would have $100,000 to spend on the remediation program (the original principal of $75,000, plus another $25,000 in interest earnings). With the remediation program we would be able to provide each youth who would actually engage in delinquency with $6,666 of intervention services (rather than the $2,500 "treatment dose" provided under the early childhood program), or else we could hold the intensity of the adolescent intervention constant at $5,000 per year and use the $25,000 interest earnings to compensate victims from the initial delinquent acts through which teenagers self-identify as delinquents.

I certainly don't mean to argue against the potential value of early intervention. I am merely suggesting caution against the uncritical acceptance that prevention need always dominate remediation. Whether that is true or not will depend on answers to a variety of empirical questions, answers that could vary across social policy applications.

IF EARLY INTERVENTION IS SO GREAT, WHY DON'T WE DO MORE OF IT?

Social scientists have been calling for more early intervention for the past 50 years (at least). And yet even now, only around perhaps half of all low-income children are enrolled in an early childhood intervention of even moderate intensity like Head Start, much less an intensive family-oriented program of the sort advocated by Welsh and Piquero. Why is that?

Some answers are so obvious, cynical, and depressing that they need not be recounted in great detail. For example I have been at meetings in Washington, DC, where people have openly said that the problem with poor children is that they don't vote, call their Congressional representative, or make large contributions to political campaigns.

Another part of the answer presumably must have to do with the timing of electoral cycles in relation to the lag associated with the benefits from early childhood interventions. Most politicians probably have a planning horizon that does not extend 10 or 15 years, the time between when early childhood interventions are implemented and when we would expect to see any benefits from reductions in criminal behavior. A similar problem of overly short planning horizons has been noted in the area of government budgeting, and has led to calls for what is called "intergenerational accounting" – the idea that we should think about government expenditures and revenues as flows over long periods of time, and make clear to the public the impact that different policy decisions will have on these long-term flows. There have also been calls to broaden the definition of Gross Domestic Product to incorporate non-monetary considerations, like the value of a country's stock of environmental quality.

Why not extend these ideas to the area of crime policy? Why not report as part of our national accounting statistics the effects of different policy decisions on the stock of human capital embedded within each cohort of children? As my friends Philip Cook and John Laub have pointed out, background is not destiny – the same early developmental influences and individual behavioral propensities can be associated with massively different levels of realized criminal behavior, depending on environmental circumstances at the time people reach peak potential offending ages (Cook & Laub, 1998, 2002). Nevertheless evidence from Perry Preschool and other studies show that holding environmental circumstances during adolescence or early adulthood constant, interventions that improve the developmental conditions of poor children can reduce lifetime criminal involvement. Why not make it easier for voters to hold politicians accountable for the criminal behavior they may be bequeathing to future society?

REFERENCES

Angrist, J. & Pischke, J. (2009). *Mosly harmless econometrics: An empiricist's companion*. Princeton, NJ: Princeton University Press.

Beirne, P. (1987). Adolphe Quetelt and the origins of positivist criminology. *American Journal of Sociology, 92*(5), 1140-1169.

Coleman, J. (1966). *Equality of Eeducational opportunity*. Washington, DC: United States Office of Education.

Cook, P. & Laub, J. (1998), The unprecedented epidemic in youth violence. *Crime and Justice, 24,* 26-64. Chicago, IL: University of Chicago Press.

Cook, P. & Laub, J. (2002). After the epidemic: Recent trends in youth violence in the United States. *Crime and Justice, Vol. 29,* 1-37. Chicago, IL: University of Chicago Press.

Currie, J. & Thomas, D. (1995). Does Head Start make a difference? *American Economic Review, 85*(3), 341-364.

Deming, D. (2009). Early childhood intervention and life-cycle skill development: Evidence from Head Start. *American Economic Journal: Applied Economics, 1*(3), 111-134.

Dodge, K. (2007). Fast Track randomized controlled trial to prevent externalizing psychiatric disorders: Findings from grades 3 to 9. *Journal of the American Academy of Child and Adolescent Psychiatry, 46*(10), 1250-1262.

Drake, E., Aos, S., & Miller, M. (2009). Evidence-based public policy options to reduce crime and criminal justice costs: Implications in Washington State. *Victims and Offenders, 4,* 170-196.

Duncan, G. & Magnuson, K. (2007). Penny wise and effect size foolish. *Child Development Perspectives, 1,* 46–51.

Evans, W. & Garthwaite, C. (2010). Estimating heterogeneity in the benefits of medical treatment intensity. working paper, Department of Management and Strategy, Kellogg School of Management, Northwestern University. Retrieved June 1, 2010, from http://www.kellogg.northwestern.edu/faculty/garthwaite/htm/paper _draft_heterogeneity.pdf

Garces, E., Thomas, D., & Currie, J. (2002). Longer term effects of Head Start. *American Economic Review, 92*(4), 999-1012.

Hanushek, E. (2003). The failure of input-based schooling policies. *The Economic Journal, 113,* F64-F98.

Jepsen, C. & Rivkin, S. (2009). Class size reduction and student achievement: The potential tradeoff between teacher quality and class size. *Journal of Human Resources, 44*(1).

Kling, J., Liebman, J., & Katz, L. (2007). Experimental analysis of neighborhood effects. *Econometrica, 75*(1), 83-119.

Kling, J., Ludwig, J., & Katz, L. (2005). Neighborhood effects on crime for female and male youth: Evidence from a randomized housing voucher experiment. *Quarterly Journal of Economics, 120*(1), 87-130.

Knudsen, E., Heckman, J., Cameron, J., & Shonkoff, J. (2006). Economic, neurobiological, and behavioral perspectives on building America's future workforce. *Proceedings of the National Academy of Sciences, 103,* 10155–62.

Krueger, A., (2003). Economic considerations and class size. *The Economic Journal, 113,* F34-F63.

LaLonde, R. (1986). Evaluating the econometric evaluations of training programs with experimental data. *American Economic Review, 76,* 604-620.

Lipsey, M. (2009). The primary factors that characterize effective interventions with juvenile offenders: A meta-analytic review. *Victims and Offenders, 4,* 124-147.

Ludwig, J. & Cook, P. (2000, August 2). Homicide and suicide rates associated with implementation of the Brady Handgun Violence Prevention Act. *Journal of the American Medical Association, 284*(5), 585-591.

Ludwig, J. & Kling, J. (2007). Is crime contagious? *Journal of Law and Economics, 50*(3), 491-518.

Ludwig, J. & Miller, D. (2007). Does Head Start improve children's life chances? Evidence from a regression discontinuity approach. *Quarterly Journal of Economics, 122*(1), 159-208.

Ludwig, J. & Phillips, D. (2007). The benefits and costs of Head Start. NBER Working Paper No. 12973.

Sampson, R., Morenoff, J., & Gannon-Rowley, T. (2002). Assessing neighborhood effects: Social processes and new directions in research. *Annual Review of Sociology, 28,* 443-478.

Sanbonmatsu, L., Kling, J., Duncan, G., & Brooks-Gunn, J. (2006). Neighborhoods and academic achievement: Results from the moving to opportunity experiment. *Journal of Human Resources, 41*(4), 649-691.

Sherman, L., Gottfredson, D., MacKenzie, D., Eck, J., Reuter, P., & Bushway, S. (1998). *Preventing crime: what works, what doesn't, what's promising.* A Report to the United States Congress, Prepared for the National Institute of Justice. College Park, MD: Department of Criminology and Criminal Justice, University of Maryland. http://www.ncjrs.gov/works/index.htm

Shonkoff, J. & Phillips, D. (2000). *From neurons to neighborhoods: The science of early childhood development.* Washington, DC: National Academy Press.

Welsh, B., Sullivan, C., & Olds, D. (2010). When early crime prevention goes to scale: A new look at the evidence. *Prevention Science, 11,* 115-125.

[*] Author's Note: Thanks to Philip Cook for helpful discussions and to David Farrington and Richard Rosenfeld for comments. Any errors and all opinions are of course my own.

Keeping Up with the Jurisdiction Next Door: Access to and Use of Evidence Regarding Effective Prevention Programs for High-Risk Families

Peter W. Greenwood

In their paper Welsh and Piquero review recent meta-analyses and systematic reviews regarding delinquency risk factors associated with family composition and parenting styles as well as programs designed to reduce them. Their focus is on early interventions before the age of 5. Not surprisingly, to those who are familiar with this field, they find consistent evidence that interventions designed to improve child development, such as home visitation, parent education, daycare, and parent management training can reduce delinquency and improve other school and employment outcomes.

Although the authors find that early family-based interventions are consistently effective, their primary conclusions are on the cautious side, reminding readers of the difficulties encountered in attempting to replicate proven programs and the possibility of attenuated effects in later years.

More specifically, Welsh and Piquero conclude that:

- There is a strong evidence base on the importance of family-based risk factors for delinquency and the effectiveness of early family-based programs designed to address these risk factors, including nurse home visits and parent management training. In fact this database was emerging in the 1980s and 90s and is now quite rigorous and accessible.
- Early childhood programs also produce a wide range of other important benefits for families, which are more difficult to monetize than the crime benefits.
- There is some evidence to suggest that these programs can pay back program costs and produce substantial monetary benefits for society.
- There is a need for this approach to play a central role in early prevention policy.
- Prevention is more effective and less costly than remediation, and earlier is far better than later. Starting with a focus on the family will help make this happen.

In responding to their paper I would like to discuss several issues: 1) differences in expected outcomes between similar types of programs; 2) early prevention versus later remediation; 3) the accessibility of this information to those who need it; 4) how this information is being used to

41

affect public policy now; and 5) how to hold public officials more accountable for its proper use in the future.

DIFFERENCES IN EXPECTED OUTCOMES BETWEEN PROGRAMS

Parent training and early childhood education programs can take a variety of forms and levels of intensity. Some are center-based, while others take place in the home. Some last only a few months, while others continue for more than two years. Some parent training programs include the child and some early childhood programs involve the parents. Some programs use highly trained professionals, while others use paraprofessional or volunteer staff.

Evidence from the research base on prevention programs provides three distinct types of advice about what works to practitioners and public officials. One is a list of specific "brand name" programs with varying degrees of research support. The best of these are those like David Olds' Nurse Family Partnership (NFP) that have been evaluated in several rigorous trials and found to be consistently effective. Less reliable are those that have been evaluated only once or where their evaluation designs have been weak.

Another type of advice is provided by the type of systematic reviews and meta-analyses which were the primary sources reviewed by Welsh and Piquero. Rather than representing the work of a single individual or research team refining a specific model, as was the case for NFP, these systematic reviews combine evaluations of similar programs developed by different individuals, such as early childhood education, parent training or family therapy.

The third type of advice comes in the form of general "principles of effectiveness" that are identified by meta-analysis and appear to apply across a broad spectrum of programs. Focusing on the higher-risk individuals, ensuring close fidelity to the original model, and ensuring appropriate dosage are principles that have been identified to date (Lipsey, 2009; Greenwood, 2010).

Although one might get the impression from the Welsh and Piquero review that many forms of home visitation are effective in reducing child abuse and delinquency, only NFP has been able to demonstrate consistent effects and provides the kind of technical assistance and training required to produce high fidelity replications of the model program. In fact, it is the multiple evaluations of NFP that provide most of the positive evidence for the generic home visitation model. Evaluations of popular home visitation programs that do not follow the NFP protocols, or which substitute less costly social workers for the nurses used in NFP, have not been found effective (Olds et al., 2004; Greenwood, 2006). Jurisdiction seeking to reduce delinquency and child abuse through early interventions need to be aware – not all members of a generic program type are created equal, or can be expected to produce similar results.

Furthermore, NFP is only cost-effective for particular types of family situations. It is only appropriate for young women dealing with their first child, and only for those who are most at-risk for negative child outcomes (Karoly et al., 1998; Greenwood, 2006).

EARLY PREVENTION VERSUS LATER REMEDIATION

While it might seem that early delinquency prevention should be more cost effective than later remediation, this is not necessarily the case. Although several cost benefit studies have found that the total benefits of NFP exceed its costs by several orders of magnitude, when implemented under appropriate conditions (Karoly et al., 1998; Drake, Aos, & Miller, 2009), similar analyses of family based interventions for older juveniles demonstrate that they produce a higher benefit to cost ratio than NFP (Drake et al., 2009). This advantage is due to the fact that the 2+ year NFP program requires more resources per case than does family therapy, while high-risk adolescents are better identified by their behavior than are high-risk young children by their family characteristics alone. Nevertheless, both NFP and family-based programs for adolescents are more cost effective than many other types of criminal justice interventions currently in use (Drake et al., 2009).

THE ACCESSIBILITY OF PROGRAM EFFECTIVENESS INFORMATION TO POLICY MAKERS

Those of us who publish regularly in academic journals must accept the fact that our peer-reviewed articles are not usually read by practitioners or policy makers. Between their technical language and extensive qualifications, their impact on policy makers is much like that of the fine print in the credit card contracts and software "terms and conditions" that most of us sign without ever reading.

Those who need this effectiveness information are most likely to obtain it from a variety of sources that attempt to package and provide it in a simpler form that meets their needs. The accuracy and coverage of the information provided by these resources varies considerably depending on when it was assembled and how it was reviewed (Greenwood, 2008). The information needs and decision-making styles of criminal justice policy makers and practitioners are issues about which most academics know very little and about which additional research needs to be conducted (Fixsen, Naoom, Blase, Friedman, & Wallace, 2005)

A recent report designed to provide this type of information to California policy makers (Greenwood, 2010) summarized information provided by four such sources: the University of Colorado's Blueprints for Violence Prevention (Elliott, 1997); reports by the Washington State Institute for Public Policy (Drake et al., 2009); the Coalition for Evidence Based Practice's Top Tier program rating system (www.toptierevidence.org/wordpress/); and analyses published by Lipsey (2009). California jurisdictions applying for recent CalGrip violence prevention grants were encouraged to select programs from this list by receiving extra points for doing so when their applications were scored (http://www.calgrip.ca.gov/index.cfm?navid=103). There is clearly a need for further research on how these lists of effective programs should be constructed and how they should be used.

HOW THIS INFORMATION IS CURRENTLY AFFECTING POLICY

Home visitation programs for new mothers is a politically popular concept that has been supported in many states for some time. NFP has been identified and promoted as the most cost-effective version of this concept for over a decade and was the first developmental program supported by the U.S. Department of Justice's Weed and Seed Program, an effort designed to "weed" out the bad element of a high-crime community with aggressive law enforcement, and then provide the "seeds" for more positive outcomes for the community's youth. When various organizations began developing their lists of what they believed to be proven programs, they all identified NFP as one of the most proven programs for child abuse and crime prevention. As part of the Obama Administration's efforts to improve youth development with Evidence Based Practice (EBP), NFP was the first EBP to receive special and significant line-item funding in the budget (http://www.acf.hhs.gov/programs/olab/budget/2010/sec3f_nhv_2010cj.pdf).

More generally, many states have taken steps to help promote the adoption of evidence based programs (EBPs) at the local level. Such steps can include: efforts to identify and promote a list of EBPs; special funding to support the adoption of EBPs; the establishment of specialized intermediary organizations or resource centers to provide guidance and technical assistance to local communities and agencies. The Communities That Care program (CTC) developed by David Hawkins and Richard Catalano at the University of Washington provides one example of how a state can can provide guidance to local communities in program selection and implementation. A recent evaluation has shown that CTC improves the likelihood of successful program implementation and positive outcomes (Hawkins et al., 2008). Efforts by the Washington State Institute for Public Policy (WSIPP) to identify and promote EBPs is another (Aos, 2002).

The state of Washington was one of the first to provide state funding to local communities for the purpose of implementing a portfolio of EBPs identified by WSIPP. Maryland has established the Innovations project within the University of Maryland Medical School. California is just beginning such an effort being run by the Governor's Office of Youth and Gang Violence with a mix of public and foundation funding (http://www.calgrip.ca.gov/index.cfm?navid=103). The point to be made here is that states have finally begun to realize that some initiative is required on their part if local communities are going to make the kinds of investments in EBPs that will eventually save the state substantial sums in operating its corrections system. Washington has already eliminated one new prison system from its building plans based on reductions in commitment rates it anticipates from increased spending on EBP prevention.

HOLDING PUBLIC OFFICIALS ACCOUNTABLE

At the present time there is very little pressure on public officials to make use of the best evidence based programs to help at-risk youth and families, reduce crime and violence, and reduce government spending on correctional facilities. While these programs have been identified and promoted by a variety of sponsors for more than a decade, fewer than ten percent of the families and youth who could be cost effectively helped by such programs are receiving their services. Until some method of measuring and publicizing the performance of those who are in a position to adopt them, the rate of adoption is likely to continue at its current glacial pace.

One measure that could be used to compare the progress of jurisdictions in adopting these programs is the total number of evidence based programs available divided by the targeted population, or some other quantity which might serve as a measure of need. Since most jurisdictions do not routinely keep track of the number of high-risk families or youths who these programs might serve, the best that can be done at this time is to divide the number of evidence based programs they offer by such available measures as their total population, correctional population, or annual number of juvenile arrests.

As an example of the differences in performance that such measures can provide, Figure 1 shows the number of NFP and two other proven family-based therapy programs, Functional Family Therapy (FFT) and Multisystemic Therapy (MST), currently provided by a sample of states, divided by their total or corrections population. Notice the difference in NFP programs per 100,000 population between states that lead in the use of NFP, such as Pennsylvania and Washington, and those with much lower rates or zero availability, such as Connecticut and Florida. Of course, explanations for this difference could be that that there are many fewer first-time births to high-risk mothers in these states compared to the others, or just ignorance about the effectiveness of NFP. However, since Pennsylvania and Washington are two states who were early promoters of EBP, it is much more likely that the low rate of availability for NFP in Connecticut and Florida reflects conscious policy choices to not serve this population, or to serve them with less effective programs.

The low rate of NFP availability in California does not reflect a lack of concern for high risk mothers and young children since that state was in the vanguard of those setting aside special funding streams to serve such individuals, when the voters passed a special ballot initiative in 1998, increasing taxes on cigarettes and providing more than 400 million dollars a year to help improve outcomes for children ages 0-5 (http://www.ccfc.ca.gov/press/prop.asp). Rather it reflects the political struggle that ensued over how such funding should be used. In many counties the special commissions that were established to oversee the distribution of these funds opted for programs with weaker evidence of effectiveness that could serve more children than the more expensive NFP. This is particularly ironic in that a RAND cost-benefit study of NFP and the Perry Preschool program (Karoly et al., 1998) had been used by supporters of the initiative in promoting its passage.

Notice that the leading NFP states are not necessarily the leaders in the use of the FFT and MST programs. Since NFP utilizes public health nurses and focuses on child health and safety issues, programs are typically operated by local public health agencies. FFT, which sends specially trained therapists into homes to improve parenting skills, and MST, which provides similar services at a more intensive level along with others forms of service brokerage and skill building, usually deal with the families of delinquent or dependent youth and are typically housed in probation departments or departments of mental health. While Pennsylvania is among the leading states in the use of FFT and MST, as well as NFP, low NFP usage states such as Connecticut and Rhode Island are among the leaders in using FFT and MST. Clearly these measures of program usage provide some indication of a state's commitment to serving at-risk families with EBP.

The indicators plotted in Figure 1 can be easily calculated because NFP, MST, and FFT all provide information on their websites regarding the location and operating agency for all of their active programs. If more EBPs, or those who fund them, provided such data, a more detailed picture of each state's progress in shifting toward EBPs could be developed.

Figure 1. Utilization of NFP, FFT and MST for selected states: Proven family-based prevention programs per capita.

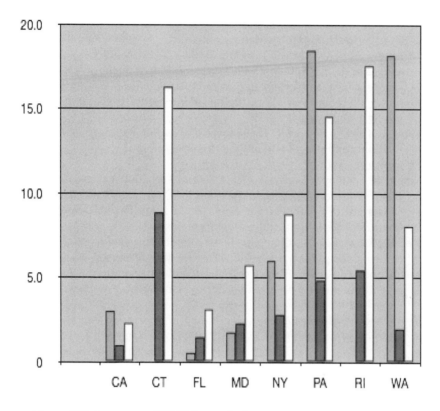

blue = NFP teams per 100,000 population

red = MST and FFT teams per million population

white = MST and FFT teams per 10,000 prison inmate

Conclusions

As Welsh and Piquero have amply demonstrated, evidence regarding the effectiveness of family-based prevention programs is strong and consistent. Implementation of appropriate programs, for the appropriate population, with a high degree of fidelity, is a cost effective policy for reducing crime and violence.

Identifying the appropriate boundaries of effectiveness, tracking fidelity, evaluating major adaptations of proven models, and holding public officials accountable for making proper use of this information remain as challenges for our field.

REFERENCES

Aos, S. (2002). *The juvenile justice system in Washington State: Recommendations to improve cost-effectiveness*, #02-10-1201. Olympia, WA: Washington State Institute for Public Policy. (www.wsipp.wa.gov/pub.asp?docid=02-10-1201)

Drake, E., Aos, S., & Miller, M. (2009). *Evidence-based public policy options to reduce crime and criminal justice costs: Implications in Washington State*. Olympia, WA: Washington State Institute for Public Policy. (www.wsipp.wa.gov)

Elliott, D. (1997). *Blueprints for violence prevention*. Boulder, CO: Center for the Study and Prevention of Violence. (www.colorado.edu/cspv/blueprints/)

Fixsen, D., Naoom, S., Blase, K., Friedman, R., & Wallace, F. (2005). *Implementation research: A synthesis of the literature*. Tampa, FL: University of South Florida, Louis de la Parte Florida Mental Health Institute, The National Implementation Research.

Greenwood, P. (2006). Changing lives: Delinquency prevention as crime control policy, Chicago, IL: University of Chicago Press.

Greenwood, P. (2008, Fall). Prevention and intervention programs for juvenile offenders: The benefits of evidence-based practice. *Future of Children,18*(2).

Greenwood, P. (2010, January). *Preventing and reducing youth crime and violence: Using evidence based practices*. Sacramento, CA: California Governor's Office of Gang and Youth Violence Policy. (www.calgrip.ca.gov/documents/Preventing and Reducing Youth Crime and Violence.pdf)

Hawkins, J., Brown, E., Oesterle, S., Arthur, M., Abbott, R., & Catalano, R. (2008). Early effects of Communities That Care on targeted risks and initiation of delinquent behavior and substance use. *Journal of Adolescent Health, 43*, 15-22.

Karoly L., Greenwood, P., Everingham, S., Hoube, J., Kilburn, M., Rydell, C., Sanders, M., & Chiesa, J. (1998). *Investing in our children: What we know and don't know about the costs and benefits of early childhood interventions* Santa Monica, CA: RAND.

Lipsey, M. (2009). The primary factors that characterize effective interventions with juvenile offenders: A meta-analytic overview. *Victims and Offenders, Special Issue*.

Olds, D., Robinson, J. Pettitt, L., Luckey, D., Holmberg, J., Ng, R., Isacks, K., Sheff, K., & Henderson Jr., C. (2004). Effects of home visits by paraprofessionals and by nurses: Age four follow-up results of a randomized trial. *Pediatrics, 114*(6), 1560-8. (http://pediatrics.aappublications.org/cgi/content/full/114/6/1560)

EDUCATION

THE INFLUENCE OF RACIAL THREAT IN SCHOOLS: RECENT RESEARCH FINDINGS

KELLY WELCH

ABSTRACT

As with the criminal justice system, educational institutions have become increasingly punitive by adopting a crime control approach for addressing student violations, resulting in many students on the "jailhouse track." This has occurred as crime rates and rates of school violation have declined. Many studies have examined possible explanations for increased school punitiveness, including myriad student and school-level influences, but only a small number of significant findings have partially predicted harsh discipline. Recent research, however, applies the racial threat perspective—which has traditionally been tested only in criminal justice contexts—within educational institutions. Rooted in conflict theory, these studies show that schools with larger proportions of black students are more likely to implement harsh disciplinary policies and less apt to endorse restorative policies. Results are maintained while controlling for other important influences, including student misbehavior and delinquency salience. This essay reviews these findings and argues that they demonstrate the relevance of applying criminological theories to educational institutions. Further, it suggests that not only do the trends in school punishments mirror those in the criminal justice system, but that part of the cause—racial threat—is similar. Thus, school disciplinary policies must be modified to rid them of race-related influences and disparate applications.

INTRODUCTION

The expansion of formal social control in American schools over the past 25 years (Beger, 2002; Noguera, 2008; Wallace, Goodkind, Wallace, & Bachman, 2008) can be seen in the greater use of harsh school discipline and punishment, despite decreases in rates of student delinquency, student drug use, and violent victimization in school (Beger, 2002; Brooks, Schiraldi, & Ziedenberg, 1999; Devoe, Peter, Noonan, Snyder, & Baum, 2005; Dinkes, Cataldi, & Lin-Kelly, 2007). It is also clear that the crime control model has become the guiding principle found in many American social institutions (Simon, 2007), including most modern urban public schools (Noguera, 2008).

Among the disciplinary innovations found in modern schools is the widespread presence of surveillance and security programs, which operate in at least 55 percent of all schools, and virtually all urban schools (Beger, 2002; Devoe et al., 2005). Metal detectors are used to prevent weapons from entering school grounds (Beger, 2002; Brooks et al., 1999; Mawson, Lapsley, Hoffman, & Guignard, 2002). Locked and monitored doors and gates prevent unauthorized individuals from entering campus and prevent students from leaving without permission (Devoe et al., 2005; Gottfredson & Gottfredson, 2001). Hallways are often supervised by school staff and administrators (Devoe et al., 2005), and many schools also hire uniformed and armed Security Resource Officers (SROs) to maintain order and catch rule-breakers (Beger, 2002; Giroux, 2003; Kupchik & Ellis, 2008; Watts & Erevelles, 2004). Many educational institutions have also installed security cameras (Devoe et al., 2005; Watts & Erevelles, 2004). Schools often use drug-sniffing dogs, perform regular locker searches, and require students to carry clear book bags to reduce the presence of contraband (Brooks et al., 1999; DeVoe et al., 2005; Giroux, 2003; Gottfredson & Gottfredson, 2001).

The actions of rule-breakers in schools are frequently defined with criminal justice language (Tredway, Brill, & Hernandez, 2007). Students, sometimes called "suspects" or "repeat offenders," are subjected to "investigations," "interrogations," and "searches" by dogs or SROs who will sometimes report "needing back-up." Students may then be involved in "line-ups" and school "courts" before receiving punishments that, among other things, exclude students from the classroom. In fact, records indicate an increase in the use of exclusionary discipline, which includes teacher referrals to the principal, detentions, in-school and out-of-school suspensions, and expulsions (Gottfredson & Gottfredson, 2001; Kupchik & Ellis, 2008; Noguera, 2008).

The consequences of the crime control approach taken by educational institutions are not insignificant. Students who are caught violating school policies are now more often referred to law enforcement instead of only being disciplined internally, a change that has largely been the result of government mandates, such as zero tolerance policies, which require legal intervention (Beger, 2002). Thus, students are not only more likely to be disciplined harshly by schools, but they are more likely to receive criminal sanctions—an outcome that is likely to only increase their odds of future involvement in the criminal justice system.

EXPLANATIONS FOR SCHOOL PUNITIVENESS

Studies have made it clear that these changes in school punitiveness do not correspond with changes in student violations and delinquency (Kupchik & Monahan, 2006; Skiba & Peterson, 1999; Wu, Pink, Crain, & Moles, 1982). Thus, myriad explanations for the intensification of formal school social controls have emerged over the last couple of decades. However, these explanations have been incomplete in certain ways.

Some argue that the punitive approach to discipline is a direct consequence of the popular anxiety that followed certain high profile school shootings (Beger, 2002; Brooks et al., 1999; Watts & Erevelles, 2004) that resulted in public and political support for harsh responses to the perceived crisis. While most schools reported no such crimes and overall school violence actually decreased from 1993 to 2000 (Devoe et al., 2005), it is likely that mandatory policies, like zero tolerance, were, in fact, implemented in part because of these crimes (Skiba, 2000; Skiba & Peterson, 2000). However, moral panic cannot totally account for the criminal justice approach to school discipline, because even before Columbine and other school shootings, the public was already concerned about what they perceived to be an urgent situation (Hirschfield, 2008).

Some have argued that because of increasing pressure to increase student academic performance, low performing students have been essentially disciplined out of the classroom in order to inflate class averages. This explanation is insufficient, however, because it is not only discretionary discipline that has expanded, but mandatory policies that cannot be used to specifically target low-scoring students have also increased (Hirschfield, 2008).

Still others suggest that the criminal justice approach to student discipline derives from teachers and principals wanting to avoid legal liability for implementing discipline that falls outside of mandatory punishment, therefore resulting in school violations being handled increasingly by law enforcement (Arum, 2003; Toby, 1998). However, because legal remedies are presumed to be most accessible to wealthier students (Arum, 2003) yet it is poorer urban schools that tend to use the harshest discipline (Noguera, 2008), this "due process" explanation for expanding school discipline is not adequate (Hirschfield, 2008).

BLACK STUDENTS AND PUNITIVE SCHOOL DISCIPLINE

Other explanations for the crime control approach to school discipline have focused on the characteristics of those students who are most likely to be punished by harsh school policies. The considerable overrepresentation of black students receiving punitive consequences to problem behavior is particularly noticeable and concerning. Research clearly documents that black students experience more intense punishment in school than white students (Ferguson, 2000; Foney & Cunningham, 2002; Gottfredson & Gottfredson, 2001; Nichols, 2004; Skiba, 2001; Skiba, Peterson, & Williams, 1997) and receive punitive treatment more frequently for less serious offenses (Brown & Beckett, 2006; McCarthy & Hoge, 1987; McFadden, Marsh II, Price, & Hwang, 1992; Nichols, 2004; Noguera, 2008; Raffaele Mendez & Knoff, 2003; Shaw & Braden, 1990; Skiba, 2000, 2001; Skiba, Michael, Nardo, & Peterson, 2002). Statistics indicate that black students are more likely to be suspended than white students (Brooks et al., 1999; Gregory & Weinstein, 2008; Gottfredson & Gottfredson, 2001; Nichols, 2004). Although black students make up only about 17 percent of those enrolled in American public schools, they account for 32 percent of out-of-school suspensions (Gottfredson & Gottfredson, 2001; Vavrus & Cole, 2002). In fact, minority students as a whole are suspended three times more frequently than white students (APA Zero Tolerance Task Force, 2006; Brooks et al., 1999). Expulsion, generally the most severe school penalty, is another punishment that is more frequently assigned for violations by black students (Gottfredson & Gottfredson, 2001; Gregory & Weinstein, 2008; Skiba et al., 2002; Skiba & Peterson, 1999). These students are also more frequently exposed to even harsher disciplinary practices like corporal punishment (Glackman et al., 1978; Gregory, 1995; Shaw & Braden, 1990; Skiba & Peterson, 2000; Skiba et al., 2002) and are less likely to receive mild disciplinary alternatives (McFadden et al., 1992; Skiba & Peterson, 2000; Skiba et al., 2002).

Racial explanations for school punitiveness

Several explanations for disproportionate punitiveness toward black students are offered in previous research. The most obvious explanation for the racially disparate discipline practices of schools would be that black students are disproportionately involved in delinquency, thereby justifying their overrepresentation in punitive disciplinary practices (Noguera, 2008; Watts & Erevelles, 2004). However, studies have shown that, in fact, black students have not misbehaved or participated in delinquency at a higher rate than whites and that racial disparities in discipline, including mandatory discipline, are not attributable to differences in offending (McCarthy & Hoge, 1987; Skiba & Peterson, 1999; Vavrus & Cole, 2002).

Another frequently cited explanation for racial disparity in school discipline is that it may be attributable to socioeconomic differences and that any relationship between race and punitive discipline is partially, if not completely, spurious (Brantlinger, 1991; Nichols, 2004; Skiba et al., 2002; Watts & Erevelles, 2004; Wu et al., 1982). This would make sense, because statistics indicate that poorer students are, in fact, more likely to be targeted by harsh school practices (Brantlinger, 1991; Skiba et al., 1997; Skiba et al., 2002). Although this argument is compelling, multivariate tests of the relationships among student race, economic status, and school discipline indicate that black students are still punished more often and more harshly by schools, regardless of their economic status (Gregory & Weinstein, 2008; McCarthy & Hoge, 1987; Skiba & Peterson, 1999; Skiba et al., 2002; Wu et al., 1982).

Since black students are not violating school policies at a greater rate than other students, yet are being treated more punitively than white students regardless of economic disadvantage, misbehavior, attitudes, academic performance, parental attention, or school organization, many have concluded that racial bias or discrimination are to blame for their disproportionate involvement in school discipline (Brown & Beckett, 2006; Ferguson, 2000; Giroux, 2003; Noguera, 2008; Skiba & Peterson, 1999; Skiba et al., 2002; Watts & Erevelles, 2004; Wu et al., 1982). Some argue that this bias may come from the mere *perception* that black students are engaged in more school delinquency (Morrow & Torres, 1995; Nichols,

2004; Noguera, 2003), a possible result of the perceived "adultification" of black boys (Ferguson, 2000). However, it is notable that there has been no empirical support for this idea that bias and discrimination contribute to harsh school discipline. Given the amount of research highlighting the racial disparity of juvenile discipline in educational institutions, it is remarkable that there are so few that explore the causes of this disproportionality, and none that have accounted for it with multivariate analyses (Skiba et al., 2002).

RESEARCH ON RACIAL THREAT AND SCHOOL PUNITIVENESS

Research has recently begun to explore whether racial threat contributes to the intensification of punitive school discipline. The racial threat hypothesis suggests that social control will expand as the proportion of blacks in an area increases in relation to whites. This theoretical orientation originated from the work of Blumer (1958) and Blalock (1967) who described "power threat" related to economic and political competition presented by racial minorities to the white majority. Perceived racial competition for limited financial and political resources is one explanation for efforts to increase social control, which are implemented to preserve the social status of whites. Tests for the influence of this threat, eventually also termed "social threat" and "racial threat," eventually included black crime as another salient source of threat to whites (Crawford, Chiricos, & Kleck, 1998; Liska, 1992).

Because crime and punishment are so closely linked with race, the racial threat perspective has traditionally been tested using a criminal justice framework. Studies have found that racial threat, usually operationalized as the proportion of minorities in various places (such as counties, cities, and neighborhoods), is associated with a number of punitive criminal justice outcomes. These outcomes include higher rates of arrest (Mosher, 2001), expansion of law enforcement capabilities (Kent & Jacobs, 2004), higher incarceration rates (Jacobs & Carmichael, 2001), and greater use of the death penalty (Tolnay, Beck, & Massey, 1992). While this perspective originally focused on the effects of the threat presumably posed by blacks, recent studies have also addressed the effects of "ethnic threat" or "Hispanic threat" on social control (Eitle & Taylor, 2008).

Considering the extent to which racial composition has been related to harsher criminal justice measures, it is not surprising that research has begun to apply the racial threat perspective to educational institutions in an attempt to explain the growing punitiveness of disciplinary policies and practices in educational institutions. The few studies that have examined racial composition of students in schools have predicted that the implicit connection between race and crime potentially made by teachers, administrators, and policymakers at the local level results in harsher punishments being sanctioned in schools with more black students to control what may be perceived as a growing threat to safety (Kupchik,

2009; Payne & Welch, 2010; Welch & Payne, 2010). Overall, the findings of this emerging research suggest that racial threat is, indeed, operating in schools much in the same way it has had an influence on the criminal justice system.

The first study to use aggregated school minority compositional data to examine a potential association with punitive school discipline was conducted by Kupchik (2009) from 2004-2005. Although this research tested cultural reproduction theory rather than racial threat, its design and findings are relevant for an examination of the effects of racial threat in schools. Kupchik's study analyzed interview and observational data that were collected from four different high schools in two U.S. states over a 6-12 month period. In each of the states, one of the schools was predominantly attended by poor minority (predominantly black or Hispanic) students while the other was attended by predominantly upper-middle class white students. According to the cultural reproduction theory explored in this research, Kupchik (2009) expected to find that school discipline would be harsher in the two schools that had a student body comprised mostly of poor minorities because of the way discipline practices reproduce and exacerbate existing social inequalities among students by socializing them into different roles within the social structure.

Although the intention of this study was not to test the minority threat explanation for social control, its findings suggest that minority composition and the economic status of schools' students do not differentially impact the severity of disciplinary policies; all four schools implemented considerably punitive tactics. However, upon closer examination, this study found that there were "important differences in the frequency of school punishments and in how school discipline takes shape across schools" (Kupchik, 2009, p. 298). A further observation supporting the apparent influence of racial threat is that the appeals process for disciplinary action is more powerful in schools with more middle-class white students; discipline is more easily contested and avoided by students in those schools. This means that although the official disciplinary policies of schools are similarly punitive regardless of economic and racial/ethnic status, the practices of schools with more minority students are likely to be harsher than those with more white students.

The first study designed to specifically test the racial threat hypothesis in the school setting was conducted by Welch and Payne (2010). Using Ordinary Least Squares (OLS) regression to analyze a national sample of 294 public, non-alternative secondary schools, Welch and Payne (2010) found that schools with a greater percentage of black students more often implemented punitive discipline (such as withdrawal of a privilege, detention, and in-school suspension), zero tolerance policies (requiring automatic suspension for the possession of items such as tobacco, drugs, or weapons), and extremely punitive discipline (such as expulsion and reporting to police) for student misbehavior. Likewise, this research found that schools with proportionally more black students were less likely to implement mild forms of discipline (such as referrals to a school counselor, parent conferences, and oral reprimands) and restitutive discipline (such as making repayments for harm caused and community service). These results were maintained while controlling for several important school level influences, including student body economic status, student delinquency and drug use, perceived lack of school safety, teacher victimization, concentrated disadvantage, urbanicity, student Hispanic composition, percent of male students, principal and administrative leadership, and discipline training of staff.

In addition, to explore the possibility of contextual differences found in previous racial threat research, Welch and Payne (2010) examined the potential moderating effects of both student economic disadvantage and student deviance, finding that a school's percentage of black students has a stronger effect on punitive and extremely punitive discipline practices in schools with lower levels of student deviance. Thus, in schools where students engage in less delinquency and drug use, it appears that schools may be more likely to respond harshly and extremely harshly to misbehavior partly because of the racial composition of the student body. In conditions where delinquency and drug use are high, it is likely that student punishment is already so intense that there is less opportunity for other factors, including the racial composition of students, to have an appreciable effect.

The racial threat perspective was supported by Welch and Payne (2010) in large part because that study was able to control for several important crime-specific influences, measured irrespective of race, which revealed an apparent residual effect of racial composition of schools on disciplinary policies. This indicates that there is some race-specific factor that persists in intensifying discipline, regardless of levels of delinquency and delinquency salience in schools.

To further investigate the findings of Welch and Payne (2010), Payne and Welch (2010) used Structural Equation Models (SEM) to examine the relationships among the various disciplinary responses, as well as with the racial composition of schools and other influences on these responses. This study argued that schools are often functioning more like correctional, rather than educational, institutions and often control and punish students in a manner that is similar to the treatment of suspected and convicted adult criminals (Giroux, 2003; Kupchik & Monahan, 2006; Mawson et al., 2002; Noguera, 2003, 2008; Tredway, Brill, & Hernandez, 2007). In addition to corroborating the influence of racial composition on punitive and restorative disciplinary responses, this study showed that significant positive relationships exist among the various disciplinary responses themselves. This indicates that schools responding to student misbehavior with one type of discipline tend to use other types of disciplinary responses as well, suggesting that when discipline is used by schools, schools may in fact become harsher simply because of the number of disciplinary measures implemented in them.

In addition, Payne and Welch (2010) found significant relationships among many of the exogenous factors, demonstrating that schools with relatively more black students are also more likely to have a greater percentage of poor and Hispanic students, be located in disadvantaged urban communities, have less effective principals, conduct more discipline training, and have higher levels of disorder and crime salience. The models of these interrelationships highlight the possibility of indirect effects on school discipline. For example, it is possible that the lack of a direct effect of urbanicity on punitive discipline is actually because urbanicity has an indirect effect on discipline through other factors, such as racial composition or student economic disadvantage.

CONCLUSIONS

Recent findings about the relationship between racial threat and social control in educational institutions are important for a number of reasons. One such reason is that they demonstrate that the effects of racial threat extend beyond the criminal justice institutions traditionally found to be influenced by it. Racial threat is not only associated with harsh crime policies, but also with punitive school policies—a conclusion that suggests racial threat may be operating even beyond criminal and educational institutions.

Another important conclusion made by these studies is that punitive school punishment is influenced by race in ways that prior research on the effects of race at the individual student level have not: Racial composition influences the degree to which schools use harsh disciplinary practices. This phenomenon of using harsher and more frequent discipline in predominantly minority schools reinforces prevailing perceptions of young minority males as delinquents and criminals, and further validates the racial disparities evident at all levels of *criminal* justice. In return, perceptions about the racial composition of criminality also appear to influence social policy relative to public schools and education (Duncan, 2000), intensifying student discipline in a seemingly endless cycle. Future studies examining influences on student discipline will want to consider the significant contributing role of the minority make-up of educational institutions.

These research results are also important because they have serious implications for school discipline. It is troubling that the size of schools' minority populations appears to partially explain the implementation and use of harsh disciplinary policies. By being subjected to more punitive discipline, punished students are not equally benefiting from education; if they are being disciplined, they are most likely not in class and, thus, will experience further academic disadvantage, eventually resulting in failing or dropping out of school altogether (Skiba & Peterson, 2000). This not only affects prospects of employment, but also the likelihood of future involvement in crime and the criminal justice system (Gregory & Weinstein, 2008; Hirschfield, 2008).

REFERENCES

APA Zero Tolerance Task Force. (2006). *Are zero tolerance policies effective in the schools? An evidentiary review and recommendations.* Washington, DC: APA Council of Representatives.

Arum, R. (2003). *Judging school discipline: The crisis of moral authority.* Cambridge, MA: Harvard University Press.

Beger, R. (2002). Expansion of police power in public schools and the vanishing rights of students. *Social Justice, 29,* 119-130.

Blalock, H. (1967). *Towards a theory of minority group relations.* New York, NY: Capricorn Books.

Blumer, H. (1958). Race prejudice as a sense of group position. *The Pacific Sociological Review, 1,* 3-7.

Brantlinger, E. (1991). Social class distinctions in adolescents' reports of problems and punishment in school. *Behavioral Disorders, 17,* 36-46.

Brooks, K., Schiraldi, V., & Ziedenberg, J. (1999). *School house hype: Two years later.* San Francisco, CA: Center on Juvenile and Criminal Justice.

Brown, L. & Beckett, K. (2006). The role of the school district in student discipline: Building consensus in Cincinnati. *The Urban Review, 38,* 235-256.

Crawford, C., Chiricos, T., & Kleck, G. (1998). Race, racial threat, and sentencing of habitual offenders. *Criminology, 36,* 481-511.

Devoe, J., Peter, K., Noonan, M., Snyder, T., & Baum, K. (2005). *Indicators of school crime and safety: 2005.* Washington, DC: U.S. Departments of Education and Justice.

Dinkes, R., Forrest Cataldi, E., & Lin-Kelly, W. (2007). *Indicators of school crime and safety: 2007.* NCES 2007-NCES 2008, U.S. Departments of Education and Justice. Washington, DC: Government Printing Office.

Duncan, G. (2000). Urban pedagogies and the celling of adolescents of color. *Social Justice, 27,* 29-41.

Eitle, D. & Taylor, J. (2008). Are Hispanics the new 'threat'? Minority group threat and fear of crime in Miami-Dade County. *Social Science Research, 37,* 1102-1115.

Ferguson, A. (2000). *Bad boys: Public schools in the making of black masculinity.* Ann Arbor, MI: University of Michigan Press.

Foney, D. & Cunningham, M. (2002). Why do good kids do bad things? Considering multiple contexts in the study of antisocial fighting behaviors in African American urban youth. *The Journal of Negro Education, 71,* 143-157.

Giroux, H. (2003). Racial injustice and disposable youth in the age of zero tolerance. *International Journal of Qualitative Studies in Education, 16,* 553-565.

Glackman, T., Martin, R., Hyman, I., McDowell, E., Berv, V., & Spino, P. (1978). Corporal punishment, school suspension, and the civil rights of students: An analysis of Office for Civil Rights school surveys. *Inequality in Education, 23,* 61-65.

Gottfredson, G. & Gottfredson, D. (2001). What schools do to prevent problem behavior and promote safe environments. *Journal of Educational and Psychological Consultation, 12,* 313-344.

Gregory, J. (1995). The crime of punishment: Racial and gender disparities in the use of corporal punishment in the U.S. Public Schools. *Journal of Negro Education, 64,* 454-462.

Gregory, A. & Weinstein, R. (2008). The discipline gap and African Americans: Defiance or cooperation in the high school classroom. *Journal of School Psychology, 46,* 455-475.

Hirschfield, P. (2008). Preparing for prison? The criminalization of school discipline in the USA. *Theoretical Criminology, 12,* 79-101.

Jacobs, D. & Carmichael, J. (2001). The politics of punishment across time and space: A pooled time-series analysis of imprisonment rates. *Social Forces, 80,* 61-89.

Kent, S. & Jacobs, D. (2004). Social divisions and coercive control in advanced societies: Law enforcement strength in eleven nations from 1975 to 1994. *Social Problems, 51,* 343-361.

Kupchik, A. (2009). Things are tough all over: Race, ethnicity, class and school discipline. *Punishment and Society, 11,* 291-317.

Kupchik, A. & Ellis, N. (2008). School discipline and security: Fair for all students? *Youth and Society, 39,* 549-574.

Kupchik, A. & Monahan, T. (2006). The new American school: Preparation for post-industrial discipline. *British Journal of Sociology of Education, 5,* 617-631.

Liska, A. (1992). *Social threat and social control.* Albany, NY: State University of New York Press.

Mawson, A., Lapsley, P., Hoffman, A., & Guignard, J. (2002). Preventing lethal violence in schools: The case for entry-based weapons screening. *Journal of Health Politics, Policy and Law, 27,* 243-260.

McCarthy, J. & Hoge, D. (1987). The social construction of school punishment: Racial disadvantage out of universalistic process. *Social Forces, 65,* 1101-1120.

McFadden, A., Marsh II, G., Price, B., & Hwang, Y. (1992). A study of race and gender bias in the punishment of handicapped school children. *The Urban Review, 24,* 239-251.

Morrow, R. & Torres, C. (1995). *Social theory and education: A critique of theories of social and cultural reproduction.* Albany, NY: SUNY Press.

Mosher, C. (2001). Predicting drug arrest rates: Conflict and social disorganization perspectives. *Crime & Delinquency, 47,* 84-104.

Nichols, J. (2004). An exploration of discipline and suspension data. *The Journal of Negro Education, 73,* 408-423.

Noguera, P. (2003). Schools, prisons, and social implications of punishment: Rethinking disciplinary practices. *Theory into Practice* 42:341-350.

Noguera, P. (2008). *The trouble with black boys...and other reflections on race, equity, and the future of public education.* San Francisco, CA: Jossey-Bass.

Payne, A. & Welch, K. (2010). Modeling the effects of racial threat on punitive and restorative school discipline practices. *Criminology 48.*

Raffaele Mendez, L. & Knoff, H. (2003). Who gets suspended from school and why: A demographic analysis of schools and disciplinary infractions in a large school district. *Education and Treatment of Children, 26,* 30-51.

Shaw, S. & Braden, J. (1990). Race and gender bias in the administration of corporal punishment. *School Psychology Review, 19,* 378-383.

Simon, J. (2007). *Governing through crime: How the war on crime transformed American democracy and created a culture of fear.* New York, NY: Oxford University Press.

Skiba, R. (2000). Zero tolerance, zero evidence: An analysis of school disciplinary practice. *Policy Research Report.* Indianapolis, IN: Indiana Education Policy Center.

Skiba, R. (2001). When is disproportionality discrimination? The overrepresentation of black students in school suspension. In W. Ayers, B. Dohrn, & R. Ayers (Eds.), *Zero tolerance: Resisting the drive for punishment in our schools: A handbook for parents, students, educators, and citizens* (pp. 176-187). New York, NY: The New Press.

Skiba, R., Michael, R., Nardo, A., & Peterson, R. (2002). The color of discipline: Source of racial and gender disproportionality in school discipline. *The Urban Review, 34,* 317-342.

Skiba, R. & Peterson, R. (1999). The dark side of zero tolerance: Can punishment lead to safe schools? *Phi Delta Kappan, 80,* 372-382.

Skiba, R. & Peterson, R. (2000). School discipline at a crossroads: From zero tolerance to early response. *Exceptional Children, 66,* 335-347.

Skiba, R., Peterson, R., & Williams, T. (1997). Office referrals and suspension: disciplinary intervention in middle schools. *Education and Treatment of Children, 20,* 295-315.

Toby, J. (1998). Getting serious about school discipline. *The Public Interest, 133,* 68-84.

Tolnay, S., Beck, E., & Massey, J. (1992). Black competition and white vengeance. Legal executions of blacks as social control in the cotton south, 1890 to 1992. *Social Science Quarterly, 73,* 627-644.

Tredway, L., Brill, F., & Hernandez, J. (2007). Taking off the cape: The stories of novice urban leadership. *Theory into Practice, 46,* 212-221.

Vavrus, F. & Cole, K. (2002). 'I didn't do nothin': The discursive construction of school suspension. *The Urban Review, 34,* 87-111.

Wallace, Jr., J., Goodkind, S., Wallace, C., & Bachman, J. (2008). Racial, ethnic, and gender differences in school discipline among U.S. high school students: 1991-2005. *Negro Educational Review, 59,* 47-62.

Watts, I. & Erevelles, N. (2004). These deadly times: Reconceptualizing school violence by using critical race theory and disability studies. *American Educational Research Journal, 41,* 271-299.

Welch, K. & Payne, A. (2010). Racial threat and punitive school discipline. *Social Problems, 57,* 25-48.

Wu, S-C., Pink, W., Crain, R., & Moles, O. (1982). Student suspension: A critical reappraisal. *The Urban Review, 14,* 245-303.

Racial Threat and Schools: Looking Beyond the Boundaries of Criminology

Aaron Kupchik

The essay by Kelly Welch offers a helpful assessment of what we know – and perhaps more importantly, what we don't know – about the influence of racial threat in schools, particularly with regard to school discipline. This is a careful, thorough review that describes the limits of our knowledge and ends with a discussion of recent research that attempts to fill in the gaps in our knowledge about how race shapes school discipline.

There is now an abundance of research that very clearly documents stark racial disproportionality in school discipline, with black and Latino/a students more likely than white students to receive school punishments such as suspensions and expulsions, even when controlling for their actual rates of misbehavior. Welch points out that many scholars attribute this disproportionality to racial bias, but states that "there has been no empirical support for this idea that bias and discrimination contribute to harsh school discipline." Though I agree in large part with this claim, I also feel that it is a bit of an overstatement, for two reasons: 1) the statement seems to expect a higher level of evidence than seems feasible, and 2) we have very strong, though indirect, evidence of racial bias leading to disproportionate discipline from researchers in other fields.

With regard to the first of these two reasons, it is unclear to me what would constitute solid empirical evidence to support the understanding that racial bias is responsible for disproportionate school discipline. Discovering causal relationships is a weakness of nonexperimental quantitative analyses, and yet this is the type of research that the leading criminology journals publish nearly exclusively, thus the research that criminologists most often produce is not well-designed for this type of problem. Instead, as Welch describes, criminologists have found that the race of a student is related to his or her likelihood of punishment, even while controlling for competing explanations such as their level of self-reported or school-reported misbehavior. But as Welch argues (and I agree), this is insufficient, since our measures of student misbehavior may be neither reliable nor valid, and we cannot claim to have controlled for all possible confounding factors. We cannot be certain, for example, whether disproportionate discipline is due to racial bias, to teachers' perceptions of the communities from which these students come, or to a lack of suitable classroom management skills among teachers who teach in urban schools.

But the problem is not just that the methods most often used by criminologists are inadequate. A very careful qualitative study likewise would not be sufficiently generalizable to satisfy those looking for convincing empirical support. It is not clear to me how to design a study that could sufficiently explain the role of bias in disproportionate school discipline, or what such empirical support would even look like. That is, how could one convincingly demonstrate that racial disproportionality is indeed due to racial bias? The fact that criminologists are still asking the same question of racial disproportionality in the criminal justice system suggests that such empirical support is difficult to obtain.

CONSULTING A BROADER LITERATURE

I suggest that we need to look beyond the specific problem at hand, and explore the literature on schools more broadly. Schools are very complex organizations that are shaped by local community politics, national politics, and internal organizational dynamics. When an administrator decides whether to suspend a student, he or she may be thinking of more than just the juvenile's character and actual misbehavior; concerns as broad as the need to appear supportive to a teacher, the need to protect the learning environment for other students, the need to maintain adequate daily attendance counts, and other pedagogical, financial, and political factors can shape the decision. Because school discipline is embedded within a dense web of issues, we need to consider school governance and school social relations from a broader perspective than criminologists often assume.

There have been several studies from the sociology of education that offer clear indirect support for the racial bias explanation of disproportionate discipline; the support is only indirect because the research is not related specifically to school discipline. I imagine that other fields as well, especially psychology, public affairs, and education, also contribute to this debate, though I am less familiar with these literatures. Sociologists such as Prudence Carter (2005), Amanda Lewis (2003), and Ed Morris (2005, 2007), to name only a few, have very clearly shown in recent research that racial biases profoundly impact how teachers and administrators evaluate students. Though these studies do not seek to explain school discipline, specifically, they clearly illustrate the racialized nature of schools. Race shapes how much and what kind of attention students receive. It affects teachers' perceptions of attributes such as students' academic abilities and whether students are obedient or defiant. Black and Hispanic youth are perceived as less academically gifted, more defiant and unruly, and less interested in academic work.

Indirectly, this body of research seems capable of explaining the racial disproportionality in discipline. Though this research is not focused on discipline *per se*, it illustrates how minority youth are perceived as having characteristics and behaviors that impede the school's academic mission, deteriorate the school social climate, and cause difficulty for teachers and administrators. Clearly, such students will be disciplined more often than others because of these perceptions. Of course, one could argue that it is unwise to assume the connection between discipline and broader perceptions of students. But given that schools "govern through crime" (Simon, 2007; see also Kupchik, 2010), in that crime control is a central organizing construct for school governance, it seems reasonable to assume a tight link between overall perceptions or school governance, and student discipline. Thus, I do believe that there is empirical support for the idea that bias and discrimination contribute to harsh school discipline, though I concede that it is indirect and based on case studies rather than large-scale quantitative research.

RACIAL THREAT AND SOCIAL REPRODUCTION

Assuming that this is true, it is worth discussing how to conceive of this relationship between race and discipline, theoretically. Welch uses a racial threat perspective to explain it. A racial threat perspective stems from the seminal work of Blalock (1967), whose concept of "power threat" referred to efforts of whites to curtail the economic and political competition of minority groups. Thus this perspective views school discipline as an effort to control the perceived threat of youth of color. I agree that this is a valid way to think about racial bias and school punishment, but I also believe that the link between race and school discipline goes beyond such efforts to punish threatening populations. I find it more helpful to conceive of this relationship using a social reproduction framework instead, since this framework draws attention to the seemingly natural way in which discipline works.

A social reproduction thesis hails primarily from Bourdieu (see Bourdieu & Passeron, 1990), who illustrates the ways that schools reproduce and exacerbate existing social inequality. Students from varying backgrounds come to school with very different skill sets and behavioral patterns, and schools must decide which of these to value and reward; the behaviors and skills demonstrated by middle-class, white youth are those so favored. This means that middle-class white students are rewarded and treated as school successes, while equally intelligent and hard-working students from other backgrounds might be treated as failures due to their use of language, the way they dress, or their mannerisms. Schools thus reward already advantaged students for what they learn in their homes and communities, while making it appear that they are being rewarded for their hard work and intelligence instead.

This perspective applies to school discipline because it explains schools' responses to non-academic behavior as well. Black male youth who dress, walk, and talk in ways that are accepted within their community are often treated as disruptive, due only to their mannerisms, not to any actual disruptive behavior. In some schools where I have done research, these racial cues are even codified in the school rules, such as the prohibition of do-rags (commonly worn by black students) but not baseball caps (commonly worn by white students). When students are disciplined because of these mannerisms, the school distinguishes them from the students who are not punished and who therefore appear to be better behaved, and in this way existing social inequality is made worse.

A social reproduction framework and racial threat theory both make the same predictions regarding school discipline; both predict that schools with larger populations of racial and ethnic minority students will practice harsher discipline, and that this operates within schools as well. I find the social reproduction thesis to be more helpful because it explains the seemingly natural way that schools punish students. A social reproduction thesis views racial (or other) bias as a universal feature of stratified society, not as a defensive response to groups perceived as threatening the power of the white majority (see Apple, 1979). It can explain how we still see racial disproportionality in schools with largely nonwhite administrators (e.g., Carter, 2005), and also how harsh discipline is enforced with benevolent motives – since the harsh discipline is understood as a natural response to the abilities and characteristics of a group of youth, and as thoughtful preparation for their expected futures. For example, in my research in schools I often heard school administrators justify the need for harsh punishment by describing it as training disadvantaged youth for their future labor roles, stating that they are trying to prepare these youth for employment under a supervisor who would fire them if they acted in such a way. It's fair to trust that for most of these administrators, their motives truly are benevolent. But this perspective assumes that these youth will be working in low-wage jobs where they are closely supervised, rather than the supervisors themselves; it is a social class-based assumption and it advances the class stratification on which it is based because it leads to distinct treatment between groups of youth.

In her book, *De-Facing Power*, political scientist Clarissa Rile Hayward (2000) illustrates this process. She studies how power and authority are exercised over young children in two fourth-grade classes: one in a poor, mostly black, urban neighborhood, and one in a middle-class, mostly white, suburban neighborhood. The students in the two schools receive very different styles of discipline and teaching, with the urban students receiving a much more authoritarian style of interaction. The teacher in the urban school is more rigid and authoritarian than the suburban teacher, because she understands the dangers lurking in these youths' communities and she wants to prevent these youth from entering "the streets;" she hopes that by teaching rules that demarcate right from wrong, she can prevent these youth from working within the drug trade, for example. Thus, the teacher in the urban school may be practicing social reproduction through harsher discipline, but she is doing so for the sake of youth, not to diminish the power or threat they pose. Though a racial threat hypothesis would have predicted the same result, a social reproduction framework better considers the complex motivations and social processes underlying social discipline.

In sum, I enjoyed reading Welch's thoughtful essay. Though I advocate for a different perspective on a few issues, these are fairly small quibbles.

Overall, I agree with Welch's analysis of the existing research and the need for additional work on this important topic.

REFERENCES

Apple, M. (1979). *Ideology and curriculum.* Boston, MA: Routledge & Kegan Paul.

Blalock, H. (1967). *Towards a theory of minority group relations.* New York, NY: Capricorn Books.

Bourdieu, P. & Passeron, J. (1990). *Reproduction in education, society and culture (2nd ed.).* Newbury Park, CA: Sage Publications.

Carter, P. (2005). *Keepin' it real: School success beyond black and white.* New York, NY: Oxford University Press.

Hayward, C. (2000). *De-facing power.* New York, NY: Cambridge University Press.

Kupchik, A. (2010). *Homeroom security: School discipline in an age of fear.* New York, NY: New York University Press.

Lewis, A. (2003). *Race in the schoolyard: Negotiating the color line in classrooms and communities.* New Brunswick, NJ: Rutgers University Press.

Morris, E. (2005). "Tuck in that shirt!" Race, class, gender and discipline in an urban school. *Sociological Perspectives, 48*(1), 25-48.

Morris, E. (2007). 'Ladies' or 'loudies'? Perceptions and experiences of black girls in classrooms. *Youth and Society, 38*(4), 490-515.

Simon, J. (2007). *Governing through crime: How the War on Crime transformed American democracy and created a culture of gear.* New York, NY: Oxford University Press.

THE IMPACT OF RECENT SCHOOL DISCIPLINE RESEARCH ON RACIAL THREAT THEORY

CYNDY CARAVELIS HUGHES

Research on questions of social threat and social control has experienced a resurgence in recent years (Baumer, Messner, & Rosenfeld, 2003; Bontrager, Chiricos, & Bales, 2005; Eitle, D'Alessio, & Stolzenberg, 2002; Greenberg & West, 2001; Jacobs & Carmichael, 2001). This is not surprising given the continually changing racial and ethnic landscape of the United States and the need to identify frameworks that help to understand the expansion of formal social control measures during a period when crime rates have been declining. The theoretical link between racial and ethnic minorities and the exercise of social control has been conceptualized on both the individual and aggregate level. Common to both is the expectation that minorities are perceived as threatening in ways that inform the mobilization of social control.

Blalock (1967) brought the threat of minority populations into focus with his seminal "power threat" concept. He developed his theory systematically in a sociological analysis of the power imbalance and competition between dominant and minority groups in society. Grounded in the conflict perspective, Blalock's formulations of the threat and social control relationship conceptualize social control responses to minority threats of a political and economic nature. More recently, the putative threat posed by minority presence has been recast in criminal terms. The "logic" of this position was first described by Liska and Chamlin (1984, p. 384) who noted that "the threat hypothesis . . . suggests that a high percentage of nonwhites produced an emergent property, 'perceived threat of crime,' which may have consequences for a variety of social control impulses."

The recent trend towards increased punitiveness has manifested beyond the bounds of the criminal justice system and has surfaced in the practices of other key social institutions. In the Presidential Panel paper entitled, *The Influence of Racial Threat in Schools: Recent Research Findings*, Welch argues that the applicability of racial threat theory can be expanded beyond explanations of enhanced criminal sentencing to elucidate the method in which discipline is handled in schools. In support of this argument, Welch draws parallels between the criminal justice system and educational institutions explain the increasing harshness in school discipline. This comparison is warranted given that the rising punitive nature of school discipline in educational institutions is occurring in light of decreased rates of delinquency and violent school victimization. Additionally, the increasing overlap between the criminal justice system and educational institutions is illustrated by a rising number of school disciplinary practices resulting in the involvement of local law enforcement, further streamlining the "school to prison pipeline" (Hirschfield, 2008).

Welch makes a compelling case for utilizing racial threat theory to examine the effects of minority threat in other institutions that have critical responsibility for social control broadly understood. As Welch notes, it is not surprising that students who are punished the most harshly in schools are male, poor and members of a racial or ethnic minority (Noguera, 2003a; Singer, 1996). It would stand to reason that, much like judicial actors, teachers and administrators might also in certain instances view a sizeable minority presence on campus and in the classroom as potentially threatening. To this end, racial threat theory might help to explain why the response to a perceived rule violation, illegal or otherwise, is met with unusually harsh sanctioning or immediate involvement of legal authorities, who may be considered more capable of dealing with threatening situations.

The application of racial threat theory to the disciplinary practices of educational institutions opens the door to a wide array of potentially fruitful research inquiries. Particularly promising would be contextual analyses using multi-level modeling that would highlight whether cross-level effects exist between the proportion of a school's minority population and the likelihood that black or Latino students would experience harsher school discipline or punishment than a similarly behaving white students. Drawing on the racial threat literature, Ulmer and Johnson noted that "racial group threat theory clearly predicts that the percent of the local black and/or Latino population will be positively associated with sentencing severity" (2004, p. 145). They also suggested that group threat theory would predict a cross-level interaction whereby "black or Latino defendants may be sentenced more severely in contexts with larger black or Latino populations" (2004, p. 145). Similarly, in his study of criminal sentencing, Britt cited media portrayals of crime that may exacerbate perceived minority threat and that could result in the sentencing of "minority offenders more severely . . . in communities with larger minority populations and greater ethnic heterogeneity" (2000, p. 711). By examining the cross-level effects of the proportion of a school's minority population and the treatment of individual minority students, perhaps the mechanisms of racial bias in the application of school discipline would be better understood.

Additionally, several individual-level theories may work well with the racial threat perspective to further illuminate the dynamics behind any observed relationship between the punitiveness of school discipline and schools with a greater proportion of minority group students. One example would be Kalvin and Zeisel's (1966) liberation hypothesis, which suggests that racial disparity in sentencing should decrease as the seriousness of the charged behavior increases. Indeed, research on criminal sentencing has shown that the possibility for racial bias is greater in situations where the crime is less serious and greater opportunities for discretionary responses exist (Albonetti, 1997; Spohn & Spears, 2000; Steffensmeier & Demuth, 2001). This pattern has effectively been established in educational institutions where research on the application of school discipline has shown that black students are generally given punishments that are more frequent and more punitive for less serious offenses (Brown & Beckett, 2006; Nichols, 2004; Noguera, 2003b; Skiba, 2000, 2001; Wacquant, 2001).

Another individual level formulation of the "threat" hypothesis that might prove insightful in an educational context is Albonetti's theory of bounded rationality, which made use of race-related threat to account for "discrimination and disparity in sentencing decisions" (1991, p. 250). She argued that judges attempt to make rational decisions in contexts that often involve incomplete information and uncertainty, particularly concerning the potential threat of future criminality. In this context, judges may rely on "stereotypical images of which defendant is most likely to recidivate" (1991, p. 250). Support for Albonetti's theory can be found in research examining the sources of gender and racial disproportionality in school punishment. Skiba et al. (2002) found that black students received referrals for rule violations that were more subject to interpretation. While white students were cited more frequently for objective infractions such as smoking and vandalism, black students were more frequently referred to the office for disrespect, threatening behavior, and loitering. As Skiba et al. notes, "Even the most serious of the reasons for office referrals among black students, *threat,* is dependent on perception of threat of the staff making the referral" (2002, p. 334).

This perceived threat posed by black students may also be explained by a similar theoretical framework outlined by Steffensmeier, Ulmer, and Kramer (1998) who argued that three focal concerns are present in judicial decision making. These include practical constraints, blameworthiness, and protection of the community. The potential interaction of race and criminal threat achieves salience in relation to the concern for community protection. In this regard, interviews conducted with Pennsylvania judges showed that young black men were "more likely to be perceived as dangerous, committed to street life and less reformable" than other defendants (Steffensmeier, et al., 1998, p. 787). While the research conducted by both Albonetti and Steffensmeier is specifically referring to criminal sentencing, it's possible that the same racial bias present in criminal sentencing proceedings may be playing a part in school discipline as well. While not expressly addressing the racial threat hypothesis, research has established that harsh disciplinary practices may be linked to perceptions of misbehavior resulting from racial stereotypes or bias (Nichols, 2004; Skiba & Peterson, 1999), and the "adultification" of minority students by school personnel (Ferguson, 2000).

As previously noted, central to the racial threat hypothesis is the inclusion of macro-level indicators to model levels of racial and ethnic threat. Most discussions of minority threat have focused on the putative danger of blacks, especially black males. However, the perceived threat of Latinos has been increasingly recognized. Portillos noted that "the assumption is frequently made that if you are a young Latino, and especially a Latino male, you are a gun wielding, drug selling gang-banger, unless proven otherwise" (1998, p. 156). Referencing the existence of stereotypes that link Latinos to drug trafficking and drug related violence, Steffensmeier and Demuth suggested that increasing numbers of Latinos "may exacerbate perceptions of their cultural dissimilarity and the 'threat' they pose in ways that contribute to their harsher treatment in criminal courts" (2001, p. 725). Recent accounts in the media of Mara Salvatrucha (MS-13), reputed to be "the most violent gang in America" with more than 10,000 members (Campo-Flores, 2005) have underscored the perception of threat associated with Latinos, especially Latino males. An important area of new research in terms of schools and social control will be to examine the potential threat posed or perceived to be associated with the presence of Latino male students. Again, this can be assessed at the individual level or in relation to the broader context of the relative size of Latino student populations.

Threat related research in the context of school discipline and punishment may well be enhanced by the examination of dynamic indicators of racial and ethnic threat. One limitation with the static indicators that have been traditionally used in threat research is that when black or Latino populations are either very small or conversely, large and constant, they are less likely to be perceived as threatening (Blalock, 1967). As Blalock and others (Jacobs & O'Brien,1998; King & Wheelock, 2007) have pointed out, it is often the growth of minority populations over time that may be perceived as threatening and subsequently the basis for mobilizing social control. From this perspective, it would be hypothesized that schools or school districts that have seen the greatest increase in minority populations over time, would be the most likely to invoke harsh disciplinary measures or engage law enforcement when less formal measures are possible.

The recent research linking the racial threat hypothesis to school discipline makes a number of noteworthy contributions to the field. First and foremost, it demonstrates that the racial threat hypothesis may well be applicable to educational settings by contributing to harsher disciplinary practices in schools with a greater proportion of minority students. As a result it may be fruitful to examine whether racial threat is applicable in other social institutions as well. Additionally, this study further serves to highlight the interdisciplinary nature of our field and serves as an apt reminder that criminal and delinquent behavior is interlaced with other aspects of social life and that subsequently, the response of other social institutions directly impacts the path to which individuals may find themselves entering the criminal justice system.

The policy implications for the racial patterns that exist in the use of discipline in schools are clear. As Welch notes, harsh school discipline is linked to performing poorly in school, grade level retention and dropping out of school (Skiba & Peterson, 2000). For those students affected, this potentially increases the likelihood of involvement in criminal behavior and eventual entry into the criminal justice system (Gregory & Weinstein, 2008; Hirshfield, 2008).

While legal reforms mandate that student involvement in certain illegal behaviors, such as weapon possession and drug use, result in referrals to law enforcement rather than being addressed internally, a considerable amount of individual-level discretion is employed in determining which student behaviors are addressed by these policies (Ferguson, 2000; Vavrus & Cole, 2002). Additionally, it appears that teachers may share a type of discretionary power that is typically associated with prosecutors, resulting in the increased punishment of certain students. As Welch and Payne note, "findings indicate that harsher student treatment is not merely a reflection of more violations punishable by mandated suspensions, but also importantly involves the discretion of teachers and administrators in identifying and acknowledging those behaviors" (2010, p. 27).

The clear policy choice facing school administrators is to institute measures that would ensure that any potential racial or ethnic biases in discipline and punishment are eliminated. One possible way to do this would be to borrow from the criminal justice system. Specifically, schools and school districts could develop "guidelines" for the applications of discipline based on the seriousness of the alleged behavior and the student's past record of school-related activity. Quality education for all students can only be established when the prevalent racial bias in schools is recognized and administrators subsequently understand the mechanisms through which this discrimination plays a role in the application of school discipline.

REFERENCES

Albonetti, C. (1997). An integration of theories to explain judicial discretion. *Social Problems, 38,* 247-265.

Baumer, E., Messner, S., & Rosenfeld, R. (2003). Explaining spatial variation in support for capital punishment: A multilevel analysis. *American Journal of Sociology, 108*(4), 844-75.

Blalock, H. (1967). *Toward a theory of minority-group relations.* New York, NY: John Wiley & Sons, Inc.

Bontrager, S., Chiricos, T., & Bales, B. (2005). Race, ethnicity, threat and the labeling of convicted felons. *Criminology, 43*(3), 589-622.

Britt, C. (2000). Social context and racial disparities in punishment decisions. *Justice Quarterly, 17,* 707-732.

Brown, L. & Beckett, K. (2006). The role of the school district in student discipline: building consensus in Cincinnati. *The Urban Review, 38,* 235–56.

Campo-Flores, A. (2005). The most dangerous gang in America. *Newsweek, 145*(13), 23-36.

Eitle, D., D'Alessio, S., & Stolzenberg, L. (2002). Racial threat and social control: A test of the political, economic and threat of black crime hypothesis. *Social Forces, 81*(2), 557-576.

Ferguson, A. (2000). *Bad boys: Public schools in the making of black masculinity.* Ann Arbor, MI: University of Michigan Press.

Greenberg, D. & West, V. (2001). State prison populations and their growth, 1971-1991. *Criminology, 39,* 615-653.

Gregory, A. & Weinstein, R. (2008). The discipline gap and African Americans: defiance or cooperation in the high school classroom. *Journal of School Psychology, 46,* 455-475.

Hirschfield, P. (2008). Preparing for prison? The criminalization of school discipline in the USA. *Theoretical Criminology, 12,* 79-101.

Jacobs, D. & Carmichael, J. (2001). The politics of punishment across time and space: A pooled time-series analysis of imprisonment rates. *Social Forces, 80*(1), 61-91

Jacobs, D & O'Brien, R. (1998). The determinants of deadly force: A structural analysis of police violence. *American Journal of Sociology, 103,* 837-862.

Kalven, Jr., H. & Zeisel, H. (1966). *The American jury.* Boston, MA: Little, Brown.

King, R. & Wheelock, D. (2007). Group threat and social control: Race, perceptions of minorities and the desire to punish. *Social Forces, 85,* 1255-1280.

Liska, A. (1992). Introduction to the study of social control. In A. Liska (Ed.), *Social threat and social control* (pp. 1-32). Albany, NY: State University of New York Press.

Liska, A. & Chamlin, M. (1984). Social structure and crime control among macrosocial units. *American Journal of Sociology, 90,* 383-395.

Nichols, J. (2004). An exploration of discipline and suspension data. *The Journal of Negro Education, 73,* 408–23.

Noguera, P. (2003a). Schools, prisons, and social implications of punishment: Rethinking disciplinary practices. *Theory into Practice, 42,* 341-350.

Noguera, p. (2003b). The trouble with black boys: The fole and influence of environmental and cultural factors on the academic performance of African American males. *Urban Education, 38,* 431–59.

Portillos, E. (1998). Latinos, gangs and drugs. In C. Mann & M. Zatz (Eds.), *Images of color, images of crime* (pp. 156-165). Los Angeles, CA: Roxbury.

Singer, S. (1996). *Recriminalizing delinquency.* Cambridge, UK: Cambridge University Press.

Skiba, R. (2000). *Zero tolerance, zero evidence: An analysis of school disciplinary practice.* (Policy Research Report #SRS2). Bloomington, IN: Indiana Education Policy Center.

Skiba, R. (2001). When is disproportionality discrimination? The overrepresentation of black students in school suspension. In W. Ayers, B. Dohrn, & R. Ayers (Eds.), *Zero tolerance: Resisting the drive for punishment in our schools: A handbook for parents, students, educators, and citizens* (pp. 176–87). New York, NY: The New Press.

Skiba, R., Michael, R., & Nardo, A. (2002). The color of discipline: Source of racial and gender disproportionality in school discipline. *The Urban Review, 34,* 317-342.

Skiba, R. & Peterson, R. (1999). The dark side of zero tolerance: Can punishment lead to safe schools? *Phi Delta Kappan, 80,* 372-382.

Skiba, R. & Peterson, R. (2000). School discipline at a crossroads: From zero tolerance to early response. *Exceptional Children, 66,* 335-347.

Spohn, C. & Spears, J. (2000). Sentencing of drug offenders in three cities: Does race/ethnicity make a difference? In D. Hawkins, S. Myers, Jr., & R. Stone (Eds.), *Crime control and social justice: A delicate balance* (pp. 197-233). Westport, CT: Greenwood Publishing Group.

Steffensmeier, D. & Demuth, S. (2001). Ethnicity and sentencing outcomes in U.S. Federal Courts: Who is punished more harshly? *American Sociological Review, 65,*(5), 705-729.

Steffensmeier, D., Ulmer, J., & Kramer, J. (1998). The interaction of race, gender and age in criminal sentencing: The punishment cost of being young, black and male. *Criminology, 36,* 763-798.

Ulmer, J. & Johnson, B. (2004). Sentencing in context: A multilevel analysis. *Criminology, 42,* 137-177.

Vavrus, F. & Cole, K. (2002). 'I didn't do nothin': The discursive construction of school suspension. *The Urban Review, 34,* 87–111.

Wacquant, L. (2001). Deadly symbiosis: When ghetto and prison meet and mesh. In D. Garland (Ed.), *Mass imprisonment: Social causes and consequences* (pp. 82-120). London, UK: Sage Publications.

Welch, K. & Payne, A. (2010). Racial threat and punitive school discipline. *Social Problems, 57,* 25-48.

"No Time to Talk": A Cautiously Optimistic Tale of Restorative Justice and Related Approaches to School Discipline

Gordon Bazemore
Mara Schiff

Abstract

In recent years, the school has become a new target for restorative justice intervention designed to provide an alternative to punitive discipline that might also improve school culture and climate. Although a key expectation of pilot programs in many schools is that they will reduce suspensions, it is at least equally likely that school based "alternative" programs will receive referrals that would not otherwise be considered for suspension.

It is possible that restorative justice, applied in significant dosages, may bring positive changes to schools and even impact disciplinary style. However, practical, theoretical, and methodological arguments suggest that restorative justice programs alone are unlikely to have significant impact on the critical suspension or expulsion decision. Drawing on organizational analogies from promising, well-intended criminal justice reforms, we consider failed efforts to increase uniformity in juvenile and criminal justice as cautionary examples of how promising efforts aimed at reducing school suspension may ultimately have little or no impact. Unfortunately, the phrase "no time to talk," illustrates the reality of many schools wherein harmful exclusionary disciplinary decisions (suspension, expulsion) are made with little or no discussion and instead with attention focused on more immediate and utilitarian concerns. Optimistically, we suggest that dialogue-driven restorative processes—coupled with whole school approaches grounded in routine activities theory and communal school approaches—may potentially create opportunities for open, problem solving discourse to inform meaningful disciplinary decisionmaking, improve overall safety, and a support a culture of belonging.

INTRODUCTION

"Zero tolerance may have a few problems but at least now we have a common standard....equal treatment... every student is judged by the same standard of discipline.
"

"This is our zero tolerance matrix...which is meant to make sure we provide a similar response to similar disciplinary incidents. We all know that's a joke."

Quotes from two middle-school principals.

Schools have long been viewed in sociological and criminological literature as critical "mediating institutions" (Bellah, Madsen, Sullivan, Swidler, & Tipton, 1991) along the pathway to pro-social adult life (Gottfredson, Gottfredson, Payne, & Gottfredson, 2005; Polk & Kobrin, 1972). Though family and early childhood experiences differentially prepare children for the school experience, the reality is that such differences between children are at a relatively minimal level in pre-K, and increase dramatically over time as traditional schools respond differently to students from different backgrounds (Rist, 1972; Lyons & Drew, 2006).

Given the strong connection between school success and life-course opportunities, the rise of zero tolerance policies has recently been identified as a potential threat to positive futures for a significant portion of students. Especially for minority children, this threat is a key component of what is now widely discussed as the "school-to-prison" pipeline (Advancement Project, 2005). While mostly unable to dismantle these zero tolerance policies (but see, Duncan, 2000), some school administrators and other education professionals have recently mounted intensive efforts to develop disciplinary alternatives to zero-tolerance suspension and other exclusionary practices (Morrison, 2002; Greene, 2004).

This paper has several basic premises. First, current alternative strategies and programs designed to mitigate zero tolerance responses seem likely to fail because they are not grounded in a clear and holistic understanding of the problem. That is, they often do not sufficiently consider the theoretical basis for understanding *why* such responses *might* work, but also be easily thwarted. Moreover, they do not adequately examine the historical precedents set by similar generally progressive interventions. In assessing this misunderstanding, we suggest that criminologists should consider parallels between current disciplinary reform initiatives in schools and criminal justice reforms of recent decades. For example, well-intended *just desserts*, or "justice model" reforms (von Hirsch, 1976) led to determinate sentencing (e.g., Tonry, 1995) and to other generally counterproductive, unanticipated consequences—notably, the greatest expansion in incarceration in modern history (Clear, 2007; Garland, 2005). Moreover, such strategies did little to accomplish even intended goals aimed at eliminating disparity.

Similarly, school disciplinary codes appear to create an aura of equal justice, but in practice allow for wide discretion and unfairness in application (Advancement Project, 2005; Green, 2004). For example, the common practice of designating students in conflict as "victim" or "offender" in what is often an ongoing dispute between two individuals, and then suspending the latter is a typical zero tolerance response that replicates retributive, punishment-based criminal justice strategies. There is certainly no basis for creating a more positive ongoing relationship among students, teacher conflict with students, nor conflicts between peers and teachers who typically must encounter one another on a daily basis.

In recent years, some school staff appear to be coalescing around the need for more prevention and intervention programs. Yet, students most at risk for school removal are clearly not those being referred to these programs. Indeed, most conversations about use of prevention and intervention programs to limit zero tolerance responses also confuse intervention *target groups*. Indeed, youth accused of very minor disciplinary violations or viewed as unlikely to receive suspension or referral in the first place are those who participate in these programs. Conversely, youth considered for suspension are *not* those most likely to be considered for referral to prevention programs. Faculty and administrators (like juvenile justice workers) love prevention programs, arguing that money and time invested in such programs will ultimately resolve disciplinary problems. Prevention and early intervention programs are, however, extremely difficult to evaluate because they are based on the premise that a youth not yet in trouble would have gotten in trouble without such a program. Meanwhile, youth not in trouble who are referred to these programs may begin to associate with those already engaged in minor problem behavior and may become exposed to the iatrogenic effects of such intervention, even including that aimed ostensibly aimed at prevention (Dishion, McCord, & Poulin, 1999; Cook, Gottfredson, & Na, 2010).

Using preliminary qualitative data from focus groups and informal interviews in several regions of one Southeastern state, this paper illustrates conceptual flaws in what appear to be commendable and well-meaning efforts to mitigate the effects of zero tolerance policies. Specifically, our concern is that limiting intervention practices to "program-based" responses will have little impact, or even negative effects, in the absence of a careful whole school analysis of the dynamics of zero tolerance discipline and its consequences. We argue that no one practice model, and no one theory of change is adequate to the task of school disciplinary reform. Rather, we propose three compatible, theory-driven, strategic approaches. *First*, we consider restorative justice disciplinary and conflict resolution models that prioritize "restorative accountability," socio-emotional learning and peacemaking (Braithwaite & Roche, 2001; Morrison, 2002), while addressing the overall need for a non-punitive disciplinary and conflict resolution approach and culture (i.e., restorative practice). *Second*, we propose a strategic focus based on routine activities theory to manage space and student flow in ways that should limit situations and opportunities for student conflict, violence and misbehavior (Felson, 1993; Eck, 1994). At the core of this model is a situational crime prevention/disciplinary approach using adult school employees as "capable guardians" who can limit unsupervised student interaction (Zimmerman, 2007), especially in various high risk spaces. Finally, strategic efforts based on recent, more holistic "communal school" culture initiatives (Gottfredson et al., 2005; Solomon, Watson, Battistich, Schaps, & Deluchi, 1992) may support the need for student belonging, foster adult and student skill building to resolve both discipline/conflict resolution, and develop a sense of community or "neighborhood," to enhance adult and youth bonding and guardianship responsibilities.

First, we offer a brief overview of the history and recent misuse of zero tolerance policies, while considering input from focus groups that illustrates problems in well intentioned, though misdirected alternative responses that typically by-pass the group of students ostensibly targeted for suspension and other forms of exclusion. The main focus of this paper is to examine critical gaps in theory and practice relevant to school discipline, safety and capacity to build and sustain a supportive and inclusive learning environment.

LITERATURE REVIEW

The focus of the first zero tolerance codes on firearms and drugs was clearly understood by most criminal justice and educational professionals as a practical response to public safety threats in schools that interfered with maintenance of the learning environment (Stinchcomb, Bazemore, & Riestenberg, 2006; Advancement Project, 2005). In recent years, however, these once limited policies now include a wide range of far more minor disciplinary violations (Green, 2004; Sughrue, 2003). Once defensible policies aimed initially at protecting teachers and students from violence and drug use have become all-encompassing disciplinary responses focused often on relatively minor forms of misbehavior.

In this context, what appears to be a massive criminalization of school misconduct (Advancement Project, 2005) has also begun to create a sense of urgency to implement alternatives to diminish this effect. Unfortunately, most zero tolerance codes have been developed in a relatively short time, and in the absence of clearly grounded conceptual guiding principles. Under such circumstances, most recent new codes seem unlikely to accomplish anything other than formal justification for a wide range of mostly unchecked, exclusively disciplinary discretion in schools (Stinchcomb et al., 2006). As the quotes at the beginning of the paper suggest, administrators, teachers, and other educational staff have mixed views about the value of zero tolerance policies. Most important, however, like determinate sentencing in criminal justice (though less precise), the new disciplinary codes create an illusion of fair punishment and justice while simply shifting discretion toward far less open and obvious moments in the decisionmaking process. Hence, disciplinary codes developed to reduce suspension or at least improve consistency, may have actually *increased* discretion (Casella, 2003). In doing so, they may have dangerously increased the numbers of minority youth excluded from school and referred into the juvenile justice system as part of an increasingly strong "school-to-jail pipeline," while also creating a more formal justification for such referrals (The Blueprint Commission, 2008).

Additionally, the inevitable emphasis on the need for more "prevention" in schools, though often valid in its own right, is typically disconnected from zero tolerance decision making, and from disciplinary processes as a whole. That is, zero tolerance codes operate in isolation from prevention efforts targeting students with special learning or behavioral needs. Disciplinary decisionmaking follows a different path once a behavior and student have been identified. Thus, there is literally *no time to talk* with, or hear from, students often already tagged for suspension who might have be able to remain in school if the offending behavior was mitigated rather than castigated. While prevention programs are important, in the absence of abolishing or restructuring zero tolerance codes, such programs will have little impact on suspension and expulsion in most schools (Casella, 2003). As one focus group participant expressed it, the availability of other intervention "programs" for youth in trouble at school is, however, often viewed as a positive benefit—even though such programs are explicitly located outside of school, and designed primarily or exclusively for suspended youth:

> *What is "going well" is that the schools are catching on to the civil citation program (a pre-arrest option for police officers). (Q): Does the civil citation then mean that students are allowed to stay in school? ... (A): Unfortunately, I was going to save that for later... but - no they usually get suspended from school anywhere from 2-10 days in addition to the citation and that's where I would like to see an in- school suspension option.....a maze of programs viewed as alternatives to suspension, are really NOT!*
> (Focus Group Participant, 2008)

Finally, like their justice system precedents, even current approaches to limiting zero tolerance typically individualize both disciplinary problems and their responses (Wearmouth, McKinney, & Glynn, 2007). The assumption in both education and juvenile justice systems and programs seems to be that if enough services, and punishment, are provided to *individual* youth engaged in disciplinary (or legal) violations, we can eliminate crime/misbehavior and threats to school safety. In schools, this assumption suggests tacit inattention to the overall educational climate, or culture, in which students and adults are expected to learn and interact peacefully with each other. This climate and culture may simultaneously encourage such behavior and ignore the underlying problems faced by "problem" students (Morrison, 2002). As in the juvenile justice analogy, prevention, treatment, and even incapacitation have their place. But by focusing only on downstream, remedial solutions, enforcement agents (e.g., police and school administrators) discount their own potential for truly preventative, street-level problem solving and community capacity building, as well as the role of social justice issues in the neighborhoods in question.

> *Law enforcement is in a precarious position... SROs are in theory placed to educate and build relationships with kids, but unfortunately they run into problems and difficult circumstances – where do they draw the line to become involved? Parents see them on the doorstep with bad news and they are labeled as the bad guys because someone else couldn't handle it.*
>
> (Focus Group Participant, 2008)

THE LIMITS OF PUNISHMENT AND A NEW DISCIPLINARY RESPONSE

In criminal and juvenile justice systems, punishment has become the primary response to crime; in schools, punishment has become the primary response to youth who violate disciplinary codes. Although a variety of treatment and service program interventions *may* be recommended for *some* students, overarching zero tolerance codes primarily prescribe punitive responses for a wide variety of rule violations. Indeed, like sentencing guidelines and mandatory minimums in criminal justice, disciplinary codes are an attempt to structure an ostensibly rational, equitable system that might range from warnings and rather minor restrictions on student freedoms to required participation in counseling or treatment, to a potential array of more severe sanctions in the school environment—e.g., suspension and expulsion (Green, 2004). Indeed, as recent focus group participants expressed:

> *There is lots of pressure for consistency, and this notion of equity; but it is not really equity. We are trapped into a template of zero tolerance and therefore, we don't allow discretion – we want consistency. However, we want that consistency to be fair and just and for the benefit of the child.*
>
> (Focus Group Participant, 2008)

> *Some of zero tolerance, if we didn't have that, it would be out of control. There are 3,000 kids in school designed for 1,500 kids. If you allow (certain behaviors) to occur, other things will also occur.*
>
> (Law Enforcement Officer, Focus Group Participant, 2008)

But, while most disciplinary codes are essentially punishment "menus," punishment is not the same thing as discipline. The latter is a larger, more complex concept than punishment that may, for example, include a range of prevention and intervention activities designed to precede, and hopefully, eliminate the need for administration of punishment. An approach to discipline may also include a variety of procedures, interventions, or environmental restrictions aimed at prohibiting, discouraging, and limiting the motivation for rule-breaking and harmful or disruptive behavior (Green, 2004). Yet, most zero tolerance codes now conflate punitive responses with discipline and indeed, these codes are for the most part lists of punishments. These codes typically specify a punishment for a rule violation, but do little to develop a process and culture for supporting effective discipline. The latter is a function of the structure and culture of schools and their administration, not of the codes, or intervention strategies themselves. Sometimes, in an attempt to restore school order, administrators may, either inadvertently or intentionally, criminalize behavior that would otherwise be handled informally.

Regardless of its perceived value as a deterrent, punishment occurs after the fact of a harmful behavior or rule violation and is rarely designed to address or remediate the actual behavior itself. While punishment is the dominant feature in most disciplinary codes, punishment is only *one* aspect of discipline, and is typically the weakest of several options (Claasen & Claasen, 2008). And no matter how much the supposedly equalizing value of disciplinary codes, they do little if anything to diminish unequal treatment:

> *We are finding that discretion creates an issue – whereas if the principal believes in zero tolerance and the SRO shows up, if it is a criminal issue, it has to be investigated by law enforcement.*
> (School Law Enforcement Officer,
Focus Group Participant, 2008)

> *The teacher should not make the decision as to what should happen – rather, an objective write up of what should happen [is needed]. …. the Dean makes the decision as to what should happen. … (there is) a vast difference when it gets to the Dean and you see what happens to the child. In one school, they get a slap on back, in another school they are suspended for 10 days.*
> (Focus Group Participant, 2008)

Based on theory and research at multiple levels of analysis, we argue in the remainder of this paper that three whole-school interventions may begin to create a climate for effective discipline. First, a restorative justice model of discipline and conflict resolution provides a dialogue-driven, problem-solving agenda for engaging all stakeholders in a process of repairing harm that, in contrast to offender-focused punishment models, offers a more robust and inclusionary form of accountability and peacemaking. Deployed as a whole-school approach to managing relationships and disseminating values, restorative justice provides a contextual framework within that may enable a cultural shift from authoritarian and punitive to democratic and responsive (Morrison, 2002). Second, at a more structural level, engaging adults in place management with a focus on guardianship and social support (Zimmerman, 2007; Riestenberg, 2007), facilitates a routine act*ivities* model in which new roles for *all adults* in prevention and dialogue with youth are potentially defined. Finally, a communal schools model (Solomon et al., 1992; Payne & Eckert, 2009) provides hope for building a disciplinary culture that reinforces youth and adult capacity to provide informal social control and support.

To be clear, despite pessimistic presumptions, we believe that use of restorative practices can bring about important and vital changes in zero tolerance. Yet, without more structural changes and a new mobilization of adults as resources for guardianship, restorative justice will—as is often the case in both school and juvenile justice contexts—impact only a very small number of youth (see Riestenberg, 2007). Finally, perhaps the most difficult macro level transformation is a cultural shift in schools as communities, or networks of neighborhoods, that provide a sense of belonging (Payne & Eckert, 2009). Ultimately, a strategic confluence of these agendas might ultimately allow for *more time to talk,* as less time is devoted to punitive responses to individual cases of misconduct, and adult (and student) roles are restructured to focus on mutual support.

RESTORATIVE JUSTICE AS A DISCIPLINARY AND CONFLICT RESOLUTION MODEL

Restorative justice practices have been implemented in a range of organizational and community contexts (Braithwaite, 2002; O'Brien & Bazemore, 2004). Based on hundreds of studies, including a number of randomized experiments, restorative approaches have achieved the status of an evidence-based practice (e.g., Sherman & Strang, 2005; Bonta, Rugge, Scott, Bourgon, & Yessine, 2008). One of the most interesting applications of restorative justice practice has been in schools as part of an effort to more effectively address concerns with bullying, classroom management and conflict resolution (Morrison, Blood, & Thorsborne, 2005; Ahmed, Harris, Braithwaite, & Braithwaite, 2001; Karp & Breslin, 2001).

Advocates of restorative justice view crime first as a violation of individuals, relationships, and communities that "creates obligations to make things right" (Zehr, 1990, p.181) in a process wherein "justice" is more than simply punishing, or *treating,* lawbreakers. Instead, a *restorative* response to crime, harm, and/or conflict seeks to "do justice" by repairing the harm caused to victims, offenders, and community and, to the greatest extent possible, rebuilding relationships damaged by these crimes and other conflicts. Achieving justice (and meaningful discipline) in a restorative way invites stakeholders to hold offenders or rule-breakers accountable, not by asking them to "take the punishment," but rather by ensuring that they take *responsibility* by making amends to their victims and the community. A restorative justice response includes two primary components: 1) a non-adversarial decisionmaking process that allows stakeholders to discuss the harm done to victims, while considering needs of all participants and, 2) an agreement for going forward based on the input of these stakeholders about what is needed to repair the harm.

The strength and integrity of a restorative intervention is determined by the degree of adherence to *core principles* which prioritize the following objectives: 1) the extent to which the response repairs the harm to victim, community, offenders, and their families; 2) the extent to which each stakeholder is involved in the discussion of the incident and is given input into the plan for repair; and 3) the extent to which community and government roles (e.g., the criminal justice system, education system, etc.) are transformed to allow communities a greater voice and increased responsibility for responding to community conflict, while criminal justice and other enforcement systems (e.g., school discipline) assume a more facilitative role (Christie, 1977; Pranis, 2001; Van Ness & Strong, 1997). At its best, restorative justice practice is ultimately also a problem-oriented approach (Goldstein, 1990; Eck & Spelman, 1987) that emphasizes weaknesses in reactive, incident-focused approaches that overlook the strengths of collective prevention and intervention (Bazemore & Boba, 2007). As Riestenberg asserts: "A restorative philosophy emphasizes problem-solving approaches to discipline, attends to the social/emotional as well as the physical/intellectual needs of students, recognizes the importance of the group to establish and practice agreed-upon norms and rules, and emphasizes prevention and early restorative intervention to create safe learning environments" (Riestenberg, 2007, p. 10).

Restorative justice and restorative discipline: Conflict, rule violations and repairing harm

As a model of school discipline, restorative justice can be contrasted with most current approaches that tend to individualize disciplinary violations by linking them to risks and needs posed by specific students. In the school context, restorative justice practice has been applied in response to several kinds of incidents, including disciplinary rule violations, harm caused by students to other students, conflicts between students, and violations of law. While such application is itself complex and highly discretionary, restorative justice responses have been effectively employed in response to both minor rule violations, as well as some of the most severe crimes of violence. Indeed, virtually all cases involving criminal behavior or rule violations can benefit from a restorative justice response, depending upon willingness of the three stakeholders and system decisionmakers.

A restorative disciplinary focus can be clearly distinguished from the three most typical responses to youth misbehavior, crime, and conflict (see Figure 1): the punitive, all-or-nothing approach of zero tolerance that is high on control/discipline and limit setting, but is also high in authoritarian, stigmatizing punishment that assumes good behavior is a function of external forces. Discipline is viewed as something done *to* young people, rather than *with* them and the threat of punitive discipline is thought to "keep them in line." In contrast, it is possible for individual adults and even entire institutions to virtually abandon any sense of control, support for positive behavior, or consequences for antisocial behavior by adopting a neglectful, passive, or indifferent approach. Also problematic is a permissive approach, based on what seems to be a widespread assumption that social services and individual treatment are enough to prevent future misbehavior and crime. While this approach can be supportive and nurturing, in doing *for* young people, adults may also deprive them of the opportunity to demonstrate the skills necessary to become competent and pro-social citizens. Rejecting the neglectful, permissive, and authoritarian approaches, restorative justice offers an *authoritative*, communitarian approach that, to the greatest extent possible, seeks to do things *with* students, in the context of a nurturing and learning collective of caring adults and students providing for maximum development of a youth's own internal controls. The restorative approach to discipline disapproves of the wrong done and sets tolerance limits (high control and support) while upholding the intrinsic worth of individuals engaged in crime, conflict, or rule-breaking the behavior (Moore, 1994; Braithwaite, 1989) While most schools, like many neighborhoods and communities, rely increasingly on school police and juvenile justice professionals to provide control and support, both are best provided by adults who take on the roles of community guardians and "natural helpers"(McKnight, 1995; Annie E. Casey Foundation, 2001) who are respected by youth and connected to them (Bazemore, 2001; Braithwaite, 1994).

Figure 1. The disciplinary window.

HIGH

	TO **punitive** authoritarian stigmatizing	WITH **restorative** collaborative reintegrative
	NOT **neglectful** indifferent passive	FOR **permissive** therapeutic protective

Control (limit-setting, discipline) ↑

LOW   Support (Encouragement, Nurture)   ➡HIGH

Source: Wachtel & McCold, 2002.

GUARDIANSHIP, ADULT SUPPORT, AND ROUTINE ACTIVITIES

Restorative justice is capable of creating new disciplinary responses that could provide an alternative to suspension in many cases. However, the presence of one, or even a few restorative programs, will likely fall short in the absence of a larger culture of responsive school discipline and dialogue. Essentially, discipline has become a problem of *adult*, rather than only student, culture. Often school policies, or perceptions of school policies, rise and fall with the actions of one individual adult. Part of the solution must expand beyond restorative programs.

> *[T]here is often times a perception by the community that certain teachers go an extra mile while others will not, and just turn it over to administrative staff. Parents talk to one another and see certain responses to one child but not with another, however their situations are similar.*
>
> (Focus Group Participant, 2008)

Routine activities theory is a broad and practical model for crime prevention and intervention through careful monitoring of the relationship between willing offenders, vulnerable victims, and the presence or absence of guardians (Cohen & Felson, 1979). The theory moves the genesis of crime beyond *cases* to the *environments* in which it is most likely to occur (Goldstein, 1990; Weisburd & Eck, 2004), and provides an important theoretical basis to inform situational crime prevention. In the school (and after-school) context (Gottfredson et al., 2005), the routine activities focus on place and space management may also provide for a less "individualizing" (Sampson & Wilson, 1995) approach to intervention, emphasizing instead the *places* and combinations that may breed and encourage criminal activity.

The goal of this social ecological approach is aimed at limiting victimization, independent of the concern with whether offender motivation is rational or spontaneous (Tunnel, 1992), or with underlying causes of offender behavior. It is a practical, utilitarian approach suggesting that antisocial behavior can be minimized by managing the environment in which crime occurs, rather than by managing the individual who may commit the crime. Whether they directly or indirectly criminalize behavior that is related to one's necessary presence in public space has been a point of contention. Nonetheless, routine activities approaches—especially in the school context—do offer a means of prevention based on wise management and surveillance of potentially dangerous places. Perhaps most importantly, routine activities approaches give emphasis to the pragmatic importance of *context* (Zimmerman, 2007).

Crime in restorative justice theory is understood as a function of the routine presence and activities of individuals who may find themselves vulnerable to being placed in the role of victim or offender by virtue of *where* they are, rather than because of *who* they are. Despite criticisms that routine activities—in the case of young people in particular—are not as value neutral as they sound (Harcourt, 2001), the presence of "capable adult guardians" has become a primary strategic factor in prevention. Conversely, the *lack* of adult supervision—specifically, unsupervised adolescent socializing—is now viewed as a major predictor of delinquency and deviant behavior in a number of recent studies (Osgood & Anderson, 2004; Haynie & Osgood, 2005; Gottfredson et al., 2005). Gottfredson's recent study of 40 After School Programs (ASPs) in Maryland, for example, found that unstructured supervision was associated with delinquency, substance use, and victimization even when a wide range of variables, including behavioral characteristics were held constant.

In the school, and afterschool context, routine activities theory would suggest that more strategic adult placement and monitoring could play an important role in preventing and/or resolving conflicts, limiting overt rule violation, reducing bullying, and facilitating peaceful interaction. There may also be much value, as some school safety practitioners suggest, in the very nonintrusive practice of assigning adult staff to the task of simply "standing around in the hall," monitoring youth peer interactions, and occasionally interacting directly with students (Riestenberg, 2007). In some schools, assistant principals and other adult staff have sought to more intentionally engage youth in a positive way in the corridors between classes, actively complimenting and "high fiving" them after, as one vice-principal put it, "catching them in the act" of *good* behavior. For example, a student in a large urban school who is out of compliance with dress code on Monday, is thanked on Tuesday for his compliance. In more threatening situations, students on the verge of conflict may also be surprised by a calming, yet authoritative, adult comment that quickly lowers the tension level, rather than an antagonizing response that might escalate it. Such active and strategic informal engagement between staff and students—assuming it became part of the routine activity of even a small minority of adults in schools—could go a long way toward creating a different culture of youth/adult, as well as student/student, interaction.

Following routine activities theory (Eck, 1994; Felson, 1993), it is then also possible to strategically differentiate roles of capable guardians. For example, in response to the aforementioned Gottfredson study of ASPs, Zimmerman (2007) builds on Eck's work (1994) to more specifically define guardian roles in a way that seems well suited to the school context. In doing so, she proposes an interesting division of labor between guardianship roles that include Eck's "place manager" role, whose occupant essentially monitors and controls a particular *space* (e.g., a hallway; a lunchroom) with little or no regard for what happens outside that space. A second adult guardian role, the "intimate handler" (Felson, 1993), on the other hand, offers both a broader form of monitoring *beyond* the space itself. This role might involve informal social control, physical monitoring, and possibly developing or building an "emotional connection" with students in the space. Finally, Zimmerman's precise designation of the target, or object, of control defines three complementary roles that work together toward related school missions: the Guardian who assumes responsibility for the larger disciplinary/safety/educational agenda; the Place Manager who attends to maintaining key safety and educational enhancement features of the "space," and Felson's "Intimate Handler" who seeks to "equip, support and monitor" the child while addressing goals of safety, prosocial behavior, academic achievement, and avoidance of substance abuse, etc. (Zimmerman, 2007).

While guardian roles may be defined somewhat differently in distinct school environments, what seems important is that occupants of each role be linked to a specific mission in certain contexts, while also clearly understanding the roles of other adults, and their specific responsibilities to support their colleagues in other guardian roles. Outcome measures regarding the effectiveness of this school-based routine activities model would include the extent to which guardians understand their specific role and that of others, the number and background of staff in these roles, and the level of collaboration between occupants of these roles.

Gottfredson's research, and Zimmerman's generalization of its findings, may also have a number of practical, policy implications for the critical, if now frequently dysfunctional, punitive role of school resource officers (SROs) in the zero tolerance context. Rather, than simply reacting to disciplinary infractions with arrests or threats, or to demands by principals to "get this kid out," some SROs could assume more problem-oriented roles in prevention and, depending on their skills and disposition, assume any of the three guardian roles. Overall, staff roles in discipline is an important discussion that fits well with the more collective emphasis on restorative problem solving by developing a variety of conflict resolution skills in both staff and students. Indeed, as Zimmerman (2007, p. 331) suggests, interventions that "link individual and community life to higher levels of social organization in an effort to reinforce societal norms...are associated with higher levels of success."

COMMUNAL SCHOOLS, SCHOOLS AS COMMUNITIES, AND A DISCIPLINARY CULTURE

The community of young people, along with staff and other professionals who work in schools, is by definition first an "instrumental community" (Bellah et al., 1991). Such communities exist to meet some specific need (e.g., educational, civic, safety, and/or rehabilitative). Length of residence is temporary, not necessarily voluntary, and generally clearly defined at the upper limit by policy or statute. Like workplaces, universities, civic organizations, prisons or other residential facilities, schools are temporary communities whose members reside, work, play, and/or learn for fixed and mandated periods for a specific purpose. Inevitably, schools vary by levels of social organization, culture and sense of community—as well as by function. Finally, because such instrumental communities cannot operate in isolation, the community surrounding the school must provide a vital bridge between students, school staff, and the real world.

For better or worse, instrumental school communities share many characteristics with other more permanent surrounding communities. Like some communities on the outside, instrumental communities can be dysfunctional or even criminogenic. As is apparent in the criminological literature on neighborhoods and crime (Sampson & Wilson, 1995; Sampson et al., (1997), school communities may also lack effective mechanisms of *informal* social control, which would encourage residents to support and help to enforce group behavioral norms, as well as processes for resolving conflict peacefully. However, this is challenged by the fact that too often schools and the communities in which they reside operate in isolation from one another, in terms of disciplinary as well as other school policies.

> *[A]mong parents and community leaders, there is a sense of frustration that exists that reaches the community level, frustration from a lack of information about how the discipline system works. When parents or guardians are faced with their child being disciplined, they are ill-prepared to deal with it; it is an interruption to their day and work schedule. As result, the communication into the community is a negative perception of the school system and also a feeling that there is inconsistency as relates to the discipline policy.*
>
> (Focus Group Participants, 2008)

Not unlike highly secure gated neighborhoods, schools may generally protect students from each other but provide little opportunity for their involvement in the business of education itself. They may also become engaged in disciplinary processes that might provide the skills to work and learn productively with others. School communities that lack participatory conflict resolution mechanisms—and disciplinary processes that go beyond individual punishment—therefore rely primarily or exclusively on more rigid, rule-based punitive discipline imposed by authorities from the top down to the "street-level bureaucrats" who must implement such policies (Lipsky, 1980). Unfortunately, such approaches feed upon themselves, and further weaken student capacity to develop *their own sense* of prosocial behavior and limits; even when students are engaged in learning such skills, they remain at best unsupported, and at worst condemned, by persons in the environment outside the school gates.

At a systemic level, as is often the case in neighborhoods where criminal justice and social service systems are responsible for most of the social control that provides at least minimal protection (McKnight, 1995), schools reliant on punishment and individualized case-by-case treatment and service referrals are likely to experience gradually decreasing informal controls and supports. This weakening may then *result* in progressively increased juvenile justice control and, to some extent, a greater reliance on individual expert treatment (e.g., by counselors or therapists) and expert social control rather than the skills of staff and students (McKnight, 1995; Bazemore, Stinchcomb, & Leip, 2004).

Conversely, communities that emerge in schools may, like some high-risk neighborhoods that develop shared values and collective efficacy, *offset* apparent risks by strong mechanisms of informal control. They may also continue to build upon and foster existing skills of conflict resolution and mutual support based on norms of reciprocity (Sampson, Raudenbush, & Earls, 1997). As we have argued, schools can also operate as restorative environments where members take responsibility to repair harm when it occurs, hold each other accountable, and build skills in collective problem-solving (Stinchcomb, et al., 2006). In such an environment, collective values and skills of pro-social behavior, conflict resolution, and support are learned primarily through modeling and practice in daily living (Bazemore & Schiff, 2005; Boyes-Watson, 2005). While reinforced as needed by classes and services, classroom experience and individual counseling alone cannot build and nurture these individual and collective problem solving skills or develop a commitment to pro-social living if the outside living environment is not aligned with restorative values.

As the above discussion suggests, the safest schools grounded in restorative justice values do not rely solely on external controls. Rather, as in well-functioning neighborhoods, social support is available not only from professional staff, but also from *all adults* and other students who—like residents of such neighborhoods—encourage mutual support between community members and institutionalize mechanisms for mutual assistance and peer learning. More generally, as Solomon et al. (1992) contend, "communal schools" would be characterized by residents and staff who: "...know, care about, and support one another, have common goals and sense of shared purpose, and actively contribute and feel personally committed" (Solomon et al., 1992; Gottfredson et al., 2005). They also have prosocial connections to surrounding communities and involve community members in school activities (including in some schools restorative disciplinary processes), while also providing services to communities that involved students and staff. A number of schools have now demonstrated how even high risk youths can connect with civic organizations and community groups through service designed to meet community needs (Karp & Breslin, 2001).

It has been argued elsewhere that restorative justice practices provide tools for building and enhancing informal controls and supports through a process of skill building and organizational learning (Carey, 2001; Senge, 1990). School communities using such tools are also more capable of developing organizational cultures that promote a sense of belonging, reciprocity and mutual support among staff and residents, relying on "informal social relations, common norms and experience, and collaboration and participation" (Payne, Gottfredson, & Gottfredson, 2003).

CONCLUSION

Zero tolerance statutes and practices impose formidable barriers for those wishing to minimize exclusion of youth from schools. Moreover, as in the case of unsuccessful criminal and juvenile justice reforms of previous decades, school programs intended for use as alternatives to suspension seem likely to be misused. Specifically, these programs appear to be often focused on youth engaged in very minor rule violations, while high rates of suspension and expulsion continues unabated for only slightly more serious infractions. If the "school-to-prison pipeline" (Advancement Project, 2005) is to be severed or even slowed, we suggest that no one disciplinary or educational strategy, informed by a single theoretical model, will be able to disrupt this process.

Restorative justice offers a promising approach for initiating the dialogue necessary to produce cultural change (Carey, 2001), as well as a new model of discipline that could effectively reduce the use of exclusionary practices. We argue, however, that restorative interventions need the support of both a routine activities model employing capable adult guardians and support staff. In addition, whole-school communal approaches specifically designed to engage students and adults in smaller networks could provide a sense of belonging that might nurture cultures of support to promote constructive discipline, conflict resolution and an inclusive sense of community (Payne et al., 2003).

Overall, transforming disciplinary policies is likely to require out-of-the box thinking about organizational cultures, and as Senge, Scharmer, Jaworski, & Flowers, (2005) suggest, a commitment to "suspend our normal discourse—(and) ways of believing and behaving....letting go of the need to control...developing trusting relationship...reflexive spaces for dialogue...while developing a new learning model." In addition, as Cavanagh (2007, p.68) observes, though schools are thought to be non-violent systems, they currently control both information and pedagogy and "have created a bifurcated culture of good versus bad..." that tends to limit the definition of discipline to a "discourse of consequences." While students are passive recipients of consequences determined by experts, a "discourse of peace," grounded in restorative values might transform the focus on passive receptors to co-creators; rules and regulations to relationships and interactions; teachers in control vs. shared power; teacher responsibility vs. shared responsibility; and punishment and retribution as deterrents vs. healing harm to relationships (2007, p.69). Such thinking may indeed provide a way forward for restorative discipline in the context of both capable guardians and supportive adults and a more communal school culture.

REFERENCES

Advancement Project. (2005). *Arresting development: addressing the school discipline crisis in Florida.* Washington, DC: Advancement Project.

Ahmed, E., Harris, N., Braithwaite, J., &Braithwaite, V. (2001). *Shame management through reintegration.* Cambridge, MA: Cambridge University Press.

Annie E. Casey Foundation. (2001). *Walking our talk in the neighborhood: Partnerships between professionals and natural helpers.* Baltimore, MD: Annie E. Casey Foundation.

Bazemore, G. (2001). Young people, trouble, and crime: Restorative justice as a normative theory of informal social control and social support. *Youth & Society, 33,* 199-226.

Bazemore, G. & Boba, R. (2007). "Doing good" to "make good": Community theory for practice in a restorative justice civic engagement reentry model. *Journal of Offender Rehabilitation. 46*(1/2), 25-56.

Bazemore, G. & Schiff, M. (2005). *Juvenile justice reform and restorative justice: Building theory and policy from practice.* Devon, UK, and Portland, OR: Willan Publishing.

Bazemore, G., Stinchcomb, J., & Leip, L. (2004). Scared smart or bored straight? Testing deterrence logic in an evaluation of police-led truancy intervention. *Justice Quarterly : JQ, 21*(2), 269-299.

Bellah, R., Madsen, R., Sullivan, W., Swidler, A., & Tipton, S. (1991). *The good society.* Berkeley, CA: University of California Press.

The Blueprint Commission. (2008). *Getting smart about juvenile justice in Florida.* Tallahassee, FL: Florida Department of Juvenile Justice.

Bonta, J., Rugge, T., Scott, T., Bourgon, G., & Yessine, A. (2008). Exploring the black box of community supervision. *Journal of Offender Rehabilitation, 47*(3), 248-270.

Boyes-Watson, C. (2005). Community is not a place but a relationship: Lessons for organizational development. *Public Organization Review, 5*(4), 359-374.

Braithwaite, J. (1989). *Crime, shame, and reintegration.* Cambridge, MA: Cambridge University Press.

Braithwaite, J. (1994). Thinking harder about democratizing social control. In C. Alder & J. Wundersitz (Eds.), *Family group conferencing in juvenile justice: The ways forward of misplaced optimism?* (pp. 199-216). Canberra, Australia: Australian Institute of Criminology.

Braithwaite, J. (2002). *Restorative justice and responsive regulation.* New York, NY: Oxford University Press.

Braithwaite, J. & Roche, D. (2001). Responsibility and restorative justice. In G. Bazemore & M. Schiff (Eds.), *Restorative community justice: Repairing harm and transforming communities* (pp. 63-84). Cincinnati, OH: Anderson Publishing Company.

Carey, M. (2001). Infancy, adolescence, and restorative justice: Strategies for promoting organizational reform. In G. Bazemore & M. Schiff (Eds.),

Restorative community justice: repairing harm and transforming communities. Cincinnati, OH: Anderson Publishing Company.

Casella, R. (2003). Zero tolerance policy in schools: rationale, consequences, and alternatives. *Teachers College Record, 105*(5), 872-892.

Cavanagh, T. (2005). *Creating safe schools using restorative practices in a culture of care: An ethnographic study conducted at Raglan Area School Te Kura a Rohe o Whaingaroa.* Wellington, New Zealand: Fulbright New Zealand.

Christie, N. (1977). Conflict as property. *British Journal of Criminology, 17,* 1-14.

Classen, R. & Classen, R. (2008). *Discipline that restores.* South Carolina: BookSurge Publishing.

Clear, T. (2007). *Imprisoning communities: How mass incarceration makes disadvantaged neighborhoods worse.* New York, NY: Oxford University Press.

Cohen, L. & Felson, M. (1979). On estimating the social costs of national economic policy: A critical examination of the Brenner study. *Social Indicators Research, 6*(2), 251-259.

Cook, P., Gottfredson, D., & Na, C. (2010). School crime control and prevention. In M. Tonry (Ed). *Crime and Justice: A Review of Research, Volume 39.* Chicago, IL: University of Chicago Press

Dishion, T., McCord, J., & Poulin, F. (1999). When interventions harm: Peer groups and problem behavior. *American Psychologist, 54,* 755-764.

Duncan, G. (2000). Urban pedagogies and the ceiling of adolescents of color. *Social Justice, 27*(3), 29–42.

Eck, J. (1994). Drug markets and drug places: A case-control study of the spatial structure of illicit drug dealing. Doctoral dissertation. College Park, MD: University of Maryland.

Eck, J. & Spelman, W. (1987). Problem-solving: Problem-oriented policing in Newport News. Washington, DC: Police Executive Research Forum.

Felson, M. (1993). Social indicators for criminology. *The Journal of Research in Crime and Delinquency, 30*(4), 400.

Focus Groups. (2008). *Florida Summits on Restorative Alternatives to Zero Tolerance – Orlando, FL August 2008 & St. Petersburg, FL September 2008.* Miami, FL: Research Grant Sponsored by The Collins Center for Public Policy.

Garland, D. (2005). *The culture of control.* Oxford: Oxford University Press.

Goldstein, H. (1990). *Problem-oriented policing.* New York, NY: McGraw-Hill.

Gottfredson, G., Gottfredson, D., Payne, A., & Gottfredson, A. (2005). School climate predictors of school disorder: Results from a national study of delinquency prevention in schools. *The Journal of Research in Crime and Delinquency, 42*(4), 412-444.

Greene, M. (2004). Reducing violence and aggression in schools. *Trauma, Violence, and Abuse, 6*(3), 236-253.

Harcourt, B. (2001). *The illusion of order: The false promises of broken windows policing.* Cambridge, MA: Harvard University Press.

Haynie, D. & Osgood, D. (2005). Reconsidering peers and delinquency: How do peers matter? *Social Forces, 84*(2), 1109.

Karp, D. & Breslin, B. (2001). Restorative justice in school communities. *Youth Society, 33*(2), 249.

Lipsky, M. (1980). *Street level bureaucracy: Dilemmas of the individual in public services.* New York, NY: Russell Sage Foundation.

Lyons, W. & Drew, J. (2006). *Punishing schools: Fear and citizenship in American public education.* Ann Arbor, MI: University of Michigan Press.

McKnight, J. (1995). *The careless society: Community and its counterfeits.* New York, NY: Basicbooks.

Moore, D. (1994, July). *Illegal action: Official reaction.* Paper presented at the Australian Institute of Criminology, Canberra.

Morrison, B. (2002). Bullying and victimization in schools: A restorative justice approach. *Trends and Issues in Crime and Criminal Justice, NIL*(219), 1-6.

Morrison, B., Blood, P., & Thorsborne, M. (2005). Practicing restorative justice in school communities: Addressing the challenge of culture change. *Public Organization Review, 5*(4), 335-357.

O'Brien, S. & Bazemore, G. (2004). A new era in governmental reform: Realizing community. *Public Organization Review, 4*(3), 205.

Osgood, D., & Anderson, A. (2004). Unstructured socializing and rates of delinquency. *Criminology, 42*(3), 519.

Payne, A. & Eckert, R. (2009). The relative importance of provider, program, school, and community predictors of the implementation quality of school-based prevention programs. *Prevention Science, 11,* 126–141

Payne, A., Gottfredson, D., & Gottfredson, G. (2003). Schools as communities: The relationships among communal school organization, student bonding, and school disorder. *Criminology, 41*(3), 749-77.

Polk, K. & Kobrin, S. (1972). *Delinquency prevention through youth development.* Washington, DC: Office of Youth Development.

Pranis, K. (2001). Democratizing social control: Restorative justice, social justice, and the empowerment of marginalized populations. In G. Bazemore & M. Schiff (Eds.), *Restorative community justice: Repairing harm and transforming communities* (pp. 357-378). Cincinnati, OH: Anderson.

Riestenberg, N. (2007). The restorative recovery school: Countering chemical dependency. *Reclaiming Children and Youth, 16*(2), 21.

Rist, R. (1972). The milieu of a ghetto school as a precipitator of educational failure. *Phylon, 33*(4), 348-360.

Sampson, R. & Wilson, J. (1995). Toward a theory of race. In J. Hagan & R. Peterson (Eds.), *Crime and urban inequality.* Stanford, CA: Stanford University Press.

Sampson, R., Raudenbush, S., & Earls. F. (1997, August). Neighborhoods and violent crime: A multi-level study of collective efficacy. *Science Magazine, 277*(4), 918-924.

Senge, P. (1990). *The fifth discipline.* New York, NY: Doubleday Currency.

Senge, P., Scharmer, C., Jaworski, J., & Flowers, B. (2005). *Presence: Exploring profound change in people, organizations and society.* London, UK: Nicholas Brealey.

Sherman, L. & Strang, H. (2005). Evidence-based justice. *The Lancet, 365*(9458), 469.

Solomon, D., Watson, M., Battistich, V., Schaps, E., & Deluchi, K. (1992). Creating a caring community: Educational practices that promote children's prosocial development. In F.Oser, A. Dick, & J. Pantry (Eds.), *Effective and responsible teaching: The new synthesis* (pp. 383-396). San Francisco, CA: Jossey-Bass.

Stinchcomb, J., Bazemore, G., & Riestenberg, N. (2006). Beyond zero tolerance. *Youth Violence and Juvenile Justice, 4*(2), 123-147.

Sughrue, J. (2003). Zero tolerance for children: Two wrongs do not make a right. *Educational Administration Quarterly, 39,* 238.

Tonry, M. (1995). Twenty years of sentencing reform: Steps forward, steps backward. *Judicature, 78*(4), 169.

Tunnel, K. (1992). 99 years is almost for life: Punishment for violent crime in bluegrass music. *Journal of Popular Culture, 26*(3), 165-181.

Van Ness, D. & Strong, K. (1997). *Restoring justice.* Cincinnati, OH: Anderson.

von Hirsch, A. (1976). Doing justice: The choice of punishments. *Report of the committee for the study of incarceration.* New York, NY: Committee for the Study of Incarceration.

Wachtel, T. & McCold, T. (2002). Restorative justice in everyday life: beyond the formal ritual. In H. Strang & J. Braithwaite (Eds.), *Restorative justice and civil society.* Cambridge, MA: Cambridge University Press.

Wearmouth, J., Mckinney, R., & Glynn, T. (2007). Restorative justice in schools: a New Zealand example. *Educational Research, 49*(1), 37 – 49.

Weisburd, D. & Eck. J. (2004) What can police do to reduce crime, disorder and fear? *The Annals of the American Academy of Political and Social Science, 593,* 42-65.

Zehr, H. (1990). *Changing lenses: A new focus for crime and justice.* Scottsdale, PA: Herald Press.

Zimmerman, C. (2007). Reaction essay: Routine activity theory and the handling of children and policy makers. *Criminology and Public Policy, 6*(2), 327-336.

From Social Control to Social Engagement: Enabling the "Time andSpace" to Talk Through Restorative Justice and Responsive Regulation

Brenda Morrison

Where, after all, do universal human rights begin? In small places, close to home – so close and so small that they cannot be seen on any map of the world. Yet they are the world of the individual person: the neighborhood he lives in; the school or college he attends; the factory, farm or office where he works. Such are the places where every man, woman, and child seeks equal justice, equal opportunity, equal dignity without discrimination. Unless these rights have meaning there, they have little meaning anywhere. Without concerted citizen action to uphold them close to home, we shall look in vain for progress in the larger world.

Eleanor Roosevelt, 1958, on presenting
In Your Hands to the United Nations,
in response to a worldwide, year-long observances
of the Tenth Anniversary of the
Universal Declaration of Human Rights.

Fifty years have passed since Eleanor Roosevelt spoke with wisdom and passion about where justice, opportunity and dignity begin; for our young people, those small spaces close to home, are our communities and schools. We have yet to heed this vision; instead, we have increased our reliance on strong institutional sanctions. Instead of building the capacity for individuals, within communities, to become more involved, the regulatory institutional system shifts responsibility to third parties, who read the rule book (be it the criminal code or the student code of conduct) and hand down the apportioned punishment, typically social exclusion in some form.

In the context of schools in the United States, zero tolerance policies are handed down from a federal and state level, mandating automatic suspension and expulsion for a range of infractions (Gregory & Cornell, 2009). Though zero tolerance expanded in the wake of school rampage shootings in predominantly white, suburban schools (Giroux, 2009), it is minority students of color that are expelled at disproportional rates. The evidence of disproportional representation is clear; it is students of color (Advancement Project, 2009; Ferguson, 2001; Gordon, Della Piana, & Keleher 2001; Losen & Edley, Jr., 2001; Welch & Payne, 2010) and working class students (Jordan & Bulent, 2009; Skiba, Nardo, & Peterson, 2002). The racial disparities in the school system are reflected in the criminal justice system, where black males are incarcerated at a rate six times that of white males (Human Rights Watch, 2009).

At the same time, school suspensions have increased for all students, not just minority students. In the United States, since 1973, the number of students suspended annually has more than doubled to 3.3 million students (Dignity in Schools, 2009). Suspension increases the likelihood of a student being expelled, dropping out, and being incarcerated (Ladson-Billings, 2001; Sandler, Wong, Morales, & Patel, 2000), a phenomenon dubbed the "school to prison pipeline" (Wald & Losen, 2003). Through zero tolerance and an increasing reliance on police presence in schools, many school officials are in effect helping to create an "institutional link" of formal social control between schools and prisons (Casella, 2003; Noguera, 2008; Wallace, Goodkind, Wallace, & Bachman, 2008). Prisoner statistics reveal further links between schools and prisons: in 1997, nearly 70 percent of prisoners never graduated high school, and approximately 70 percent of juvenile offenders had learning disabilities (Wald & Losen, 2003, p. 11). Through the strengthening of these formal institutional mechanisms of social control, individuals and communities have become less involved in enabling justice, opportunity and dignity in those small places close to home.

The practice of restorative justice enables schools and communities to tap into the rich ecologies of an individual's life through creating the "time and space" to talk, in places close to home. Communities cut across institutional domains, and can respond in ways that broaden the scope for achieving safe and productive schools and communities. Restorative justice draws on three broad leverage points that offer a distinct perspective to typical institutional responses of social control. First, rather than focusing on external sanctioning systems (rewards and punishment) as a motivational lever, restorative justice focuses on relational ecologies as a motivational lever that foster a rich value based internal sanctioning systems. Thus, in responding to threats to school safety and well being, instead of asking "who did it" and "what punishment do the offenders deserve?", the questions center around "what happened?", "who has been affected?", and "how do we repair the harm done?" (Zehr, 2002). Second, the process of answering these questions includes those closest to the harm, and those closest to the community affected. This is distinct to current institutional practice, wherein the decision making is often left to third parties, removed from the direct incident, particularly in the context of serious threat or harm. In the context of courts, the system has been characterized as stealing conflict from those most affected (Christie, 1977). Third, restorative justice does not trump emotion with reason, but finds reason for emotion (Sherman, 2003). This is distinct from most institutional responses that focus on establishing the facts, with little focus on the social, emotional and spiritual dimensions the make up the rich ecologies within the lives of individuals and communities.

The practice of restorative justice is theoretically eclectic, cutting across disciplinary silos, with a range of normative and explanatory theories making a case for restorative justice (Braithwaite, 2002). Normative theories draw on a range of world views: from indigenous and faith-based to sociologists, such as Durkheim and Foucault (see Braithwaite, 2002). Explanatory theories, in different way drawing on normative theory, include re-integrative shaming theory, which builds understanding of the role of the moral emotion of shame, and the process of shaming (see Ahmed, Harris, Braithwaite, & Braithwaite, 2001; Morrison, 2007); defiance theory (Sherman, 1993), which builds understanding of when punishment increases crime, decreases crime and has no effect; social identity theory (Tajfel & Turner, 1979) and self-categorization theory (Turner, Hogg, Oakes, Reicher, & Wetherell, 1987), which builds understanding of the social psychological mechanism that bridges the self and society. Building on the latter theoretical analysis, Tyler (2006; see also Okimoto, Wenzel, & Platow, 2010) in an article on rule breaking, procedural justice and restorative justice concludes that a shift from regulation by external sanctions, to self-regulation, is important:

> "Sanctioning-based models, which dominate current thinking about managing criminals, have negative consequences for the individual wrongdoer and for society. It is argued that greater focus needs to be placed on psychological approaches whose goal is to connect with and activate internal values within wrongdoers with the goal of encouraging self-regulatory law-related behavior in the future (p. 305)."

This analysis resonates with that of Valerie Braithwaite (2009a, 2009b) who brings together her work on social values and motivational postures, within a responsive regulation framework. In particular her work identifies institutional practices that generate defiance, undermining individual's capacity and willingness to cooperate in core facets of social life from family and school to work and governance. Responsive regulation is contrasted with formalized regulatory responses (Braithwaite, J., 2002), which Valerie Braithwaite argues are institutionally siloed. Within a formalized regulatory system the implicit belief is that clear rules and laws within the architecture of the system, backed up by clear and consistent sanctions, will elicit the desired behavior. The basic assumption is that at some level all actors are rational, assuming individuals and groups are uniformly programmed in the way they respond to rules and laws. In contrast, Braithwaite (2009a, 2009b) has identified five motivational postures: commitment, capitulation, resistance, disengagement, and game playing. In summary, Braithwaite (2009a, 2009b) argues that traditional sanction based rational actor models ignore the science of how individuals, groups and society function.

Social identity and self-categorization theory offer further insights beyond standard rational choice theory. The conceptual shift can be framed through an understanding the nature of power. Turner (2005) proposes a new theory of power emphasizing group identity, social organization, and ideology, rather than dependence as the basis of power.

The theory proposes that processes of power, underlying basic mechanisms of social control—persuasion, authority and coercion—can account for more explanatory variance by reversing the causal sequence of the standard theory. The latter argues that control of resources produces power, power is the basis of influence and that mutual influence leads to the formation of the psychological group. The three-process theory argues that psychological group formation produces influence, that influence is the basis of power and that power leads to control of resources (Turner, 2005, p. 1).

This conceptual shift has implications for theories of social change, emphasizing that power is leveraged as a function of social relationships, in the context of "definite social, ideological and historical content rather than reifying it as an abstract external force producing generic psychological effects" (Turner, 2005, p. 1). In other words, differential social engagement across ideology and context, as a basis for social identification, leads to enhancing the power base for access to resources.

Roca, in Chelsea, MA, has developed a community-based intervention model for very high risk youth, which resonates with these theoretical shifts that emphasize social engagement over social control. This outcome driven organization has a clearly defined mission: to help disengaged and disenfranchised young people, ages 14-24, move out of violence and poverty. Their vision is clear: "Young people will leave the streets and gangs to take responsibility for their actions and have jobs. Young immigrant mothers will raise their children in safety and will be recognized for their contributions to society. Our communities will have the ability to keep young people out of harm's way and in turn, thrive through their participation and leadership" (Roca, 2010). Roca's innovative theory of change has two levers that work hand in hand: programmatic and organizational. These two levels of change mirror the framework developed by Braithwaite (2002) in coupling the practice of restorative justice within a responsive regulatory framework at an institutional or organizational level. The key fundamental premise is the recognition that individual change is best leveraged through responsive regulation within the institution. The programmatic lever "theorized that Roca participants would experience positive outcomes through the implementation of relentless outreach, relationships for the purpose of change, peacemaking circles and skill-building opportunities" (Pierce, 2009, p. 2). The organizational theoretical lever "recognized that single programs were not sufficient to impact the trajectories of high risk people. Instead it is the combination of strategies and programs that would bring about change. The theory also documented that in order to reach the desired outcomes, leadership had to be strong and program performance tracked over time" (Pierce, 2009, p. 4). These theoretical shifts required Roca to move from programs to programming, wherein the key strategy was the management and tracking of transformational relationships (Pierce, 2009, p. 4). At the heart of all programming are two core premises: (1) change is possible for all young people and (2) people change in relationships. Relationships are built on a foundation of trust, truth and transformation (Pierce, 2009, p. 9):

> Trust: Youth workers build trusting, long-term relationships with young people and others in their lives, including family, other adults and institutions.
>
> Truth: Youth workers are truthful with young people. They are truthful about what is going on in the lives of young people, the challenges, the realities of their families and communities, and that change is possible.
>
> Transformation: The trusting and truthful relationships support and encourage personal transformation through participation in life skills, education and employment.

Outcomes are tracked and measured within the programmatic and organizational theory of change, in reference to Roca's clearly defined mission and vision, which specify three areas of focus: engagement, economic independence, and living out of harm's way. It is expected that this process of change will take 4-5 years. The key theoretical shift resonates with that specified in Turner's (2005) analysis of power; in that, transformational power, in reference to economic, social, and emotional well being, emerges as a function of social relationships.

An additional factor that is important to Roca's community-based strategy is their Engaged Institution Strategy, which recognizes that a range of institutions that are important and influential to the economic, social and emotional well being of a young person's life – schools, local government, agencies, and organizations. As such, Roca creates partnerships with these institutions and organizations. Wheeler (2006) articulates the purpose and outcomes of the Engaged Institutions Strategy as being to "ensure that the systems and institutions contribute to young people's self-sufficiency and help them to be out of harm's way" (p. 44). As a community-based organization, Roca seeks to: (1) increase institutions ability to understand and be more responsive to youth needs; (2) be accountable for services they provide; and (3) understand the impact they have on young people's lives. The processes of engaging institutions mirrors that of those used to engage young people (Pierce, 2009, p. 44):

> "The strategy is marked by an investment in building trusting relationships no matter how long it takes, frequent, consistent, honest communication between Roca staff and staff within the institutions or organizations, and the use of peacemaking circles to hear and understand each other and the young people."

The long term aim is to enact alternative restorative policies in communities that will, in turn, result in a systemic change of how our communities address the needs of this high-risk youth population.

The evidence to date is very promising: in the 2009 financial year, Roca actively served 664 youth and young adults through our High Risk Youth Intervention Model. While most programs struggle with serving and retaining this population, Roca does not lose these young people: 91 percent of the target population participants who were initially engaged in FY08 were retained through Roca's High Risk Youth Intervention Model through FY09 and are still engaged in relationships and programming to support their change processes. Of young people in Transformational Relationships (Phase 1 & Phase 2): 84 percent participated in stage based life skills, education, and/or employment programming; 72 percent of participants in a Phase 2 made positive progress through the stages of change related to specific behavior changes indicated on their service plans; 76 percent engaged in educational programming made academic gains; 88 percent engaged in pre-vocational training achieved skill gains; 91 percent being worked with toward employment obtained employment; 81 percent who successfully completed transitional employment were placed in jobs; 74 percent of these retained their employment. Roca is now involved in further implementation, outcome and impact evaluations, including a replication, with possible random assignment, in Springfield, MA. Through Roca's commitment to youth, they are building the foundation of a rich evidence base of innovation and change at the individual, community and institutional level.

Bazemore and Schiff (this volume) propose that routine activity theory, a sub-field of rational choice theory, when coupled with the practice of restorative justice will strengthen schools ability to break the school to prison pipeline, through a focus on dialogue, place management and a communal school model. While each of these factors are important to recognize, this paper argues that breaking the pattern of routine activities of young people at risk requires a more fundamental paradigm shift, from social control to social engagement. To some extent this bears out in the randomized control trial of routine activities theory in the context of an after-school program which found that the "minor increase in frequency of involvement for students who were already highly engaged did not have an influence on routine activities" (Cross, Gottfredson, Wilson, Rorie, & Connell, 2009, p. 406). The findings suggest that supervision alone was not enough to break routine activities. The sampling of participants in this study also suggests that the students in the treatment group were not particularly at high risk. In comparison to the intensive outreach by Roca, supervision, by an adult guardian alone, was a not strong enough lever for behavioral change, particularly within the context of a single program.

Restorative justice, in theory and practice, in the context of responsive regulation which reverses the causal chain of traditional rational actor models offer much more fertile ground for addressing the school to jail pipeline, particularly for youth that are disconnected and disengaged. Routine activities theory offers a rational choice theory of change through a time space analysis that is dislocated from a motivational analysis, particularly motivations evoked within a particular institutional culture (see Zimmerman, 2007). The social psychological analysis of motivational postures (Braithwaite, 2009a, 2009b), coupled with Turner's (2005) analysis of power, within a responsive regulatory framework offers further fertile explanatory variance in understanding and responding to youth who are disconnected and disengaged. This is particularly relevant to minority students of color, where power dynamics are particularly salient. In agreement with Bazemore and Schiff, current strategies and programs designed to mitigate zero tolerance responses are likely to fail, particularly within current formalized institutional responses of social control, that fail to engage individuals and communities, such that they have the "time and the space" to talk about what matters in those small places close to home.

The evidence from a recent report, *Redefining Dignity in our Schools* (Chin, 2010), reiterate the same points that Eleanor Roosevelt identified: "Human rights only have value if they are part of people's lived experiences and not just policy standards that fail to make it into the lives of the community" (p. v). There will need to be patient investment of time and resources to link theory and practice, wherein theories born of the paradigm of social control are conversant with theories born of the paradigm of social engagement. It will take this level of dialogue and engagement to shift the school-to-prison pipeline, to the school-to-dignity pipeline.

REFERENCES

Advancement Project. (2009). *Key components of a model discipline policy.* Retrieved December 10, 2009, from http://www.stopschoolstojails.org/content/model-discipline-policies

Ahmed, E., Harris, N., Braithwaite, J., & Braithwaite, V. (*2001*). *Shame management through reintegration.* Melbourne, Australia: Cambridge University Press.

Braitwaite, J. (2002). *Restorative justice and responsive regulation.* New York, NY: Oxford University Press.

Braithwaite, V. (2009a, June 25-26). *Dismissive and resistant defiance.* Paper presented at Legitimacy and Compliance in Criminal Justice: An International Symposium, University of Leeds, Leeds.

Braithwaite, V. (2009b, November 5-6). *Introducing responsive regulation.* Paper presented at the Child Protection as Regulation: Clarifying Principles Conference, Australian National University, Canberra.

Casella, R. (June 2003). Zero tolerance policy in schools: Rationale, consequences, and alternatives. *Teachers College Record, 105*(5), 872-892.

Chin, M. (2010, June). *Redefining dignity in our schools - executive summary: A shadow report on school-wide positive behavior support implementation in South Los Angeles, 2007-2010.* Los Angeles, CA: Community Asset Development Re-defining Education (CADRE); Mental Health Advocacy Services, Inc.; and Public Counsel Law Center.

Christie, N. (1977). Conflicts as property. The British Journal of Criminology, 17, 1-15.

Cross, A., Gottfredson, D., Wilson, D., Rorie, M., & Connell, N. (2009). The impact of afterschool programs on routine activities of middle school students: Results from a randomized, controlled trial. *Criminology and Public Policy, 8*(2), 391-412.

Dignity in Schools. (2009). *Fact sheet: School discipline and the push out problem.* Retrieved August 17, 2010, from http://www.dignityinschools.org/files/DSC_Pushout_Fact_Sheet.pdf

Ferguson, A. (2000). *Bad boy: Public schools in the making of black masculinity.* Ann Arbor, MI: University of Michigan Press.

Giroux, H. (2009). Ten years after Columbine: The tragedy deepens. *Policy Futures in Education, 7*(3).

Gordon, R., Della Piana, L., & Keleher, T. (2001). Zero tolerance: A basic racial report card. In W. Ayers, B. Dohrn, & R. Ayers (Eds.), *Zero tolerance: Resisting the drive for punishment in our schools* (pp. 77-88). New York, NY: The New Press.

Gregory, A. & Cornell, D. (2009). "Tolerating" adolescent needs: Moving beyond zero tolerance policies in high school. *Theory into Practice, 48*(2), 106-113.

Human Rights Watch. (2009, April). *US: Prison numbers hit new high.* Retrieved August 17, 2010, from http://www.hrw.org/en/reports/2008/05/04/targeting-blacks

Jordan, J., & Bulent, A. (2009). Race, gender, school discipline, and human capital effects. *Journal of Agricultural and Applied Economics, 41*(2).

Ladson-Billings, G. (2001). America still eats her young. In W. Ayers, B. Dohrn, & R. Ayers (Eds.), *Zero tolerance: Resisting the drive for punishment in our schools* (pp. 77-88). New York, NY: The New Press.

Losen, D. & Edley, J. (2001). The role of law in policing abusive disciplinary practices: Why school discipline is a civil rights issue. In W. Ayers, B. Dohrn, & R. Ayers (Eds.), *Zero tolerance: Resisting the drive for punishment in our schools* (pp. 256-264). New York, NY: The New Press.

Morrison, B. (2007). Restoring safe school communities: A whole school response to bullying, violence and alienation. Sydney, Australia: Federation Press.

Noguera, P. (2008). *The trouble with black boys ... and other reflections on race, equity, and the future of public education.* San Francisco, CA: Jossey-Bass.

Okimoto, T., Wenzel, M., & Platow, M. (2010). Restorative justice: Seeking a shared identity in dynamic intragroup contexts. In E. Mannix & M. Neale (Eds.), *Fairness and groups (Research on Managing Groups and Teams, Volume 13,* pp. 205-242). Bingley, UK: Emerald Group Publishing Limited.

Pierce, B. (2009). *Roca's high risk youth intervention model: Initial implementation evaluation report.* San Francisco: Jossey-Bass.

Roca. (2010). *Vision statement.* Retrieved on August 17, 2010, from http://www.rocainc.org/about.php.

Sandler, S., Wong, F., Morales, E., & Patel, V. (2000). *Turning "to" each other not "on" each other: How school communities prevent racial bias in school discipline. A preliminary report.* San Francisco, CA: Justice Matters Institute.

Skiba, R., Michael, R., Nardo, A., & Peterson, R. (2002). The color of discipline: Sources of racial and gender disproportionality in school punishment. *The Urban Review, 34*(4), 317-342.

Sherman, L. (1993). Defiance, deterrence, and irrelevance: A theory of the criminal sanction. *Journal of Research in Crime and Delinquency, 30,* 445-473.

Sherman, L. (2003). Reason for emotion: Reinventing justice with theories, innovation, and research. *Criminology, 41,* 1–38.

Tajfel, H. & Turner, J. (1979). An integrative theory of intergroup conflict. In W. Austin & S. Worchel (Eds.), *The social psychology of intergroup relations.* Monterey, CA: Brooks-Cole.

Turner, J. (2005). Explaining the nature of power: A three-process theory. *European Journal of Social Psychology, 35,* 1 – 22.

Turner, J., Hogg, M., Oakes, P., Reicher, S. & Wetherell, M. (1987). *Rediscovering the social group.* Oxford, England: Basil Blackwell.

Tyler, T. (2006). Restorative justice and procedural justice. *Journal of Social Issues, 62,* 305-323.

Van Ness, D. & Johnstone, G. (2007). *Handbook of restorative justice*. Devon, UK: Willan Publishing.

Wallace, J., Goodkind, S., Wallace, C., Bachman, J. (2008). Racial, ethnic, and gender differences in school discipline among U.S. high school students: 1991-2005. *Negro Educational Review, 59*, 47-62.

Wald, J. & Losen, D. (2003, May 16-17). *Defining and redirecting a school-to-prison pipeline: Framing paper for the school-to-prison pipeline Research conference*. Cambridge, MA: Harvard University and Northeastern University's Institute on Race and Justice.

Welch, K. & Payne, A. (2010). Racial threat and punitive school discipline. *Social Problems, 57*(1), 25-48.

Wheeler, W. & Edlebeck, C. (2006, spring). Learning, leading and unleashing potential: Youth leadership and civic engagement. *New Directions for Youth Development, spring*(109), 89-97. Retrieved August 17, 2010, from http://www.theinnovationcenter.org/news-events/articles-and-publications.

Zehr, H. (2002). *The little book of restorative justice*. Intercourse, PA: Good Books.

Zimmerman, C. (2007). Reaction essay: Routine activity theory and the handling of children and policy makers. *Criminology and Public Policy, 6*(2), 327-336.

TALKING BACK TO BAZEMORE AND SCHIFF: A DISCUSSION OF RESTORATIVE JUSTICE INTERVENTIONS IN SCHOOLS

HILARY CREMIN

INTRODUCTION

Over past decades, restorative justice has made significant inroads into the fields of youth justice and education throughout the world. For those of us who have been promoting restorative justice in schools, this is both wonderful and terrifying: wonderful because of the benefits of restorative justice for social and educational inclusion; terrifying because of the potential for it to be misapplied. There are three elements in this excellent paper by Bazemore and Schiff that I would like to pick up and address from an educationalist's point of view: firstly, the complex and multifaceted nature of schools as organisations; secondly, parallels between poorly theorised research in education and in criminology that fails to identify unintended consequences of interventions to reduce youth offending; and thirdly, characteristics of policy and practice in schools that are most likely to further the aims of restorative justice interventions. In addressing these three elements I hope to contribute to debates about how best to promote safer and more peaceful schools and communities.

SCHOOLS AS COMPLEX AND MULTIFACETED ORGANISATIONS

As suggested in the Bazemore and Schiff paper, schools have long been identified as mediating institutions by criminologists and others considering ways of reducing youth offending. Questions remain, however, as to the extent to which schools shape or reflect the society in which they are imbedded, and the extent to which they are amenable to change through any one intervention. What is more, young people are subject to a range of influences, many of them competing, both within and outside of school. Despite calls for restorative justice interventions to be used to reduce school suspensions (or exclusions as they are known in the United Kingdom) it is by no means clear that this will, in turn, reduce juvenile offending. School suspension may well be a factor in the lives of young offenders, but the two are not necessarily correlated. They may well both be a function of another variable, such as poverty or disadvantage. Reducing school suspensions does not necessarily result in a reduction in offending behaviour, other than at the level of displacing offending to out-of-school hours (Skinns, Du Rose, & Hough, 2009).

107

Yet there is a growing feeling that restorative justice interventions might improve school culture and climate, leading to less violence in schools, reduced suspensions and improved educational outcomes for all, including those from disadvantaged backgrounds. Advocates of restorative justice interventions tend to be passionate and persuasive, claiming, as Ted Wachtel from the International Institute of Restorative Practice (IIRP) for example does that:

> "The emerging new field of study, restorative practices, has the potential to transform our schools and our communities.... When systematically employed on a whole-school basis, restorative practices transform negative school environments by engaging students in taking responsibility for making their own schools better." (Wachtel, in Lewis, 2009, p. 4)

The language that is used by advocates of restorative justice interventions, in common with advocates of other educational interventions, often assumes that schools are simple organisations that function as isolated and integrated communities. Language used is often an uneasy combination of evangelism and science, borrowing words from Newtonian physics ("levers of change" "driving force") and medicine ("healing practice" "ailing communities") and implying that restorative justice might, "in significant dosages" bring about positive change. Bazemore and Schiff point out that schools are subject to competing influences and that restorative justice interventions are not a magic pill. Too many project workers and researchers in this area have assumed that schools are unidimensional, and have been unable to adapt to local contexts and underlying conditions of schooling (Cremin, Mason, & Busher, 2010). Reflecting on the general lack of sustainability of peer mediation programmes, Sellman (2009, p. 15) reflects that those involved, "perhaps underestimate the degree to which principles of power and control underpinning the traditional activity have to be transformed in order for new models of activity to be implemented."

Research that was carried out among 60 disaffected students in Lancashire, UK, to identify the reasons behind their educational exclusion and implement change is a case in point (Riley & Rustique-Forrester, 2002). As well as talking to the young people themselves, the authors interviewed both school-based and non-school-based professionals, and parents. The research unearthed frustration and mistrust, but it also revealed a surprisingly convergent set of ideas about what needed to change. Students in schools and adults with a variety of roles all agreed that the key to change lay in rethinking the nature of teaching and learning, and the interplay between teachers and students. The solutions to most of the problems, it was felt, lay within the grasp of those affected. There was agreement that head teachers and teachers have too little time for reflection, that they should not be forced to respond to competing external and internal demands, and that they should have time and space to work with individual students. A blueprint for change was put to 80 secondary head teachers at a conference in Lancashire, and was enthusiastically agreed as relevant and applicable. There was equal agreement, however, that significant change could not and would not occur. Change in schools is highly problematic in the face of tight regulation and external control. The heads in these Lancashire schools felt that high stakes testing of students and regimes of surveillance and inspection of teachers had resulted in feelings of powerlessness and a lack of ownership of processes of teaching and learning. Another study of 48 primary school students talking about their experiences of the government-mandated Literacy Hour, found that children raised important theoretical and practical issues, but that, "At a time when the primary school curriculum is increasingly defined by those outside the classroom, children are at risk of not being seriously considered or consulted" (Hancock & Mansfield, 2002, p. 197). It is, therefore, important to take account of the sociopolitical context of schooling when advocating and researching restorative justice interventions in schools. More generally, Brown and Jones ask themselves:

> "When did we start thinking that research into education improved our teaching? What sorts of success can we claim since then? Teacher practice is probably governed to a much greater extent by social norms and the policies generated within these. As such it may be more appropriate for research to focus on how these norms constitute what we teach and how it is taught."(Brown & Jones, 2001, p. 169)

None of the above is intended as an argument for not carrying out research into promising interventions in schools – indeed the opposite. According to my own extensive practice and research in this area, restorative justice interventions can and do transform the lives of students and teachers in schools. The case made here is that they will only do so if project workers and researcher are able to take account of the complex and multifaceted nature of schools. Restorative justice interventions (or any other interventions) cannot be used as cheap and easy solutions to complex social and political problems.

POORLY THEORISED INTERVENTIONS

In common with criminology, advocates of particular educational interventions regularly fail to consider underlying theory, or the nature of the field into which interventions are introduced. Not only does this leave researchers and participants ill-prepared and unsupported, but it also limits understanding, and can result in effects, both intended and unintended, that are counterproductive, or even the opposite of what was envisaged. An example of this from both criminology and education is the "net-widening" effect of interventions that seek to divert young people at risk of social or educational exclusion from engaging in offending behaviour. In both schools and community contexts, socioeconomically disadvantaged young people (and it is almost always the poor) find themselves having increased contact with peers who my already have an offending background. As Bazemore and Schiff point out, these young people, who perhaps might not otherwise have come to the attention of the authorities, find themselves under increased surveillance, and therefore at greater risk of entering the criminal justice system. My research from elsewhere (Cremin, Harrison, Mason, & Warwick, 2009) suggests that when young people from socio-economically disadvantaged communities are supported within inclusive contexts to become more civically engaged, they are able to build on existing non-traditional forms of citizenship, thus increasing life opportunities through volunteering and participation at local, national and global levels. The key here is to avoid pathologising disadvantage – working *with* young people to tackle the effects of poverty and discrimination, rather than *on* them as objects in need of intervention and healing. Drawing on theorists such as Putnam, Bourdieu, Bernstein, and Sen, it is possible to shift from a medical model of disadvantage to an environmental model which places the locus for struggle and change within existing social structures, rather than within individuals or particular social groupings. Theories of social and cultural capital, symbolic violence and capability have much to offer to the fields of both education and criminology, and can go far towards explaining why interventions might not always work in the ways envisaged, and what can be done to respond to schools as complex organisations embedded within diverse and globalised communities.

POLICY AND PRACTICE FOR EFFECTIVE RESTORATIVE JUSTICE INTERVENTIONS IN SCHOOLS

It is certainly the case, as Bazemore and Schiff argue, that restorative justice interventions are necessary, but not sufficient, to bring about safer and more peaceful communities. My own PhD research revealed just that, that peer mediation was able to impact significantly on levels of violence and bullying in one school out of three. In two schools the intervention failed, peer mediation made no impact on levels of violence and bullying. In the school where it worked, the head teacher used the intervention of peer mediation to support her efforts to improve self-discipline among students, and feelings of participation and belonging among staff, students, and parents. In the other two schools, the head teachers saw peer mediation as 'something for the kids", a bolt-on curriculum intervention that might help students from disadvantaged background develop better social skills, but not something that would involve real change for adults who "mediate all the time anyway" (contrary to the evidence of my research). Schools are often reluctant to consider the kinds of change that are necessary to transform relationships. Restorative justice interventions are countercultural, and it can be painful for adults to revisit their own attitudes towards power, control and childhood.

Although it is clear that other elements are needed for restorative justice interventions to be successful, what those other elements are is open to debate. There are countless interventions and programmes that claim to promote student wellbeing, and reduce school suspensions and indiscipline (e.g., healthy schools initiatives, resiliency training programmes, anger-management courses, peer mentoring, etc.). Many have been evaluated, often by their funders and proponents, and found to be effective. Most educationalists would agree that successful interventions share two common elements – a focus on the quality of relationships in school, including, but not exclusively, relationships between teachers and students, and a focus on teaching and learning. Those two elements are, after all, core processes of schooling. Success here will result in success across the school.

There is not the capacity within this short paper to respond in any detail to the question of how best to promote effective teaching and learning for student well-being and reduced suspensions and indiscipline, but it is possible to respond briefly to Bazemore and Schiff's points about routine activities theory and communal schools. Whilst I would agree that flooding a school with adults (including non-teaching staff and community volunteers) can promote high expectations of behaviour and reduce opportunities for negative peer interaction, the key here is in the quality of relationships in school, and the extent to which students are supported to develop self-discipline, rather than adult-mandated discipline. There is a risk that if adults see their role as a form of policing, however benign, opportunities for quality interaction based on genuineness, empathy, and unconditional positive regard (three elements grounded in humanistic psychology) may be lost, and unintended consequences might flow from young people being denied opportunities to develop strong peer relationships outside of direct adult supervision. Humanistic psychology, and particularly the work of Carl Rogers, is useful here. Figure One shows how Rogers and Freiberg conceptualise the person-centred classroom, and how this contrasts with the teacher-centred classroom (for longer discussion, see Cremin, 2007). The person-centered classroom shares the characteristics of the restorative classroom, but is grounded in a longer theoretical tradition.

Figure 1. Rogers & Freiberg's (1994) comparison of discipline in teacher-centred and person-centred classrooms.

Teacher-centred classrooms	Person-centred classrooms
Teacher is the sole leader	Leadership is shared
Management is a form of oversight	Management is a form of guidance
Teacher takes responsibility for all the paperwork and organisation	Students are facilitators for the operations of the classroom
Discipline comes from the teacher	Discipline comes from the self
A few students are the teacher's helpers	All students have the opportunity to become an integral part of the management of the classroom.
Teacher makes the rules	Rules are developed by the teacher and students in the form of a classroom contract
Consequences are fixed for all students	Consequences reflect individual differences
Rewards are mostly extrinsic	Rewards are mostly intrinsic.
Students are allowed limited responsibilities	Students share in classroom responsibilities
Few members of the community enter the classroom.	Partnerships are formed with business and community groups to enrich and broaden the learning opportunities of students.

Unfortunately, as discussed above, these methodologies have fallen out of favour, and have been replaced in many schools with initiatives that increase teacher control under the flag of raising standards and ensuring "zero tolerance" of misbehaviour. To achieve the function of getting students to do well in tests and to engage in activities that they may find boring or irrelevant, schools have increasingly relied on behaviourist methods of behaviour management, especially with those students who find it hardest to defer gratification. Behaviourist methods in schools (e.g., Cantor, 1989) have grown out of behaviourist psychology, and experiments on animals, most famously Pavlov's dogs (classical conditioning) and Skinner's rats (operant conditioning) which entail the manipulation of rewards and punishments to encourage desirable behaviour and to reduce unwanted behaviour. Some argue that the use of behaviourist methods on children is unethical (e.g., Hall & Hall, 1988) and others oppose the use of external rewards and punishments altogether. Rogers & Freiberg (1994, p. 239) argue that "fixed consequences" for undesirable behaviour, used in many behaviourist programmes, operate as if all students were the same, with identical needs and intent. They suggest that consequences for undesirable behaviour should be rational and that, "unlike fixed consequences, rational consequences have the students try to undo what has been done. If a student spills something, then he or she knows to clean it up. Placing a child's name on the board, or adding a check, does little to remedy the situation." Learning, they feel, should be intrinsically motivating, and this should be sufficient to ensure a positive learning environment. They go on to argue that, although self-discipline is what most teachers would say they are aiming for, they frequently impose discipline, denying students opportunities to develop an internalised set of behavioural norms. Self-discipline requires a learning environment that provides opportunities to learn from one's experiences – including mistakes – and to reflect on those experiences. Powerful psychological tools (the human equivalent of electric shocks and food pellets) should not be used to impose order amongst students who baulk at being forced to engage in boring test-driven activities in school. Unlike authoritarian and behaviourist methods, person-centred behaviour management does not rely on adult surveillance and control. Project workers and researchers involved in the promotion of restorative interventions in schools would do well to ground their arguments in these important theoretical considerations.

CONCLUSION

In summary, restorative justice interventions in schools need to take account of the complexity of schools, and the different ways in which they are embedded within diverse local, national and global communities. They need to encompass theoretical perspectives that strengthen policy and practice, and to consider other dimensions of schooling, especially aspects of teaching and learning, relationships, and behaviour management that impact on intended outcomes. Restorative approaches in schools need to be grounded in an expanded view of conflict and justice, and a reinvigoration of civic spaces and discursive democracy. Public dialogue can begin to articulate difference, revealing and challenging the ways in which divisions of power and opportunity have become obscured. As Braithewaite argues, "disputing over daily injustices is where we learn to become democratic citizens. And the learning is more profound when those daily injustices reveal deeply structured patterns of injustice" (2002, p. 131). This is the real potential of restorative justice interventions in schools. We ignore them at our peril.

REFERENCES

Braithwaite, J. (2002). *Restorative justice and responsive regulation.* Oxford, UK: Oxford University.

Brown, T. & Jones, L. (2001). Action research and postmodernism: Congruence and critique, Buckingham, UK: Open University Press.

Cantor, L. (1989). Assertive discipline: More than names on the board and marbles in the jar. *Phi-Delta Kappa, 71*, 57-61.

Cremin, H. (2007). *Peer mediation: Citizenship and social inclusion revisited,* Buckingham, UK: Open University Press.

Cremin, H., Mason, C., & Busher, H. (2010). Problematising pupil voice using visual methods: Findings from a study of engaged and disaffected pupils in an urban secondary school. *British Educational Research Journal*, 1–19. iFirst Article
http://www.informaworld.com/smpp/content~db=all~content=a922 465861

Cremin, H., Harrison, T., Mason, C., & Warwick, P. (2009). *Building voice, civic action and learning: What can we learn from young people living in socio-economically disadvantaged communities?* Cambridge, UK: University of Cambridge Available from http://engaged.educ.cam.ac.uk/publications

Hall, E. & Hall, C. (1988). *Human relations in education.* London: Routledge.

Hancock, R. & Mansfield, M. (2002). The Literacy Hour: A case for listening to children. *The Curriculum Journal, 13*(2), 183 – 200.

Lewis, S. (2009). *Improving school climate: Findings from schools implementing restorative practices.* Bethlehem, PA: IIRP Graduate School.

Riley, K. & Rustique-Forrester, E. (2002). *Working with disaffected students.* London: Paul Chapman.

Rogers, C. & Freiberg, H. (1994). *Freedom to learn.* New York, NY: Macmillan.

Sellman, E. (2009). Peer mediation services for conflict resolution in schools: What transformations in activity characterise successful implementation? *British Educational Research Journal, ifirst* Article 1469-3518.

Skinns, L., Du Rose, N., & Hough, M. (2009). *An evaluation of Bristol RAiS,* London: ICPR, King's College London.

RELIGION

CRIME AND RELIGION: ASSESSING THE ROLE OF THE FAITH FACTOR

BYRON R. JOHNSON
SUNG JOON JANG

ABSTRACT

The paper traces the role of religion in contemporary criminology as well as reviewing the development of scholarly interest in religion within the field of criminology. We begin with a systematic review of 270 published studies to better understand the state of the literature examining the relationship between religion and crime. Our systematic review provides support for the notion that religious involvement is a relevant protective and prosocial factor. We then discuss how various dimensions of religiousness may explain crime and delinquency (directly and indirectly) and contribute to criminological theories and research. Additionally, we offer several potentially fruitful avenues for research examining the efficacy of the "faith factor" in both reducing crime and promoting prosocial behavior. We conclude with methodological and theoretical recommendations designed to assist scholars interested in research on the role of religion within criminology as well as prosocial studies more generally.

Over the last five decades there has been growing interest in the nature of the relationship between religion and crime. In general, researchers have sought to determine if being more or less religious has anything to do with why people do or do not break the law. Scholars from diverse disciplines, including criminologists, interested in this line of inquiry have sought to test hypotheses, and cumulated research provides empirical insights to this important question.

Criminologists should be interested in religion not only because it may be useful in explaining why people do or do not commit crime, but because religion may be helpful in understanding why people engage in prosocial activities – something criminologists have generally tended to ignore. We argue it is important to understand how religiousness keeps individuals from engaging in criminal behavior, but also significant is isolating the effects, if any, of faith-motivated individuals, groups and organizations in fostering prosocial activities because prosocial behaviors decrease the probability of antisocial behaviors including crime.

As one considers the possible linkages between religion and prosocial activities as well as crime, many important questions in need of serious research come to mind: How might spiritual interventions or transformative experiences play a pivotal role as "turning points" in helping offenders reverse a history of antisocial behaviors to one characterized by prosocial actions? Based on evaluation research, what do we know about the effectiveness of faith-based prison programs in reducing recidivism of ex-prisoners? What are the similarities and differences between processes and outcomes associated with offender rehabilitation on the one hand, and spiritual transformation on the other? To what extent do religious congregations and faith-based organizations have the capacity to become serious allies in confronting problems like prisoner reentry and aftercare? Providing answers to these questions may prove meaningful not only for advancing criminological theory, but in practical ways for the field of criminal justice and crime-related policies.

A BRIEF HISTORY: RELIGION WITHIN CRIMINOLOGY

Contemporary research on the religion-crime relationship is often traced to Travis Hirschi and Rodney Starks's (1969) important study entitled *Hellfire and Delinquency*. Their primary finding was that religious commitment among youth was not related to measures of delinquency. To their surprise, the study created quite a stir in the academic community, and became the subject of considerable debate and speculation.[1] The "hellfire" study, as it was referred to by some, became the catalyst for new research on religion and crime, and a number of scholars sought to quickly replicate the study. Those replications both supported and refuted the original finding (Albrecht, Chadwick, & Alcorn, 1977; Burkett & White, 1974; Higgins & Albrecht, 1977; Jensen & Erickson, 1979). After a series of studies over a decade or so, the question of whether religion helped reduce delinquency among youth was still very much in question

Later, Stark and his colleagues returned to the issue and suggested that the contradictory findings were likely the result of the "moral" makeup of the community being studied. That is to say, areas with high church membership and attendance rates represented "moral communities," while areas with low church membership typified more "secularized communities" (Stark, Kent, & Doyle, 1982). Stark's hypothesis predicted religion would successfully deter delinquency in moral communities only. Conversely, little or no effect of religiosity would be expected for individuals residing in largely secularized communities. This moral communities thesis provided an important theoretical framework for understanding why some studies of delinquency yielded an inverse relationship between religious commitment and delinquency, and other studies failed to generate such inverse relationship (Stark, 1996; Stark et al., 1982). Though the moral communities thesis remains a perspective of interest, scholars have approached the religion-crime nexus from a number of different methodological as well as theoretical perspectives and by doing so have helped to clarify the role of religion.

One of the first studies to shed new light on the religion-crime relationship was conducted by an economist. Richard Freeman's (1986) study was particularly helpful in placing attention on one of the factors that helped at-risk teens become "resilient youth" – kids who stay out of trouble in spite of residing in disadvantaged environments. Analyzing data on black, male youth living in poverty tracts in Philadelphia, Boston, and Chicago, Freeman found church-attending youth were significantly less likely to engage in a series of illegal behaviors than youth who did not attend church. Additionally, Freeman found that frequent church attendance was also associated with improved academic performance as well as positive employment indicators.

More than a decade later, focusing on crime, we replicated Freeman's study and found evidence consistent with Freeman's original conclusions (Johnson, Larson, Li, & Jang, 2000). That is, we found the frequency of attending religious services to be inversely related to the likelihood that disadvantaged youth would commit illegal activities, use drugs, and be involved in drug selling. Specifically, the probability of committing a non-drug crime was 39 percent smaller for youth who attended church more than once a week compared to youth who did not attend, and the difference for drug use was found to be 46 percent. Finally, the probability of youth selling drugs was 57 percent smaller among regular church-attendees than non-attendees (Johnson & Siegel, 2002).

In a subsequent study, we analyzed the fifth wave of the National Youth Survey (NYS) data, focusing on black youths given the historical as well as contemporary significance of the African-American church for black Americans. An individual's religious involvement was found not only to mediate but also buffer the effects of neighborhood disorder on crime and, in particular, serious crime (Johnson, Jang, Li, & Larson, 2000). We extended this line of research to estimate a multilevel model of illicit drug use, using the NYS' first five waves of data (Jang & Johnson, 2001). First, we found that religiosity has a significant effect on illicit drug use, controlling for social bonding and social learning variables that partly mediate the effects. Second, cross-level interactions were found to be significant, indicating religiosity buffering the effects of neighborhood disorder on illicit drug use. Stated differently, religious teenagers from low-income families are less likely to use illicit drugs than otherwise comparable teenagers living in the same high-poverty neighborhoods. Finally, the age-varying effect of religiosity on illicit drug use was found to become stronger throughout adolescence. While most previous studies, including ours, have focused on samples of juveniles, research on adult samples also shows the same general pattern – religion is associated with reductions in criminal activity (e.g., Evans, Cullen, Dunaway, & Burton, 1995)

Finally, in a systematic review of 40 studies that focus on the relationship between religion and delinquency, Johnson, Li, Larson, and McCullough (2000) found that most of these studies reported an inverse relationship between measures of religiosity and delinquency. Several studies found no relationship or were inconclusive and only one found a positive link between religiosity and delinquency. Interestingly, the more sophisticated research design and methodology, the more likely it was they reported an inverse relationship between the two. In a meta-analysis, Baier and Wright (2001) reviewed 60 studies within the religiosity-delinquency literature and reached much the same conclusion as Johnson, Li, et al. (2000). That is, they found studies using larger and more representative datasets to be more likely to report expected inverse effects than studies that utilized smaller, regional, or non-probability samples. These initial reviews were helpful in demonstrating that the contemporary religion-crime literature was not nearly as ambiguous or unsettled as previous researchers had often suggested.

RELIGION AND CRIME: AN UPDATED STATE OF THE FIELD

In this paper we report the most comprehensive assessment of the religion-crime literature to date by reviewing 270 studies published between 1944 and 2010. In our systematic review, as can been seen in Appendix A, we examined the type of study (e.g., cross-sectional, prospective cohort, retrospective, experimental, case control, or descriptive), the sampling method (e.g., random or population-based, systematic sampling, or convenience/purposive sample), the number of subjects in the sample population (e.g., children, adolescents, high school students, college students, or adults), location, religious variables included in the analysis (e.g., religious attendance, scripture study, subjective religiosity, religious commitment, religious belief, or religious experience), controls, and findings (e.g., no association, mixed evidence, beneficial association, or harmful association).

The results of this current review confirm that the vast majority of the studies report prosocial effects of religion and religious involvement on various measures of crime and delinquency. Approximately 90 percent of the studies (244 of 270) find an inverse or beneficial relationship between religion and some measure of crime or delinquency. Only 9 percent of the studies (24 of 270) found no association or reported mixed findings, whereas only two studies found that religion was positively associated with a harmful outcome.[2]

Researchers over the last several decades have made steady contributions to this emerging religiosity-crime literature, and yet, until recently, there was a lack of consensus about the nature of this relationship between religion and crime. Stated differently, in studies utilizing vastly different methods, samples, and research designs, increasing religiosity is consistently linked with decreases in various measures of crime or delinquency. These findings are particularly pronounced among the more methodologically and statistically sophisticated studies that rely upon nationally representative samples. We find religion to be a robust variable that tends to be associated with the lowered likelihood of crime or delinquency. Also, the vast majority of studies document the importance of religious influences in protecting youth from harmful outcomes as well as promoting beneficial and prosocial outcomes. The weight of this evidence is especially important in light of the fact that religion has been the "forgotten factor" among many researchers and research initiatives.

However, our updated review of the extant literature identifies major deficit in two research areas. One concerns a lack of a developmental approach to study the religion-crime relationship. Despite the increasing significance of the life-course perspective in criminology, previous research on religion and crime continues to be mostly non-developmental. For example, we know little about a long-term influence of childhood involvement in religion on adolescent and adult criminality as well as religiosity and few studies have examined reciprocal relationships between religion and crime over time (but see Jang, Bader, & Johnson, 2008). Also, we need to learn more about the relevance of religion to desistance research, like potential "turning point" effects stemming from religious conversions or spiritual transformations among offenders, for which we have preliminary evidence (but see Clear & Sumter, 2002; Kerley, Allison, & Graham, 2006; Kerley & Copes, 2009; Giordano, Longmore, Schroeder, & Seffrin, 2008; Johnson, 2003, 2004).

A second area that requires more research is the subject of resiliency given that the potential linkages between resilient and prosocial behavior are clearly understudied. For example, we know that youth living in disorganized communities, are at particular risk for a number of problem behaviors including crime and drug use. However, we also know that youth from disorganized communities who participate in religious activities are less likely to be involved in deviant activities. These findings suggest religiously committed youth are "resilient" to the negative consequences of living in communities typified by disadvantage, but we do not have sufficient research to answer why this might be the case. Perhaps religious involvement may provide networks of support that help adolescents internalize values that encourage behavior that emphasizes concern for others' welfare. Such processes may contribute to the acquisition of positive attributes that give adolescents a greater sense of empathy toward others, which in turn makes them less likely to commit acts that harm others. Similarly, as indicated above, once individuals become involved in deviant behavior, it is possible that participation in specific kinds of religious activity can help steer them back to a course of less deviant behavior and, more important, away from potential career criminal paths.

MICRO-CRIMINOLOGY OF RELIGION

Our systematic review focused on micro- or individual-level research because theoretical explanations of the influence of religion on crime have been predominantly social psychological. This orientation may be partly due to the intellectual climate within criminology at the time research interest in religion was ignited by Hirschi and Stark's (1969) hellfire study.

Religion had been primarily viewed as a social psychological phenomenon since the opening days of the classical school of criminology. For example, Bentham (1970 [1789]) recognized the constraining influence of religion on human behavior, and Beccaria (2008 [1764]) discussed potential limitations of religious influence due not only to the perceived delay of divine punishment but also deceitful intent on the part of the "wicked" who abuse religion to rationalize their deviance. While their discussions of religion were limited, "it was common in the classical tradition to note that ... religious sanctions are a potentially powerful influence on behavior" (Gottfredson & Hirschi, 1990, p. 7).

On the other hand, the positivist school of criminology "eschewed religious influence on behavior" (Gottfredson & Hirschi, 1990, p. 7). For example, Lombroso (2006 [1876]), who rarely mentioned religion throughout the entire five editions of his book, *Criminal Man*, suggested no relationship between religion and crime. If there were one, he implied it would be a positive association, though likely to be spurious due to higher levels of education among atheists than religionists in Europe at that time. However, based on the contributions of early social theorists, and especially Durkheim (1981 [1912]; 1984 [1893]) the concept of religion as something eminently "social" and a source of group solidarity resonated with scholars. As a result of these influences, modern criminology applied various micro-criminological theories to explain potential intervening mechanisms between an individual's religiosity and crime (Baier & Wright, 2001). For example, many of the contemporary criminological theories being studied are based primarily on concepts of deterrence/rational choice, social bonding, differential association/social learning, and, more recently, self-control and strain (Agnew, 2006; Akers, 1998; Cornish & Clarke, 1986; Gibbs, 1986; Gottfredson & Hirschi, 1990; Hirschi, 1969; Sutherland & Cressey, 1970 [1924]).

While none of these theories focus on religion as a key cause or correlate of crime, they all offer explanations of the religion-crime relationship by identifying processes, by which religiosity is expected to decrease the probability of crime. Specifically, religious individuals are less likely to commit crime than their less religious counterparts (Nye, 1958) because they are more likely to: (1) *fear* supernatural sanctions[3] as well as this temporal criminal punishment and feel *shame* and *embarrassment* associated with deviance; (2) be bonded to conventional society in terms of *attachment, commitment, involvement*, and *beliefs*; (3) exercise high *self-control* attributable to effective child-rearing by their parents likely to be also religious; (4) have frequent and intimate *associations* with peers who *reinforce* conventional *definitions* and behaviors and become a model for *imitation* relative to those who do not; and (5) cope with life's *strains* or stressors and their resultant *negative emotions* in a legitimate, non-deviant manner. Thus, individual religiosity is expected to be negatively associated with crime.

Empirical research tends to show these intervening variables help explain the religion-crime relationship, and more often than not the estimated effect of religion remains significant after controlling for explanatory variables (e.g., Johnson, Jang, Larson, & Li, 2001). This unexplained, "direct" effect of religion should be further explained by novel concepts and new measures. In fact, such conceptual and operational improvement should be made for religion and crime as well as their explanatory variables given that the explanation's validity and reliability depend on the substantive and measurement quality not only of the mediators but also the independent and dependent variables. For example, the multidimensional concept of religiosity requires a use of multiple indicators tapping different aspects of religious involvement for content validity (e.g., Levin, Taylor, & Chatters, 1995), and given the abstract nature of religion, whenever possible, latent-variable modeling needs to be applied to study the religion-crime relationship (e.g., Jang & Johnson, 2005; Johnson et al., 2001).

In addition, criminologists need to broaden the scope of their explanatory models by taking into account intrinsically religious explanations as well as those criminologists have been using. For example, various types of *religious coping*, such as spiritual coping and religious reframing, are likely to offer a new explanation of why strained but religious individuals are less likely to turn to crime in response to life's adversity than their equally strained but non- or less religious peers (Pargament, 1997). In fact, religious coping might be harmful as well as helpful and thus be useful explaining possible linkages between religion and increases in crime or deviance. Another example is the concept of *forgiveness*, a concept highly encouraged by most world religions (McCullough, Pargament, & Thorensen, 2000). Like religious coping, the forgiveness concept can easily be incorporated into Agnew's (2006) general strain theory framework to explain how an individual's religiosity decreases the likelihood of his or her engaging in a vengeful act in reaction to some of most criminogenic types of strains, like racial discrimination and violent victimization (Agnew, 2006).

On the other hand, some researchers looking for explanations of the empirical association between religion and crime are interested in variables that help explain *away* the observed relationship. A good example is Ellis' (1987) arousal theory, which posits delinquents are neurologically predisposed to criminality in that their under-aroused nervous system causes them to be unusually prone to seek intense stimulation from their environment through various activities, including delinquency. In addition, those with suboptimal arousal tendencies (a general tendency to get bored) are less likely to be voluntarily religious because they would find religious activities (e.g., church service) boring and failing to satisfy their arousal need. Thus, Ellis hypothesizes the religion-crime relationship is "coincidental (spurious), not causal" (p. 225). Ellis' own test and another study found support for the hypothesis (Cochran, Wood, & Arnelklev, 1994; Ellis & Thompson, 1989), but their findings tend to be plagued by measurement issues. Specifically, their measures of the neurological concept (i.e., arousal) are non-neurological proxies, and have less face-validity than claimed.[4] Regardless, research on spurious explanations of the crime-religion relationship is important as well to avoid model misspecification in criminological research on religion.

RELIGION IN MACRO-CRIMINOLOGY

The number of micro-criminological studies on religion far exceeds that of their aggregate-level counterparts, but contributions made by macro-criminology to the study of religion and crime are substantively no less significant. First, although the original social disorganization theory paid little attention to the role of local religious institutions (Shaw & McKay, 1942), its revised systemic theory recognizes religion as a potential source of community control. According to Bursik and Grasmick (1993), local religious congregations represent a community organization that provides, in Hunter's (1985) term, the "parochial" level of social control (grounded in the local interpersonal networks and institutions, such as stores, schools, churches, and voluntary organizations) operating between the "private" (based on the intimate primary groups) and "public" (a community's ability to secure public goods and services available outside the community) levels of control. Similarly, Sampson and Wilson (1995, p. 51) implied the black church may not only play a role as an agency of informal social control but also provide an opportunity to have "contact or sustained interaction with individuals and institutions that represent mainstream society." However, social disorganization researchers have generally failed to put these propositions to an empirical test (Johnson, Larson, et al., 2000, p. 480).

Another macro-level explanation of the religious influence on crime is the "moral communities" thesis, which Stark (1996) offered as a way to make sense of his own micro-level, null finding regarding the religion-crime relationship (Hirschi & Stark, 1969). Based on an alternative assumption that religion as context is a social structure (or a group property) rather than an individual trait (e.g., beliefs and practices), Stark (1996, p. 164) posits the negative association between religion and crime depends on aggregate-level religiosity, such as "the *proportion* of persons in a given ecological setting who are actively religious." Stark proposed a paradigm shift from a micro to macro perspective and thus a new research question on religion. His thesis, however, was not intended to replace or even reject a micro-criminology of religion. For Stark, individual religiosity is still a necessary, though not sufficient, condition: "... what counts is ... whether [individual] religiousness is or is not ratified by the social environment" (Stark & Bainbridge, 1996, p. 72). Consistent with this interpretation, the moral communities thesis has been tested not only at the macro-level, but also the multi-level context. An example of the latter is a study conducted by a sociologist of religion, Mark Regnerus (2003).

Using school- and county-level as well as individual-level variables drawn from the Add Health data, Regnerus operationalized the concept of religion as context by employing not only Stark's suggested approach, but also by measuring "religious homogeneity" (i.e., the extent to which community residents adhere to a single religion or to a small number of faiths) to expand the original thesis. Specifically, Regnerus hypothesized religiously homogeneous places are more likely to be moral communities than those with a generic religiosity or religious adherence.[5] Interestingly, the notion of religious homogeneity parallels social disorganization theory, which postulates community crime rates are partly a function of community heterogeneity. In fact, Regnerus (2003, p. 524) correctly points out "social disorganization's ambivalence about religion as a key socializing and social control institution and its reticence in identifying religion as an important type of cultural influence" on crime.

A group of macro-criminologists have made a similar observation, pointing out a gap in the social disorganization literature: that is, a lack of interest in religion as a local social institution (Lee & Bartkowski, 2004; Lee, 2006, 2008; Lee & Thomas, 2010). While examining Stark's moral communities thesis in their models of violent crime in rural areas, Lee and his associates focus on their civic community concept based on the "civic engagement" thesis (Putnam, 2000; Tolbert, Lyson, & Irwin, 1998). According to the civic community/engagement thesis, local civic institutions are essential to community social control, a key concept of social disorganization theory, because they facilitate civic engagement: that is, participation in locally based social and civic activities, such as voting, organizing church-based charity events, participating in neighborhood associations, and joining hobby or recreational clubs. Active civic engagement, in turn, generates social capital by fostering social ties and network multiplexity and density (Krohn, 1986), promoting mutual trust and civility, and developing shared community norms and values. These factors, of course, are important for community stability as well as well-being and tend to be related to reductions in community crime rates (e.g., Rosenfeld, Messner, & Baumer, 2001).

From the civic community perspective, religious institutions are fundamental to civic engagement in America because of their ubiquity and widespread religiosity among Americans (Lee, 2008; Lee & Thomas, 2010). For example, Baylor Religion Surveys conducted by the Gallup organization in 2005 (n = 1,721) and 2007 (n = 1,648) reveal: (1) about 85 percent of contemporary American adults identified themselves with a particular religion, Judeo-Christian religion 95 times out of 100; (2) 75 to 81 percent surveyed said they believed in God with "no doubts" (63 to 67 percent) or "a higher power or cosmic force" (12 to 14 percent); and (3) about a third (36 to 38 percent) reported they attended religious services "about weekly" or more often.[6] Thus, "the civic community perspective places much more emphasis on religious institutions and religious aspects of community organization" (Lee & Thomas, 2010, p. 125) than the systemic social disorganization perspective. More importantly, the civic community perspective's emphasis on religious institutions generates an interesting new research question.

Specifically, applying Putnam's notion of "bonding" and "bridging capital" to two distinct religious denominations, Lee (2008) developed a hypothesis that civically engaged denominations are more likely to be negatively associated with violent crime rates than their conservative counterparts because the former enhance bridging capital that contributes to community organization via active civic engagement, whereas the latter tend to build in-group ties and unity, promoting bonding capital that does not directly help strengthen community integration and community control. The hypothesis received preliminary support, although the evidence was found only for rural communities. That is, as expected, the county-level proportion adhering to civically engaged denominations, primarily Catholics and mainline Protestants, was negatively related to a violent crime index (i.e., homicide, robbery, and aggravated assault) and juvenile homicide rates (Lee, 2006, 2008; Lee & Bartkowski, 2004), whereas the proportion adhering to conservative Protestant denominations was either not significant or was positively related to community crime rates.

If this positive association reflects a possible link between conservative Protestant religious culture and violence in the South (Ellison, Burr, & McCall, 2003), it might suggest the potential for a conservative Protestant religion to have the opposite effect on crime at two different levels of analysis: positive at the macro-level (Lee, 2006), but negative at the micro-level (e.g., Regnerus, 2003). Further, a recent ecological study indicates this macro-level religious effect is more attributable to Fundamentalist and Pentecostal denominations and their "otherworldliness" that tends to promote bonding capital. On the other hand, Evangelical denominations may be more similar to those civically engaged denominations because of their "engaged orthodoxy" (Smith, Emerson, Gallagher, Kennedy, & Sikkink, 1998) that develop bridging capital (Blanchard, Bartkowski, Matthews, & Kerley, 2008).

Finally, another important macro-level perspective relevant to the religion-crime relationship is Messner and Rosenfeld's (2001) institutional anomie theory. Expanding Merton's (1938) anomie theory, Messner and Rosenfeld argue the American Dream is a part of the American crime problem because it contributes to criminogenic pressures in the cultural state of anomie, where the cultural goal (i.e., material success) is overemphasized compared to the cultural means to achieve the goal. Such an anomic environment leads to an institutional imbalance of power, in which the economy exerts an unusually dominant influence on three noneconomic institutions: the polity, the family, and education.

While the number of social institutions might have been restrained by the theory's basic need for parsimony, religion seems to be an important omission in light of the deteriorating prosocial and protective function of the family and education in America, especially among the disadvantaged (Sampson & Wilson, 1995). Though religion is not exempt from the pressures of a market-oriented culture (e.g., Sargeant, 2000), religious institutions are likely to be more resilient than their noneconomic counterparts given their allegiance to the sacred and transcendent matters which fall beyond the strictly material. To the extent that religion counterbalances the economy and tempers the pressures associated with the American Dream, institutional anomie theory may exaggerate the criminogenic influence of the economy in America.

CONCLUSION: FUTURE DIRECTIONS

Based on our review of the micro- and macro-criminological literatures on religion, any effort to explain away the religion-crime relationship as entirely spurious is likely to be as futile as claiming crime can be completely explained by a lack of religion. Indeed, some studies show an initially observed religion-crime association can be fully explained by "third" and "secular" variables (e.g., Cochran et al., 1994). Scholars need to take into account methodological limitations (e.g., modeling and measurement quality) and relevant contingency factors, such as social contexts and the ascetic nature of crime (e.g., Tittle & Welch, 1983) when interpreting such findings. Thus, the effect of religion on crime "explained" by non-religious variables might be partly religious, though not detected because of model misspecification. This is a reminder that causation is both an empirical and theoretical issue.

For example, suppose that a significant effect of adolescent religiosity on drug use in reaction to strain (e.g., death of a close friend) became non-significant when attachment to parents was introduced as an intervening variable to the relationship (i.e., adolescent religiosity → attachment to parents → drug use). This result is typically interpreted as the effect of religion being explained in non-religious terms. However, whether the indirect effect is religious in nature or not is a separate issue. The actual explanatory mechanism may have involved a religious process, attributable to an omitted variable, say, religious coping, encouraged by religious parents, to whom the adolescent was strongly attached (i.e., adolescent religiosity → attachment to [religious] parents → religious coping → drug use). If this were the case, the effect of religiosity on drug use may be religious after all. Unfortunately, we cannot test this hypothesis with currently available delinquency data.

According to the 1998 General Social Survey (Davis, Smith, & Marsden, 2006), almost two-thirds (64.1 percent) of American adults (n = 1,416) engage in religious coping by "[looking] to God for strength, support, guidance" when trying to understand and deal with major problems in their lives. While the percentage might be smaller among adolescents due to their relative lack of religious maturity, criminologists may be missing an interesting research opportunity. The failure to collect even the most basic data on religion in surveys is well known, and is largely responsible for hindering research explicitly examining religion within criminology. This oversight would seem to be the result of a general lack of interest or worse, an outright bias against religion within criminology.[7] As a remedy, we offer two future directions for research in criminology, one at the micro-level and the other at the macro-level.

First, we propose criminologists look beyond biological, psychological, and social dimensions and seriously consider the religious or spiritual dimension.[8] According to a prominent sociologist of religion, Christian Smith (2003, p. 54), "all human persons ... are, at bottom, *believers*. We are all necessarily trusting, believing animals, creatures who must and do place our faith in beliefs that *cannot themselves be verified except by means established by the presumed beliefs themselves*." Also, he argues, we are "moral" agents in that we are motivated to act out and sustain moral order that helps constitute, directs, and makes human life significant, clarifying "what is right and wrong, good and bad, worthy and unworthy, just and unjust" (p. 8). For Smith, religion plays a crucial role for the moral order by affirming the reality of "superempirical" orders as real and consequential.

To the extent that we humans are *homo credens*, contemporary criminology is unlikely to be successful in providing a holistic and balanced explanation of criminal behavior. On the other hand, criminologists with a renewed interest in the religious and spiritual dimension of human behavior are likely to discover research questions rarely asked before. For example, while previous studies show religious individuals are less likely to commit crime than their non-religious counterparts, we know little about criminality of "religious seekers" or those who claim to be "spiritual but not religious" (Fuller, 2001), which make up as much as 10 percent of American adults (Dougherty & Jang, 2008).[9]

In his book, *Moral, Believing Animals*, Smith (2003) also points out a longstanding false dichotomy in sociological theory between culture and social structure, drawing our attention to the intimate connection between the two, a society's moral order (culture) and social institutions (structure). This leads to our second suggestion for criminology's future direction at the macro-level. While such a false dichotomy or a tension between culturalists and structuralists has existed in criminology (e.g., Bursik & Grasmick, 1993; Kornhauser, 1978), anomie theorists tend to be more conscious of including both culture and structure in a coherent theoretical framework than others (e.g., Merton, 1938). An excellent case in point is the institutional anomie theory that emphasizes the interrelationships between culture and institutional structure in understanding crime in America. For Messner and Rosenfeld (2001, p. 62), the American Dream "embodies the basic value commitments of the culture: its achievement orientation, individualism, universalism, and peculiar form of materialism ... described as the 'fetishism of money.'" This powerful cultural force is responsible for the economy dominating its noneconomic institutions by devaluating their functions and roles, forcing them to accommodate economic rules of engagement, and penetrating economic norms into those institutions. Thus, the American Dream puts criminogenic pressures on society, resulting in higher crime rates than other industrial nations.

Messner and Rosenfeld emphasize the invasive power of the economy in transforming noneconomic institutions into semi-economic ones. As a result, an unrealistic burden is placed on government, family, and education in promoting allegiance to normative rules as their prosocial cultural messages get overwhelmed by the anomic tendencies of the American Dream. Unfortunately, little attention is given to the religion – the noneconomic institution we believe may best be suited to push back against this cultural force. We suggest religion is a major source of "living narratives" for Americans to live by and that it produces a collective consciousness that provides the basis of social integration (Durkheim, 1984 [1893]; Smith, 2003). However, the potential contribution of religion to criminology, as a perspective as well as social institution, goes well beyond this particular theory as it has been illustrated by a religion-inspired theory of crime and practice in criminal justice (Braithwaite, 1989; Cullen, Sundt, & Wozniak, 2001).

Specifically, religious perspectives on human nature[10] and criminal behavior, whether chosen or determined (e.g., Agnew, 1995), can contribute to a new criminological perspective that focuses on human personhood (i.e., moral, believing animal), motivation, and action, which has often been neglected by modern criminology under the influence of the naturalistic, utilitarian, and non-cultural tradition of Western social theory (Smith, 2003). Just as cultural sociology has been resurgent in the last three decades to provide rich cultural accounts of human social life and action, criminology should complement the disproportionately deterministic and structural explanations of crime at both the micro- and macro-level.[11]

In conclusion, we know from decades of survey research that the influence of religion is broad and not relegated to any one segment of the population. Consequently, future research on crime and delinquency should include multiple measures of religious practices and beliefs. Churches, synagogues, mosques, inner-city storefront ministries, and other houses of worship represent one of the key institutions remaining within close proximity of most adolescents, their families, and their peers. New research will allow us to more fully understand the ways in which religion may directly and indirectly impact crime, delinquency, or faith-based approaches to criminal justice problems (offender treatment, alternative sentencing, mentoring of at-risk youth, prisoner reentry and aftercare). Finally, our updated systematic review suggests the beneficial relationship between religion and crime is not simply a function of religion's constraining function or what it discourages – opposing drug use, violence, or delinquent behavior – but also through what it encourages – promoting prosocial behaviors. Failure to consider religion variables will cause researchers to be needlessly shortsighted in estimating models designed to explain its direct and indirect influences on antisocial as well as prosocial behavior.

REFERENCES

Agnew, R. (1995). Determinism, indeterminism, and crime - an empirical exploration. *Criminology, 33,* 83-109.

Agnew, R. (2006). *Pressured into crime: An overview of general strain theory.* Los Angeles, CA: Roxbury Publishing Company.

Akers, R. (1998). *Social learning and social structure: A general theory of crime and deviance.* Boston, MA: Northeastern University Press.

Albrecht, S, Chadwick, B., & Alcorn, D. (1977). Religiosity and deviance - application of an attitude-behavior contingent consistency model. *Journal for the Scientific Study of Religion, 16,* 263-74.

Bader, C., Mencken, F., & Froese, P. (2007). American piety 2005: Content and methods of the Baylor religion survey. *Journal for the Scientific Study of Religion, 46,* 447-63.

Baier, C. & Wright, B. (2001). "If you love me, keep my commandments": A meta-analysis of the effect of religion on crime. *Journal of Research in Crime and Delinquency, 38,* 3-21.

Beccaria, C. (2008 [1764]). *On crime and punishments and other writings.* Toronto, Canada: University of Toronto Press.

Bentham, J. (1970 [1789]). *An introduction to the principles of morals and legislation.* London, UK: The Athlone Press.

Blanchard, T., Bartkowski, J., Matthews, T., & Kerley, K. (2008). Faith, morality and mortality: The ecological impact of religion on population health. *Social Forces, 86,* 1591-620.

Braithwaite, J. (1989). *Crime, shame and reintegration.* New York, NY: Cambridge University Press.

Burkett, S. & White, M. (1974). Hellfire and delinquency: Another look. *Journal for the Scientific Study of Religion, 13,* 455-62.

Bursik, R. & Grasmick, H. (1993). *Neighborhoods and crime: The dimensions of effective community control.* New York, NY: Lexington Books.

Clear, T. & Sumter, M. (2002). Prisoners, prison, and religion: Religion and adjustment to prison. *Journal of Offender Rehabilitation, 35,* 127-59.

Cochran, J., Wood, P., & Arneklev, B. (1994). Is the religiosity-delinquency relationship spurious - a test of arousal and social-control theories. *Journal of Research in Crime and Delinquency, 31,* 92-123.

Cooper, H. (2010). *Research synthesis and meta-analysis: A step-by-step approach.* Los Angeles, CA: Sage.

Cornish, D. & Clarke, R. (1986). The reasoning criminal: Rational choice perspective on offending. In A. Blumstein & D. Farrington (Eds.), *Research in criminology.* New York, NY: Springer-Verlag.

Cullen, F., Sundt, J., & Wozniak, J. (2001). The virtuous prison: Toward a restorative rehabilitation. In H. Pontell & D. Schichor (Eds.), *Contemporary issues in crime and criminal justice: Essays in honor of Gilbert Geis* (pp. 265-286). Upper Saddle River, NJ: Prentice Hall.

Davis, J., Smith, T., & Marsden, P. (2006). General social surveys, 1972-2006 [Cumulative File] [Computer file]. ICPSR04697-v4. Storrs, CT: Roper

Center for Public Opinion Research, University of Connecticut/Ann Arbor, MI: Inter-university Consortium for Political and Social Research [distributors], 2009-12-04. doi:10.3886/ICPSR04697.

Dougherty, K. & Jang, S. (2008). Spirituality: Religion and spirituality are not mutually exclusive. In R. Stark (Ed.), *What Americans really believe* (pp. 87-94). Waco, TX: Baylor University Press.

Durkheim, E. (1981 [1912]). *The elementary forms of the religious life.* London, UK: Allen and Unwin.

Durkheim, E. (1984 [1893]). *The division of labor in society.* New York, NY: Free Press.

Ellis, L. (1987). Religiosity and criminality from the perspective of arousal theory. *Journal of Research in Crime and Delinquency, 24,* 215-32.

Ellis, L. & Thompson, R. (1989). Relating religion, crime, and arousal and boredom. *Sociology and Social Research, 73,* 132-9.

Ellison, C., Burr, J., & McCall, P. (2003). The enduring puzzle of southern homicide: Is regional religious culture the missing piece? *Homicide Studies, 7,* 326-52.

Evans, T., Cullen, F., Dunaway, R., & Burton, V. (1995). Religion and crime reexamined - the impact of religion, secular controls, and social ecology on adult criminality. *Criminology, 33,* 195-224.

Ferrell, J. (1999). Cultural criminology. *Annual Review of Sociology, 25,* 395-418.

Frankl, V. (1984 [1946]). *Man's search for meaning.* New York, NY: Pocket Books.

Freeman, R. (1986). Who escapes? The relation of churchgoing and other background factors to the socioeconomic performance of black male youth from inner-city tracts. In R. Freeman & H. Holzer (Eds.), *The black youth employment crisis* (pp. 353-376). Chicago, IL: University of Chicago Press.

Fuller, R. (2001). *Spiritual, but not religious: Understanding unchurched America.* New York, NY: Oxford University Press.

Gibbs, J. (1986). Punishment and deterrence: Theory, research, and penal policy. In L. Lipson & S. Wheeler (Eds.), *Law and the social sciences* (pp. 319-368). New York, NY: Russell Sage.

Giordano, P., Longmore, M., Schroeder, R., & Seffrin, P. (2008). A life-course perspective on spirituality and desistance from crime. *Criminology, 46,* 99-132.

Gottfredson, M. & Hirschi, T. (1990). *A general theory of crime.* Stanford, CA: Stanford University Press.

Higgins, P. & Albrecht, G. (1977). Hellfire and delinquency revisited. *Social Forces, 55,* 952-8.

Hirschi, T. (1969). *Causes of delinquency.* Berkeley, CA: University of California Press.

Hirschi, T. & Stark, R. (1969). Hellfire and delinquency. *Social Problems, 17,* 202-13.

Hunter, A. (1985). Private, parochial, and public school orders: The problem of crime and incivility in urban communities. In G. Suttles & M. Zald

(Eds.), *The challenge of social control: Citizenship and institution building in modern society* (pp. 230-242). Norwood, NJ: Ablex.

Jang, S., Bader, C., & Johnson, B. (2008). The cumulative advantage of religiosity in preventing drug use. *Journal of Drug Issues, 38*, 771-98.

Jang, S. & Johnson, B. (2001). Neighborhood disorder, individual religiosity, and adolescent use of illicit drugs: A test of multilevel hypotheses. *Criminology, 39*, 109-44.

Jang, S. & Johnson, B. (2005). Gender, religiosity, and reactions to strain among African Americans. *The Sociological Quarterly, 46*, 323-357.

Jensen, G. & Erickson, M. (1979). The religious factor and delinquency: Another look at the hellfire hypothesis. In R. Wuthnow (Ed.), *The religious dimension* (pp. 157-177). New York, NY: Academic Press.

Johnson, B. (2003). *The InnerChange Freedom Initiative: A preliminary evaluation of a faith-based prison program.* ISR Research Report, Institute for Studies of Religion. Waco, TX: Baylor University. http://www.isreligion.org/publications/reports/

Johnson, B. (2004). Religious programs and recidivism among former inmates in prison fellowship programs: A long-term follow-up study. *Justice Quarterly, 21*, 329-54.

Johnson, B., Jang, S., Larson, D., & Li, S. (2001). Does adolescent religious commitment matter? A reexamination of the effects of religiosity on delinquency. *Journal of Research in Crime and Delinquency, 38*, 22-44.

Johnson, B., Jang, S., Li, S., & Larson, D. (2000). The 'invisible institution' and black youth crime: The church as an agency of local social control. *Journal of Youth and Adolescence, 29*, 479-98.

Johnson, B., Larson, D., Li, S., & Jang, S. (2000). Escaping from the crime of inner cities: Church attendance and religious salience among disadvantaged youth. *Justice Quarterly, 17*, 377-91.

Johnson, B., Li, S., Larson, D., & McCullough, M. (2000). A systematic review of the religiosity and delinquency literature: A research note. *Journal of Contemporary Criminal Justice, 16*(1), 32-52.

Johnson, B. & Siegel, M. (2002). *The great escape: How religion alters the delinquent behavior of high-risk adolescents.* ISR Research Report, Institute for Studies of Religion. Waco, TX: Baylor University. http://www.isreligion.org/publications/reports/

Kerley, K., Allison, M., & Graham, R. (2006). Investigating the impact of religiosity on emotional and behavioral coping in prison. *Journal of Crime and Justice. 29*, 71-96.

Kerley, K. & Copes, H. (2009). 'Keepin' my mind right': Identity maintenance and religious social support in the prison context. *International Journal of Offender Therapy and Comparative Criminology, 53*, 228-244.

Kornhauser, R. (1978). *Social sources of delinquency: An appraisal of analytic models.* Chicago, IL: University of Chicago Press.

Krohn, M. (1986). The web of conformity - a network approach to the explanation of delinquent-behavior. *Social Problems, 33*, S81-93.

Lee, M. (2006). The religious institutional base and violent crime in rural areas. *Journal for the Scientific Study of Religion, 45*, 309-324.

Lee, M. (2008). Civic community in the hinterland: Toward a theory of rural social structure and violence. *Criminology, 46,* 447-478.

Lee, M. & Bartkowski, J. (2004). Love thy neighbor? Moral communities, civic engagement, and juvenile homicide in rural areas. *Social Forces, 82,* 1001-1035.

Lee, M. & Thomas, S. (2010). Civic community, population change, and violent crime in rural communities. *Journal of Research in Crime and Delinquency, 47,* 118-147.

Levin, J., Taylor, R., & Chatters, L. (1995). A multidimensional measure of religious involvement for African-Americans. *Sociological Quarterly, 36,* 157-173.

Liska, A., Krohn, M., & Messner, S. (1989). Strategies and requisites for theoretical integration in the study of crime and deviance. In S. Messner, M. Krohn, & A. Liska (Eds.), *Theoretical integration in the study of deviance and crime: Problems and prospects* (pp. 1-19). Albany, NY: State University of New York Press.

Lombroso, C. (2006 [1876]). *Criminal man.* Durham, NC: Duke University Press.

Maume, M. & Lee, M. (2003). Social institutions and violence: A sub-national test of institutional anomie theory. *Criminology. 41,* 1137-1172.

McCullough, M., Pargament, K., & Thorensen, C. (2000). *Forgiveness: Theory, research, and practice.* New York, NY: Guilford Press.

Merton, R. (1938). Social structure and anomie. *American Sociological Review, 3,* 672-682.

Messner, S. & Rosenfeld, R. (2001). *Crime and the American dream.* Belmont, CA: Wadsworth.

Nye, F. (1958). *Family relationships and delinquent behavior.* New York, NY: Wiley.

Pargament, K. (1997). *The psychology of religion and coping: Theory, research, practice.* New York, NY: Guilford Press.

Pargament, K., Maton, K., & Hess, R. (1992). *Religion and prevention in mental health: Research, vision, and action.* New York, NY: The Haworth Press.

Post, S. (1992). DSM-III-R and religion. *Social Science & Medicine, 35,* 81-90.

Putnam, R. (2000). *Bowling alone: The collapse and revival of American community.* New York, NY: Simon and Schuster.

Regnerus, M. (2003). Moral communities and adolescent delinquency: Religious contexts and community social control. *The Sociological Quarterly, 44,* 523-554.

Rosenfeld, R., Messner, S., & Baumer, E. (2001). Social capital and homicide. *Social Forces, 80,* 283-310.

Sampson, R. & Wilson, W. (1995). Toward a theory of race, crime, and urban inequality. In J. Hagan & R. Peterson (Eds.), *Crime and inequality* (pp. 37-54). Stanford, CA: Stanford University Press.

Sargeant, K. (2000). *Seeker churches: Promoting traditional religion in a nontraditional way.* New Brunswick, NJ: Rutgers University Press.

Shaw, C. & McKay, H. (1942). *Juvenile delinquency and urban areas*. Chicago, IL: University of Chicago Press.

Smith, C. (2003). *Moral, believing animals: Human personhood and culture*. New York, NY: Oxford University Press.

Smith, C. & Denton, M. (2005). *Soul searching: The religious and spiritual lives of American teenagers*. New York, NY: Oxford University Press.

Smith, C., Emerson, M., Gallagher, S., Kennedy, P., & Sikkink, D. (1998). *American evangelicalism: embattled and thriving*. Chicago, IL: University of Chicago Press.

Stark, R. (1996). Religion as context: Hellfire and delinquency one more time. *Sociology of Religion, 57*, 163-173.

Stark, R. & Bainbridge, W. (1996). *Religion, deviance, and social control*. New York, NY: Routledge.

Stark, R., Kent, L., & Doyle, D. (1982). Religion and delinquency - the ecology of a lost relationship. *Journal of Research in Crime and Delinquency, 19*, 4-24.

Sutherland, E. & Cressey, D. (1970 [1924]). *Criminology*. Philadelphia, PA: J. B. Lippincott Company.

Tittle, C. & Welch, M. (1983). Religiosity and deviance - toward a contingency theory of constraining effects. *Social Forces, 61*, 653-682.

Tolbert, C., Lyson, T., & Irwin, M. (1998). Local capitalism, civic engagement, and socioeconomic well-being. *Social Forces, 77*, 401-427.

ENDNOTES

[1] In a relatively recent interview, both Hirschi and Stark remarked they were surprised at the reaction generated by the publication (personal communication, April 15, 2009).

[2] We acknowledge that the current systematic review does not carry the same weight as a meta-analysis, where effect sizes for individual studies are considered in the overall assessment of research literature under consideration. While meta-analysis is a more rigorous and transparent (i.e., standardized) method than traditional narrative synthesis or systematic reviews, its utility for summarizing past research is limited for non-experimental, correlational studies which make up a majority of the criminological research (Cooper, 2010). We are, however, currently conducting a separate meta-analysis of this same research literature.

[3] While irreligionists might not be interested in the validity of such religious sanctions, they might not be completely immune from "supernatural" sanctions cognitively. Survey research confirms non-religious people tend to be more superstitious than religious people.

[4] For example, Cochran et al. (1994) operationalized the arousal construct by using the scales of self-reported thrill seeking, impulsivity, and physicality, which might have measured instead Gottfredson and Hirschi's (1990) low self-concept, which is a sociological rather than a neurological concept.

[5] Specifically, Regnerus constructed not only measures of generic religiosity at the county (the proportion of residents who are religious adherents) and

school levels (the percentage of students in the school that attend church weekly and the percentage of students who consider themselves "born again" Christians), but also a county-level measure of religious homogeneity (the proportion of adherents who belong to conservative Protestant churches).

6 While there are differences in wording, the 2006 General Social Survey (Davis et al., 2006) documents similar findings: (1) 83 percent of respondents (*n* = 4,510) indicated having a religion or religious denomination preference – 95 percent responded "Protestant," "Catholic," or "Jewish;" (2) 73 percent said they "know God exists" without a doubt (63 percent) or believe in "some high power" (10 percent); and (3) 31 percent reported they attended religious service "nearly every week" or more often. For a detailed description of methods and findings from the 2005 Baylor Religion Survey, see a special section in the 2007 December issue of the *Journal for the Scientific Study of Religion* (Bader, Mencken, & Froese, 2007).

7 Bias against religion has been documented in the social and behavioral sciences. For example, until recently, religiosity was linked to mental illness rather than mental health (Pargament, Maton, & Hess, 1992), and the DSM-III-R contained considerable negative bias against religion, contributing to unfair stereotypes of religious persons (Post, 1992). This bias against religion was corrected in the DSM-IV.

8 Viktor Frankl (1984 [1946]), a Nazi concentration camp survivor who later became the leader of the Third Viennese School of Psychotherapy, made a similar appeal to psychiatrists not to exclude the spiritual dimension *a priori* based on their naturalistic presupposition about human behavior. Other behavioral (e.g., psychology) and medical sciences generally appear to be more open to the spiritual dimension of human personhood than ever before.

9 The percentage among American teenagers varies, depending on whether we count only those who say it is "very true" that they are "spiritual but not religious" (8 percent) or those who say it is "somewhat true" as well (46 percent), while the estimate is said to be generally unreliable because a majority of teenagers tend to have no clue what it means to be "spiritual but not religious" (Smith & Denton, 2005).

10 For example, Judeo-Christian religion offers an alternative, non-dualistic view on human nature, combining the underlying assumptions of "original sin" and "original virtue" in criminological theories (Kornhauser, 1978, p. 35). These "incompatible" assumptions have been an issue for debate on theoretical integration (Liska, Krohn, & Messner, 1989).

11 We avoid the "cultural criminology" label because it has already been used to refer to a perspective within criminology and criminal justice; drawn from cultural studies, postmodern theory, critical theory, and interactionist sociology, and on ethnographic methodologies as well as media/textual analysis (Ferrell, 1999).

APPENDIX A. A SYSTEMATIC REVIEW OF THE RELIGION AND CRIME LITERATURE

No	Investigators	Type	Method	N	Population	Location	Religious Variable	Control	Findings
1	Adamcyzk (2008)	PC	R	1,449	Ad	National US	SR, ORA, RE	MC	B
2	Adelekan (1993)	CS	S/R	636	CS	Nigeria	SR, D	N	B
3	Adlaf (1985)	CS	R	2,066	Ad	Ontario	D, ORA, SR	N	B
4	Albrecht (1977)	CS	C	244	Mormon teens	Utah, Idaho, LA	SR, ORA	MC	B
5	Albrecht (1996)	PC	R	12,168	HS	National US	ORA	MC	B
6	Alford (1991)	PC	C	157	Ad, PP	Nebraska	Misc.	N	B
7	Allen (1967)	CS	S	179	HS (16-18)	Youth fac.	D, ORA, SR	MC	B
8	Amoateng (1986)	CS	R	17,000	HS	National US	SR, ORA	MC	B
9	Amey (1996)	CS	R	11,728	HS	National US	OR, SR, D	MC	B
10	Bahr (1993)	CR	C/P	322	Ad	3 west counties US	SR	MC	M
11	Bahr (1998)	CS	R	13,250	HS	Utah	ORA, SR	MC	B
12	Bahr (2008)	PC	R	18,517	Ad	National US	A, S. R	MC	B
13	Barnes (1994)	PC	R	658	Ad	Buffalo, NY	ORA	MC	B
14	Barrett (1988)	CT	S	326	Ad	Texas	ORA	MC	B
15	Bell (1997)	CS	R	17,952	CS	National US	SR	MC	B
16	Benda (1994)	CS	R	1,093	HS	OK, MD, AR	ORA, SR	MC	B
17	Benda (1995)	CS	S	1,093	HS	Arkansas & MD	ORA, SR	MC	B
18	Benda (1997)	CS	S	724	HS	Arkansas & OK	ORA, SR	MC	B

No	Investigators	Type	Method	N	Population	Location	Religious Variable	Control	Findings
19	Benda (1997b)	CS	R	1,093	HS	5 US cities	ORA, SR	MC	B
20	Benda (1999)	CS	R	1,093	Ad	OK, MD, AR	Misc.	MC	B
21	Benda (2000)	CS	R	1,057	HS	OK, MD, AR	Misc.	MC	B
22	Benda (2001)	CS	R	837	HS	South-east	Misc.	MC	M
23	Benda (2002)	CS	C	326	M (15-24)	Arkansas	SR	SC	B
24	Benda (2006)	CS	R	3,551	Ad	Southern State	SR	MC	B
25	Benson (1989)	CS	R	> 12,000	HS	National US	SR	MC	B
26	Bjarnason (2005)	CS	R	3,524	HS	Iceland	SR	MC	B
27	Bliss (1994)	CS	C	143	CS	Ohio	ORA, SR	N	M
28	Bowker (1974)	CS	R	948	CS	College	ORA, D	N	B
29	Brizer (1993)	CC	C	65	PP	New York	ORA, NORA	N	B
30	Brook (1984)	CS	C/P	403	CS	College in NJ	ORA	MC	B
31	Brown T L (2001)	CS	R	899	Ad	OH, KY	ORA, IR, Misc.	N	B
32	Brown T N (2001)	CS	R	188,000	HS	National US	RCM	MC	B
33	Brownfield (1991)	CS	C/P	800+	HS	Seattle	SR, ORA, D	MC	B
34	Burkett (1974)	CS	C	855	HS	Pacific NW	ORA	SC	B
35	Burkett (1977)	CS	S	837	HS	Pacific NW	ORA, RB	SC	B
36	Burkett (1980)	CS	S	323	HS	Pacific NE	ORA, SR, RB	N	B
37	Burkett (1987)	PC	C	240	HS	Pacific NW	ORA, SR, RB	MC	B
38	Burkett (1993)	PC	R	612 & 428	HS	Pacific NW	RB, SR, ORA	MC	B
39	Cancellaro (1982)	CC	C	74	Drug Addicts	Kentucky	NORA, RE	N	B

No	Investigators	Type	Method	N	Population	Location	Religious Variable	Control	Findings
40	Caputo (2004)	PC	R	1,911	Ad	National US	Misc.	MC	B
41	Caputo (2005)	PC	R	1,911	Ad	National US	Misc.	MC	B
42	Carlucci (1993)	CS	R	331	CS	Eastern US	D	N	B
43	Carr-Saunders (1944)	CC	C	276-551	Delin-quents	London, UK	ORA	N	B
44	Cecero (2005)	CS	C/P	237	CS	NE University	Misc.	MC	B
45	Chadwick (1993)	CS	R	2,143	Ad (Mormons)	Eastern US	ORA, RB	MC	B
46	Chandy (1996)	PC	R	1,959	Ad	National US	SR	MC	B
47	Chawla (2007)	CS	R	1,442	CS	West Coast	SR	MC	B
48	Chen (2004)	CS	R	12,797	HS	Panama & DR	D, ORA,	MC	B
49	Christo (1995)	PC	C	101	Poly-drug abuse	London	RB	N	B
50	Chu (2007)	PC	R	1,725	Ad	National US	ORA, SR	MC	B
51	Cisin (1968)	CS	R	2,746	CDA	National US	ORA, RC, RB	MC	B
52	Clark (1992)	CS	R	2,036	Medical students	Great Britain	D	N	B
53	Clear (2002)	PC	S	769	Pri-soners	DE, TX, IN, MS	SR, D	MC	B
54	Cochran (1989)	CS	R	3,065	Ad	Midwest US	ORA, SR, D	MC	B
55	Cochran (1991)	CS	R	3,065	Ad	Midwest US	ORA, SR, D	MC	B
56	Cochran (1993)	CS	R	3,065	Ad	Midwest	Misc.	MC	B
57	Cochran (1994)	CS	C	1,600	HS	Oklahoma	ORA, SR	MC	B
58	Cohen (1987)	PC	S	976	Mother/caretaker	New York	ORA	MC	B
59	Coleman (1986)	CC	S	50	Opiate addicts	Philadelphia	ORA, SR	MC	M

No	Investigators	Type	Method	N	Population	Location	Religious Variable	Control	Findings
60	Cook (1997)	CS	R	7,666	Youth (12-30)	United Kingdom	RCM	N	B
61	Coombs (1985)	PC	C	197	Ad	Los Angeles	RB, ORA	N	B
62	Crano (2008)	PC	R	2,111	Ad, HS	National US	RA	MC	B
63	Cretacci (2003)	CS	R	6,500	Ad, youth	National US	SR, ORA, RCM, D	MC	B
64	Cronin (1995)	CS	C	216	CS	Maryland	D, SR	N	B
65	Dennis (2005)	Q	D	1,725	(15-21)	National US	SR	SC	B
66	Desmond (1981)	PC	C	248	PP addicts	San Antonio	Misc.	N	B
67	Desmond (2009)	PC	R	1,725	Ad	National US	ORA, SR	MC	B
68	Dudley (1987)	CS	R	801	SDA Youth	National US	ORA, NORA, CM	SC	B
69	Dunn (2005)	CS	R	6,029	HS	National US	SR	MC	B
70	Elifson (1983)	CS	R	600	Ad, HS	Atlanta, GA	RB, SR, NORA	SC	NA
71	Ellis (1989)	CS	C	354	CS	North Dakota	RB, Misc.	SC	B
72	Ellis (2002)	P	C	11,000	CS, R	US & Canada	D	SC	B
73	Ellison (1999)	CS	R	13,017	CDA	National US	ORA, D, Misc.	MC	B
74	Ellison (2001)	CS	R	13,017	CDA	National US	ORA	MC	B
75	Ellison (2007)	CS	P	3,666	CDA	National US	ORA	MC	B
76	Engs (1980)	CS	S	1,691	CS	Australia	D, SR	N	B
77	Engs (1996)	CS	C	12,081	CS	National	SR, D	N	B
78	Engs (1999)	CS	C	4,150	CS	Scotland	D, SR	N	B
79	Evans (1995)	CS	S	477	CDA	Midwest US	OR, SR, RB, D	MC	B
80	Evans (1996)	CS	R	263	HS	Midwest City	ORA, SR, RC	MC	B

No	Investigators	Type	Method	N	Population	Location	Religious Variable	Control	Findings
81	Fernquist (1995)	CS	—	180	CS	—	ORA, NORA	N	B
82	Forliti (1986)	CS	C	10,467	Ad/ parents	United States	RB, ORA, SR	NS	B
83	Forthun (1999)	CS	R	526	CS	South-western	ORA	N	B
84	Foshee (1996)	PC	R	1,553	Ad	Southeast US	ORA, RB, SR, D	MC	B
85	Francis (1993)	CS	S	4,753	HS	England	ORA, RB	N	B
86	Francis (1997)	CS	S	16,734	Ad	England & Wales	A, D	N	B
87	Fraser (1967)	CS	R	282	Ad	New Zealand	Misc.	MC	B
88	Free (1992)	CS	C/P	916	CS	SW & Midwest	ORA, SR	N	B
89	Free (1993)	CS	C/P	916	CS	SW & Midwest	ORA, SR	N	B
90	Free (1994)	CS	C/P	916	CS	SW & Midwest	ORA, SR	N	B
91	Freeman (1986)	CS	R/R	4,961	Ad	Boston, Chi, Phil	ORA	MC	B
92	Galen (2004)	CS	C/P	265	CS	--	D, MD	MC	B
93	Gannon (1967)	CS	C/P	150	Ad	Chicago, IL	Misc.	N	M
94	Gardner (2007)	CC	C/P	202	Ad	Jamaica	Misc.	MC	B
95	Garis (1998)	PC	R	25,000	Ad	National US	ORA	MC	B
96	Grasmick (1991)	CS	R	304	CDA	Oklahoma City	D, ORA, SR	SC	M
97	Grasmick (1991)	CS	R	285	Adults	Oklahoma City	D, SR	MC	B
98	Grunbaum (2000)	CS	R	441	HS	Texas	ORA	MC	B
99	Guinn (1975)	CS	S/R	1,789	HS	Texas	ORA	N	B
100	Hadaway (1984)	CS	R	600	Ad, HS	Atlanta	ORA, SR, NORA	SC	B

No	Investigators	Type	Method	N	Population	Location	Religious Variable	Control	Findings
101	Hamil-Lucker (2004)	CS	PC	2,509	14-22	--	Misc.	N	B
102	Hammer-meister (2001)	CS	C/P	462	CS	Pacific Northwest		N	B
103	Hansell (1990)	PC	R	908	Ad	NJ	ORA	MC	B
104	Hanson (1987)	PC	R	6,115	CS	US	D	N	B
105	Hardert (1994)	CS	C	1,234	HS, CS	Arizona	ORA, SR	MC	NA
106	Hardesty (1995)	CS	C	475	HS, CS (16-19)	Midwest US	Family religiosity	SC	B
107	Harris (2003)	CS	R	1,393	Ad, LDS	7 US states	ORA, SWB, RE	MC	B
108	Hater (1984)	CS	S	1,174	PP	National	ORA, SR	MC	NA
109	Hawks (1994)	CS	R	293	Ad and Parents	3 Utah counties	D	MC	NA
110	Hays (1986)	CS	R	1,121	Ad (13-18)	National	Religiosity scale	MC	B
111	Hays (1990)	CS	--	415	HS	--	D	MC	B
112	Heath (1999)	PC	R	1,687	twins only	Missouri	Misc.	MC	B
113	Hercik (2004)	PC	C	413	Prisoners	Florida	Religious Program	MC	B
114	Herronkohl (2005)	CS	R	680	HS	Pacific NW	Misc.	MC	B
115	Higgins (1977)	CS	R	1,410	HS (10th)	Atlanta, GA	ORA	SC	B
116	Hill (1999)	PC	R	808	HS (1985-1993)	Seattle	ORA	N	M
117	Hillman (2000)	CS	C/P	292	HS	Midwest	D, SR	N	B
118	Hirschi (1969)	CS	R	4,077	HS	Northern CA	ORA	N	NA

No	Investigators	Type	Method	N	Population	Location	Religious Variable	Control	Findings
119	Hodge (2001)	CS	R	414	HS	New Mexico	ORA, RB	MC	B
120	Humphrey (1989)	CS	R	1,097	CS	South-eastern US	ORA	MC	B
121	Hundleby (1982)	CS	C	231	HS	Ontario	ORA, NORA	N	NA
122	Hundleby (1987)	CS	C	2,048	HS	Ontario	ORA	MC	B
123	Isralowitz (1990)	CS	R	7,671	CS	Singapore	RB	N	NA
124	Jang (2001)	PC	R	1,087	Youth (13-22)	National US	ORA, SR	MC	B
125	Jang (2003)	CS	R	2,107	CDA	National US	ORA, NORA SR	MC	B
126	Jang (2004)	CS	R	659	CDA	National US	ORA, NORA SR	MC	B
127	Jang (2005)	CS	R	659	CDA	National US	ORA, NORA SR	MC	B
128	Jang (2007)	PC	R	1,250	CDA	National US	ORA, NORA SR	MC	B
129	Jang (2008)	PC	R	1,044	Ad	National US	D, ORA, SR	MC	B
130	Jang (2010)	PC	R	1,033	Ad	National US	ORA, SR, D	MC	B
131	Jessor (1973)	PC	R	605-248	HS, CS	Colorado	ORA	N	B
132	Jessor (1977)	PC	R	432-205	HS, CS	Colorado	ORA, NORA SR	N	B
133	Jessor (1980)	CS	R	13,122	Ad	National US	ORA, SR	MC	B
134	Jeynes (2006)	PC	R	18,726	Ad, HS	U.S.	R	MC	B
135	Johnson (1987)	RS	S	782	Former pri-soners	Florida	ORA, SR	MC	NA

No	Investigators	Type	Method	N	Population	Location	Religious Variable	Control	Findings
136	Johnson (1997)	CC	S	201-201	Former prisoners	New York	ORA, NORA	MC	B
137	Johnson (2000a)	CS	R/R	2,358	Youth	Boston, Chicago, Phil	ORA	MC	B
138	Johnson (2000b)	PC	R	207	Ad	National US	ORA	MC	B
139	Johnson (2001a)	PC	R	1,087	Ad	National US	SR	MC	B
140	Johnson (2001b)	PC	R	1,305	Youth	National US	ORA, SR	MC	B
141	Johnson (2002)	CC	S	148-247	Former prisoners	Brazil	Religious program	SC	B
142	Johnson (2003)	PC	C	177-177	Former prisoners	Texas	Religious program	MC	B
143	Johnson (2004)	CC	S	201-201	Former prisoners	New York	ORA, NORA	MC	B
144	Jones (2004)	CS	R	3,395	HS	Midwestern State	Misc.	MC	B
145	Junger (1993)	CS	R	788	Ad	Netherlands	ORA	MC	B
146	Kandel (1976)	PC	R	1,112	Ad	New York	ORA	MC	B
147	Kandel (1982)	CS	R	1,947	Ad	New York	D	MC	B
148	Kandel (1986)	PC	R	1,004	Ad/ young adults	New York	ORA	MC	NA
149	Kerley (2005)	RS	R	386	Prisoners	Mississip-pi	ORA, SR, RB	MC	B
150	Kerley (2005b)	RS	R	386	Prisoners	Mississip-pi	ORA	MC	B
151	Kerley (2006)	RS	R	386	Prisoners	Mississip-pi	ORA	MC	B
152	Kerley (2009)	RS	C/P	63	Prisoners	Mississip-pi	ORA, SR, RB	MC	B
153	Kvaraceus (1944)	CS	S	700+	Ad	New Jersey	ORA, D	N	NA

No	Investigators	Type	Method	N	Population	Location	Religious Variable	Control	Findings
154	Lee J (1997)	CS	R	7,658	Ad/ Parents	US & Canada	ORA, Misc.	MC	B
155	Lee M (2004)	CC	R	1,889	homicide	National	D	MC	B
156	Leigh (2005)	CS	R	196	CS	Intro Psych Class	Misc.	MC	B
157	Linville (2005)	CS	R	235	Teens	Virginia	ORA	MC	B
158	Litchfield (1997)	PC	R	>1,500	Ad	--	ORA, RB, RCM	MC	B
159	Lo (1993)	CS	R	160	CS	Deep south	D	MC	B
160	Long (1993)	PC	R	625	HS	Montana	CM, ORA, SR	MC	B
161	Longest (2008)	PC	R	1,680	Ad	National US	ORA, SR, NORA	MC	B
162	Longshore (2004)	PC	R	1,036	Drug offenders	5 US Cities	RB, SR, D	MC	B
163	Lorch (1985)	CS	S/R	13,878	HS	Colorado Springs	CM, ORA, SR	MC	B
164	MacDonald (2005)	CS	R	5,414	HS	South Carolina	ORA	MC	M
165	Mainous (2001)	--	P/C	191	Ad, HS	Kentucky	A,R	MC	B
166	Marcos (1986)	CS	R	2,626	HS	Southwest US	ORA, RCM	MC	B
167	Mason (2001)	PC	R	840	Ad	New York	S, A, D	MC	B
168	Mason (2002)	PC	L	6,504	Ad	National US	Misc.	MC	B
169	Mauss (1959)	CS	S	459	HS	California	D	N	B
170	McIntosh (1981)	CS	R	1,358	HS	Texas	D, ORA, SR	MC	B
171	McLuckie (1975)	CS	R	27,175	HS	Pennsylvania	D, RA	MC	B
172	Merrill (2001)	CS	R	1,036	CS	US	RCM	MC	B

No	Investigators	Type	Method	N	Population	Location	Religious Variable	Control	Findings
173	Merrill (2005)	CS	C	1,333	CS	Utah	D, A, R	MC	B
174	Middleton (1962)	CS	—	554	CS	California, FL	RB, ORA, SR	N	B
175	Miller (2000)	CS	R	676	Ad	National US	ORA, NORA RE	MC	B
176	Miller (2001)	CS	C	279	C	New York	ORA, RCM, D	MC	B
177	Mitchell (1990)	CS	R	694	CS	2 universities	ORA	MC	B
178	Montgomery (1996)	CS	—	392	HS	Great Britain	NORA	SC	B
179	Moon (2000)	PC	R	788	mother/child	National US	ORA	MC	M
180	Moore (1995)	CS	C	2,366	Ad	Israel	D, SR	N	B
181	Morris (1981)	CS	C	134	CS	Tennessee	IR, ER	N	B
182	Mullen (2001)	CS	R	1,534	HS	Netherlands	D, ORA, RB	N	B
183	Muller (2001)	PC	P	--	HS	US	ORA	MC	B
184	Nelsen (1982)	CS	R	4,531	HS	NE US	ORA, D	N	B
186	Newcomb (1986)	PC	R	994	Ad	Los Angeles	SR	N	B
187	Newman (2006)	CC	C/P	827	HS	Thailand	D	N	B
188	Nonnemaker (2003)	PC	R	16,306	Ad	National US	IR, ER	MC	B
189	O'Connor (2002)	CS	C/P	1,597	Prisoners	South Carolina	ORA, NORA	SC	B
190	Oetting (1987)	CS	S	415	HS	Western US	SR, ORA	MC	B
191	Oleckno (1991)	CS	C	1,077	CS	Northern IL	ORA, SR	N	B
192	Onofrio (1999)	CS	C	1,127	C, Ad, HS	US-Mid Atlantic	D, R	MC	B
193	Parfrey (1976)	CS	R	444	CS	Ireland	ORA, RB	N	B

No	Investigators	Type	Method	N	Population	Location	Religious Variable	Control	Findings
194	Park (1998)	CS	R	1,081	HS	National US	RB	MC	B
195	Park H (2002)	PC	R	7,692	HS	National US	D	MC	B
196	Parsai (2008)	CS	C/P	1,087	Ad	Southwest	ORA, D	MC	B
197	Patock-Peckham (1998)	CS	C/P	364	CS	Arizona	D, IR, ER	MC	M
198	Pearce L (2003)	PC	R	1,703	6th & 8th grade	Northeastern US	ORA, NORA SR	MC	B
199	Pearce M (2004)	PC	R	10,444	Ad & mothers	US	SR, D	MC	B
200	Peek (1985)	PC	R	817	HS	National US	RCM	MC	M
201	Perkins (1985)	CS	S	1,514	CS 17-23	New York	D, S	MC	B
202	Perkins (1987)	CS	S	860	CS	New York	SR, D, Misc.	MC	B
203	Pettersson (1991)	CS	R	118	Police districts	Sweden	ORA	SC	B
204	Petts (2007)	PC	R	1,259	National survey	US	Misc.	MC	B
205	Piko (2004)	CS	R	1,240	Ad	Szeged, Hungary	ORA, prayer	MC	B
206	Piquero (2000)	CC	C/P	150	Ad	Detention facility	Misc.	MC	B
207	Pirkle (2006)	PC	R	929	Ad	National US	SR	MC	B
208	Powell (1997)	CS	S	521	HS high risk	Birmingham, AL	ORA, SR	MC	B
209	Preston (1969)	CS	R	516	HS	Southern US state	ORA, RCM, RB	MC	B
210	Pullen (1999)	CS	R	217	Ad	Southeast US	ORA	MC	B
211	Regnerus (2003)	PC	R	9,667	HS	National US	ORA, SR	MC	B
212	Regnerus (2003b)	PC	R	9,234	HS	National US	ORA, IR	MC	B
213	Regnerus (2003c)	PC	R	9,200	HS	National US	ORA, IR	MC	B

No	Investigators	Type	Method	N	Population	Location	Religious Variable	Control	Findings
214	Regnerus (2003d)	PC	R	11,890	Ad, Parents	National US	ORA, RC, D	MC	B
215	Resnick (1997)	CS	R	12,118	Ad	National US	SR	MC	NA
216	Ritt-Olson (2004)	CC	C/P	382	HS	California	ORA, RB, SR	MC	B
217	Rhodes (1970)	CS	R	21,720	HS	Tennessee	ORA, D, Misc.	MC	B
218	Rohrbaugh (1975)	CS	C	475-221	HS/CS	Colorado	ORA, RB, RE	N	B
219	Ross (1994)	CS	R	271	CS	Seton Hall	Misc.	MC	M
220	Schiff (2006)	CS	R	600	HS	Jerusalem	ORA	MC	B
221	Schlegel (1979)	CS	R	842	HS	Ontario, Canada	ORA, D	N	B
222	Schulenberg (1994)	PC	R	3,399	HS	National US	ORA, RC	MC	B
223	Scholl (1964)	CC	C/P	52-28	Ad delinquents	Illinois	RB, RE	N	H
224	Simmons (2004)	CS	R	451-867	families/children	Iowa	Misc.	MC	B
225	Singh (1979)	CS	C	54/59	CA/HS	Ottawa, Can	SR	N	B
226	Sinha (2007)	CS	R	2,004	Ad	National US	ORA, SR	MC	B
227	Sloane (1986)	CS	R	1,121	HS	National US	ORA, SR	MC	B
228	Sorenson (1995)	CS	R	1,118	HS	Seattle	ORA, D	MC	B
229	Stark (1982)	CS	R	1,799	Ad M	National US	RB, SR, ORA	N	B
230	Stark (1996)	CS	R	11,955	Ad	National US	D, ORA	SC	B
231	Steinman (2004)	CS	C	705	HS	Midwest City	ORA	N	B
232	Steinman (2008)	CS	R	33,007	Ad	Columbus, OH	ORA	MC	B
233	Stewart (2001)	--	C/P	337	CS	Southern US	SR, RB	N	B
234	Stewart (2002)	CS	R	2,317	Ad	National	ORA, SR, NORA	N	B

No	Investigators	Type	Method	N	Population	Location	Religious Variable	Control	Findings
235	Stylianou (2004)	CS	R	275	CS	Pacific NW	RCM	MC	B
236	Sussman (2005)	CS	R	501	Ad	Southern CA	Misc.	MC	M
237	Sussman (2006)	CS	R	501	Ad	Southern CA	Misc.	MC	B
238	Taub (1990)	CS	R	3,500	HS	National US	ORA, SR	MC	B
239	Tenent-Clark (1989)	CC	C	25-25	Ad	Colorado	SR	N	B
240	Tepmlin (1999)	CS	C/P	277	CS	Catholic College	RC	MC	B
241	Tibbetts (2002)	CS	C/P	598	CS	Into courses	SR	MC	B
242	Tittle (1983)	CS	R	1,993	15 and older	IA, NJ, OR	ORA, SR	MC	B
243	Travers (1961)	--	C/P	223	10-17	NE urban area	RCM	MC	B
244	Trawick (2006)	--	R	120	counties	Kentucky	Misc.	N	B
245	Turner C (1979)	CS	R	379	CS	Private school, NJ	Misc.	N	B
246	Turner N (1994)	CS	R	247	HS	Austin, TX	D, ORA	MC	B
247	Valliant (1982)	PC	R	456	Ad	Boston	ORA	N	B
248	Vakalahi (2002)	CS	R	4,983	Ad	Utah	D	MC	B
249	Van Den Bree (2004)	CS	PC	14,133	Ad, CS	National US	ORA, SR, Misc	MC	B
250	Veach (1992)	CS	C	148	CS	Nevada	RE, Misc.	N	H
251	Vener (1977)	CS	C	4,220	Ad, CS	3 midwest cities	RB	N	B
252	Wallace (1991)	CS	R	--	Ad	National US	ORA, SR	N	B
253	Wallace (1998)	CS	R	5,000	HS	National US	D, ORA, SR	MC	B
254	Wallace (2003)	CS	R	47,738	HS	UW	SR, ORA, D	MC	B

No	Investigators	Type	Method	N	Population	Location	Religious Variable	Control	Findings
255	Wallace (2007)	CS	R	16,595	HS	National US	ORA, SR, Misc.	MC	B
256	Walsh (1995)	CS	R	480	CS	Boise State	ORA, SR	MC	B
257	Wattenburg (1950)	CS	S	2,137	Ad	Detroit, MI	ORA	N	B
258	Weschler (1979)	CS	R	7,170	CS	New England	D, ORA	N	B
259	Wechsler (1995)	CS	R	17,592	CS	National	SR	MC	B
260	Weill (1994)	PC	R	437	HS	France	ORA	N	B
261	White (2008)	PC	R	825	CS/Ad	Washington	ORA	MC	B
262	Wickstrom (1983)	CS	C/P	130	CS	4 states	IR, ER	MC	B
263	Willis (2003)		R	7,123	HS	New York	Misc.	MC	B
264	Wills (2003)	PC	R	1,182	Ad	New York	RB, SR, Misc.	MC	B
265	Windle (2005)	PC	R	760	Ad	New York	ORA, SR	MC	B
266	Wright (1971)	CS	C	3,850/ 1,574	CS	England	RB, ORA, Misc.	N	B
267	Yarnold (1995)	CS	R	1,694	Ad	Dade County, FL	SR	MC	B
268	Youniss (1997)	CS	R	3,119	HS	National US	ORA, SR	MC	B
269	Zhang (1994)	CS	C	1,026	CS	China, Taiwan, US	SR, NORA ORA	MC	B
270	Zimmerman (1992)	--	C/P	218	Ad	Inner city Balti-more	Misc.	MC	B

TOWARD A CRIMINOLOGY OF RELIGION: COMMENT ON JOHNSON AND JANG

FRANCIS T. CULLEN

Johnson and Jang make a persuasive case that religion is an empirically established predictor of antisocial conduct, is implicated in direct and complex ways in criminal involvement, can be integrated profitably into existing criminological theories, and is a potentially useful target for change in interventions with offenders. They have discovered, much to my astonishment, 270 studies examining the association between religion and crime. I express astonishment for two reasons: first, because I had no idea this body of evidence existed, and second, because it is paradoxical that, despite these empirical works, religion remains largely ignored as a cause of crime in most major investigations of crime and in most textbooks on criminological theory. I start by commenting on possible reasons for this criminological omission. As part of a call for a "criminology of religion and crime," I then map out three lines of inquiry that scholars might fruitfully explore.

CRIMINOLOGISTS' NEGLECT OF RELIGION

In a non-scientific, yet illuminating attempt to test the thesis that religion is neglected in criminological theory, I reached to my bookshelf, pulled off 16 conveniently located titles, and turned to the books' indices. Religion was not mentioned in the indices of three classic theoretical works (Akers, 1998; Gottfredson & Hirschi, 1990; Sampson & Laub, 1993), of five theory textbooks (Akers & Sellers, 2004; Cao, 2004; Lilly, Cullen, & Ball, 2007; Mutchnick, Martin, & Austin, 2009; Vold, Bernard, & Snipes, 2002), and of six books on the development of offending (Andrews & Bonta, 2006; Benson, 2002; Farrington, 2005; Moffitt, Caspi, Rutter, & Silva, 2001; Thornberry & Krohn, 2003; Wright, Tibbetts, & Daigle, 2008). "Religiosity" was noted in the index of one book that nicely summarizes research on criminological theory, but the topic received only a cursory, one-paragraph treatment (Kubrin, Stucky, & Krohn, 2009, p. 177). Only Robert Agnew (2001), in his *Juvenile Delinquency: Causes and Control*, focused on the issue in a clear way. His textbook included a heading, "Does Religion Reduce Delinquency?", and a two-page discussion. Agnew (2001, p. 188) concluded that "religion appears to have a small effect on delinquency, especially victimless crimes. The effect of religion is overshadowed by that of other groups, such as the family, peer group, and school."

151

Why do criminologists have a blind spot with regard to religion? Perhaps the most manifest reason is what might be called the "secular humanist (or heathen) effect." Similar to other social sciences, criminology is a secular humanist profession in which faith is marginalized, if not implicitly discouraged. There is no controversy over public displays of faith at our ASC meetings, because they would be virtually unthinkable. Imagine a Society president opening a session with a prayer or an award-winner thanking Jesus for his or her success! Although exceptions exist, life-histories of prominent theorists rarely mention religion or do so only to note that the reformist impulses of these secularized scholars might be traced to their now-rejected early religious upbringing (Cullen, Jonson, Myer, & Adler, 2010). This is not to say that there is not a silent majority—or at least a silent minority—of faithful criminologists. But the point is that this religious commitment remains silent.

Beyond secular humanism, I would suspect that two other considerations have limited criminologists' interest in making religion a more central part of the discipline. I will refer to these as the "Hirschi effect" and the "blame-the-culture effect."

First, in the same year that he published *Causes of Delinquency* (1969), Hirschi joined with Rodney Stark to author his classic study *Hellfire and Delinquency*. As Johnson and Jang note, Hirschi and Stark (1969) failed to detect a religious influence on youthful misconduct. To be sure, this finding did not stop research on religion and offending and, if anything, may have inspired a number of empirical studies. But the key point is that given the lack of a significant effect in his Hellfire article, Hirschi felt no compulsion to incorporate religion systematically into his social bond theory. He did not assert that scholars must explore the impact on delinquency of attachment to ministers and church, commitment to or a stake in religion, belief in or a respect for the Ten Commandments, and involvement in church activities. Moreover, if Hirschi had detected a religion effect, he might well have used this result to further debilitate strain theory (which, as an economic-goal theory, ignored religion) and as a point of contention with social learning theory (claiming that religion reduces crime through social bonds and not as a conduit for prosocial learning). But in the absence of a strong finding, religion was largely pushed aside as a concern central to determining which theory—whether social bond or a competing perspective—should rule criminology.

Over four decades later, it is perhaps difficult for younger scholars to appreciate how much—indeed, how masterfully—Hirschi shaped the criminological enterprise, especially through *Causes of Delinquency* (1969). For example, his measure of strain—the gap between aspirations and expectations—was subsequently used repeatedly in empirical tests, even though its validity was highly questionable (Burton & Cullen, 1992). His dismissal of racial discrimination as a cause of crime also arguably redirected scholars' attention away from this topic (Unnever, Cullen, Mathers, McClure, & Allison, 2009). The point is that had Hirschi and Stark argued that religion was a *theoretically central correlate of delinquency*—an empirical fact that all theories must explain—the history of the study of religion and crime might well have been different. Tests of criminological theories would have been seen as incomplete if religion were omitted from the analysis. But this did not happen. The "Hirschi effect" was in the opposite direction, rendering moot any requirement to include religion as a standard measure within criminological investigations.

Second, criminologists dislike any theory that blames culture for crime unless the culture itself is explained by structural disadvantage. Thus, Elijah Anderson's (1999) *Code of the Street*, which traces inner-city moral codes to joblessness and destitution, is okay, but Walter Miller's (1958) lower-class culture theory, which is seen as saying that people are poor and criminal due to their cultural values (or "focal concerns"), is not okay. In this context, scholars thus are wary of religious explanations because they are easily (though not necessarily) portrayed as a rejection of structural theories that link crime to concentrated disadvantage. Put another way, religion attributes crime to bad morals, not to bad social conditions. Thus, the blame-the-culture effect is that criminologists are inclined to reject a religious theory of crime as a reductionist cultural argument that acquits inequitable social arrangements from any complicity in crime.

The exemplar of this mode of thinking is found in *Body Count*, the provocative work of William Bennett, John DiIulio, and James Walters. Bennett et al. (1996, p. 56) argue that the root cause of "predatory street crime" is not poverty or "material want" but rather "moral poverty." Moral poverty is not somehow linked to economic deprivation but rather is the lack of loving parents who, through example and instruction, fail to inculcate a firm sense of right and wrong. For Bennett et al., religion is the "most important dimension" of moral poverty (p. 207). With Original Sin implicitly informing their view, they claim that we have forgotten something that was once widely assumed: "the *good requires constant reinforcement and the bad needs only permission*" (p. 208, emphasis in the original). In this task, "religion is the best and most reliable means we have to reinforce the good" (p. 208).

Setting aside the accuracy of these claims, the key insight is that *Body Count* consciously juxtaposes a moral, religious explanation of crime against a (rejected) structural, economic explanation—claiming, in essence, that only one can be true. After all, not all poor people break the law. Faced with daily disadvantage, resilience to crime is nonetheless a moral choice: Those with a strong religious fiber can resist criminal temptation. Of course, this kind of logic ignores the notion of poverty as a criminogenic risk factor (alas, resilience is not needed in affluent neighborhoods) and the persistent reality that so-called "super-predators" are concentrated in impoverished areas. Regardless, my sense is that to the extent that religion is portrayed— or understood—as a conservative culture war that attacks structural root-cause thinking about crime, it is inconsistent with the professional ideology of criminologists and thus will inspire little interest (see also Wilson, 1975).

The genius of Johnson and Jang's essay, however, is that they ask fellow criminologists to set aside any preexisting predilections and to consider religion in a very secular scientific way: What do the data tell us about the impact of religion on crime? With 270 studies reviewed, they have done the heavy lifting to convince us that religion is likely a modest predictor of crime that rivals the effects of other variables typically included in empirical studies and tests of theories of crime. With this foundation laid, the issue is what next steps should be taken in the study of religion and crime. One obvious task, which they are undertaking, is a sophisticated meta-analysis of the extant empirical literature that can provide a more precise estimate of the overall effect size for the impact of religion on crime and a more complete specification of how various substantive and methodological factors condition this effect size. Beyond this important work, I will briefly suggest three potentially fruitful lines of inquiry to pursue: belief in a loving God, an age-graded religious theory of antisocial conduct, and—with some caution—the role of faith-based interventions in the lives of offenders.

A LOVING GOD

As I was growing up in Boston, it was common to be asked what *parish*, rather than what neighborhood, I was from. In my case, it was St. Gregory's parish. Even in the land of the liberalism and the Kennedy's, church was a central point of our lives. Every Sunday morning, all children would attend a special mass at 8:30. To this day, I recall a sermon by Father Sweeney. We typically rejoiced when Father Sweeney entered the altar. He was a microwave priest, saying mass in about 38 minutes (the norm was over 50 minutes). On this one day, however, Father Sweeney was swift but scary. He warned us to be careful not to sin, for Hell was, he reminded us, hotter than a Westinghouse oven!

In this context, it is perhaps understandable that the first major work in my generation on religion and crime—by Hirschi and Stark—would carry the title of *Hellfire and Delinquency*. Religion had long been seen as exerting a controlling function. In studying youths, it thus was easy to examine religion as potentially the ultimate form of direct control. Since God is omnipresent and knows everything, all bad acts will be punished. Celerity might be lacking (unless guilt was immediately felt after a delinquent act), but both certainty (detection was inescapable) and severity (Hellfire loomed) were present. In any event, Hirschi and Stark's work was salient because it framed thinking about the effect of religion. It led scholars to debate whether "supernatural sanctions," as they were called by Hirschi and Stark, reduced or were redundant with more secular controls (see, e.g., Evans, Cullen, Dunaway, & Burton, 1995).

My sense is that the Hellfire approach got the research agenda on religion and crime off on the wrong foot—or at least off on only one foot. My own work has expressed the view that, in general, criminology is too focused on "control." I have felt that although social control matters, there is a whole other side to life—one that I suggested might be captured by the construct of social support (Cullen, 1994). Thus, in the socialization process, parents not only detect and punish bad conduct but also hug, help, and love their kids. In a similar vein, religion cannot be reduced to fear of damnation—to the Hellfire effect. In Christianity, for example, there is an invitation to have a personal relationship with a God (Jesus in particular) who forgives, guides, and loves. In no way intending any sacrilege, Jesus is, in criminological terms, the ultimate provider of powerful social support. This is received through individual belief and, when writ large, through membership in a community that is mandated to help those inside and outside the congregation.

Notably, Andrew Greeley (1995) has observed that people's Godly image can vary on a continuum from loving, intimate, and nurturing at one end to distant, harsh, and judgmental at the other end. (He measured this variation through his "gracious image of God" scale.) In fact, research suggests people embrace different images of God and that notions of a loving versus a Hellfire deity arise in childhood (Dickie et al., 1997; Unnever, Cullen, & Bartkowski, 2006; Unnever, Bartkowski, & Cullen, in press). The criminological point is whether Godly images shape involvement in crime.

Building on my work with James Unnever and John Bartkowski, I suggest that that such an image might exert a meaningful influence. I am particularly interested in the side of God neglected by criminologists: the extent to which He is seen as loving. Our research reveals that belief in a close personal relationship with a loving God reduces punitive sentiments, such as support for the death penalty (see also Applegate, Cullen, Fisher, & Vander Ven, 2000). Taking the logic of this finding one step farther, I would submit that the embrace of a loving God is incompatible with conduct that inflicts pain on others. The Biblical prescription, of course, is to live by the Golden Rule, to turn the other cheek, and to forgive others' trespasses. In more secular terms, modeling a loving God may well create both the capacity and the mandate to feel empathy towards others—not because of fear of damnation but because this is "what Jesus would do." Notably, although still in its beginning stages of development, a growing literature exists suggesting that empathy is negatively related to criminal offending (Jolliffe & Farrington, 2004, 2007). The unique effect of religiously-inspired empathy, however, remains to be investigated.

In short, despite what many criminologists might have experienced in their childhood, religion is not strictly about a retributive God who seeks to evoke guilt when His commandments are violated and who threatens Hellfire for transgressions. Religion also is about God's love and about the invitation to spread the good word and to be good. Exploring the impact of faith in a loving God thus appears worthy of further exploration.

AN AGE-GRADED THEORY OF RELIGION AND CRIME

In *Hellfire and Delinquency*, Hirschi and Stark (1969) included a measure not only of Hellfire (belief in the afterlife and in the devil) but also of church membership. As Johnson and Jang's research survey shows, subsequent studies have sought to extend this early work by using diverse measures to capture what being religious entails (e.g., denomination, church membership, church attendance, church activities, reading the Bible, religious beliefs). Their subsequent meta-analysis will, I suspect, give us a more precise reading of the effect size of each of religion's multi-faceted dimensions. My concern is slightly different and is suggested by Johnson and Jang. To wit: To develop a clearer demarcation of the religion and crime nexus, we need to explore how the various dimensions of religion have potentially varying impacts across the life course. That is, we need to develop an age-graded theory of religion and crime.

It is beyond my expertise to map out such a theory, but a few obvious insights can be supplied. Thus, we might start by examining the nature of religious socialization in childhood and how it might affect the expression of conduct disorders, especially among high-risk children. As youngsters move into adolescence, how does religious belief change and how is it challenged? Does participation in church-related youth groups insulate against wayward conduct? What will we discover if we measure not only how many delinquent peers a youth has but also how many friends with a personal relationship to their deity? As individuals make the transition to adulthood, the role of religion in desistance (as Johnson and Jang note) is of intriguing importance, especially as it might relate to the kinds of cognitive transformations that ending crime appears to involve (Giordano, Cernkovich, & Rudolph, 2002; Maruna, 2001). But I would suggest one other fruitful line of inquiry: What is the impact of religious belief on participation in white-collar crime? Scholars from Sutherland (1940) onward note the respectable breastplate worn by upperworld offenders—going to church on Sunday and price-fixing and polluting on Monday. It remains to be seen, however, whether religious belief is compartmentalized and easily neutralized or whether it distinguished those who resist from those who succumb to the lure of profitable white-collar schemes.

FAITH-BASED INTERVENTION:
OPPORTUNITY AND TWO WORDS OF CAUTION

Although a personal observation, I have little doubt that religious volunteers—from Quakers to evangelicals—spend more time visiting prison inmates than criminologists. We scholars thus should be wary of dismissing the humanizing influences that religious people—of all faiths—have inside the correctional system. Religious faith is a shared experience that traverses ideological boundaries and can nourish the view, across the political spectrum, that offenders are capable of being saved. Survey research also shows that, in general, the American public supports faith-based correctional initiatives (Cullen et al., 2007).

Another reason for considering faith-based interventions, as Johnson and Jang point out, is science. To the extent that religion is established empirically as a predictor of crime, it becomes a legitimate target for intervention. Increasing faith and involving offenders in a community that will reinforce such prosocial beliefs can potentially reduce recidivism. Further, it also is a legitimate treatment target because unlike other recidivism predictors—say, gender or a past criminal history—it is capable of being changed. Andrews and Bonta (2006) call predictors that have the potential to change "dynamic risk factors."

Still, I offer two words of caution. First, religion is only one predictor of reoffending, and it remains to be seen if it rivals the effect of other, major dynamic predictors of recidivism (e.g., antisocial attitudes) (Andrews & Bonta, 2006). Even if so, designing a program that only focuses on one predictor—while ignoring other relevant known criminogenic risks—is questionable.

This leads to the second word of caution. Faith-based interventions have been implemented in the absence of a sound criminological foundation. In this sense—but only in this sense—they are similar to boot camps. Faith-based and boot camp programs draw their legitimacy not from science but from powerful common-sense beliefs about crime. After all, if we use the boot camp to break down wayward youth and then build them back up, won't we save them from a life in crime? If we transform sinners into believers, is not redemption assured? Of course, the answer to this might well be "no." For programs to be effective, they must address stubborn criminological realities. If they do not target for change the known predictors of recidivism with programming capable of altering offender thinking and behavior, they will not be effective (Andrews & Bonta, 2006).

To be sure, as Johnson and Jang note, evidence exists that faith-based interventions can be effective (see Johnson, 2004). But this is not enough. There are opportunity costs to subjecting offenders to untried or modestly effective faith-based programs when they might be treated with programs based on the principles of effective intervention—an approach to offender correction rooted in sound social psychological theory and in decades of evaluation research (Cullen & Smith, in press). In the least, faith-based approaches cannot remain purely sacred; they must embrace and learn lessons from scientific criminology so as to more effectively deliver treatments to offenders. For example, it is now well-established that cognitive-behavioral programs are among the most effective intervention strategies (MacKenzie, 2006). In this context, I can imagine a faith-based intervention that uses the principles and techniques of cognitive-behavior psychology but infuses them with religious content. Regardless, the more general point is that religion should not be juxtaposed as an opponent of scientific criminology. Rather, advocates of religion-informed interventions should use science as a powerful tool in an effort to save offenders through faith from a life in crime.

A CRIMINOLOGY OF RELIGION AND CRIME

As a sociologist, I took it for granted during my graduate training that religion was an inextricable part of grand theory (Marx, Durkheim, and Weber all had something to say about religion's influences!), and that the "sociology of religion" was an important subfield in the discipline. By contrast, as a criminologist, I have long wondered why religion has remained so much on the periphery of our theory, research, and understanding of correctional policy. I think that the broader significance of Johnson and Jang's essay is that it focuses our attention on the salience of religion in American life and in the lives of those who do and do not choose to offend. Indeed, their work might best be seen as making a persuasive case for developing a systematic *criminology of religion*.

Such an undertaking, which should involve (as it does in sociology) criminologists both with and without religious faith, is long overdue. Indeed, rich lines of inquiry remain to be mined—many of them identified nicely by Johnson and Jang. Religion is a multi-faceted experience that potentially affects the onset, persistence, and desistance of crime across the life course. Our prisons, founded as "penitentiaries," are still places where religious influences exist, not just through faith-based programs but through chaplains and religious good works (Sundt & Cullen, 1998). Correctional policies, from support of capital punishment to a belief that the criminally wayward can be saved, have been shown to have a religious foundation (Applegate et al., 2000; Unnever & Cullen, 2006). We also might wish to explore how faith affects decision-making by police and court officials. These comments only outline in a beginning way what the contours of a criminology of religion might entail. But I trust that they are sufficient to convey my chief message: The study of religion should be an integral part of the criminological enterprise and a vibrant subfield within our discipline.

REFERENCES

Agnew, R. (2001). *Juvenile delinquency: Causes and control*. Los Angeles, CA: Roxbury.

Akers, R. (1998). *Social learning and social structure: A general theory of crime and deviance*. Boston, MA: Northeastern University Press.

Akers, R. & Sellers, C. (2004). *Criminological theories: Introduction, evaluation, and application*, 4th ed. Los Angeles, CA: Roxbury.

Anderson, E. (1999). *Code of the street: Decency, violence, and the moral life of the inner city*. New York, NY: W. W. Norton.

Andrews, D. & Bonta, J. (2006). *The psychology of criminal conduct*, 4th ed. Cincinnati, OH: LexisNexis/Anderson.

Applegate, B., Cullen, F., Fisher, B., & Vander Ven, T. (2000). Forgiveness and fundamentalism: Reconsidering the relationship between correctional attitudes and religion. *Criminology, 38*, 719-753.

Bennett, W., DiIulio, Jr., J., & Walters, J. (1996). *Body count: Moral poverty and how to win America's war against crime and drugs*. New York, NY: Simon and Schuster.

Benson, M. (2002). *Crime and the life course: An introduction*. Los Angeles, CA: Roxbury.

Burton, Jr., V. & Cullen, F. (1992). The empirical status of strain theory. *Journal of Crime and Justice, 15*(2), 1-30.

Cao, L. (2004). *Major criminological theories: Concepts and measurement*. Belmont, CA: Wadsworth.

Cullen, F. (1994). Social support as an organizing concept for criminology: Presidential Address to the Academy of Criminal Justice Sciences. *Justice Quarterly, 11*, 527-559.

Cullen, F., Jonson, C., Myer, A., & Adler, F. (eds.). (2010). *The origins of American criminology: Advances in criminological theory* (Vol. 16). New Brunswick, NJ: Transaction Publishers.

Cullen, F., Pealer, J., Santana, S., Fisher, B., Applegate, B., & Blevins, K. (2007). Public support for faith-based correctional programs: Should sacred places serve civic purposes? *Journal of Offender Rehabilitation, 43*(3-4), 29-46.

Cullen, F. & Smith, P. (In press). Treatment and rehabilitation. In M. Tonry (Ed.), *The Oxford handbook of crime and criminology*. New York, NY: Oxford University Press.

Dickie, J., Eshleman, A., Merasco, D., Shepard, A., Vander Wilt, M., & Johnson, M. (1997). Parent-child relationships and children's image of God. *Journal for the Scientific Study of Religion, 36*, 25-43.

Evans, T., Cullen, F., Dunaway, R., & Burton, Jr., V. (1995). Religion and crime reexamined: The impact of religion, secular controls, and social ecology on adult criminality. *Criminology, 33*, 195-224.

Farrington, D. (ed.). (2005). *Integrated developmental and life-course theories of offending: Advances in criminological theory* (Vol. 14). New Brunswick, NJ: Transaction.

Giordano, P., Cernkovich, S., & Rudolph, J. (2002). Gender, crime, and desistance: Toward a theory of cognitive transformation. *American Journal of Sociology, 107*, 990-1064.

Gottfredson, M. & Hirschi, T. (1990). *A general theory of crime.* Stanford, CA: Stanford University Press.

Greeley, A. (1995). *Religion as poetry.* New Brunswick, NJ: Transaction.

Hirschi, T. (1969). *Causes of delinquency.* Berkeley, CA: University of California Press.

Hirschi, T. & Stark, R. (1969). Hellfire and delinquency. *Social Problems, 17*, 204-213.

Johnson, B. (2004). Religious programs and recidivism among former inmates in prison fellowship programs. *Justice Quarterly, 21*, 329-354.

Jolliffe, D. & Farrington, D. (2004). Empathy and offending: A systematic review and meta-analysis. *Aggression and Violent Behavior, 9*, 41-476.

Jolliffe, D. & Farrington, D. (2007). Examining the relationship between low empathy and self-reported offending. *Legal and Criminological Psychology, 12*, 265-286.

Kubrin, C., Stucky, T., & Krohn, M. (2009). *Researching theories of crime and deviance.* New York, NY: Oxford University Press.

Lilly, J., Cullen, F., & Ball, R. (2007). *Criminological theory: Context and consequences*, 4th ed. Thousand Oaks, CA: Sage.

MacKenzie, D. (2006). *What works in corrections: Reducing the criminal activities of offenders and delinquents.* New York, NY: Cambridge University Press.

Maruna, S. (2001). *Making good: How ex-convicts reform and rebuild their lives.* Washington, DC: American Psychological Association.

Moffitt, T., Caspi, A., Rutter, M., & Silva, P. (2001). *Sex differences in antisocial behaviour: Conduct disorder, delinquency, and violence in the Dunedin Longitudinal Study.* Cambridge, UK: Cambridge University Press.

Miller, W. (1958). Lower class culture as a generating milieu of gang delinquency. *Journal of Social Issues, 14*(3), 5-19.

Mutchnick, R., Martin, R., & Austin, W. (2009). *Criminological thought: Pioneers past and present.* Upper Saddle River, NJ: Prentice Hall.

Sampson, R. & Laub, J. (1993). *Crime in the making: Pathways and turning points through life.* Cambridge, MA: Harvard University Press.

Sundt, J. & Cullen, F. (1998). The role of the contemporary prison chaplain. *The Prison Journal, 23*, 271-298.

Sutherland, E. (1940). White-collar criminality. *American Sociological Review, 5*, 1–12.

Thornberry, T. & Krohn, M. (eds.). (2003). *Taking stock of delinquency: An overview of Findings from contemporary studies.* New York, NY: Kluwer Academic/Plenum.

Unnever, J., Bartkowski, J., & Cullen, F. (In press). God images and opposition to abortion and capital punishment: A partial test of religious support for the consistent life ethic. *Sociology of Religion.*

Unnever, J. & Cullen, F. (2006). Christian fundamentalism and support for capital punishment. *Journal of Research in Crime and Delinquency, 43,* 169-197.

Unnever, J., Cullen, F., & Bartkowski, J. (2006). Images of God and public support for capital punishment: Does a loving God matter? *Criminology, 44,* 833-864.

Unnever, J., Cullen, F., Mathers, S., McClure, T., & Allison, M. (2009). Racial discrimination and Hirschi's criminological classic: A chapter in the sociology of knowledge. *Justice Quarterly, 26,* 377-409.

Vold, G., Bernard, T., & Snipes, J. (2002). *Theoretical criminology,* 5th ed. New York, NY: Oxford University Press.

Wilson, J. (1975). *Thinking about crime.* New York, NY: Vintage.

Wright, J., Tibbetts, S., & Daigle, L. (2008). *Criminals in the making: Criminality across the life course.* Thousand Oaks, CA: Sage.

Religion as a Unique Cultural Influence on Crime and Delinquency: Expanding on Jang and Johnson's Agenda

Jeffery T. Ulmer

In recent years, high-profile critics of religion such as Richard Dawkins and Christopher Hitchens have asserted that religion causes more harm than good, and that religion fosters as much antisocial as prosocial behavior. Dawkins and Hitchens make their cases primarily with the strength of rhetoric. However, the question of how religion influences prosocial and/or antisocial behavior is best answered with evidence, rather than polemics. Jang and Johnson's systematic review of the research on religion and crime/delinquency calls for religion to assume a central place in the study of crime and delinquency, as well as prosocial behavior.

Sociologists since Durkheim have recognized that religion is a core element of culture, and that it therefore is a powerful potential motivator of and control on behavior (Smith, 2003; see also Vaisey, 2009). Foundational theorists in the social sciences such as Emile Durkheim, Max Weber, G.H. Mead, Charles Horton Cooley, and Talcott Parsons all speak explicitly (though in different ways) about the important role of religion in society and culture. The study of religion seems to be enjoying a renewed vitality in sociology, and new thinking in psychology (e.g., Pargament, 2008; Geyer & Baumeister, 2005), but criminology has yet to locate religion centrally in the field. Yet religion has powerful but insufficiently understood effects on behavior (Pargament, Magyar-Russell, & Murray-Swank, 2005; Pargament, 2008).

Jang and Johnson's review of the crime and religion literature shows us where we have been and how far we still need to go. They also lay out a rich research agenda, noting many important and under-researched directions of inquiry at the micro and macro levels. These directions fall under two major deficits they identify: a) a lack of a developmental/life course focus approach to the question of how religion influences criminality, and b) a lack of attention to the theme of "resiliency," that is, the degree to which religion acts as a protective factor against strain, structural disadvantage, and social disorganization and other community-level criminogenic factors.

Jang and Johnson correctly note the limitations of quantitative meta-analysis, and opt for a systematic review approach. Given the nature of the literature, this is probably a beneficial choice, because they can include a wider variety of studies. My interest was piqued for a finer grained analysis of the 270 studies reviewed. For example, I would find useful a more explicit teasing out of what we know now, beyond the reviews of Baier and Wright (2001), or Johnson, Li, Larson, and McCullough (2000). What are some particular ways that studies since the late 1990s/early 2000s have improved our understanding of the religion-crime/delinquency relationship? Of the 9 percent of studies that found no, or mixed, religiosity effects, what features of these studies might account for this discrepancy with the rest of the literature. What might account for null findings? What of the two studies that found harmful effects—what accounts for their discrepant findings? Jang and Johnson will likely provide a more granular analysis in the future.

I will spend the rest of my commentary elaborating on two themes embedded in their calls for future research. By doing so, I hope to locate and contextualize their review and its recommendations in terms of two key general theories of crime and delinquency. First, I discuss the role of religion as a key cultural phenomenon that is intertwined with social learning theory and its causal mechanisms. Second, I discuss possibilities for how religion provides a cultural framework that augments self control, which in turn decreases crime and delinquency. In doing so, I make some suggestions about religion as a path toward alternative ways to think about self control as compared to the Gottfredson and Hirschi (1990) approach (and to a lesser extent, Hirschi's 2004 statements). Then, I raise some questions about what it means to characterize religion as a unique influence on crime/delinquency. Finally, I discuss religion as a fundamental aspect of culture, whose potential causal power goes beyond and encompasses more proximal variables (such as peers, social bonds, self control, strain, opportunity) that we in criminology tend to focus on.

RELIGION AND SOCIAL LEARNING OF CRIME, DELINQUENCY, AND PROSOCIAL BEHAVIOR

Jang and Johnson note that research on religion's influence has been predominantly social psychological. Part of that social psychological focus includes attention to how religion influences the likelihood of associating with deviant or conforming peers, and identification with/imitation of deviant or conventional role models. I would argue that specifying the mechanisms by which religion can be deeply intertwined in social learning processes is a research agenda that deserves further attention. As Jang and Johnson note, religiosity and spirituality likely fosters social learning processes that are favorable to prosocial behavior and unfavorable to delinquency, and there is support for this in the literature.

Edwin Sutherland (1947) and Ronald Akers (1998) emphasize the learning of definitions or messages favorable or unfavorable to delinquency and crime as a major cause of these behaviors. Religion, in turn, is a source of definitions and moral messages that discourage interpersonal violence, stealing, dishonesty, illicit substance use, etc. Religion thus likely involves differential association processes entailing exposure to and internalization of *definitions*—values, attitudes, and beliefs that reject crime and delinquency.

Peer influences are among the strongest predictors of delinquency

(Akers, 1998). As Jang and Johnson note, previous research focuses on the idea that religious and non-religious youth differ in their rates of delinquency because they are differentially exposed to delinquent friends (see, for example, Simons, Simons, & Conger, 2004; Johnson, Jang, Larson, & Li, 2001). Alternatively, however, religious and nonreligious adolescents may differ in their rates of delinquency because they are differentially *affected* by exposure to the *same* influences. In other words, religious and non-religious youth may both be exposed to delinquent friends, but religiosity may serve as a protective factor that reduces the effect of exposure. Thus a key research question is, when religious youth are friends with delinquent peers, does their religiosity serve as a protective factor that reduces the effect of criminal or delinquent peer influences? Theoretically, religiosity could reduce the impact of exposure to peer influences for many reasons (see Glanville, Sikkink, Hernandez, 2008). For example, religiosity should strengthen moral beliefs about the wrongfulness of delinquent behaviors. When religious adolescents are encouraged to engage in delinquent behaviors by peers, their religious beliefs could help them to resist peer influences.

Further, religiosity and spirituality likely foster prosocial imitation, role modeling, and self definitions, and discourage delinquent imitation, role modeling, and self definition. Religiosity and spirituality may foster identification with role models who represent prosocial behavior rather than delinquency (Geyer & Baumeister, 2005). Religiosity and spirituality would involve exposure to prosocial spiritual role models. Indeed, much of the teaching in most religious traditions involves defining one's identity and behavior around those of exemplary religious figures and principles. Church attendance and participation in spiritual activities and rituals also involves identification of oneself as a member of a religious group or spiritual tradition, and interacting with co-believers on the basis of these religious or spiritual identities. Religiosity and spirituality likely also foster definitions of self that revolve around prosocial characteristics and behaviors rather than deviant or criminal ones.

In addition, for those individuals already involved in delinquency, religious or spiritual change might be associated with desistence from delinquency and crime (Giordano, Longmore, Schroeder, & Seffrin, 2008; Giordano, Schroeder, & Cernkovich, 2007; Giordano, Cernkovich, & Rudolph, 2002). That is, the development of a religious identity and definition of self may encourage desistence from delinquency and may foster prosocial life course outcomes, including involvement in prosocial family or work oriented emotions and behavior (Giordano et al., 2008; Chu, 2007; Schroeder & Frana, 2009).

Finally, religiosity and spirituality likely affect the differential reinforcement of delinquency and prosocial behavior. Participation in religious activities such as church attendance and church activities, would increase the degree to which youth are under conventional adult supervision, and increase the degree to which they could be informally sanctioned for deviance. We expect that religiosity and spirituality would increase the degree to which individuals are enmeshed in networks of people who disapprove of delinquent or criminal behavior, and who would provide emotional and social rewards for prosocial behavior. As mentioned below, Geyer and Baumeister (2005) argue that religion in particular should increase the degree to which people experience guilt if they engage in delinquent or antisocial behavior, or behavior that violates their personal norms (see also Akers, 1998). On the other hand, religiosity and spirituality may foster emotional rewards for prosocial behavior.

RELIGION AND SELF CONTROL

Jang and Johnson note that religious individuals may exercise greater self control, and this may be a mediating factor in the religion-crime/delinquency relationship. I agree that self control may be a potentially important intervening mechanism in the religion-crime/delinquency connection that has received little empirical attention. Previous research suggests that religious individuals indeed often exhibit greater levels of self control (Aziz & Rehman, 1996). Geyer and Baumeister (2005) theorize that religiosity should strengthen and improve self control, and thereby increase "morally virtuous" behavior, through a variety of psychological mechanisms. However, Hay and Forrest (2006, p. 740) note that "little is known about the process by which [self control] develops over time."

In Gottfredson and Hirschi's terms (1990; see also Hirschi, 2004), any effect of religiosity on delinquency should be mediated by self control (except for perhaps any effects religion might have on opportunities for deviance), though this theory would accept the possibility that certain religious beliefs might foster parenting practices that increase self control (see Sherkat & Ellison, 1999). However, Akers (1998, p. 162) argues that: "Self control is itself a product of social learning, and therefore any variation that it accounts for ultimately depends on social learning." Religious socialization and participation would seem to be a potentially important social learning process by which self control could be developed and increased. Indeed, self control could be pervious to religious influence, even after the late childhood/early adolescence period posited by Gottfredson and Hirschi to be the point at which one's relative self control stabilizes. In fact, some scholars have moved away the notion of self control as a stable individual trait and towards treating it as a dynamic capacity, conditioned by factors, such as prior self control depletion, moral beliefs and choice, or community characteristics (Muraven, Pogarsky, & Shmueli, 2006; Piquero & Buffard, 2007; Tittle, Ward, & Grasmick, 2004; Wikstrom & Treiber, 2007).

Furthermore, Gottfredson and Hirschi (1990) say that *between-individual differences* in self control stabilize after late childhood (see the discussion of this point by Hay & Forrest, 2006). However, this leaves open the possibility that religion might increase an individual's *absolute* levels of self control, even if it might not equalize stable differences between individuals. For example, imagine two religious adolescents: one with higher self control and one with lower self control. Religion might augment the absolute self control of both individuals, such that both develop greater self control than they would have without religion's influence, but the relative difference between them would remain the same.

A major development in conceptualizing self control is the "muscle" or "strength" model (Baumeister, Bratlafsky, Muraven, & Tice, 1998; Muraven & Baumeister, 2000; Muraven, Tice, & Baumeister, 1998). This model depicts self control as a cognitive resource that is temporarily depleted whenever it is exercised, just as a muscle is temporarily fatigued when it is used (Baumeister & Exline, 1999, 2000; Geyer & Baumeister, 2005). Importantly, this model also implies that self control should grow stronger with regular "exercise." That is, repeated efforts at self control should make one's self control stronger over time (Muraven et al., 1998). Geyer and Baumeister (2005) argue that religion should decrease a variety of deviant behaviors by augmenting self control, it should do so at any age, and implicitly, that it should do so regardless of individuals' relative base levels of self control. In other words, religion may fortify this psychological muscle of self control by encouraging its repeated use in everyday life.

Religion likely augments the three main elements in the operation of self control: 1) it fosters internalization of *behavioral standards*, 2) it fosters *self monitoring*, and 3) it exorts individuals to *control or alter their own behavior*. Geyer and Baumeister (2005, p. 430) argue:

> "Religion may promote self control by upholding specific moral standards, by motivating people to want to be good, by exploiting the prosocial power of guilt, by linking the religious individual to a stable network of relationships with other believers and with God, by promoting character strength through regular exercise of moral muscle, by fostering self criticism, and by making people feel that their good and bad deeds are being observed and recorded."

WHAT DOES IT MEAN TO SAY THAT RELIGION HAS UNIQUE INFLUENCES?

Jang and Johnson's review and agenda also calls for research on how religiosity may exert *unique* influences that are not mediated by specific non-religious predictors. This echoes Pargament et al.'s (2005; Pargament, 1997) notion that religion is a unique phenomenon, with unique influences on behavior.

What does it mean to say that religion has unique affects on crime and delinquency? According to Pargament (2008, p. 32), "...the sacred is more than a source of solutions and problems, it is a distinctive source of significance." "Religion may be a unique aspect of human functioning, one that cannot simply be reduced to or explained away by presumably more basic psychological, social, or physical processes" (Pargament et al., 2005, p. 680). In addition, Jang and Johnson call attention to Christian Smith's (2003) work, which argues that religion provides individuals with distinctive moral narratives and cultural meanings that guide behavior (on the importance of narrative and biography, see also Maines, 1993). Thus, religion likely entails complex processes of socialization, identity formation, and personal narrative, and their effects on behavior may not be reducible to the effects of peer influence, opportunity, social bonds, self control, or shaping how individuals experience strain. Indeed, Jang and Johnson's review finds that often the effects of religiosity on delinquency and crime are not fully mediated by peers, social bonds, self control, or strain.

Jang and Johnson state, "...any effort to explain away the religion-crime relationship as entirely spurious is likely to be as futile as claiming crime can be completely explained by a lack of religion." However, this raises the question: by what mechanisms does religion affect crime and delinquency (and perhaps behavior in general)?

Throughout their conclusion, Jang and Johnson return to the notion of religion and culture. In my view, herein lies the answer to the question of what it means to say that religion's influence is unique. Perhaps religion is a fundamental and ubiquitous dimension of culture, and should be treated as such. If so, religion would fundamentally shape selfhood and socialization, morality and motivation (Smith, 2003; Vaisey, 2009). It would even structure cognition (see Pargament, 2008; Geyer & Baumeister, 2005). In fact, Emile Durkheim argued that religion fundamentally shaped the construction of social reality (Rawls, 1996).

The take-away point for criminology would be that religion might not be merely a significant predictor in regression models that retains some unmediated effects on crime or delinquency measures once the usual predictors derived from the core criminological theories are accounted for. In the larger picture, religion is likely a truly exogenous factor in our theoretical models, the way other dimensions of culture are (such as language, meaning, legal culture, etc.). That is, religion is likely a fundamental and nearly ubiquitous cultural institution that, when present in individual or group life, can shape and conditions socialization, identity, learning and opportunity structures, relationships and social bonds, social capital, and coping mechanisms in the face of strains. Thus, one reason research is likely to find that religion's effects on behavior are not fully mediated by any particular non-religious variable or set of variables is that religion's influence is likely holistic, simultaneously affecting the whole social person. I think this is what lies behind Jang and Johnson's skepticism about the literature's frequent preoccupation with identifying proximal variables (peers, self control, bonds, etc.) that would mediate or "explain away" the effects of religious measures. This constitutes what could be called an unhelpful *proximal variable bias*, to coin a phrase, in the approach to understanding religion's likely multifaceted and complex but pervasive effects on crime and delinquency. It is not that our standard theoretical explanations of crime and delinquency are incorrect, but rather that their causal factors can all be profoundly shaped by, and interact with, religion. Ultimately, this is broadest implication of Jang and Johnson's discussion, one that locates religion, and ultimately culture, solidly in the heart of criminological inquiry.

REFERENCES

Akers, R. (1998). *Social learning and social structure: A general theory of crime and deviance.* Boston, MA: Northeastern University Press.

Aziz, S. & Rehman, G. (1996). Self control and tolerance among low and high religious groups. *Journal of Personality and Clinical Studies, 12*(1-2), 83-85.

Baier, C. & Wright, B. (2001). If you love me, keep my commandments: A meta-analysis of the effect of religion on crime. *Journal of Research in Crime and Delinquency, 38,* 3-21.

Baumeister, R., Bratlafsky, E., Muraven, M., & Tice, D. (1998). Ego depletion: Is the active self a limited resource? *Journal of Personality and Social Psychology, 74,* 1252-1265.

Baumeister, R. & Exline, J. (1999). Virtue, personality, and social relations: Self control as the moral muscle. *Journal of Personality, 67,* 1165-1194.

Baumeister, R. & Exline, J. (2000). Self control, morality, and human strength. *Journal of Social and Clinical Psychology, 19,* 29-42.

Chu, D. (2007). Religiosity and desistence from drug use. *Criminal Justice and Behavior, 34.* 661-679.

Geyer, A. & Baumeister, R. (2005). Religion, morality, and self control. In F. Paloutzian & C. Park (Eds.), *Handbook of the psychology of religion and spirituality* (pp. 412-434). New York, NY: Guilford Press.

Giordano, P., Cernkovich, S., & Rudolph, J. (2002). Gender, crime, and desistence: Toward a theory of cognitive transformation. *American Journal of Sociology, 107,* 990-1064.

Giordano, P., Longmore, M., Schroeder, R., & Seffrin, P. (2008). A life course perspective on spirituality and desistence from crime. *Criminology, 46,* 99-131.

Giordano, P., Schroeder, R., & Cernkovich, S. (2007). Emotions, and crime over the life course: A neo-median perspective on criminal continuity and change. *American Journal of Sociology, 112,* 1603-1661.

Glanville, J., Sikkink, D., & Hernandez, E. (2008). Religious involvement and educational outcomes: The role of social capital and extracurricular participation. *The Sociological Quarterly, 49,* 105-138.

Gottfredson, M. & Hirschi, T. (1990). *A general theory of crime.* Stanford, CA: Stanford University Press.

Hay, C. & Forrest, W. (2006). The development of self control: Examining self control theory's stability thesis. *Criminology, 44,* 739-774.

Hirschi, T. (2004). Self control and crime. In R. Baumeister & K. Vohs (Eds.), *Handbook of self regulation: research, theory, and applications* (pp. 537-552). New York, NY: Guilford Press.

Johnson, B., Jang, S., Larson, D., & Li, S. (2001). Does adolescent religious commitment matter? A reexamination of the effects of religiosity on delinquency. *Journal of Research in Crime and Delinquency, 38,* 22-44.

Johnson, B., Li, S., Larson, D., & McCullough, M. (2000). A systematic review of the religiosity and delinquency literature: A research note. *Journal of Contemporary Criminal Justice, 16*(1), 32-52.

Maines, D. (1993). Narrative's moment and sociology's phenomena: Toward a narrative sociology. *The Sociological Quarterly, 34*(1), 17-38.

Muraven, M. & Baumeister, R. (2000). Self regulation and depletion of limited resources: Does self control resemble a muscle? *Psychological Bulletin, 126*, 247-259.

Muraven, M., Pogarsky, G., & Shmueli, D. (2006). Self control depletion and the general theory of crime. *Journal of Quantitative Criminology, 22*, 263-277.

Muraven, M., Tice, D., & Baumeister, R. (1998). Self control as a limited resource: Regulatory depletion patterns. *Journal of Personality and Social Psychology, 74*, 774-789.

Pargament, K. (1997). *The psychology of religion and coping: Theory, research, practice.* New York, NY: The Guilford Press.

Pargament, K. (2008). The sacred character of community life. *American Journal of Community Psychology, 41*, 22-34.

Pargament, K., Magyar-Russell, G., & Murray-Swank, N. (2005). The sacred and the search for significance: Religion as a unique process. *Journal of Social Issues, 61*, 665-687.

Piquero, A. & Buffard, J. (2007). Something old, something new: A preliminary investigation of Hirschi's redefined self control. *Justice Quarterly, 24*, 1-27.

Rawls, A. (1996). Durkheim's epistemology: The neglected argument. *American Journal of Sociology, 102*(2), 430-482.

Schroeder, R. & Frana, J. (2009). Spirituality and religion, emotional coping, and criminal desistence: A qualitative study of men undergoing change. *Sociological Spectrum, 29*(6), 718-741.

Sherkat, D. & Ellison, C. (1999). Recent developments and current controversies in the sociology of religion. *Annual Review of Sociology, 25*, 363-394.

Simons, L., Simons, R., & Conger, R. (2004). Identifying the mechanisms whereby family religiosity influences the probability of adolescent antisocial behavior. *Journal of Comparative Family Studies, 35*, 547-563.

Smith, C. (2003). *Moral, believing animals: Human personhood and culture.* New York, NY: Oxford University Press.

Sutherland, E. (1947). *Principles of criminology.* Philadelphia, PA: Lippincott.

Tittle, C., Ward, D., & Grasmick, H. (2004). Capacity for self control and individuals' interest in exercising self control. *Journal of Quantitative Criminology, 20*, 143-173.

Vaisey, S. (2009). Motivation and justification: A dual process model of culture in action. *American Journal of Sociology, 114*(6), 1675-1715.

Wikstrom, P. & Treiber, K. (2007). The role of self control in crime causation. *European Journal of Criminology, 4*, 237-264.

PRISONER RADICALIZATION AND SACRED TERRORISM: A LIFE COURSE PERSPECTIVE

MARK S. HAMM

ABSTRACT

Studies show that Islam is the fastest growing religion among prisoners in Europe and North America. Experts claim that more than 250,000 U.S. inmates have converted to the Muslim faith since the terrorist attacks of 9/11, sparking an unprecedented interest in the issue of prisoner radicalization. Research is divided on the threat posed by radicalization, however. Some studies suggest that Western prisons are incubators for radical Islam and terrorist ideology; other studies claim that there is no such relationship; and still others maintain that radicalization occurs only under specific conditions of confinement. This paper begins with a review of the literature, and concludes that radicalization is based on a prison gang model whereby inmates are recruited into radical networks through a process of one-on-one proselytizing by charismatic leaders.

But researchers have yet to discover a definitive relationship between prisoner radicalization and terrorism. This paper addresses that deficiency in two ways. First, it presents a database of cases where prisoner radicalization has been linked to terrorism against Western targets. The database features background information on terrorists, their involvement in radical religious movements, the nature of their terrorist plots, criminal competence, and the time lag between release from custody and violence. Second, in an effort to accurately explain this temporal ordering of events, a paradigmatic case is selected for qualitative analysis and interpretation within the context of life course theory.

The analysis shows that prison-based terrorism is inimically linked to inmate subcultures via religious extremism. Prison-based terrorists are predominantly African or African-American. They are older than other terrorists, though most were radicalized in their early twenties. Far from ubiquitous, the problem of prison-based terrorism can be traced to specific institutions, reflecting what is known about the clustering of international jihadists around friendship and kinship arrangements. In the United States, most prison-based terrorists belong to homegrown jihad groups inspired by al-Qaeda. Prison-based terrorists demonstrate a respectable level of competence in criminal affairs. They typically wage their attacks within three years of release from custody. Consistent with the life course perspective, the case study indicates that these terrorist acts are triggered by decisive micro-level turning points—including those that may have occurred both before and after imprisonment—and macro-level political developments beyond the individual's control.

Since the terrorist attacks of September 11, 2001, much attention has been paid to the global spread of radical Islam, leading researchers to examine the influence of extremist websites, jihadist chat rooms, and incendiary fatwa issued by Muslim clerics. There is also growing concern about various social networks where people are introduced to radical Islam through contact with other like-minded individuals. Since 9/11, such networks have been discovered in mosques, bookstores, barbershops, military barracks, sports clubs, community centers, and perhaps most disconcertingly, prisons.

PRISONER RADICALIZATION

Prisoner radicalization was of little interest to researchers until the 9/11 attacks. Central to this development was the discovery of an al-Qaeda training manual, seized during a 2000 police raid on a safe house in Manchester, England, which identified Western prisoners as candidates for conversion to Islam because they may harbor hostility toward their governments (Pistole, 2003). Since then, Islam has become the fastest growing religion among prisoners in Europe and North America (Beckford, Daniels, & Khosrokhavar, 2005; Spalek & Wilson, 2002). Experts estimate that among those who seek faith while imprisoned in the United States, an astounding 80 percent turn to the Muslim faith (Ammar, Weaver, & Saxon, 2004). The yearly number of conversions to Islam in municipal, state, and federal correctional institutions is estimated at 30,000 (Dix-Richardson, 2002) or perhaps as many as 40,000 (Waller, 2003). Based on these estimates, some 250,000 American prisoners have converted to Islam since 9/11. Research on this issue is divided into three camps.

The first camp claims that Western prisons are incubators for radical Islam and terrorist ideology. Because Islam feeds on resentment and anger all too prevalent in prison, Islam is thought to pose a threat of "unknown magnitude" to U.S. security (e.g., Cilluffo & Saathoff, 2006). The second camp claims that there is no security threat. If anything, just the opposite is true. Islam is thought to have a moderating effect on inmates that plays a crucial role in their rehabilitation (e.g., Ammar et al., 2004; Spalek & El-Hassan, 2007). According to Zoll's (2005) nationwide investigation of radicalization, administrators insist that there is no evidence of terrorist recruitment by Muslims in their prisons. Likewise, Useem and Clayton (2009) argue that officials in Pennsylvania, New York, and Texas—states with large Muslim inmate populations—have seen no signs of prisoner radicalization whatsoever.

A third camp offers a more nuanced approach, arguing that radicalization occurs only under specific conditions. According to a landmark survey of U.S. prisons conducted by the FBI in 2005, these conditions are: (1) most cases of prisoner radicalization involve domestic extremists with few or no foreign connections; (2) some radicalized Islamic inmates are current or former members of street or prison gangs, indicating an emerging "crossover" from gang members to Islamic extremists; (3) radicalization activity appears to be higher in densely populated areas on the West Coast and in the Northeast; and (4) charismatic leadership may be the single most important contributing factor to prisoner radicalization (Van Duyn, 2006; Trout, 2007).

Criminologists have independently confirmed several of these findings, beginning with the discovery of a crossover between prison gangs and Islamic extremism. This point is made in Knox's (2002) study of a Michigan prison gang called the Melanic Islamic Palace of the Rising Sun, who used their own brand of Islam to wage a holy war against other prisoners, culminating in a 1999 riot at the Chippewa Correctional Facility—two years before the 9/11 attacks. More than anything, Knox argues, the Melanics represent a mutating form of "Prison Islam"—small inmate cliques known for using gang methods of coercion and "cut-and-paste" interpretations of the Koran to recruit new members. International researchers have made similar findings (Brandon, 2009; Warnes & Hannah, 2008), including a study by Britain's Chief Inspector of Prisons which reports "a rising problem of prisoner radicalization and an increase in Muslim conversions," adding that some Muslim prisoners "operated as a gang and put pressure on non-Muslims to convert [and] conform to a strict and extreme interpretation of Islamic practice" (HM's Chief Inspector of Prisons, 2008, p. 43).

These findings are also consistent with my own study (Hamm, 2009) which discovered a pattern of radicalization among Islamic gang members in California's overcrowded maximum security prisons. In addition to Islamic prisoners, I interviewed inmates affiliated with the Aryan Brotherhood.[1] In both instances, radicalization was based on a prison gang model whereby inmates are radicalized through a process of one-on-one proselytizing by charismatic leaders.

RESEARCHING PRISONER RADICALIZATION AND TERRORISM

Any attempt to understand the relationship between prisoner radicalization and terrorism is faced with two research puzzles. The first relates to the criminological implications of prisoner radicalization. If radicalization is "the process by which prisoners adopt extreme views, including beliefs that violent measures must be taken for political or religious purposes" (U.S. Department of Justice, 2004, p. 85), then it is not enough to simply discover "extreme views" held by convicts. Researchers must also take into account the social processes by which prisoners adopt such views, and show how they translate these views into violence. The surest way to understand the phenomenon, then, is to examine specific cases in which violent measures have actually been taken, or attempted, by inmates for political or religious purposes. In other words, research must focus on specific *incidents* (not incidence in the traditional criminological sense) where radicalization has led to terrorism (Webb, 2010).[2]

The second puzzle involves temporal ordering. There are three ways that a prisoner can become involved in terrorism. The most likely way is for an inmate to wage a terrorist plot upon release from custody. Less likely, a prisoner can collaborate with a parolee and/or fellow travelers in the community to wage a plot. Less likely still, a prisoner can wage a plot from behind bars without assistance from outsiders. The first instance involves a time lag between release from prison and terrorism, and a time lag will occur in the second instance with respect to the parolee. (In all other instances there will be a zero time lag because the prisoner has not been released.)

Accordingly, the relationship between radicalization and terrorism is best conceptualized in terms of the theoretical perspective most attuned to temporal ordering: life-course criminology (Laub & Sampson, 1993). The life-course perspective concentrates on a criminal's changing personal choices and life experiences over time, and seeks to uncover trajectories or "turning points" which form critical periods in the process of violent development. In this way, prisoner radicalization is conceived as one of what may be *several* decisive experiences—including those that may have occurred both before and after imprisonment—in the developmental process leading to terrorism.

The purpose of this research is twofold. First, the study presents a database of cases where prisoner radicalization has been linked to terrorism. And second, a paradigmatic case study is examined through the lens of life-course theory.

THE PRISONER RADICALIZATION/TERRORISM DATABASE

The database is displayed in Appendix 1. It features 46 domestic and international cases based on open sources (prior research, prisoner memoirs, media accounts, and court documents). Cases were selected based on the FBI's (2001) definition of terrorism, which defines the crime as "a violent act or an act dangerous to human life in violation of the criminal laws...to intimidate or coerce a government, the civilian population, or any segment thereof, in the furtherance of political or social objectives." The database is concerned only with cases where offenders were radicalized in prison and subsequently involved in either executed or attempted acts of terrorism upon release, or while in custody. In other words, the database represents a purposive sample of offenders who were not terrorists when they went to prison, but became terrorists upon release or during confinement. All terrorism databases contain flaws, and this one is no exception. Its limitations are as follows.

First, sources used to construct the database were created for purposes other than the study of prisoner radicalization. Often missing in these sources were such crucial facts as the offender's incarceration history and gang involvement. Moreover, the database is limited by the vagaries of open-source reporting. Second, although the database includes domestic and international cases, it is limited to attacks and threats against Western targets. Missing are attacks by terrorists in such hotbeds of extremism as Pakistan, Sri Lanka, and the Middle East. As Brandon (2009) observes, many modern Islamic terrorist movements in these parts of the world have been dominated and led by individuals who were radicalized in prison. Such a limitation has the dual effect of significantly underreporting incidents of radicalization and terrorism, while biasing the data toward democratic nations (especially the United States) where free media and open source materials are more available than in non-democratic countries. Finally, the database underreports terrorism's connection to prisoner radicalization due to legal reasons. For example, case 18 in the database presents details on Mohammed Achraf, convicted of plotting to bomb Spain's National Court in 2004. Sources reveal that Achraf organized the operation from a Spanish prison and was assisted by four other prisoners, but their identities have never been disclosed by the courts. For these reasons, then, the database represents a conservative estimate of the problem at hand.

FINDINGS

Background

The 46 cases cover a period of 41 years. Cases are listed in Appendix 1 by year of the terrorist event, beginning with Eldridge Cleaver in 1968 (case 1) and ending with Kevin Gardner in 2009 (case 46). Background data are displayed in Table 1. (All were men but one.) Table 1 shows that 34 of the 46 cases (74 percent) have occurred since 2001. Contrary to research suggesting that prisoner radicalization is non-existent, these data indicate a growing trend in the opposite direction: The largest increase in prison-based terrorist events over the past four decades has occurred since 9/11, mirroring a global trend in support for jihadist ideologies (Sageman, 2008).

Table 1 shows that most of the cases originated in U.S. prisons. The majority of terrorists were African-American or African; one-fourth was Caucasian and the rest were of Arab or Hispanic ethnicity. The mean age at the time of the terrorist event was 31.4 years old, confirming research showing that terrorists tend to be somewhat older than common criminals (Smith, 1994). But more to the point of this study, the finding indicates that prison-based terrorists are somewhat older than other terrorists. In his seminal study of 400 Afghan mujahedeen, Sageman (2004) found that the average age for joining the jihad was 25.6 years old, some six years younger than the prison-based terrorists.

Table 1. Background characteristics of prisoners involved in terrorism (N=46).

	N	(%)
Year of attack/plan		
1968 - 1974	2	4%
1983 - 1986	2	4%
1992 - 1995	6	14%
1996 - 2000	2	4%
2001 - 2005	15	29%
2006 - 2009	19	41%
Country of Incarceration		
United States	29	63%
Britain	6	13%
Spain	5	11%
France	4	9%
Jordan	1	2%
Egypt	1	2%
Ethnicity		
Caucasian	12	26%
African-American	14	30%
African	13	28%
Arab	5	11%
Hispanic	2	4%
Age at attack/plan		
20-24	7	15%
25-29	9	19%
30-34	18	39%
35-39	5	11%
40-44	1	2%
45-49	2	4%
50 and over	2	4%
Unknown	3	6%
Mean age = 31.4		

Prisoner radicalization

This study uses the U.S. Justice Department's definition of prisoner radicalization.[3] A measure of this process is conversions to religions that may be perceived as espousing ideologies of intolerance and violence. This would include not only various interpretations of Islam, but also a constellation of white supremacy faiths including Christian Identity and

Odin/Asatru.[4] Prisoner conversions are summarized in Table 2. Table 2 shows that 62 percent of the terrorists underwent a conversion to some form of Islam in prison: be it to traditional Islam, Sunni Islam, Salafi Jihadist,[5] Nation of Islam, Moorish Science Temple, or a strain of Sunni-inspired Prison Islam. Another 18 percent converted to a white supremacy faith while in custody.

Table 2 also includes eight terrorists (17 percent of the sample) in the No Conversion category. Importantly, all of them were either Sunni Muslims or Salafists when they began their incarceration. Sources indicate that these inmates were nevertheless radicalized in prison through their associations with fellow inmates and/or the conditions of their confinement. A well-known example is al-Qaeda's top lieutenant, Ayman al-Zawahiri (case 14), incarcerated and tortured in Egyptian prisons in the early 1980s following the assassination of Anwar Sadat. Already an Islamic militant when he entered prison, al-Zawahiri's ideology became even more extreme as a result of the torture. This has led some analysts to view his terrorist career—including the 9/11 attacks—as an attempt to exact revenge on Western allies of the Egyptian government for the treatment he endured in prison (Brandon, 2009; Scheuer, 2008; Wright, 2006).

Moreover, the data suggest that prison-based terrorism is inimically linked to inmate subcultures through religious extremism. Table 2 indicates that these subcultures have a strong appeal among younger inmates—those who may be most vulnerable to radical ideologies supporting terrorism (Merari, 1990). In this study, the average age of conversion was 24.7.

Table 2. Radicalization characteristics of prisoners involved in terrorism (N=46).

	N	(%)
Prisoner Religious Conversions		
Islam	7	15%
Sunni Islam/Salafi Jihadist	13	28%
Nation of Islam	1	2%
Moorish Science Temple	2	4%
Prison Islam (Wahhabi)	6	13%
Christian Identity	3	7%
Odinism/Asatru	5	11%
No Conversion (Already Sunni/Salafi)	8	17%
Other (Marxism)	1	2%
Age at Conversion (Approximate)		
Under 20	5	
20-24	10	
25-29	10	
30-34	4	

	N	(%)
35-39	1	
Unknown	8	
Not Applicable	8	
Mean age = 24.7		
Place of Conversion		
United States	26	68%
California	5	
Texas	4	
Pennsylvania	4	
New York	3	
Michigan	2	
Arizona	1	
Florida	1	
Washington	1	
Colorado	1	
Illinois	1	
Bureau of Prisons	1	
U.S. Military	1	
Unknown	1	
Britain	6	16%
Young Offender Institution	4	
Adult Prison	2	
Spain	2	5%
France	3	7%
Jordan	1	2%
Suwaqah	1	
Not Applicable	8	

Pockets of radicalization

Table 2 concludes with Place of Conversion. As expected, most conversions occurred in U.S. prisons, primarily in state institutions. Six conversions occurred in British prisons; three took place in France and two in Spain. Closer inspection of Place of Conversion in Appendix 1 reveals a link between small inmate groups confined to specific penal institutions, and incidents of radicalization and terrorism—reflecting what is known about the clustering of international jihadists around friendship and kinship arrangements (Sageman, 2008).

An important example is Abu Musab al-Zarqawi (case 17), the founder of al-Qaeda in Iraq. Al-Zarqawi did not convert to Islam in prison (he was raised by a Sunni family in Jordan), but according to the terrorist's biographer, "it was in prison that his magnetism and strength appeared in a new light" (Brisard, 2005, p. 43). Prior to al-Zarqawi's incarceration at Jordan's high-security Suwaqah prison in 1996, his "reputation was that of a hoodlum with vague religious learning" (Brisard, 2005, p. 40). Al-Zarqawi thrived under the harsh conditions of the desert prison where he received extensive religious instruction from fellow prisoner Abu Muhammad al-Maqdisis, a renowned Salafi scholar. Based on al-Maqdisis' tutelage, al-Zarqawi developed the body of a fighter and the proselytizing techniques of a zealot. These organizational skills allowed al-Zarqawi to recruit a gang of ordinary criminals and drug addicts from the Suwaqah population that would later prove vital to his terrorist campaign in Iraq (Scheuer, 2008).

The importance of a specific institution is even more apparent in Britain. According to the database, shoe-bomber Richard Reid, Taliban member Martin Mubanga, Sulayman Keeler of al-Muhajiroun (designated a terrorist organization under U.K. law), and would-be bomber Kevin Gardner (cases 15, 16, 38, and 46, respectively) all converted to Islam while serving time in British young offender institutions. Reid and Mubanga underwent conversions at the Feltham Young Offenders Institution in London in 1995 and 1992, respectively; and though he did not convert there, as a teenager Muktar Ibrahim (case 24), leader of the foiled London subway bombing plot of 2005, was incarcerated at several young offender institutions, including a bit at Feltham in 1992.[6] The other British terrorist in the database is Mohammad al-Figari (case 27), convicted of attending a terrorist training camp in 2006. Al-Figari was radicalized by a fellow prisoner named Mohammed Hamid, who was also imprisoned at Feltham during the early 1990s. That the radicalization of all British terrorists in the database can be traced to England's young offender penal system suggests the presence of not only a social network of prisoners who became terrorists, but an ongoing social network. The point of departure for understanding this network is the Feltham Young Offenders Institution.

A similar network was found in Spain. While serving time in a Spanish detention center for immigration fraud in 2000, Jamal Ahmidan (case 19) met fellow inmate Jose Trashorras (case 22), who introduced Ahmidan to the jihadist principles of radical Islam. Both were released in 2001. Three years later, using proceeds from drug dealing Ahmidan singlehandedly financed the historic Madrid train bombings of March 11, 2004; Trashorras played a supporting role. On April 3, Ahmidan and six other plotters died in an apparent suicide explosion in a Madrid suburb. Sageman discusses the presence of a "jihadi cool" in Europe, "where it is fashionable to emulate terrorists" (2008, p. 159). Indeed, later that year Spanish authorities charged 18 members of the Martyrs for Morocco (a North African Salafist group with ties to al-Qaeda) for plotting a sequel to the Madrid train bombings—an attack on the Madrid headquarters of the National Court. Algerians Mohamed Achraf and Abdel Bensmail (cases 18 and 20) had recruited for and planned the National Court plot while incarcerated at Topas Prison in the Salamanca Province of western Spain. Sources link Bensmail to Allekema Lamari (case 21), another ringleader of the Madrid train bombings who died alongside Jamal Ahmidan. At least four other suspects in the National Courts plot were former Topas prisoners. Once again, radicalization led to terrorism through a circumscribed social network of prisoners linked to one institution—Topas Prison.

Several U.S. cases reveal the importance of social networks within specific institutions. Lawrence Brewer and John King (cases 12 and 13) met in 1994 while serving time at the Beto One Unit of the Texas prison system. There they joined the neo-Nazi gang Aryan Circle and embraced the tenants of Odin/Asatru. Brewer and King were paroled in January 1998 and moved to King's hometown of Jasper, Texas. Nine months later they murdered African-American James Byrd in one of the most brutal hate crimes of the 20th century.[7] In 2005, Kevin James and Levar Washington (cases 25 and 26), converts to a fringe group of Sunni inmates at California's New Folsom Prison known as Jam'iyyat Ul-Islam Is-Saheed (the Assembly of Authentic Islam, or JIS), initiated what the FBI called a "fully operational terrorist plot" to commit mass murder at two Los Angeles army recruiting centers on the symbolic date of September 11.

The database shows that no U.S. prison has produced more terrorists than the military garrison at Guantanamo Bay, Cuba. Taliban members Abdullah Mehsud and Abdullah Rasoul (cases 23 and 29), along with a Saudi named Said Ali al-Shihri (case 33), were taken into U.S. custody in Afghanistan and Pakistan during the early years of the war on terrorism and detained as enemy combatants at Guantanamo. All were eventually released after the government failed to uncover any evidence of potential terrorism (i.e., they were not terrorists when they entered prison). Similar to the treatment of Ayman al-Zawahiri by the Egyptians—and the violence that would ensue—official documents indicate that the U.S. military subjected Guantanamo prisoners to torture-based techniques as part of an "enhanced interrogation" protocol (Mayer, 2009). Upon his release in 2004, Mehsud returned to Pakistan, joined a Taliban unit with ties to al-Qaeda, and participated in the kidnapping of two Chinese engineers employed by coalition forces. Rasoul was released to the Afghan government in late 2007 and became an operations officer for the Taliban in southern Afghanistan where he mounted a series of lethal attacks against U.S. and British forces. Al-Shihri was released to Saudi Arabia in 2007 where he entered a government-sponsored de-radicalization program. Upon completion of the program, al-Shihri moved to Yemen, Osama bin Laden's ancestral home, where he became a leader of al-Qaeda's Yemen branch. Al-Shihri was subsequently involved in the September 2008 car-bombing of the U.S. Embassy in Yemen's capital, Sana, killing 16. Months later he killed six Christian missionaries in Yemen. Then, in late 2009, al-Shihri was implicated in the failed Christmas Day bombing of a Northwest Airlines flight from Amsterdam to Detroit (Erlanger, 2010).

International and homegrown organizations

Terrorism scholars are well aware of the recent debate between Bruce Hoffman and Marc Sageman over the nature of the terrorist threat to

Western democracies. Hoffman argues that al-Qaeda is, and will continue to be, the major threat to Western interests. Sageman contends that the main threat no longer comes from al-Qaeda, but from the bottom up—from radicalized individuals who meet and plot in informal social networks. Table 3 considers this debate as it relates to prison-based terrorism.

In the United States, nearly 80 percent of the terrorists belonged to homegrown groups. However, some were inspired by al-Qaeda. Examples include JIS out of New Folsom Prison—who actually referred to themselves as "Al-Qaeda of California"—and Luqman Ameen Abdullah's Ummah (cases 39 and 40), designers of a plot to bomb the 2006 Super Bowl in Detroit. In the remaining cases, an international connection was clearly present. In addition to the former Guantanamo detainees, these include Jeff Fort (case 4), leader of the El Rukn street gang, who in 1986 as a prisoner at the Federal Correctional Center in Bastrop, Texas, forged ties with representatives of the Libyan government to bomb a federal building in Chicago; and Aqil Collins (case 7), an ex-offender from a California juvenile boot camp who traveled to Afghanistan in 1994 where he trained with future members of al-Qaeda.

Nature of plots

Researching incidents of prisoner radicalization and terrorism has been described as "a daunting task" (Webb, 2010, p. 368). The most daunting task is the cataloguing of terrorist criminality. Some cases examined here (like Michael Finton [case 42], convicted of plotting to bomb the federal courthouse in Springfield, Illinois, in 2009) have participated in only one terrorist event. Others (most notably al-Zarqawi and al-Zawahiri) have been involved in terrorist campaigns involving dozens of events (killing thousands, it must be said), making it impossible to squeeze all pertinent information into a database. For those involved in multiple events, then, Table 3 offers a summary estimate of their overall competence. Nature of Plots is categorized as Executed, Operational, or Aspirational. Executed means the plot was carried out. Operational means that the terrorist had the means to execute a plot; but it was aborted for one reason or another. An Aspirational plot indicates that the terrorist may have had the motive to carry out a plot, but lacked the operational resources to do so.

In the majority of cases (28 out of 46, or 61 percent), a terrorist plot was executed, suggesting a fairly sophisticated level of criminal competence. Twenty-two percent of the cases were operational and 20 percent were aspirational. The figures for U.S. prisoners are especially revealing given this criticism of prisoner radicalization by James Austin:

> [L]et us remind ourselves that the number of actual cases in which terrorist acts have been led by released U.S. prisoners who were radicalized while incarcerated is zero....Existing intelligence and self-regulating prisoner control systems—coupled with the general *lack of competence* to become an effective terrorist cell—

make the whole issue mute and unworthy of serious inquiry (Austin, 2009, p. 645 emphasis added).

Table 3. Characterisics of terrorism or threatened terrorism (N = 46).

Country	Types of Organization	
	International Group*	*Homegrown Group**
United States (29 Terrorists)	6	23
Britain (6)	4	2
Spain (5)	5	0
France (4)	4	0
Jordan (1)	1	0
Egypt (1)	1	0

Nature of Plots

	Executed	*Operational*	*Aspirational*
United States (29)	19	4	6
Britain (6)	0	4	2
Spain (5)	3	0	2
France (4)	4	0	0
Jordan (1)	1	0	0
Egypt (1)	1	0	0
	28	8	10

* Number of terrorists reported

According to Table 3, the number of actual cases in which executed terrorist acts have been led by released or incarcerated U.S. prisoners who were radicalized in prison, is at least 19 (some were involved in multiple events), accounting for 65 percent of all U.S. cases. In addition to the executed U.S. cases already discussed (the ex-Guantanamo detainees and the Jasper murder), are the following.

After escaping from California's Soledad Prison in 1973, where he was radicalized into the prevailing black consciousness movement, Donald DeFreeze (case 2) founded the Symbionese Liberation Army and went on to commit bank robberies, assassination, and the famous kidnapping of newspaper heiress Patty Hearst. As a founding member of the Order, considered by the FBI as the most competent domestic terrorist group they have ever faced, Gary Yarbrough (case 3)—a prison convert to Christian Identity—took part in counterfeiting, assassination, and several spectacular 1984 Brinks armored truck robberies (one netting over $3.6 million). As founding members of the Aryan Republican Army, focal point of one of the most extensive FBI terrorism investigations of the 1990s, Richard Guthrie and Peter Langan (cases 5 and 6)—both prison converts to Christian Identity—robbed 22 Midwestern banks and distributed robbery proceeds throughout the American terrorist underground. In 2007, Aryan Circle leader Dennis Clem and his AC girlfriend Tonya Smith (cases 28 and 31)—both prison converts to Odin/Asatru—committed multiple homicides, including the killing of two police officers in Houston, Texas. In 2008, Howard Cain, Eric Floyd and Levon Warner (cases 34, 35, and 37), all converts to Prison Islam, committed bank robbery and the murder of a Philadelphia police officer. The same year, from a jail cell in Denver, Colorado, inmate Marc Ramsey (case 36)—a prison convert to Moorish Science Temple—executed a successful anthrax hoax against United States Presidential candidate John McCain.

Time lag between prison release and terrorism
    Last, Table 4 shows the time lag between release from custody and the terrorist event. In the United States the mean lag time between release and terrorism was 2.6 years. This compares to Britain (at 7.4 years) in a way that is not favorable to U.S. security.

Table 4. Time lag between prison release and terrorism (N = 46).

	0	<1 yr	1-2 yrs	3-5 yrs	6-10 yrs	>10yrs	Not known	Mean years
United States (29)	5	6	6	4	1	2	5	2.6 yrs
Britain (6)			1	1	3	1		7.4 yrs
Spain (5)			3	2				2.4 yrs
France (4)	1		2				1	1 yr
Jordan (1)				1				-
Egypt (1)							1	-

A LIFE-COURSE PERSPECTIVE ON TERRORISM

    Howard Becker points out that case studies focus on process, or "the temporal dimension in which phenomena occur in specific settings" (1995, p. 208). According to Becker, social processes form a narrative analysis which has a story to tell. To the extent that the processes identified in the following story are similar to those in other stories of radicalization and terrorism across time and place, then something may be said about the generality of life-criminology.
    Ruben Luis Leon Shumpert (case 30) was born in Seattle, Washington, in 1977 to a Mexican mother and an African-American father. Reflecting on his upbringing in a court filing years later, Shumpert wrote: "My life has

been peppered with...hardships so severe it would have completely destroyed most people."[8] Perhaps emblematic of his attempts to adapt to these hardships, when Shumpert was twelve years old he bought a gun and tattooed a large cross on his arm representing his love for Jesus. Although Shumpert claimed that his background "neither defines me nor is it a contributing factor to my current situation," these two personal obsessions—guns and religion—would play an essential role in what lay ahead for him.

As a teenager, Shumpert was arrested and remanded to juvenile detention on a firearms violation. Once released, Shumpert became a major Seattle drug dealer, thereby setting the stage for a series of life-course events that became turning points in his pathway to terrorism—events made possible by four interrelated social networks.

Network 1: The Prison. In 1998, Shumpert was convicted of drug trafficking and sentenced to the Monroe State Prison near Everett, Washington. He learned to cut hair in prison, and is likely to have associated mainly with other minority inmates. Shortly before his release on August 6, 2002, Shumpert converted from the Catholic religion to Sunni Islam. Like most all converts, Shumpert chose a Muslim name to mark his new symbolic birth to the faith: Amir Abdul Muhaimeen. He was 25 years old.

Network 2: The Barbershop. Returning to Seattle, Shumpert gave up drinking and drug dealing and vowed to stay away from guns. He quickly became destitute and homeless, though, and sought shelter in a local mosque. There he met a man who owned the Crescent Cuts Barbershop in the Rainer Valley area of Seattle, a low-income black community. Shumpert went to work at Crescent Cuts (Crescent being the symbol of Islam); thereby putting to use both the skill and the religion he had learned in prison. As in many African-American communities, the barbershop was a neighborhood gathering place. According to a federal court document, "The shop served as a casual meeting place for...like-minded individuals, mostly African American men with criminal histories who had converted to Islam, either in prison or after contact later with prison converts."[9] Sensing the potential for radicalization among these Muslim converts in the year following 9/11, the Seattle office of the FBI developed an undercover informant to monitor activities inside the barbershop (Shukovsky, 2004).

The investigation went on for three years (2002-2005), during which time Shumpert emerged as the most outspoken member of the barbershop group. He was also the most devout. By this point Shumpert had developed a "raisin" in the middle of his forehead, the mark of a pious Muslim who grinds his forehead into the ground during prayer. Shumpert also got married, became a father, opened a homeless shelter, and conducted clothing drives for the poor. Shumpert was an asset to his community. Yet on one occasion he supplied the FBI informant with a counterfeit $100 bill. And on another, Shumpert sold the informant a handgun. Meanwhile, barbershop discussions about the war in Iraq were likely at fever pitch. Shumpert described his grievance like this: "Nineteen extremists kill over

3,000 Americans on 9/11 and over 30,000 Iraqis are killed as an indirect result....The Muslim community always pays the price."[10]

With his grievance at an all-time high, Shumpert announced that he was going to Iraq to fight alongside Abu Musab al-Zarqawi. Yet before he could do so, on April 15, 2005, Shumpert was arrested on an assault charge and locked up in Seattle's King County Jail. Before Shumpert could post bail, the FBI unsealed charges in federal court accusing him of passing counterfeit money and being a felon in possession of a firearm.

Network 3: The Jail. Facing a federal prison sentence, Shumpert took his most important step toward terrorism. In King County, Shumpert met a group of Somali inmates who advised him to accept a plea agreement, pleading guilty on the counterfeiting charge in exchange for dropping the assault and firearms violations, allowing Shumpert to be released on bond so that he could flee America and join the cause of jihad in Somalia. He would do just that.

Network 4: Transnational Terrorist Organization. In late summer 2006, Shumpert jumped bail and fled the country on forged travel documents provided to him by the Somalis. Upon his arrival at Mogadishu airport, Shumpert was met by members of al-Shabaab—"the youth" in Arabic—a militia of violent Islamist guerrillas at war against Somalia's weak U.S.-backed transitional government because it is not based on Islam. By 2007, al-Shabaab had gained the support of Osama bin Laden and was designated a terrorist organization by the U.S. State Department (Anderson, 2009), due to its rendering of "summary justice" against enemies in the form of suicide bombings, kidnappings, beheadings and amputations, and a mortar attack against a plane carrying a U.S. Congressman (Elliott, 2009).

Al-Shabaab arranged for Shumpert to purchase an assault rifle and took him to a jihad training camp. According to a statement released by al-Shabaab, in late 2007 Shumpert's brigade traveled to Adale, about 150 km north of Mogadishu, where Shumpert was shot in the back during a battle with secular warlords and evacuated to Mogadishu for treatment. After his recovery, the militia retreated to a forest near Mogadishu where a group boarded a boat, destination unknown. Acting on intelligence from an informant inside al-Shabaab, the group was targeted by a U.S.-supported rocket attack, killing three. Months later, Senator Joseph Lieberman, Chairman of the Senate Homeland Security Committee, announced that among the dead was Ruben Shumpert (Hsu & Johnson, 2009).

CONCLUSION

Essentially, the debate over prisoner radicalization turns on a matter of logic. Criminologists who find no threat work from a deductive model by estimating the *prevalence* of radicalization within the general U.S. prison population. With that population now soaring above the 2 million mark, this approach is like looking for a needle in the haystack. Criminologists who do recognize a threat work from an inductive model by focusing on actual *incidents* of prisoner radicalization and terrorism. They begin with a handful of needles and try to find consistencies in how the things were made.

The present study found several consistencies, beginning with the significance of radical religion as part of a cycle of ideologically-motivated violence. This is not necessarily a direct cause-and-effect relationship where a young man goes off to prison, converts to a radical religion, and becomes a terrorist. The process appears to be more complicated. It seems to involve a course of action that happens within little-known social networks, both in prison and out, that is sequenced yet progressive.

Sampson and Laub apply such an interactive process to the influence of incarceration, arguing that: "The effect of confinement may be indirect and operative in a developmental, cumulative process that reproduces itself over time...its indirect effect may well be criminogenic (positive) as structural labeling theorists have long argued" (2001, p. 159). From the life-course perspective, Ruben Shumpert is seen as a career criminal who would have never become involved with the transnational terrorist organization al-Shabaab had he not met Somalis in jail who were sympathetic to their cause. For it was through these jailed Somalis that Shumpert not only took up the jihadist banner, but he obtained the forged travel documents necessary for him to become an international fugitive. This was a major turning point for Shumpert but it was not his only one. Shumpert may have never gone to jail in the first place were it not for the associations he formed at the barbershop, most importantly, the association he formed with an FBI informant. It follows that Shumpert may have never gone to work at the Islamic barbershop had he not converted to Islam in prison.

Yet Shumpert's experiences within these social networks do not tell the whole story. Shumpert was also deeply affected by the war in Iraq. Sampson and Laub leave no doubt about the potential influence of sociopolitical events on adult criminality: "The idea is that turning points in the adult life course matter, and that a change in life direction may stem from macro-level events largely beyond individual control (e.g., war)" (1996, p. 347). Shumpert's terrorist development was therefore a combination of turning points involving both micro-and-macro-level events. In the end, then, it is not just time that matters but timing. And it is for these reasons that life-course theory matters to the study of terrorism. With its focus on the duration and sequencing of major life events and their consequences for later criminality, the life-course perspective provides a portal through which criminologists may understand how people *evolve* into terrorists.

REFERENCES

Ammar, N., Weaver, R., & Saxon, S. (2004). Muslims in prison: A case study from Ohio state prisons. *International Journal of Offender Therapy and Comparative Criminology, 48*, 414-28.

Anderson, J. (2009, December 14). The most failed state: Letter from Mogadishu. *The New Yorker,* 64.

Austin, J. (2009). Prisons and fear of terrorism. *Criminology & Public Policy, 8*, 641-46.

Becker, H. (1995). The epistemology of qualitative research. In C. Ragin & H. Becker (Eds.), *What is a case? Exploring the foundations of social inquiry* (pp. 192-211). New York, NY: Cambridge University Press.

Beckford, J., Daniels, J., & Khosrokhavar, F. (2005). *Muslims in prison: Challenges and change in Britain and France.* Basingstoke, Hampshire (UK): Palgrave Macmillan.

Blazak, R. (2009). The prison hate machine. *Criminology & Public Policy, 8,* 633-40.

Brandon, J. (2009). *Unlocking Al-Qaeda: Islamist extremism in British prisons.* London, UK: Quilliam.

Brisard, J. (2005). *Zarqawi: The new face of Al-Qaeda.* New York, NY: Other Press.

Cilluffo, F. & Saathoff, G. (2006). *Out of the shadows: Getting ahead of prisoner radicalization.* George Washington University/University of Virginia, Critical Incident Analysis Group.

Dix-Richardson, F. (2002). Resistance to conversion to Islam among African-American women inmates. *Journal of Offender Rehabilitation, 35*, 109-26.

Elliott, A. (2009, July 12). A call to Jihad, answered in America. *New York Times.* Retrieved August 17, 2010, from http://www.nytimes.com/2009/07/12/us/12somalis.html

Erlanger, S. (2010, January 3). Yemen's chaos aids evolution of Qaeda cell. *New York Times.* Retrieved August 17, 2010, from http://www.nytimes.com/2010/01/03/world/middleeast/03yemen.html

FBI. (2001). Definition of terrorism. Retrieved July 6, 2010, from http://www.fbi.gov/publications/terror/terror2000_2001.htm

HM's Chief Inspector of Prisons. (2008). *Report on unannounced full follow-up inspection of HMP Whitemoor.* London, UK: HM's Inspectorate of Prisons.

Hamm, M. (2009). Prison Islam in the age of sacred terror. *British Journal of Criminology, 49*, 667-85.

Hsu, S. & Johnson, C. (2009, March 11). Somali Americans recruited by extremists. *Washington Post.* Retrieved August 17, 2010, from http://www.washingtonpost.com/wp-dyn/content/article/2009/03/10/AR2009031003901.html?nav=emailpage

Kaplan, J. (1997). *Radical religion in America: Millenarian movements from the far right to the children of Noah.* Syracuse, NY: Syracuse University Press.

Knox, G. (2002). Melanics: A gang profile analysis. *Journal of Gang Research, 9,* 1-76.

Laub, J. & Sampson, R. (1993). Turning points in the life course: Why change matters to the study of crime. *Criminology, 31*(3), 301-325.

Mayer, J. (2009). *The dark side: The inside story of how the war on terror turned into a war on American ideals.* New York, NY: Anchor Books.

Merari, A. (1990). The readiness to kill and die: Suicidal terrorism in the Middle East. In W Reich (Ed.), *Origins of terrorism: Psychologies, ideologies, theologies, states of mind* (pp. 192-207).. Washington, DC: Woodrow Wilson Center Press.

Pistole, J. (2003, October 14). Statement for the record, John S. Pistole, Assistant Director, Counterterrorism Division, Federal Bureau of Investigation. Testimony before the United States Senate Committee on the Judiciary. Terrorist Recruitment and Infiltration in the United States: Prisons and Military as an Operational Base.

Sageman, M. (2004). *Understanding terror networks.* Philadelphia, PA: University of Pennsylvania Press.

Sageman, M. (2008). *Leaderless Jihad: Terror networks in the twenty-first century.* Philadelphia, PA: University of Pennsylvania Press.

Sampson, R. & Laub, J. (1996). Socioeconomic achievement in the life course of disadvantaged men: Military service as a turning point. *American Sociological Review, 61,* 347-367.

Sampson, R. & Laub, J. (2001). A life-course theory of cumulative disadvantage and the stability of delinquency. In A. Piquero & P. Mazerolle (Eds.), *Life-course criminology: Contemporary and classic readings* (pp. 146-170). Belmont, CA: Wadsworth.

Scheuer, M. (2008). *Marching toward hell: America and Islam after Iraq.* New York, NY: Free Press.

Shukovsky, P. (2004, November 19). 14 Arrested in Raids by Terror Task Force. *Seattle Post Intelligencer.* Retrieved August 17, 2010, from http://www.seattlepi.com/local/200337_raid19.html

Smith, B. (1994). *Terrorism in America: Pipe bombs and pipe dreams.* Albany, NY: SUNY Press.

Spalek, B. & El-Hassan, S. (2007). Muslim converts in prison. *The Howard Journal of Criminal Justice, 46,* 99-114.

Spalek, B. & Wilson, D. (2002). Racism and religious discrimination in prison: The marginalization of Imams in their work with prisoners. In B. Spalek (Ed.), *Islam, crime and criminal justice* (pp. 996-112). Portland, OR: Willan Publishing.

Trout, C. (2007, August 14). The Correctional Intelligence Initiative (CII): Preventing prison radicalization. Presentation at the American Correctional Association 137th Annual Congress of Corrections, Kansas City.

U.S. Department of Justice. (2004). *A review of the Federal Bureau of Prisons' selection of Muslim religious service providers.* Washington, DC: Office of Inspector General.

Useem, B. & Clayton, O. (2009). Radicalization of U.S. prisoners. *Criminology & Public Policy, 8,* 56-92.

Van Duyn, D. (2006, September 19). Testimony of Donald Van Duyn, Deputy Assistant Director, Counterterrorism Division, Federal Bureau of Investigation, Senate Committee on Homeland Security and Governmental Affairs.

Waller, M. (2003, October 14). Terrorist recruitment and infiltration in the United States: Prisons and military as an operational base. Testimony before the U.S. Senate Committee on the Judiciary.

Warnes, R. & Hannah, G. (2008). Meeting the challenge of extremist and radicalized prisoners: The experiences of the United Kingdom and Spain. *Policing, 2*(4), 402-11.

Webb, V. (2010). Searching for a needle in the haystack: A look at hypotheses and explanations for the low prevalence of radicalization in American prisons. In N. Frost, J. Freilich, & T. Clear (Eds.), *Contemporary issues in criminal justice policy* (pp. 367-370). Belmont, CA: Wadsworth.

Wright, L. (2006). *The looming tower: Al-Qaeda and the road to 9/11.* New York, NY: Knopf.

Zoll, R. (2005, June 4). American prisons become political, religious battleground over Islam. Associated Press.

Legal Cases

USA v. Ruben Luis Leon Shumpert. CR04-494MJP.

ENDNOTES

[1] Officials estimate that 10 percent of the U.S. prison population is involved in white supremacy gangs. In California prisons, the Aryan Brotherhood alone has some 15,000 members (Blazak, 2009).

[2] Within criminology, incidence refers to the number of crime events that have occurred during a specific period of time in a specified population. Incidence is used to study risk to that population. An incident is different. It is a definite, distinct occurrence, or an event that occurs anywhere and at any point in time.

[3] "The process by which prisoners adopt extreme views, including beliefs that violent measures must be taken for political or religious purposes" (U.S. Department of Justice, 2004, p. 85).

[4] Christian Identity is a theology that gives the blessing of God to the racist cause. The Identity creed holds that Jews are the children of Satan, while Aryans are God's chosen people. Odin/Asatru is a pre-Christian pagan religion calling for the return to a mythical age of the Nordic gods (see Kaplan, 1997).

[5] Salafists advocate a pure interpretation of the Koran and strict observance of the original texts of Islam and the traditions of "pious ancestors" (Sageman, 2004).

[6] Unless otherwise noted, claims made about the cases are based on information found in the database column marked Sources. Sources are referenced in Appendix 2.

[7] Debate over the distinction between terrorism and hate crime is longstanding. Hate crime is defined as an act of prejudicial violence based on race, religion, ethnicity, or sexual preference. The Jasper murder fits that definition, yet it was also an act of violence intended to intimidate the civilian population of Jasper, in the furtherance of political objectives associated with the white supremacy movement, thus qualifying it as an act of domestic terrorism as well (Blazak, 2009).

[8] Letter from Amir Abdul Muhaimeen to U.S. District Judge Marsha J. Pechman, June 5, 2006.

[9] *USA v. Ruben Luis Leon Shumpert.* CR04-494MJP.

[10] Letter to Judge Pechman, June 5, 2006.

APPENDIX 1

TABLE A1, PART 1 (* Plot waged from prison)

Case #	Name	Year of Attack/Plan	Age at AttackPlan	Prison religious conversion	Age at conversion (approx)	Place of conversion/ incarceration	Lag release/ violence
1	Cleaver, Eldridge (1935 -1998), U.S. Black Panther Party	1968	33	Nation of Islam	23	San Quentin, California	2 yrs
2	DeFreeze, Donald "Cinque" (1943-1974), U.S. Symbionese Liberation Army	1973 /74	31	No (Marxism)	30	Soledad, California	7 months
3	Yarbrough, Gary (1955-), U.S. The Order	1983 /84	26	Christian Identity	24	Arizona State Prison, Arizona	4 yrs
4	Fort, Jeff (1947-), U.S. El Rukn	1986	39	Moorish Science Temple	28 (1975)	U.S.P. Leaven-worth, Kansas	0* (reincar-nated, 1983) FCC-Bastrop, Texas
5	Guthrie, Richard (1958-1996), U.S. Aryan Republic Army	1992-1995	32	Christian Identity/ Phineas Priesthood	25	Navy, Brig (Unknown Location)	8 yrs
6	Langan, Peter (1958-), U.S. Aryan Republic Army	1992-1995	32	Christian Identity/ Phineas Priesthood	19	Raiford Prison, Florida	13 yrs
7	Collins, Aqil (1974-), U.S.	1994	20	Sunni-Islam	18	Juvenile Boot Camp, California	2 yrs
8	Vallat, David (1971-), France GIA	1994 /95	22	Salafi-Jihadism	22	French Prison, France	1 yr
9	Kelkal, Khaled (1972-1995), France Algerian Armed Islamic Gropu (GIA)	1995	24	Salafi-Jihadism	22	French Prison, France	2 yrs

Case #	Name	Year of Attack/Plan	Age at AttackPlan	Prison religious conversion	Age at conversion (approx)	Place of conversion/ incarceration	Lag release/ violence
10	Raime, Joseph (u/k), France GIA	1995	u/k	Salafi-Jihadism	u/k	French Prison, France	u/k
11	Bourada, Safe (1970-) (Plus other prisoners), France Partisans of Victory	(1995) 2003-08	33	No (Already Salafi Jihadist)		French prison, France	0 (immediate involvement after release)
12	Brewer, Lawrence (1967-) U.S. Aryan Circle	1998	32	Odin	27	Beto One, Texas	9 months
13	King, John (1975-), U.S. Aryan Circle	1998	23	Odin	19	Beto One, Texas	9 months
14	Al-Zawahiri, Ayman (1951-), Egypt al-Qaeda	1998-2009	47 at first attack	No (Already Wahhabist)		Egyptian Prison, Egypt	24 yrs
15	Reid, Richard (1973-), Britain Al-Qaeda	2001	28	Sunni-Islam	22	Feltham Young Offenders Institution Britain	6 yrs
16	Mubanga, Martin (1972-), Britain	2001	28	Islam	19	Feltham Young Offenders Institution Britain	6 yrs
17	Al-Zarqawi, Abu-Musab (1966-2006), Jordan Al-Qaeda in Iraq	2003-06	37	Wahhabi-Islam	33	Suwaqah, Jordan	4 yrs
18	Achraf, Mohamed (1973-) (Plus 4 ex-prisoners), Spain Martyrs for Morocco	2004	30	No (Already Sunni-Muslim)		Topas Prison Salamanca Spain	2 yrs
19	Ahmidan, Jamal (1970-2004), Spain	2004	34	Sunni-Islam	31	Spanish Prison	3 yrs

Case #	Name	Year of Attack/Plan	Age at AttackPlan	Prison religious conversion	Age at conversion (approx)	Place of conversion/ incarceration	Lag release/ violence
20	Bensmail, Abdel (U/K), Spain Martyrs for Morocco	2004	u/k	No (Already Sunni-Muslim)		Topas Prison Salamanca Spain	2 yrs
21	Lamari, Allekema (U/K), Spain GIA	2004	u/k	No (Already Sunni-Muslim)		French Prison, France	2 yrs
22	Trashorras, Jose (1976-), Spain	2004	28	Sunni-Islam	25	Spanish Prison	3 yrs
23	Mehsud, Abdullah (1974-2007), U.S. Taliban	2004-07	30	No (Guan-tanimo Detainee, 2002-03)			6 months
24	Ibrahim, Muktar (1976-), Britain	2005	29	Sunni-Islam	21	Woodhill Prison, Britain	7 yrs
25	James, Kevin (1976-), U.S. Jam'iyyat Ul-Islam Is-Saheed (JIS)	2005	29	JIS (Prison Islam)	21	State Prison, Tahachapi, California	0*
26	Washington, Levar (1980-), U.S. JIS	2005	25	JIS (Prison Islam)	25	New Folsom Prison, California	2 months
27	Al-Fiqari, Mohammad (1964-), Britain	2006	42	Sunni-Islam Salafi-Jihad	33	Wands-worth Prison, Britain	4 yrs
28	Clem, Dennis (1983-2007), U.S. Aryan Circle	2007	24	Odin	u/k	Texas Prison, Texas	u/k
29	Rasoul, Abdullah (1973-), U.S. Taliban	2007	34	No (Guan-tanimo Detainee, 2001-2007)			2 months
30	Shumpert, Rueben (1977-2007), U.S. Al-Sheebab	2007	30	Sunni-Islam	25	Monroe State Prison, Wash-ington	2 yrs

Case #	Name	Year of Attack/Plan	Age at AttackPlan	Prison religious conversion	Age at conversion (approx)	Place of conversion/ incarceration	Lag release/ violence
31	Smith, Tonya (1984-), U.S. Aryan Circle	2007	23	Odin	u/k	Texas Prison, Texas	u/k
32	Adolf, Shawn (1974-), U.S. Aryan Nations	2008	34	Wicca/Odin	22	Colorado Prison, Colorado	11 yrs
33	Al-Shihri, Said Ali (1973-), U.S. Al-Qaeda in Yeman	2008	35	No (Guan- tanimo Detainee, 2001-2007)			1 yr
34	Cain, Howard (1975-2008), U.S.	2008	33	Prison Islam	29	State Prison, Pennsyl- vania	2 yrs
35	Floyd, Eric (1975-), U.S.	2008	33	Prison Islam	u/k	State Prison, Pennsyl- vania	0* (half-way house resident)
36	Ramsey, Marc (1969-), U.S.	2008	39	Morrish Science Temple	u/k	U/K	0*
37	Warner, Levon (1972-), U.S.	2008	38	Prison Islam	u/k	State Prison, Pennsyl- vania	u/k
38	Keeler, Sulayman (1972-), Britain al-Muhajiroun	2008	35	Islam	24	Young Offenders Institution Britain	12 yrs
39	Abdullah, Luqman Ameen (Christopher Thomas) (1956- 2009), U.S. Ummah	2009	53	Sunni-Islam	29	Michigan Prison, Michigan	U/K
40	Bassir, Mohammad (Franklin Williams) (1951-), U.S. Ummah	2009	50	Sunni-Islam	u/k	Michigan Prison, Michigan	0*
41	Cromitie, James (1964-), U.S.	2009	45	Islam	39	Fishkill, New York	5 yrs

Case #	Name	Year of Attack/Plan	Age at AttackPlan	Prison religious conversion	Age at conversion (approx)	Place of conversion/ incarceration	Lag release/ violence
42	Finton, Michael (1980-), U.S.	2009	29	Islam	25	Illinois Prison, Illinois	4 yrs
43	Payen, Laguerre (1981-), U.S.	2009	28	Islam	23	New York Prison New York	5 yrs
44	Scruggs, Rasheed (1975-), U.S.	2009	33	Prison Islam	u/k	State Prison, Pennsyl- vania	u/k
45	Williams, Onta (1976-), U.S.	2009	33	Islam	19	New York/BOP New York	2 yrs
46	Gardner, Kevin (1986-), Britain	2009	23	Islam	20	Stoke Heath Young Offenders Institution Britain	2 yrs

TABLE A1, PART 2

Case #	Name	Nature of Offense	Nature of Plots	International/ Homegrown	Ethnicity	Source
1	Cleaver, Eldridge (1935 -1998), U.S. Black Panther Party	Attempted murder of police officers	Executed	Home- grown	African American	Cleaver, 1968
2	DeFreeze, Donald "Cinque" (1943-1974), U.S. Symbionese Liberation Army	Assassina- tion, kidnapping, bank robbery	Executed	Home- grown	African American	McLellan & Avery, 1977

Case #	Name	Nature of Offense	Nature of Plots	International/ Homegrown	Ethnicity	Source
3	Yarbrough, Gary (1955-), U.S. The Order	Counter-feiting, murder, bank robbery	Executed	Home-grown	Caucasian	Smith, 1984; Flynn & Gerhardt 1989
4	Fort, Jeff (1947-), U.S. El Rukn	Attempted bombing of federal buildings (Libya)	Opera-tional	Inter-national	African American	Schmidt, 2007
5	Guthrie, Richard (1958-1996), U.S. Aryan Republic Army	Attempted assassina-tion (G.H.W. Bush), bank robbery, bombing	Executed	Home-grown	Caucasian	Hamm, 2002
6	Langan, Peter (1958-), U.S. Aryan Republic Army	Attempted assassina-tion (G.H.W. Bush), bank robbery, bombing	Executed	Home-grown	Caucasian	Hamm, 2002
7	Collins, Aqil (1974-), U.S.	Trained with al-Qaeda ('94); Islamic Chechen	Executed	Inter-national	Caucasian	Cnn.com 2002
8	Vallat, David (1971-), France GIA	Trained with al-Qaeda ('94); French bombing ('95)	Executed	Inter-national	African (Algerian)	Mili, 2006
9	Kelkal, Khaled (1972-1995), France Algerian Armed Islamic Group (GIA)	Assassina-tion, bombing campaign (France)	Executed	Inter-national	African (Algerian)	Mili, 2006

Case #	Name	Nature of Offense	Nature of Plots	International/ Homegrown	Ethnicity	Source
10	Raime, Joseph (u/k), France GIA	French bombing campaign	Executed	Inter-national	African (Algerian)	Mili, 2006
11	Bourada, Safe (1970-) (Plus other prisoners), France Partisans of Victory	Plotting terrorist attack in France, Iraq, Paris Metro Bombing	Opera-tional	Inter-national	North African (Algerian)	*Global Jihad*, *2008*
12	Brewer, Lawrence (1967-), U.S. Aryan Circle	Murder, hate crime Jasper, Texas	Executed	Home-grown	Caucasian	Blazak, 2009 Texas DCJ Records
13	King, John (1975-), U.S. Aryan Circle	Murder, hate crime Jasper, Texas	Executed	Home-grown	Caucasian	Blazak, 2009 Texas DCJ Records
14	Al-Zawahiri, Ayman (1951-), Egypt al-Qaeda	East African bombings, 9/11 attacks, etc.	Executed	Inter-national	Arab	Wright, 2006; Brandon, 2009
15	Reid, Richard (1973-), Britain Al-Qaeda	Trained w/ al-Qaeda; 2001 shoe-bomb plot	Opera-tional	Inter-national	African-Carribean	Brandon, 2009; Elliot, 2002
16	Mubanga, Martin (1972-), Britain	Terrorist related activity	Aspira-tional	Inter-national	African (Zambia)	Brandon, 2009
17	Al-Zarqawi, Abu-Musab (1966-2006), Jordan Al-Qaeda in Iraq	Multiple terrorist attacks; beheading Nicholas Berg	Executed	Inter-national	Arab	Brandon, 2009; Brisard, 2005
18	Achraf, Mohamed (1973-) (Plus 4 ex-prisoners), Spain Martyrs for Morocco	Plot to bomb Spain's National Court	Aspira-tional	Inter-national	North African (Algerian)	AP, 2004; Haahr, 2004

Case #	Name	Nature of Offense	Nature of Plots	International/ Homegrown	Ethnicity	Source
19	Ahmidan, Jamal (1970-2004), Spain	Madrid train bombing (2004)	Executed	International	North African	Rotella, 2005
20	Bensmail, Abdel (U/K), Spain Martyrs for Morocco	Plot to bomb Spain's National Court	Aspirational	International	North African (Algerian)	Bakker, 2006
21	Lamari, Allekema (U/K), Spain GIA	Madrid train bombing (2004)	Executed	International	North African (Algerian)	History Commons, 2004
22	Trashorras, Jose (1976-), Spain	Madrid train bombing (2004)	Executed	International	Hispanic	Cuthbertson, 2004
23	Mehsud, Abdullah (1974-2007), U.S. Taliban	Kidnap-ping, Mass murder; Coalition attacks	Executed	International	Arab	Masood, 2007
24	Ibrahim, Muktar (1976-), Britain	London subway bomb plot (2005)	Operational	International	African (Eritrea)	Brandon, 2009; Lyall, 2007
25	James, Kevin (1976-), U.S. Jam'iyyat Ul-Islam Is-Saheed (JIS)	Plot to attack Army recruiting offices, L.A. 2005	Operational	Homegrown	African American	Hamm, 2007
26	Washington, Levar (1980-), U.S. JIS	Plot to attack Army recruiting offices, L.A. 2005	Operational	Homegrown	African American	Hamm, 2007
27	Al-Fiqari, Mohammad (1964-), Britain	Attending terrorist camps, UK	Aspirational	Homegrown	African (Trinidad)	Brandon, 2009
28	Clem, Dennis (1983-2007), U.S. Aryan Circle	Multiple homicide 2 police officers 2007	Executed	Homegrown	Caucasian	ADL, 2008

Case #	Name	Nature of Offense	Nature of Plots	International/ Homegrown	Ethnicity	Source
29	Rasoul, Abdullah (1973-), U.S. Taliban	Bombing coalition forces, Afghani- stan	Executed	Inter- national	Arab	Evans, 2009
30	Shumpert, Rueben (1977- 2007), U.S. Al-Sheebab	Counter- feiting; weapons; joined Somali network	Executed	Inter- national	Hispanic/ African American	Shum- pert 2006; NEA, 2008
31	Smith, Tonya (1984-), U.S. Aryan Circle	Mulitple homicides	Executed	Home- grown	Caucasian	ADL, 2008
32	Adolf, Shawn (1974-), U.S. Aryan Nations	Attempted assassina- tion Barack Obama	Opera- tional	Home- grown	Caucasian	Cardona, 2009
33	Al-Shihri, Said Ali (1973-), U.S. Al-Qaeda in Yeman	Bombing U.S. Embassy, Yemen 2008	Executed	Inter- national	Arab	Worth, 2009
34	Cain, Howard (1975-2008), U.S.	Bank robbery, murder of police officer	Executed	Home- grown	African American	Schilling, 2009
35	Floyd, Eric (1975-), U.S.	Bank robbery, murder of police officer	Executed	Home- grown	African American	Teauge, 2008
36	Ramsey, Marc (1969-), U.S.	Attempted anthrax attack on John McCain	Executed	Home- grown	African American	AP, 2008
37	Warner, Levon (1972-), U.S.	Bank robbery, murder of police officer	Executed	Home- grown	African American	Schilling, 2009

Case #	Name	Nature of Offense	Nature of Plots	International/ Homegrown	Ethnicity	Source
38	Keeler, Sulayman (1972-), Britain al-Muhajiroun	Supporting terrorism	Operational	International	Caucasian	Brandon, 2009
39	Abdullah, Luqman Ameen (Christopher Thomas) (1956-2009), U.S. Ummah	Multiple felonies, shooting at FBI; plot to bomb Super Bowl	Aspirational	Homegrown	African American	U.S.A. v Abdullah
40	Bassir, Mohammad (Franklin Williams) (1951-), U.S. Ummah	Multiple felonies, shooting at FBI; plot to bomb Super Bowl	Aspirational	Homegrown	African American	U.S.A. v Abdullah
41	Cromitie, James (1964-), U.S.	Plot to bomb synagogues, military	Aspirational	Homegrown	African American	Wakin, 2009
42	Finton, Michael (1980-), U.S.	Plot to bomb federal building	Aspirational	Homegrown	Caucasion	Robinson 2009
43	Payen, Laguerre (1981-), U.S.	Plot to bomb synagogues, military	Aspirational	Homegrown	African (Haiti)	Wakin, 2009
44	Scruggs, Rasheed (1975-), U.S.	Murder of police officer	Executed	Homegrown	African American	Schilling, 2009
45	Williams, Onta (1976-), U.S.	Plot to bomb synagogues, military	Aspirational	Homegrown	African American	Wakin, 2009
46	Gardner, Kevin (1986-), Britain	Bomb plot, UK military	Operational	Homegrown	Caucasian	Brandon, 2009

APPENDIX 2

Database sources

ADL. (2008, November 5). *Extremism in the news.* Washington, DC: Anti-Defamation League.

Associated Press. (2004, October 20). *Spain says terrorist plotted "big blow."*

Associated Press. (2008, August 22). *Officials: Threat sent to McCain Colorado Office.*

Bakker, E. (2006). *Jihadi terrorists in Europe, their characteristics and the circumstances in which they joined the Jihad: An exploratory study.* The Hague: Clingendael Institute.

Blazak, R. (2009) The prison hate machine. *Criminology & Public Policy, 8,* 633-40.

Brandon, J. (2009). *Unlocking Al-Qaeda: Islamist extremism in British prisons.* London, UK: Quilliam.

Brisard, J. (2005). *Zarqawi: The new face of Al-Qaeda.* New York, NY: Other Press.

CNN.com. (2002, July 3). *Insight.* (Transcript).

Cardona, F. (2009, January 30). Obama-plot figure sentenced. *Denver Post.* Retrieved August 17, 2010, from http://www.denverpost.com/politics/ci_11586042?source=pkg

Cleaver, E. (1975). Excerpt from Soul on Ice. In J. Trupin (Ed.), *In prison: Writings and poems about the prison experience* (pp. 174-182). New York, NY: New American Library.

Cuthbertson, I. (2004). Prisons and the education of terrorists. *World Policy Journal, 21,* 15-22.

Elliott, M. (2002, February 16). The shoe bomber's world. *Time.*

Evans, M. (2009, March 13). Afghans pressed to explain release of Abdullah Ghulam Rasoul. *The Times* (London).

Flynn, K. & Garhardt, G. (1989). *The silent brotherhood: Inside America's terrorist underground.* New York, NY: Free Press.

Global Jihad. (2008). Safe Bourada. Retrieved July 6, 2010, from http://www.globaljihad.net/view_page.asp?id=904

Haahr, K. (2002). Algerian Salafists and the new face of terrorism in Spain. *Terrorism Monitor* 2, online version. Retrieved July 6, 2010, from http://www.jamestown.org/single/?no_cache=1&tx_ttnews%5Btt_news%5D=346

Hamm, M. (2002). *In bad company: America's terrorist underground.* Boston, MA: Northeastern University Press.

Hamm, M. (2007). *Terrorist recruitment in American correctional institutions: An exploratory study of non-traditional faith groups.* Washington, DC: National Institute of Justice.

History Commons. (2004). *Allekema Lamari.* Retrieved July 6, 2010, from http://www.historycommons.org/entity.jsp?entity=rachid_oulad_akcha_1

Lyall, S. (2007, July 6). Britain convicts 4 in separate terrorism trials. *New York Times.* Retrieved August 17, 2010, from

http://query.nytimes.com/gst/fullpage.html?res=9F0CEFD6123EF935
A35754C0A9619C8B63&sec=&spon=&pagewanted=2

Masood, S. (2007, July 25). Taliban leader is said to evade capture by blowing himself up. *New York Times*. Retrieved August 17, 2010, from http://query.nytimes.com/gst/fullpage.html?res=9801EEDF103CF936 A15754C0A9619C8B63&sec=&spon=

McLellan, V. & Avery, P. (1977). *The voices of guns; the definitive and dramatic story of the twenty-two-month career of the Symbionese Liberation Army, one of the most bizarre chapters in the history of the American Left.* New York, NY: Putnam.

Mili, H. (2006). Al-Qaeda's caucasian foot soldiers. *Terrorism Monitor, 4,* online version.

NEA. (2008). Al-Shebaab, 'stories from the Muhajireen: Ruben Shumpert.' Retrieved July 6, 2010, from http://revolution.thabaat.net/?p=741

Robinson, M. (2009, September 24). Michael Finton charged by FBI for attempting to bomb the Springfield Federal Courthouse. Associated Press.

Rotella, S. (2004, February 23). Holy water, hashish and Jihad. *Los Angles Times.*

Schilling, C. (2009, February 17) 'Jailhouse Islam' converts gun down U.S. cops. *WorldNetDaily.*

Schmidt, W. (1987, November 5). Chicago Journal; U.S. squares off against tough gang. *New York Times*. Retrieved August 17, 2010, from http://www.nytimes.com/1987/11/05/us/chicago-journal-us-squares-off-against-tough-gang.html?scp=437&sq=&st=nyt

Shumpert, R. (2006, June 5). Letter transmitted from Amir Abdul Muhaimeen to U.S. District Judge Marsha J. Pechman.

Teague, M. (2008). The radicals among us. *Militant Islam Monitor.org*. Retrieved July 6, 2010, from http://www.militantislammonitor.org/article/id/3877

Texas DCJ Records. (n.d.). John King. Retrieved July 6, 2010, from http://www.tdcj.state.tx.us/stat/offendersondrow.htm

Texas DCJ Records. (n.d.). Lawrence Brewer. Retrieved July 6, 2010, from http://www.tdcj.state.tx.us/stat/brewerlawrence.htm

Wakin, D. (2009, May 23). Imams reject talk that Islam radicalizes inmates. *New York Times*. Retrieved August 17, 2010, from http://www.nytimes.com/2009/05/24/nyregion/24convert.html

Worth, R. (2009, January 23). Guantanamo detainee resurfaces in terrorist group. *International Herald Tribune.*

Wright, L. (2006). *The looming tower: Al-Qaeda and the road to 9/11.* New York, NY: Knopf.

Legal Cases

USA v. Luqman Ameen Abdullah. Case: 2:09-mj-30436.

Politicization of Prisoners Is an Old and Contemporary STory

Todd R. Clear

Ever since the people invented the prison, they have been trying to figure out ways to avoid having prisons make problem people worse. Occupying a position at the far extreme of "getting worse" is, one might suppose, the act of becoming a terrorist. Mark Hamm's paper is about the way imprisonment now contributes to making some people worse through embracing terrorism.

Searching international databases of prisoner records, Hamm identifies 46 cases of prisoner radicalization in which a stretch of time in prison contributed to the radicalization process, leading eventually to a willingness to engage in terroristic acts. The case of Reuben Shumpert is described in detail to help illuminate the link between imprisonment, radicalization, and the life course of people who are incarcerated.

The paper shows that through the influence of prison and life-course events, a few people in prison end up embracing violent terrorism. Hamm does not say this directly, but the implication is that this is a potentially serious problem that deserves new policy development. Some of this will no doubt occur. I worry about it.

Prison as Political

When I was a first-year graduate student, back in the early 1970s, I wrote a paper for a class on incarceration in which I argued that every person behind bars could be considered a "political prisoner." The professor called me "naïve," scribbled a few ironic comments, and gave me an "A-."

I mention this little bit of personal history, because two of the cases contained in this database, Eldridge Cleaver and Donald DeFreeze, influenced my argument. George Jackson, the *Soledad Brother*, did not make this list but remains on mine.

These days, I am a bit less naïve than I was in my heady graduate school days. But the central argument I made in that paper, that the laws that put people behind bars do not protect the interests of the classes of people who go to prison equally to the interests of the classes who benefit most from the dominant social order (and, of course, capitalism) is no doubt as true today as it was then. When I first figured this out, back in my 20s, it was a very important idea to me. I can well imagine that it has similar salience for people who go to prison today, when *they* first figure it out.

Politics and power are closely affiliated forces, and if anything is true about prison, it is that power permeates the place. It should not surprise us that politics comes along for the ride. Many people who go to prison—maybe most—find themselves facing a painful self-accusation: "why am I here in this awful place?" Over the course of time behind bars, numerous explanations offer themselves, from sin to bad luck. One of the answers, inevitably, is that "the system" is stacked to produce a prison filled with young, poor—and, especially black—men. Once this idea is planted, radical thought is a natural, though not necessary, consequence.

GETTING HIT BY LIGHTNING AND WINNING THE LOTTERY

To me, it is surprising how limited the radical terror connection is for prisons. The Hamm database covers 42 years and half-dozen Western countries. In that time, perhaps 12 million people have left prisons in the United States, alone. To find only 46 cases of radical terror conversion among them is pretty extraordinary. Surely, as Hamm recognizes, the 46 cases underestimate the phenomenon. But even if we multiply the number of cases found by a factor of 100, the radical conversion rate is still something on the order of .0004. This is a bit better than the odds of winning the lottery, but not noticeably so.

To say that radicalization is remarkably rare is to say that it matters *not* as a substantive issue, but as a symbolic one.

To illustrate, let us consider the general case of the intervention principles that we would apply to preventing a rare event. When the base rate of an undesirable event is but .0004, we might be cautious in applying preventative interventions. We might consider doing so under three conditions: (1) the intervention is not very costly, (2) the intervention is not particularly intrusive into peoples' lives, and (3) the consequences of failing to intervene are extremely undesirable. That is, as a matter of fiscal and strategic principal, we should intervene to prevent rare events only if by doing so we avert the problem at very little cost for everyone else.

Of course this calculus does not apply to radical conversion to terrorism in prisons, any more than it applies to airport security from terrorism. That is because the *symbolic* importance of terrorism far exceeds its actual importance. It may be indisputably true that terrorist conversions in prison are about as rare as being hit by lightning, but that fact will have no policy bearing on the importance we might place on preventing such conversions. Some dissembling happens to the reasoning mind when the subject turns to terror.

DEPRIVATION OR IMPORTATION

There is a longstanding debate about the nature of the prison subculture; whether the cause of the particular normative subculture that arises in prisons is primarily due to the way a prison treats people, or to the values people who go to prison bring with them. What this debate has always missed is that prison deprivations and prior life experiences have always interacted in the prison context to produce the people who leave it.

Part of Hamm's point is that to understand the way people become drawn to radical terrorism as a philosophy of action, you have to understand both the gang-related experiences they bring with them to the prison and the influence of prison life, and these have to be integrated with the events that make radical action possible. Shumpert's story, as Hamm tells it, is an integration of pre-prison experiences, exposure to prison conditions in particular "pockets" of terrorism activity, and post-prison events.

Put in the correctional theory context, we might deduce from Hamm's data that homegrown terrorism in prison contexts arises when a ready convert is exposed to personally convincing rationales that resonate with those experiences while incarcerated, then engages a post-release network that provides opportunities to act on them.

Of course this is true. What a wildly unlikely story it would be if prison-based, homegrown terrorism arose in a different way other than this construction of the event-sequence of a life-course model. A feeling of injustice outside the prison, combined with a radical network inside, is undeniably the seed for radical conversion. Maybe the more noteworthy point is that, with so much social justice outside, and so much proselytizing inside, it is remarkable that radical conversion is as rare as it seems to be.

TERRORISTIC CONVERSION AND THE LIFE COURSE OF PEOPLE WHO GO TO PRISON

Offhand, if I were asked to name the most pressing problems of incarceration in the United States, my list would be pretty long before it got to "conversion-to-radical-terrorism." More than that, if I were asked to worry about aspects of the life course for people who go to prison, again I would have a bit of a list before getting to this topic. There are two reasons. One is that radical conversion that becomes operable in acts of terror is so rare. The other is that myriad problems besetting the prison system are not.

It does not belittle the broader problem of terroristic acts to say that prison-based terrorism is rare enough that we need not think of it as a major concern for US prison policy. Yet to the contrary, it is hard to imagine a US prison administrator who could say with conviction that radical ideologies of violence are of no concern. The administrator who ignores the ideology of mass violence is by any measure unwise.

But it is equally hard to imagine a response to this concern that—at least under current regimes—would not entail increased suppression. Thus is unfortunate, not only because history teaches that ideas are rarely successfully suppressed by overt power, but also because suppression is itself the kind of experience that has such deleterious impact on the life course for those who go to prison. Faced with the threat of terrorism arising from our prisons, the response will be predictable: we will make those prisons more likely to generate the kind of resentment that promotes radical ideological violence.

Conversion, Radicalization, and the Life Course: Future Research Questions

Margaret A. Zahn

WITH ASSISTANCE OF CHELLI PLUMMER

Professor Hamm's study attempts to shed some light on the controversial and insufficiently studied area of prison radicalization. He analyzes, using open sources, 46 cases over a 41-year time span, of prior prisoners who sometime post release (within months to 24 years) executed or attempted a terrorist attack. He suggests that certain institutions had higher numbers of radicalized prisoners, including Topas Prison in Spain and Britain's young offenders' penal system, especially Feltham Young Offender Institution in London. He suggests using a life course perspective as a way of studying prisoner radicalization and uses a case study of Ruben Shumpert; later convert Amir Abdul Muhammeen, to demonstrate its use. Hamm hopes, by tracing Shumpert's life course, he will demonstrate how inductive approaches will shed light on the degree of threat posed by prison radicalization. His attempt to study a very difficult area is to be applauded, and collecting many open source cases in one place is certainly helpful. There are however conceptual and methodological problems that it would be important to address.

Conceptual and Methodological Problems

Hamm uses open sources for the analysis, ranging from court documents to CNN reports. While he identifies his sources, he does not say how and why they were selected and what the similarities or differences between the various sources are. This may be particularly important since there is such a long time span involved and sources may differ substantially in different time periods and the quality of the sources vary as well.

Two, there are really a very small number of cases over a very long period of time. The small number may indicate the lack of radicalization in prisons, or it may indicate the lack of attention to these issues in open source reports. However, the small number across such a long time span fails to address the changing contexts which would occur over this lengthy period and how that may impact radicalization. This problem is exacerbated by the fact that cases from multiple nations from different time periods are used. Hamm includes both US prisoners and those in Europe and in the Middle East. While each situation is worth examination, the contexts of the prison experience in each of these settings may be sufficiently different to warrant separate analyses. For example, many homegrown Muslim terrorists in Europe derive from a situation of discriminatory practices against Muslims in France and England. There may be less discrimination against Muslims in the United States and so less source for this grievance (Sageman, 2008). There are not enough cases in his examination to do a good comparison between radicalization in these multiple countries or to provide a good picture of how prisons serve as a context for radicalization (such would require deeper analysis of prison systems). Nor is there enough information on individuals who become radicalized to determine similarities in individual level change. More in-depth information on each case could augment this.

An additional significant problem is Hamm's definition of radicalization, i.e., conversion to religions that may be perceived as espousing ideologies of intolerance and violence.

While some of the religions he lists, e.g., Moorish Science Temple and Salafi-Jihadism would seem to fit the definition, Sunni-Muslim may not. Further, converting to a belief system that espouses violence and actually committing violence are related but not coterminous. In fact, as McCauley and Moskalenko (2008) indicate separate additional factors may influence executing a violent act. For example, evidence from terrorist groups suggests that attacks against the group may accelerate the desire for violent action. Further, radicalization within the group can intensify personal radicalization as members may be in competition to prove their commitment to the cause. Additionally, the lag time between conversion and terrorist attack (five or more years in a quarter of the cases) with some being as long as 24 years, can be problematic in drawing any conclusions. It is difficult to suggest that radicalization in prison is the key element, because there are so many other transitions (occurrences) along the life course, that lengthy time lags do not take into account.

He also does not determine how the radicalization actually occurred and what the evidence of this is. The time of radicalization is hazy, leaving the assumption that radicalization occurred in prison. For cases such as Al-Zawahiri, it is difficult to determine exactly when Islamic faith became radicalized belief. Further, as Useem and Obie (2009) point out, the fact that you commit a terrorist act following a stint in prison doesn't prove that prison is the radicalizing influence. He suggests that radicalized people go on to commit violent acts subsequent to prison. However, without a comparison group of inmates who were not radicalized, it is less tenable to suggest that radicalization has led to these violent outcomes. In sum, how these changes relate to violence in support of ideology remains a question.

Hamm also suggests based on his study that certain institutions are more likely to foster radicalization. He, however, does not indicate what the nature of these institutions, their structure, and the ways that structure of prisons can impact radicalization. Mark Colvin's (2007) discussion of Coercion and Social Support theory, in relation to a penitentiary in New Mexico, may be of special relevance here. In particular, he suggests that periods of reduced coercive restrictions and higher levels of institutional social support produce higher levels of pro-social behavior and positive relations between staff and inmates. Perhaps Marquart's (2007) assertion that in regard to authority and power in prison either you run it or they will is part of the explanation. Strong leadership can be a deterrent to prison violence and the spread of violent thinking. It would be especially helpful if Hamm spelled out in more detail the characteristics of these "high radicalization prisons" to determine the way that contexts affects violence and radicalization. Similarly, other research, including Hamm's past research (2008, 2009), regarding radicalization suggests that charismatic leaders are of importance to recruiting and sustaining the radical impulse. Hamm confirms this with discussion of the Al-Zarqawi case; however, he could go much further by determining who leaders were in the other prisons during the time period. This would be a feasible exploration that would add to the substance of the claim that certain institutions were more conductive to radicalization than others. This may be a feasible next step for this research.

Hamm suggests that the life course perspective would be of value in understanding radicalization. He includes only one case and tries to show how the life course of Shumpert demonstrates this. However, life course is affected by opportunity and incentives so perhaps opportunity theory and incentives to engage in terrorism need more attention in this particular trajectory. The inclusion of life course and developmental perspectives, however, are of value

In ways that need further exploration, as Hamm finds, young inmates are more vulnerable to conversion to radical ideologies. Studies of conversion, more generally, have found the majority of conversions to any faith occur in young adulthood. This age-related stage, then, is the same in the prison community as in the wider community. Young adulthood seems to be a time of "cognitive opening" and conversion to faiths occur with that opening. In fact, it would seem that a developmental perspective involving development from adolescence to young adulthood plays a role in the prison radicalization issue.

Age-graded transitions may occur simultaneously with changes in social settings. This occurs when a young adult goes to college or to prison. It would seem that when times of transitions in life settings coincide with age graded transitions the most personal change will occur. Conversion in prison (whether of the radicalized or non-radicalized form) serves purposes for prisoners which are important in the inmate creating a new life narrative. Maruna, Wilson, and Curran (2006) suggest that Islam in particular serves to empower the powerless and give one's life a higher meaning. All the more important when transitioning to adulthood. Examining further how developmental and life course perspectives enhance studies of radicalization is proposed in Hamm's paper. Future studies must develop this further.

POLICY IMPLICATIONS

While Hamm proposes some new leads in prison radicalization research, the very small number of cases over such a long time span suggests that radicalization to "Jihadist" activities may not be a major risk in American prisons. Radicalization to other ideologies, such as the Aryan Brotherhood, may need more attention as the incidents of hate crimes rises nationally, conversion to radical Islam may not warrant extensive attention, even with high levels of conversions to Muslim traditions. Useem and Obie (2009), based on interviews in ten correctional departments and one municipal jail system, including interviews with 210 prison officials and 270 inmates who volunteered to be interviewed, concluded that the chances for terrorist radicalization are fairly low and falling. This conclusion suggests that inmates are focused more on wanting to get home, and they do not perceive America as the enemy. They may see the judicial and/or penal system as the enemy, but they are Americans. The fact that they are somewhat patriotic would suggest that it would be more difficult for terrorist cells to be highly supported among prison inmates. Further, prisons have become more orderly and under control in the past two decades, suggesting that all forms of violence from internal murder to supporting terrorism have been reduced (Useem & Obie, 2009). In addition, with the increasing vigilance of administrators, as well as patriotic leanings of inmates, the chances of a number of radicalized cells in prisons would seem to be low. This would be consistent with the notion that the need for social support is important for an ideology to be adopted, and while the Muslim faith may be widely adopted, killing in the name of a fringe element of it may not.

The RAND report *Social Science for Counterterrorism: Putting the Pieces Together* (2009) provides a long list of research-identified factors that can contribute to the radicalization process. While this report does not focus on radicalization in prisons many of these factors would not seem to apply well to US prison situations, although others may. According to the report , radicalization to Islamic "jihad" is more likely in the following situations: religious settings advocating violence; family members encourage involvement in radical ideology; feelings of alienation from a current situation or setting (as when a Muslim becomes a student at an American university) desire for an independent state or removal of some from their current nation state; perceived social economic, political discrimination; desire to respond to grievance including revenge against those who have harmed one or one's family; perceived rewards including religious rewards, social status, or economic rewards; excitement. For many of these factors (not all), there would seem to be small incentives for US-born inmates to find "jihad" as an attractive an alternative, as an Egyptian or Palestinian may. For example, most prisoners want to "go home" not see themselves as wanting to leave the United States; and discrimination may be viewed as racially based, not politically or religiously based. Further, rewards for suicide bombing (such as a place in heaven) may not be attractive to those more oriented to going home—meaning Detroit, Chicago, LA.

While conversion to Islam may provide a structure and meaning to their lives in prison, and perhaps beyond, it is a greater leap to take that structure and meaning to include attacking other Americans in their home communities in order to secure a "new world" or join an afterlife. Some of the factors associated with radicalization would suggest that American prisons may be more of a breeding ground for radicalization to race based hate groups than radicalization to holy war against the United States. In either case, while vigilance may be warranted, panic and high levels of counterterrorist action would appear not to be.

REFERENCES

Colvin, M. (2007). Applying differential coercion and social support theory to prison organizations: The case of the penitentiary of New Mexico. *The Prison Journal, 87*, 367-387.

Davis, P. & Cragin, K. (2009). *Social science for counterterrorism: Putting the pieces together.* Santa Monica, CA: Rand Corporation, Rand Monograph Series.

Hamm, M. (2008). Prisoner radicalization: Assessing the threat in U.S. correctional institutions. *NIJ Journal, 261, 14*-19.

Hamm, M. (2009). Prison Islam in the age of sacred terror. *British Journal of Criminology, 49,* 667-85.

Marquart, J. (2007). Addicted to prisons and asking 'Why don't they riot?' *Criminology and Public Policy 7*(1), 153-158.

Maruna, S., Wilson, L., & Curran, K. (2006). Why God is often found behind bars: Prison conversions and the crisis of self-narrative. *Research in Human Development. 3*(2&3), 161-184.

McCauley, C. & Moskalenko, S. (2008). Mechanisms of political radicalization: Pathways toward terrorism. *Terrorism and Political Violence 20,* 415-433.

Sageman, M. (2008). *Leaderless Jihad: Terrorist networks in the twenty-first century.* Philadelphia, PA: University of Pennsylvania Press.

Useem, B. & Clayton, O. (2009). Radicalization of U.S. prisoners. *Criminology & Public Policy, 8*(3), 561-592.

Webb, V. (2010). Searching for a needle in the haystack: A look at hypotheses and explanations for the low prevalence of radicalization in American prisons. In N. Frost, J. Freilich, & T. Clear (Eds.), *Contemporary issues in criminal justice policy* (pp. 367-370). Belmont, CA: Wadsworth.

ECONOMY

FAMILY AND NEIGHBORHOOD EFFECTS ON YOUTH VIOLENCE: DOES COMMUNITY ECONOMIC DEVELOPMENT INCREASE ADOLESCENT WELL-BEING?

JOHN M. MACDONALD
RICKY BLUTHENTHAL
ROBERT STOKES
BEN GRUNWALD

ABSTRACT

There is a well established link between structural disadvantage and negative outcomes for youth including criminal victimization. Yet, there are few examples of community-level responses that show measurable effects on the underlying community conditions that lead to these disparities. Community economic development models like the business improvement district (BID) that focus on improving neighborhood environments of areas may be useful framework for fostering systemic changes in areas and reducing the prevalence of criminal victimization. In this article, we analyze the relationship between family and neighborhood features and victimization outcomes through a neighborhood-matching strategy that compares households in BID and non-BID areas exposed to similar neighborhood structural characteristics. Our analysis shows that the presence of a BID in a neighborhood is not strongly associated with victimization outcomes. Rather, traditional measures of family social control and neighborhood collective efficacy remain key covariates of violence outcomes. Youth living in immigrant households also are at a reduced risk for experiencing victimization compared to similarly situated youth with U.S.-born parents. These findings occur in cross-sectional and longitudinal analyses. We discuss the implications of this work for theories of neighborhood dynamics and public policy discussions on the role of community economic development.

INTRODUCTION

Social inequalities in crime and violence remain a stable feature of American city life. Neighborhoods characterized by high rates of family disruption, unemployment, concentrated poverty, and inaccessibility to economic opportunities appear particularly vulnerable to youth violence (Sampson & Lauritsen, 1994; Moore & Tonry, 1998). Eighty years of social science research has generated numerous theoretical explanations for these relationships, but few answers for how to create public policies that lead to necessary community change.

Urban sociology in the first half of the 20th century chronicled the correlation between neighborhood environmental factors (e.g., poverty, percentage of single-parent households, population mobility, percentage foreign born) and juvenile delinquency, positing that neighborhood attributes influenced crime through their impact on community-level disorder, residential cohesion, and informal social control. Poverty and family disruption, for example, make it difficult for residents to establish common values and engage in relationships of mutual trust that establish neighborhood social control (Park, 1915; Shaw & McKay, 1942; Kornhauser, 1978). A broad literature has focused on identifying these patterns of community social disorganization and their relationship to violent behaviors, including those that occur among youth (Sampson & Lauritsen, 1994). Another line of research examines the role of community-based economic development and its broader role in facilitating community stability (Porter, 1997). Both of these streams of research have raised attention to community-level processes and their influence on health outcomes including youth violence (see Kawachi & Berkman, 2003).

Public-policy research, however, has yet to identify specific, actionable community-level interventions that show effective results in mediating the influence of social and economic disparities on crime and violence (see Sampson, 1995; Taylor, 2001). For example, the majority of evaluations of community-level and community-based crime or violence prevention initiatives find that they have had little or no impact on modifying the social forces associated with these outcomes (Welsh & Hoshi, 2002).

In this article, we examine the community economic development model of the business improvement district (BID) as an example of a community-level intervention that may produce sustainable positive changes in neighborhood environments and reduce the incidence of youth violence. BIDs, by design, are grassroots, community-level interventions—though centered on the business community rather than the residential community—that are theoretically tied to the social processes outlined in community-based theories of neighborhood disorder and violence. BID activities often focus on addressing community-level processes, such as order maintenance, formal and informal social control, and neighborhood cohesion that research has identified are associated with lower rates of interpersonal violence.

Drawing on prior literature on the relationship among economic development, community organization, and violence, we argue that the social connections established through BIDs could reduce youth violence rates in surrounding residential communities through their efforts at fostering collective community action toward enhancing the safety and attractiveness of neighborhood commercial areas. We link community economic development literature to social disorganization theory in suggesting that a key ingredient to improvements in youth violence is community-level change driven by local actors. To examine the effects of

BIDs we analyze longitudinal self-reported responses from 626 households situated in 213 Los Angeles neighborhoods that assess family and neighborhood features of life and exposure to youth violence outcomes over time. We apply a sampling strategy that matches households in neighborhoods exposed to BIDs to households in non-BID exposed neighborhoods with similar structural features of neighborhood disadvantage. We thus bring together a research design and data collection strategy that provides an opportunity for examining the role of this community economic development approach in improving cross-sectional and longitudinal outcomes for youth in disadvantage neighborhoods.

THEORETICAL LINKS BETWEEN COMMUNITY FEATURES AND VIOLENCE

Despite declines in violent offending and victimization rates for youth during the 1990s (see Blumstein, Rivara, & Rosenfeld, 2000; Cook & Laub, 2002), violence remains a serious social policy concern for adolescents, especially among poor and minority youth, who continue to suffer the negative impact of persistent social inequalities (McLaughlin, Yelon, Ivatury, & Sugerman, 2000). Homicide remains a leading cause of death for African American youth and second leading cause of death among Hispanic youth, and less-than-lethal forms of violence remain prevalent and reflect similar racial disparities (see Anderson & Smith, 2009; Grunbaum et al., 2004; Sampson & Lauritsen, 1994; Hawkins et al., 1998). Although there has been a proliferation of research examining community-based factors related to violence most often committed and experienced by youth and young adults (Krivo & Peterson, 2000; Land, McCall, & Cohen 1990; Sampson, 1987; Sampson, Raudenbush, & Earls, 1997; Sampson, Morenoff, & Raudenbush, 2005), few studies have examined how changes in community conditions influence youth violence (see Messner, Raffalovich, & McMillan, 2001).

Research indicates that African Americans, whites, and Hispanics live in vastly different neighborhood contexts (Krivo & Peterson, 2000; Sampson & Wilson, 1995), and that aggregate measures of family disruption (e.g., single-parent heads of household) are particularly important for explaining aggregate age patterns of violence for African American youth (Glaeser & Sacerdote, 1999; Ousey, 2000; Sampson, 1987; Sampson et al., 1997; Shihadeh & Steffensmeier, 1994). Racial differences in youth-violence outcomes are largely accounted for by the rate of single-parent households and concentrated poverty in inner-city neighborhoods (see Sampson et al., 2005).

The structural covariates of youth violence found in contemporary research are consistent with the early work on neighborhood dynamics and their relationship to gangs and juvenile delinquency pioneered by sociologists at the University of Chicago (Thrasher, 1927; Shaw & McKay, 1942). Sprung from the theory of *social ecology*—that is, the idea that communities develop through a natural, organic process—this research suggested that community rates of juvenile delinquency and violence could be explained through the principle of *social disorganization*, or the inability of residents to form common values and maintain effective social controls (Bursik, 1988; Kornhauser, 1978; Sampson & Groves, 1989).

There are various community-level mechanisms for explaining how the presence of economic deprivation for families places children at an increased risk of living in communities characterized by higher rates of violence. The opportunity structure for youth violence appears to change with higher rates of poverty and its association with greater concentrations of delinquent or unsupervised peer groups (Elliott, Huizinga, & Menard, 1989). Communities immersed in problems associated with gangs and drug distribution, for example, are more likely to have predatory environments that disable informal social control and invite violent and otherwise illegal activity by youth (Anderson, 1998; Herrenkohl et al., 2000; McLaughlin et al., 2000; St. Jean, 2007).

The lack of economic opportunities for families in inner-city neighborhoods is associated with increased idleness, a decreased pool of employed men who are attractive spousal partners, a decreased level of community supervision of youth, and a lower rates of participation in social organizations that bond youth to larger institutions of social control (e.g., church, prosocial youth activities; school programs) (Sampson, 1987; Wilson, 1987; Janowitz, 1975; Kornhauser, 1978).

Social disorganization theory suggests that community organization is an important resource on which parents can draw to maintain supervision and control of youth (Bursik, 1988; Coleman, 1988; Sampson, 1987; Shaw & McKay, 1942). A key to this perspective is the influence of community normative social control exercised by residents themselves on youth (Bursik, 1988; Kornhauser, 1978; Sampson & Groves, 1989). Results from work on the Project on Human Development in Chicago Neighborhoods further confirms the social disorganization perspective and finds that concentrated poverty affects violence, but its impact is mediated by the willingness of residents to come together to form a common set of values and engage in informal social-control practices, commonly referred to as *collective efficacy* (Sampson et al., 1997; Sampson & Raudenbush, 1999; Morenoff, Sampson, & Raudenbush, 2001).

The literature is clear in pointing to the importance of community-contextual factors in understanding the variation in adult and adolescent violence at various levels of aggregation (Sampson & Lauritsen, 1994; Sampson et al., 2005). Importantly, research suggests that economic disadvantage is concentrated within ecological contexts or specific types of neighborhoods (Sampson et al., 2005). Furthermore, increases in crime and violence at the community-level appear to further disintegrate communities by making them even less attractive to business investment, thus producing a continued spiral of decay (Porter, 1997; Skogan, 1990). Communities characterized by these social and economic problems associated with crime and violence also have a decreased ability to marshal city services to help ameliorate poor physical and social conditions (Bursik & Grasmick, 1993).

In other words, concentrated poverty is associated with a lack of both economic and political capital to create change, both important aspects to community revitalization.

It is distressing that there are few examples in the social science literature demonstrating how communities can effectively reduce these social disparities. Early work on the community-level dynamics of delinquency led to the creation of community organizations—such as the Chicago Area Project (CAP)—that were designed to engage delinquent youth, as well as provide economic opportunities and job-training programs in disadvantaged neighborhoods. CAP was designed specifically to mobilize local, informal social control in disadvantaged Chicago neighborhoods by providing alternative prosocial activities for youth, improving the physical environment of communities (e.g., fixing dilapidated housing and sanitation), and improving coordination with city and social services (e.g., police, social work agencies). Unfortunately, evaluations of CAP found that it had only modest success (Kobrin, 1959; Finestone, 1976). Research indicates that positive community-level change is possible even in disadvantaged areas (Taub, Taylor, & Dunham, 1984; Boston & Ross, 1997), but there is no record of substantial success in modifying community-level processes associated with negative youth outcomes associated with concentrated disadvantage. Very little work has identified and tested actionable ways of modifying the social and physical environment to facilitate improved economic opportunities and reduce negative outcomes for youth in distressed environments. This work seeks to assess whether demonstrable improvements in local commercial areas illicit positive social externalities to families in adjacent residential communities.

EXISTING POLICY TARGETING COMMUNITY-LEVEL FACTORS

Some scholars point to economic revitalization efforts in many downtown or inner-city neighborhoods as examples of community-level change, but these case studies often describe examples of neighborhoods that have undergone significant gentrification through the influx of upper-class individuals and the subsequent decamping of poverty-stricken residents (Simon, 2001).

Over the past three decades, policymakers have pursued a wide range of publicly funded programs designed to combat concentrated poverty and related social disadvantage in urban areas. Many state governments, for example, began designating Enterprise Zones in poor urban neighborhoods in the 1980s. The federal government followed suit by enacting its own Enterprise Zone program in the early 1990s. Enterprise Zones attempt to revitalize urban neighborhoods by attracting business investment through commercial and industrial deregulation and tax abatement (Riposa, 1996). These efforts seek to improve community economic development primarily through job creation. Research into the efficacy of Enterprise Zones has yielded inconsistent findings with a number of studies examining an array of zones, outcome variables, and programmatic efforts. In sum, the most recent evaluations of Enterprise Zone programs indicate little evidence of significant improvement in employment for residents of Enterprise Zone communities (Elvery, 2009; Neumark & Kolko, 2010 [unpublished]; Bondonio & Greenbaum, 2005; Greenbaum & Engberg, 2004).

The shift in federal urban policy came as the Democrats took over the White House in 1992. This shift led to the federal Empowerment Zones (EZs) program. Federal EZs were first established in 1993 and added social services and employment training to the existing tax incentive and regulatory relief strategies embodied by local Enterprise Zone programs. In short, EZs were designed to constitute a "comprehensive attack on urban distress by blending economic tax incentives and social services in a coordinated effort among federal agencies and local communities" (Riposa, 1996, p. 545). EZs combine two important community development strategies. First, they provided substantial financial incentives to local businesses: including tax-exempt loans, accelerated tax write-offs for property depreciation, and tax credits for employers of EZ residents. In 1999, the General Accounting Office (GAO) estimated that these financial incentives would cost roughly $2.5 billion over the first ten years of the program (U.S. GAO, 1999). Second, federal EZs promoted local community engagement by requiring funding recipients to engage community partners in the planning and delivery of their social service programming. A total of six EZs were authorized and each received block grants of $100 million. Additional EZs were established later, but these sites received less funding for social service and community programs.

Few rigorous evaluations of the EZ program are available. An interim assessment conducted by Abt Associates finds that EZs have a substantial effect on job creation (Hebert, Vidal, Mills, James, & Gruenstein, 2001). A number of methodological concerns, such as the lack of equivalent comparison groups, suggest these findings are inconclusive (Busso & Kline, 2008). Oakley and Tsao (2006) examined the impact of the EZ designation on poverty, employment and income in Baltimore, Chicago, Detroit, and New York City, four of the six original sites and found a few, albeit inconsistent effects. Busso and Kline (2008) found modest improvements in employment and poverty by comparing areas in cities that were designated EZs to areas that applied for EZ designation, but ultimately did not receive funding. Krupka and Noonan (2009) found that EZ designation was correlated with increased property values. It is not clear, however, whether the increase in property values helps the quality of life of existing residents, or is merely an increase in the perceived value of properties due to EZ designation. Overall, the effects of EZs on local communities appear positive but unimpressive, particularly given the cost of the program. One assessment of the Chicago Empowerment Zone suggests that zones may insufficiently emphasize community involvement and local partnerships (Oakley & Tsao, 2007). This observation may help explain the modest economic outcomes, while outcomes related to participatory politics have gone largely unexamined.

The seeming failure of publicly funded urban revitalization efforts to show measurable results has led to a call for community economic development (CED) models. CED models typically utilize established local community-based nonprofits in both policy development and implementation efforts. In effect, these organizations take the place of traditional governmental funded programs in developing housing, employment, or business opportunities to enhance the quality of life for local residents in defined community boundaries (Simon, 2001). Such an approach to community revitalization fits within a sociological perspective of social disorganization by focusing on fostering change at the grassroots, community level. CED models attempt to facilitate change at the community level relying on the existing social, political, and economic capital of residents and business merchants within recognized community boundaries to foster community revitalization (DeFilippis & Saegart, 2008). Perhaps local development initiatives, which place greater emphasis on the collective participation of local leaders, organizations, and businesses, may provide greater opportunity for neighborhood improvement.

Business improvement districts (BIDs) are one example of such an approach. Under the BID model special assessments are charged on commercial properties located within designated business areas to augment traditional municipal services including sanitation, security, place marketing, and urban planning (Mitchell, 2001). Some BIDs in the United States offer a wider range of services, including homeless outreach, employment and youth programming, and school-based youth activities (Stokes, 2002). Although organized by private-sector interest groups, the majority of BIDs are publicly controlled entities, chartered and regulated by general-purpose governments (Briffault, 1999). Services delivered through BID assessment schemes do not replace public services, but rather offer an enhancement in a geographically defined district. BID services typically are directed toward sanitation and security in commonly used areas. These services and their delineation are analogous to the common-area security and social control functions seen in shopping centers, apartment complexes, and with home owners associations that attempt to regulate conduct and norms in common areas.

Many BIDs have increased their service roles in an attempt to broaden their impact on economic-development and community change. While some have challenged the private sector interests of BIDs and the potential conflicts that arise when business interests become involved in the management of public spaces (Harcourt, 2005), their growth is congruent with a general movement away from publicly controlled redevelopment efforts, toward nonprofit development corporations (Fainstein, 1994; Hall & Hubbard, 1998). Consistent with sociological theories of neighborhood control (Shaw & McKay, 1942), BIDs fit into a movement away from wide-scale collective action toward a geographically targeted, place- or community-based solution to public problems, including crime and violence (Mallet, 1993).

The BID model represents a type of community organization in which board members consist of commercial landowners, merchants, elected officials, and local resident groups who interact with and public agencies in charge of delivering services to their areas (e.g., police, sanitation, public works, parks). BIDs bring additional resources to bear, both in fiscal and political terms, and use these resources to provide their own services, as well as advocate for more attentive public services. To this end, BIDs offer improved defensible space (Newman, 1995) and territorial functioning (Taylor, Gottfredson, & Brower, 1984), as well as providing a place-management function that was missing from many public urban-management schemes (Felson, 1995). Thus, BIDs can be seen as providing an answer to social disorganization by fostering increased interaction between the community and public service providers in increasing the overall level of informal social control within a geographic area.

Collectively, businesses have a strong interest in establishing and maintaining a safe place to attract customers, whereas individually, business owners have an interest in preserving safety for themselves and their employees. Commercial districts are thus often characterized by high levels of community organization through business member organizations and offer higher levels of informal and formal surveillance than do residential areas (Mazerolle, Kadleck, & Roehl, 1998). They possess more resources to deal with local community problems. Moreover, the political importance of promoting commercial activity in urban areas often results in significant public resource allocation to promote this end. Relatedly, CED models have become inextricable linked to revitalization in communities struggling to create employment options for under skilled residents (Wiewel, Teitz, & Giloth, 1993).

Economic-development planners in urban areas can no longer ignore crime and other incivilities in their attempts to foster redevelopment in urban neighborhood settings. Some research has examined the effects of BID on officially reported crime and found significant associations between the establishment and presence of BIDs and a lower than expected incidence of property, robbery, and total reported index offenses in Philadelphia, Pennsylvania, and Los Angeles, California (see Hoyt, 2004; Brooks, 2008; MacDonald, Golinelli, Stokes, & Bluthenthal, 2010; Cook & MacDonald, 2010). These studies rely on official statistics and do not examine the broader social context of crime and violence experienced by the most vulnerable segments of neighborhoods – youth. Nor do they link localized crime prevention successes with more generalized positive social outcomes for communities. Research indicates that crime commission and victimization rates are highest during adolescent years (Farrington, 1989; Thornberry & Krohn, 2000). If community economic development models like BIDs truly change the level of social control for surrounding neighborhoods, these changes should be apparent in the adolescent share of the population most prone to criminal victimization.

HYPOTHESIS

BID activities are consistent with prior research on the social ecological correlates of crime and violence and may thus be a useful framework for assessing policy innovation on community change. We theorize that variations across communities in the levels of concentrated disadvantage, residential stability, and the concentration of disadvantaged ethnic and racial minorities act as structural antecedents of social disorganization (e.g., poor residential cohesion, physical and social deterioration of the physical environment, and lack of employment opportunities), which, in turn, fosters an environment in which violence is more likely to occur. According to this theoretical perspective, BIDs can mediate the effects of these structural sources of disadvantage by increasing the likelihood of community organization and helping improve the social and physical environment of communities. BID activities aimed at improving the physical environment and increasing economic viability should, in turn, aid in increasing the level of residential social cohesion and foster neighborhood environments less conducive to criminal victimization.

We examine the hypothesized relationship between BIDs and victimization through an examination of residents living in and around neighborhoods exposed to BIDs in Los Angeles, California. Los Angeles was selected because of its racially and ethnically diverse population and its large number of BIDs in a variety of city locations. Los Angeles is a major destination for immigrants, presenting an additional opportunity for examining how neighborhood dynamics of crime reflect racial, ethnic, and economic disparities are similar to other large U.S. cities. The L.A. BID program started in 1994 with the establishment of a single, merchant-based district. At the start of this study, there were a total of 30 established BIDs in L.A., located in 14 of the city's 15 council districts. Neighborhoods exposed to BIDs in L.A. vary greatly in their demographic and income characteristics, from considerably lower-to-lower levels of concentrated poverty and higher-to-lower levels of immigrant and Hispanic households than the city average, reflecting a presence of BIDs in areas of both relative poverty and relative affluence.[1] The geographic diversity of BIDs in Los Angeles and the variation in the demographic and income profile of households in their surrounding neighborhoods allowed us to study their association with youth violence outcomes across a diverse set of neighborhoods over two points in time.

DATA AND METHOD

Neighborhood data

To examine whether BIDs are associated with community-level processes linked to youth violence, we conducted a household survey of parents and adolescents living in L.A. neighborhoods exposed to BIDs and a matched group of neighborhoods not exposed to BIDs. The primary purpose of the household survey was to assess the dynamics of youth violence at both the individual and neighborhood levels and to examine whether BIDs have any effect on incidence of youth violence in neighborhoods. To develop a sampling frame whereby residents living in BID areas could be compared to those living in comparable non-BID areas, we relied on census tract–level data detailing various household-, family-, and individual-level indicators that have been shown in prior research to be correlated with area differences in crime and other negative health outcomes (see Land et al., 1990; Sampson, Morenoff, & Gannon-Rowley, 2002; Sampson et al., 2005).

These categories include race and ethnicity, economics and earnings, household characteristics, and residential unit characteristics. Race and ethnicity data include the percentage of various racial representations in a given neighborhood, as well as the percentages of Latino and non-Latino populations. Also represented in this category is the percentage of residents born outside the United States. Economics and earnings variables include mean household earnings, the percentage of households receiving governmental assistance (welfare), and the percentage of households with incomes below the poverty line. Household characteristics include the percentage of female-headed households.[2] Residential-unit characteristics include the age of dwelling, whether they are owner occupied, and the residential density in an area.

To investigate the effects that the presence of a BID has on youth violence, geographic shape files for the census tracts in the city of Los Angeles were used to map the locations of all tracts (U.S. Census 2000 Summary File 1 (SF 1), (SF 2), (SF 3) undated)[3] and their relationship to BID areas. A shape file containing the 30 established BIDs was obtained from the City of Los Angeles Office of the City Clerk (undated) and overlaid with the census-tract files. These census-tract measures were then applied to a matching algorithm to establish a comparison group of neighborhoods that look like BID neighborhoods. In addition to census-level data and BID locations, crime data provided by the LAPD were also integrated into a geographic file. Specifically, crime offense codes were abstracted for the smallest geographic unit reported by the police—the police reporting district (RD). RD data include the count of each offense classification for years 1994 to 2005. There are, on average, about 1.2 RDs per census tract, and each is, on average, 2.1 square miles.[4] We included only the counts for homicide and robbery because they are less susceptible to differences in under-reporting and have consistently been shown to have higher reliability than other reported crime outcomes (Sampson, 1987; Hindelang, Hirschi, & Weis, 1981).

All three data sources (census, BID locations, and crime reports) were spatially integrated with ArcMap™ software, a GIS program. In ArcMap software, tabulated data were merged with corresponding geographic area (tracts, RDs, and BIDs). Once mapped, the various shape files were then layered and integrated by using a distance function for all tracts adjoining

BIDs, which serve as the treatment group of neighborhoods. Because census tracts, BID areas, and police RDs all have different geographic shapes, areal interpolation was used to reconfigure all data sources into the same geographic unit. For the purposes of the present analysis, census tracts were chosen as the target geographic zone, and BID areas and police RDs were interpolated into tract areas using a spatial weight that calculated the proportion of area overlap between the source and target zones.

Neighborhood census tracts were not randomly assigned to receive a BID. Therefore, it is likely that there are household and economic features of areas that are associated with BID formation. If one compares neighborhoods with BIDs to a set of neighborhoods without a BID but does not take into account the differences in selection, the effects observed will be confounded by these characteristics of BID assignment. In particular, it is important to match the BID neighborhoods with the non-BID neighborhoods with respect to all those characteristics that are associated with both the BID-assignment process and the outcome of interest: youth violence.

Based on prior literature on neighborhood effects on youth violence, we selected 10 features for matching BID and non-BID tracts (see Sampson et al., 2005). This matching was based on tract-level characteristics taken from the 2000 census related to (1) *concentrated disadvantage* (percentage of people with incomes below the poverty line, percentage of female single parents with children under 18, percentage of families on welfare, and percentage unemployed) (see Sampson et al., 2005); (2) *age structure* (percentage of the population who are male and under 25 years of age); (3) *residential stability* (percentage of units occupied for five years or more, percentage of housing units that are owner occupied); (4) *racial composition* (e.g., percentage Latino, percentage foreign born); and (5) *population density* (e.g., population per square mile) (see Table 1).

Census tracts were chosen as the sampling unit for analysis because they are designed to enclose populations and neighborhoods that are relatively homogenous and contain populations in the range of 2,000–10,000 (mean: 4,000). They are small enough to study population-level effects in a homogenous population but large enough to sample, from an estimate, neighborhood effects for the entire set of neighborhoods that are exposed to BIDs and their relationship with the social, economic, and environmental factors in the proposed study. We recognize that the selection of census tracts provides some limitations to the refinement of approximating neighborhoods and therefore conducted a series of sensitivity analyses that specifically compares the results using other levels of neighborhood aggregation (e.g., neighborhood clusters that are larger than census tracts).[5]

Sampling strategy

Respondents for this study were selected from households in neighborhoods (census tracts) that have an established BID program and from the comparison group of matched neighborhoods lacking an established BID program. To select households in BID and non-BID areas that were exposed to similar structural features, we designed a sample allocation that would match residents living in BID neighborhoods to those living in non-BID neighborhoods in Los Angeles. There were a total of 147 census tracts that bordered the 30 established BIDs in Los Angeles. The sample design for the neighborhood household survey allocated a minimum number of observations (approximately 10) from each of the 147 census tracts that overlap with a BID in Los Angeles. From 2000 census data, we obtained an estimate of what the sample of a household would look like, on average, from neighborhoods (BID sample) that are exposed to the BID treatment. The second column of Table 1 indicates the characteristics of the BID sample that we expected to observe from census data.

When selecting households from non-BID comparison tracts, random sampling would not likely generate a sample with characteristics similar to those living in BID exposed neighborhoods. Therefore, we developed a targeted sample allocation algorithm that samples from non-BID areas so that the control sample has household characteristics similar to those of the expected BID sample (see Cormen, Leiserson, Rivest, & Steine, 2001). This approach effectively creates a balance between BID (treatment) and non-BID (control) neighborhoods.

There were 690 non-BID census tracts in Los Angeles. Census data indicate that these tracts each have up to 2,300 households with children. We constrained the allocation so that we would sample no more than 50 households in a census tract, nor would we allocate more than half of those households with children within a census tract to the sample. Furthermore, if we allocated any sampling effort to a census tract, we required that at least 10 households be surveyed from that census tract. The sample-allocation algorithm proceeded sequentially through the following seven steps:

> Set the sample allocation for each of the 690 non-BID census tracts to 0.
> Find the census tract, i, that has a distribution of households most similar to the BID sample's distribution.
> Allocate at least 10 households from census tract i to the sample.
> Find the census tract, j, such that, if allocating one household from that census tract to the sample, the non-BID sample would be most similar to the BID sample.
> If the allocation to census tract j exceeds 50 or exceeds half of the number of households with children, then discard census tract j and return to step 4.
> Increase the sample allocation for census tract j by one household. If the allocation to census tract j is less than 10, then set the allocation to 10.
> If the total allocation is less than 750 households, then return to step 4.

We measured distribution similarity in steps 2 and 4, using the mean absolute difference in the standardized household characteristics between the BID and non-BID census tracts. This sequential algorithm allocated between 10 and 50 households to 85 non-BID census tracts. Table 1 indicates that the BID and non-BID households are expected to have a nearly identical feature distribution if we select random samples within each census tract with the sample size given in the allocation.[6]

Table 1. Expected characteristics of the BID and non-BID samples.

Variable	Expected Characteristic	
	BID Sample	**Non-BID Sample**
Female head of household + children under 18 (%)	25	25
Unemployed (%)	8	8
Below poverty line (%)	15	15
Receiving welfare (%)	8	8
Population male + under 25 (%)	21	21
Latino (%)	50	50
Foreign born (%)	40	40
Owner occupied (%)	63	59
Units occupied more than 5 years (%)	51	51
Population per square mile	9,870	9,883

Source: US Census 2000 Summary File 1 (SF 1), (SF 2), (SF 3)

This methodology has, in effect, created a matched comparison group of neighborhoods from which to sample households in non-BID areas that are similar to those sampled from neighborhoods intersecting BIDs. The BID treatment area was defined in terms of 147 census tracts that covered the combined area of the 30 BIDs in Los Angeles. The comparison areas consisted of 85 census tracts with sampled households of similar socio-demographic characteristics. A visual depiction of the size, locations, and census-tract neighborhoods adjoining these BIDs and their comparison neighborhoods is displayed in Figure 1.[7]

Figure 1. BID and comparison neighborhoods.

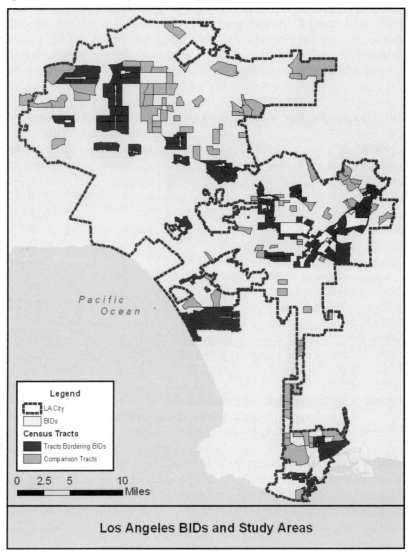

Los Angeles BIDs and Study Areas

Sample

Our examination of the relationships between the individual and neighborhood features and their association with youth violence are based on a survey undertaken by the RAND Corporation through a subcontract to Research Triangle International (RTI) and the Social Science Research Center (SSRC) at California State University Fullerton. Between October 2006 and February 2007, RTI conducted telephone survey interviews with randomly selected adult parents and youth (ages 14 to 17) in the targeted neighborhoods.[8]

As previously discussed, a quota system was established to ensure that samples of adults and youth were allocated to achieve a balance between BID and non-BID neighborhoods on key demographic features. A sampling frame of list-assisted telephone numbers, with geo-coded matching addresses, was initially used to limit respondents to the targeted neighborhoods. This approach was used instead of a random-digit dial (RDD) because of the difficulty of determining through RDD whether unlisted households are located within the target census tracts. Limiting the sample to listed numbers created the potential for bias because of unknown differences between listed and unlisted households. Obtaining street addresses was a necessary step for the study design, therefore negating the feasibility of using RDD. In addition to list-assisted numbers additional steps were taken, including the use of marketing data and driver's license data, to identify households in sampled neighborhoods with a higher likelihood of containing an eligible adolescent.[9]

A comparison of target quota and sample obtained for each of the selected census tract neighborhoods indicates that approximately 41 percent (n = 89) did not meet the quota goal and 24 percent (n = 52) exceeded the target quota. The allocation of under- and oversampling, however, was distributed evenly across census tracts such that it did not effect the overall study design to balance household features of BID and non-BID tracts.[10] A final total sample of 737 eligible households agreed to participate in the survey. The overall effective response rate was 40.2 percent. Of these 737 interviews, 85 percent (n = 626) completed a parent/youth dyad.[11] The sampling plan yielded a probability sample of residents with a large enough sample allocated to BID and non-BID neighborhoods to estimate between-neighborhood differences. Follow-up interviews were conducted by SSRC with 635 (86 percent retention) households 18 months later, 83 percent (n=535) completing a parent/youth dyad. This sample should not be considered a probability sample of the population of all households with adolescents. The variety of unknown features of this population and the difficulty in obtaining respondents suggests that the sample represents only those in the population with listed numbers who were willing to participate in the survey.

Measures

The outcome measure of this analysis focuses on self-reported violent victimization among youth participants aged 14 to 17. Each youth was asked to indicate whether, during the previous 12 months, he or she had experienced (1) another youth trying to steal something from him or her by force; (2) another youth threatening him or her with a gun, knife, or club; (3) another youth hitting him or her badly enough to require bandages or a doctor; (4) a physical attack by a group of two or more youth; and/or (5) seeing someone in the neighborhood being assaulted by a group of two or more youth.[12] The prevalence of experiencing violent victimization ranged from a low of 2.3 percent for being seriously injured from violence to a high of 16 percent for seeing someone in the neighborhood being assaulted by a group of two or more youth. The prevalence of these items was slightly lower at follow-up for all outcomes (e.g., 16 percent for seeing someone assaulted drops to 13 percent), reflecting a general downward trend in victimization in later adolescence. Individual items from the household surveys were combined into a single hierarchical scale, with witnessing violence in the neighborhood serving as the least serious category with the highest prevalence (see Sampson et al., 2005, for a similar approach).

Family attributes
A number of measures were derived from extant literature to assess the association between individual- and family-related contextual variables and youth violence. To assess ethnic and immigrant disparities in youth violence, subjects' ethnicities were derived from the adult household interviews. Subjects were identified first as immigrants (non–U.S. born) and second by race and ethnicity. Approximately 57 percent of subject households were identified as immigrants (parents non-U.S. born), and 52 percent self-identified as Latino. Approximately 83 immigrant parents indicated that they were Latino. Because of the relative minority of households comprised of other racial and ethnic groups (African American – 6 percent, Asian – 5 percent, white – 34 percent), the present analyses focus only on differences between Latinos and other ethnicities and between immigrants and non-immigrants in the sample.[13]

To assess the extent to which family and individual background factors are related to individual differences in the likelihood of experiencing violence, we selected a common set of predictors, including age of teen, gender, socioeconomic status of household, years living in the current neighborhood, levels of youth bonds to family and school, family kinship network, and the importance of religion in the household. Age of the teen was included as a covariate because older teens are at greater risk for violence due to a number of factors, including reduced parental monitoring (Loeber & Farrington, 1998). Gender was included because a large body of research indicates that males experience a disproportionate share of violent offending and victimization (see McCord, Widom, & Crowell, 2001). Prior research suggests that exposure to youth violence varies across social class gradients (Loeber & Farrington, 1998). To assess socioeconomic status (SES), we included an average summed index of the parental respondent's reported level of education, household mortgage or rent, and household income. Education was measured on a six-point scale from less than high school diploma to a graduate or professional degree. Household mortgage or rent was measured on a six-point scale from $500 or less to more than $2,500 per month. Household income was measured on a six-point scale from $20,000 or less to $100,000 or more.[14]

Research also suggests that offending and victimization are associated with the extent to which youth are bonded to institutions of family and school (Lipsey & Derzon, 1998; McCord et al., 2001). Bonds to family and school were assessed based on eight five-point scaled items that gauged how much—with responses ranging from "not at all" to "very much"—they agreed with the following statements about school and family: (1) You are close to people at school; (2) You are part of your school; (3) You are happy to be at school; (4) The teachers treat you fairly; (5) Your parents care about you; (6) People in your family understand you; (7) You and your family have fun together; and (8) Your family pays attention to you. These items were combined into an average summed scale, and the alpha reliability for this scale was 0.76. Higher scores on this scale reflect greater levels of bonding to family and school.

Some research also indicates that familial religious beliefs and participation may provide a protective factor from violence (see Hawkins et al., 1998). To assess the importance of religion in the household, parents were asked on a four-point Likert-type scale the relative importance—with response options ranging from "very important" to "very unimportant"—that the family practice religion. Higher scores reflect less religious importance in the family.

Extant literature suggests that youth residing in married-parent households are at reduced risk for violence and other negative life outcomes (McCord et al., 2001). Therefore, we included a dummy variable to indicate whether the responding parent was legally married (= 1) or living an alternative familial arrangement (= 0).

Finally, to control for the relative influence of local neighborhood kinship ties, a dummy variable was included that measured whether (= 1) or not (= 0) the household had relatives or family members living in the neighborhood. We also include the number of years that the respondents had lived in the neighborhood as a measure of household stability, because frequent moving can be a signal of a number of factors that place youth at greater risk for experiencing violence (McCord et al., 2001).

Neighborhood attributes

As the relative importance of neighborhood context in explaining dissimilarities in exposure to youth violence is at the heart of this study, we incorporated a set of neighborhood-specific measures derived from the literature.[15] Prior research, for example, suggests that perceptions of neighborhood disorder differ significantly between high- and low-crime and violence areas (Skogan, 1990). We recognize there is debate about the relative importance of disorder as a distinct concept that is not endogenous to crime and its meaning across racial and ethnic groups (see, e.g., Sampson & Raudenbush, 1999, 2004; Skogan, 1990; Taylor, 2001). To measure disorder, respondents were asked on a three-point scale—with response options ranging from "big problem" to "not a problem"—their view of 10 signs of physical and social disorder in their neighborhoods, including (1) litter or trash in the streets; (2) graffiti; (3) vacant housing or vacant storefronts; (4) poorly maintained property; (5) abandoned cars; (6) drinking in public; (7) selling or using drugs; (8) homeless people or street panhandlers causing disturbances; (9) groups of teenagers hanging out on street corners without adult supervision; and (10) people fighting or arguing in public. The 10 items were combined into an average summed scale, and the alpha reliability for the scale was 0.93.[16] Higher scores indicated that respondents perceived more social and physical disorder in their neighborhood.

Research also indicates that the level of area social cohesion is linked to violence and crime, in addition to other negative life outcomes (see Sampson et al., 2002, for a review). This study attempted to assess the level of perceived neighborhood social cohesion by asking respondents 15 items related to this concept, now commonly referred to as *collective efficacy*. The level of neighborhood social cohesion was assessed from nine items that asked parents their level of agreement—with responses ranging from "strongly agree" to "strongly disagree"—the following statements about their neighborhood: (1) People around here are willing to help their neighbors; (2) This is a close-knit neighborhood; (3) People in this neighborhood can be trusted; (4) People in this neighborhood generally don't get along with each other; (5) People in this neighborhood do not share the same values; (6) Parents in this neighborhood know their children's friends; (7) Adults in this neighborhood know who the local children are; (8) Parents in this neighborhood generally know each other; and (9) People in this neighborhood are willing to do favors for each other, such as watching each other's children, helping with shopping, or watching each other's houses when someone is out of town. The level of perceived informal social control in the neighborhood was assessed from six items that asked residents how likely—with responses ranging from "very likely" to "very unlikely"—that neighbors would do something if (1) children were skipping school and hanging out on a street corner; (2) children were spray painting graffiti on a sidewalk or building; (3) children were showing disrespect to an adult; (4) a fight broke out in public; (5) a youth gang was hanging out on the street corner selling drugs and intimidating people; and (6) a local school near home was threatened with closure due to budget cuts. Consistent with previous work (Sampson et al., 2005), these two scales were closely associated ($r = 0.60$; $p < 0.01$) and were combined into a single average summed scale, with higher scores representing lower levels of collective efficacy. The alpha reliability for this scale was 0.86. The scores on this scale were coded so that higher scores on the scale would reflect lower levels of neighborhood collective efficacy.

ANALYTIC PLAN

We estimate a multilevel variance components model[17] that takes into account the hierarchical structure of victimization outcomes and respondent households being nested within BID and non-BID neighborhoods. First, we construct a multilevel model of violence according to the following form:

$$\eta_{ijkt} = \mu + \sigma_i + \beta bid_{jkt} + \delta x_j + \lambda_k + \pi_t + \varepsilon_{ijkt} \qquad (1)$$

Here, the outcome represents the odds ratio of experiencing a violent victimization [P($Yikjt$ = 1)/ P($Yikjt$ = 0)], for respondent household j residing in neighborhood census tract k during interview occasion t. In Equation 1, we include a dummy variable denoting whether the respondent household lives in a BID neighborhood and x represents the matrix of individual, family, and neighborhood attributes (immigrant or ethnic status, SES, age of teen, gender of teen, social bonds, religious importance, years in neighborhood, disorder, collective efficacy). Random intercept parameters λ and π are included to shift the model up or down according to each neighborhood location and interview wave, and σ represents a fixed effect parameter for each youth-violence item i (witnessing neighborhood violence is the reference category) (see Sampson et al., 2005, for a similar specification). Thus, μ represents the intercept, or the average probability of youth violence adjusting for individual, family, neighborhood attributes, neighborhood location, and interview wave. The error structure for this model is composed of fixed (individual respondent) and random variance (neighborhood and interview wave) that is assumed to be normally distributed with mean 0 and variance $\square$.[18] This model simply compares youth-violence outcomes for youth living in BID areas to those in non-BID comparison areas after conditioning for the effects of observed family and neighborhood differences over time.

To test the sensitivity of these estimates to the small number of households in each neighborhood census tract, we also constructed a second set of analyses based on estimated neighborhood clusters (NCs). We constructed neighborhood-specific estimates of the incidence of youth violence using a NC approach that combines adjacent census tracts into large enough geographic units to estimate between-neighborhood differences with reasonable precision. To create these NCs, we used the following four rules. First, census tracts were clustered among BID and non-BID tracts separately. Second, census tracts were clustered together if they were geographically contiguous, with a maximum of four census tracts making up any one NC. Third, areas in which five tracts bordered each other were divided so that no single tract could have more than two-thirds the balance of the total number of household interviews. Fourth, NCs for BID areas were chosen so that they would cluster around their most proximal BID location. Applying these rules resulted in a total of 71 NCs representing 587 households over both time periods.

It is clear that several trade-offs were made to generate reasonable estimates from these NCs. These estimates, therefore, should not be interpreted as representing actual neighborhoods in Los Angeles. Rather, the NCs should be interpreted as geographically proximal census tracts with sufficient enough sample to yield an area estimate.[19] It is worth noting that the definition of *neighborhood* in the household survey more closely applies to an actual census tract and not these larger NC aggregations. To construct NC estimates, we followed the same logic and estimated a variance components model that is identical to that specified in equation 1 for neighborhoods, but the random intercept was estimated at the cluster (c) rather than neighborhood (k) level.[20]

RESULTS

Sample description

The descriptive statistics for the measures of individual/household and neighborhood attributes between BID and non-BID comparison groups are displayed in Table 2. Sixty-nine percent of respondent households were married and, on average, had lived in the current neighborhood for almost 15 combined years. The average age of youth respondents was 16. A comparison of these descriptive data indicates that few differences between those living in BID and non-BID areas were observed. A significantly higher proportion of respondents in BID households were immigrant, Latino, and of lower socioeconomic status (p<.05). In addition, BID respondents reported slightly lower levels of collective efficacy (p<.05) than those living in comparison areas.[21] These differences in samples suggest the need to adjust for these differences in our subsequent analysis of BID effects on community-level processes and youth violence. On average, however, the distribution of the observed features of each household were essentially equivalent between those living in BIDs compared to non-BID comparison areas, suggesting that the sample-allocation algorithm was an effective tool in sampling equivalent households across areas.[22]

Table 2. Descriptive statistics of key measures.

Variable	Overall (n=1,372)	Comparison (n=700)	BID Areas (n=672)	(t-value)	Range
Demographics					
Immigrant household (%)	56.7	53.0	60.6	2.79*	0–1
Latino (%)	52.2	48.4	56.3	2.92*	0–1
SES (z-units)	3.09	3.19	2.99	2.73*	1–6
Age of teen (years)	16.37	16.37	16.37	0.05	13–19
Gender (=male)	53.6	53.0	54.2	0.42	0–1
Married (%)	68.8	68.7	68.0	0.10	0–1
Great social bonds	4.12	4.12	4.12	0.07	2–5
Religion (> less)	1.58	1.57	1.60	0.53	1–4
Kinship network (%)	21.7	20.2	23.3	1.38	0–1
Years in neighborhood	14.61	14.69	14.54	0.59	0–76
Neighborhood attributes					
Disorder	1.69	1.66	1.71	1.51	1–3
Collective efficacy (> means less)	2.18	2.16	2.21	2.23*	0.8–3.87

Notes:

n=1,372 = 737 baseline + 635 follow-up interviews.

*p<.05

Fifty-seven percent of sampled household adult respondents were immigrants, and 52 percent identified as Latino. These figures exceed the most recent (2000) census population estimates for the sampled neighborhoods, which indicated that 40 percent of the population was foreign born and 50 percent were of Latino ethnicity. The sample may be a closer representation of the population of households with teenage children, or reflective of more recent immigration trends of residents from Latin American countries into L.A. neighborhoods. Because of the potential changes in demographics in these areas since the 2000 census, we did not reweight the sample to mirror that of the census population. The analysis presented in this study is, therefore, unweighted. Because the sample allocation between neighborhoods was designed to be self-weighting, we also do not weight neighborhoods (see Sampson et al., 2005, for a similar approach). The results from the subsequent multivariate analyses are based on a final sample of 635 households clustered in 189 census tract neighborhoods interviewed at two periods in time (n=1270), with mean/median imputation adjustments made for missing data on the variables considered.[23]

Multilevel models

The results from the multilevel logistic regression analysis are reported in odds ratios (ORs) with respective p-values. Table 3 examines the direct association between BIDs and youth violence, as well as the role of neighborhood mediators of collective efficacy and disorder, controlling for individual/household-related covariates. There is no direct association between BIDs and youth violence. The results, however, indicate that immigrant status, social bonds, importance of religion to the family, perceptions of neighborhood disorder, and collective efficacy are significantly associated with youth-violence victimization.

Model 1 presents estimates for household and neighborhood attributes, contrasting immigrants with all others. The results indicate that several of these household-related covariates are significantly associated with the odds of experiencing youth violence. Specifically, residing in an immigrant household reduces the odds of experiencing youth violence by 45 percent compared to those of non-immigrants (OR = 0.55; 95% CI= 0.39- 0.78). Youth with increased bonds to family and school are also associated with a reduced risk experiencing youth violence. Greater social bonds were associated with a 0.68 odds of victimization (95% CI = 0.56-0.83). Specifically, a standard deviation increase in one's reported social bonds to family and school reduced the odds of meeting youth violence by 0.79.[24] The less important religion was to a family the higher odds of violence (OR=1.18; 95% CI=1.01-1.36). The presence of kinship (relatives or family) in one's neighborhood is associated with a 93 percent higher odds (95% CI=1.43-2.60) of youth violence. In terms of neighborhood features, both perceived social and physical disorder and collective efficacy are associated with youth violence. The results indicate that youth violence is 1.55 times higher in areas with increased disorder (95% CI = 1.21–1.97). Converting the effect size into standard-deviation units, we see that a one standard-deviation increase in disorder is associated with a 1.30 increase in odds of violence. Lower levels of collective efficacy in a respondent's neighborhood was associated with a 49% increase in the odds of youth violence (OR = 1.49; 95% CI = 1.09–2.03). Living in a BID neighborhood, however, is not significantly associated with experiencing more or less youth violence.

Given that a high proportion of immigrant households in this sample are also Latino and that the two covariates, when entered separately, had different effects in opposite directions, this provides evidence for a nonlinear relationship. Model 2 captures the potential nonlinear relationship between ethnicity and youth violence by including the dummy variable to capture different intercepts and an interaction term (Latino X immigrant) to estimate different slopes. The results from model 2 indicate a significant interaction term and suggest that youth from immigrant households of Latin American origin have a significantly reduced odds of more serious forms of youth violence relative to non-Latinos (OR = 0.27;

95% CI = 0.17–0.45); whereas nonimmigrant Latino youth are at increased odds of experiencing more serious forms of youth violence (OR = 4.05; 95% CI = 2.50–6.55) relative to non-Latinos. These findings are consistent with work by Sampson et al. (2005) that found immigration status to be associated with significantly reduced odds of committing youth violence in the community, even when compared with youth residing in the same neighborhoods with similarly situated social and economic circumstances. BIDs, however, have no systematic effect on youth-violence experience. The results from model 2 also indicate that higher perceptions of neighborhood disorder are associated with an increase in the seriousness of youth violence (OR = 1.43; 95% CI=1.11-1.84) and that collective efficacy continues to be significantly associated with a reduced odds in the likelihood of experiencing more serious forms of youth violence. A one-unit decrease in reported collective efficacy is associated with a 55 percent increase in the odds of youth violence (OR = 0.55; 95% CI = 1.12–2.12).

Table 3. Individual- and neighborhood-level covariates of violence.

	Model 1		Model 2	
Variable	**OR**	**P-Value**	**OR**	**P-Value**
Immigrant household	0.55	0.001	—	—
Latino	—	—	4.05	<0.001
Immigrant X Latino	—	—	0.27	0.001
SES	0.79	0.001	0.88	0.091
Age of teen	1.01	0.732	1.01	0.747
Married	1.05	0.712	0.96	0.823
Social bonds	0.68	<0.001	0.64	<0.001
Religion (>less)	1.18	0.028	1.22	0.009
Kinship network	1.93	<0.001	1.86	<0.001
Years in neighborhood	0.98	0.111	0.98	0.103
BID	1.09	0.644	0.99	0.980
Disorder (> more)	1.55	<0.001	1.43	0.004
Collective efficacy (> less)	1.49	0.011	1.55	0.006
X^2	96.41	<0.001	100.29	<0.001

Notes:
n = 5,770 item responses, 577 households, 178 census tracts, 352 waves.
X^2= Likelihood ratio test comparing multilevel variance component to single variance logistic regression.

Because there has been some debate about the relative importance of disorder itself in creating signals of neighborhood incivility and increasing the likelihood that crime and violence will flourish (Wilson & Kelling, 1982; Sampson & Raudenbush, 1999), we also estimated models that included disorder and collective efficacy in separate equations. The results indicated that disorder and collective efficacy[25] are more correlated with youth violence when estimated separately than together, suggesting that collective efficacy and disorder slightly offset each other in their associations with youth violence.[26]

Table 4. Structural predictors of youth violence.

Variable	OR	95% CI	P-Value
Model 1 (concentrated disadvantage)			
BID	0.98	0.66-1.46	0.948
Disorder	1.45	1.12–1.86	0.004
Collective efficacy	1.43	1.04–1.95	0.025
Concentrated disadvantage	1.08	0.93–1.25	0.312
Violent-crime rate (log)	1.00	0.67–1.450	0.983
X^2	84.12*		
Model 2 (percentage of males under 25)			
BID	1.03	0.69-1.55	0.849
Disorder	1.45	1.13–1.87	0.003
Collective efficacy	1.42	1.03–1.95	0.028
% of males under 25	1.01	0.96–1.07	0.475
Violent-crime rate	1.04	0.70–1.54	0.827
X^2	84.69*		
Model 3 (immigrant concentration)			
BID	1.01	0.68-1.49	0.955
Disorder	1.46	1.13–1.87	0.003
Collective efficacy	1.43	1.04–1.97	0.024
Immigrant concentration	1.19	0.31–4.56	0.796
Violent-crime rate	1.08	0.73–1.60	0.691
X^2	84.58*		
Model 4 (residential stability)			
BID	0.97	0.64-1.46	0.905
Disorder	1.45	1.13–1.87	0.003
Collective efficacy	1.43	1.04–1.96	0.024
Residential stability	0.64	0.18–2.24	0.496
Violent-crime rate	1.06	0.73–1.54	0.720
X^2	84.46*		
Model 5 (population density)			
BID	0.97	0.65-1.46	0.911
Disorder	1.45	1.13–1.87	0.003
Collective efficacy	1.43	1.04–1.96	0.024
Population density	1.08	0.85–1.37	0.498
Violent-crime rate	1.10	0.77–1.57	0.594
X^2	84.89*		

Notes:

Controlling for individual- and family-related variables shown in Table 3.

n = 5,485 item responses, 558 individual households, 178 census-tract neighborhoods.

X^2 = Likelihood ratio test comparing multilevel variance component to single variance logistic regression.

*$p < 0.01$

Structural covariates

Our findings indicated that BIDs are not significantly associated with youth violence. A significant proportion of individual/household differences in youth-violence experience are associated with neighborhood location and perceptions of collective efficacy in one's neighborhood. The sampling algorithm used in this study was designed to assess households in BID and non-BID areas so that they were exposed to similar neighborhood environments. The algorithm was not designed to assess the overall city-level effect of neighborhood structural features on youth violence. This raises the question of whether neighborhood perceptions of collective efficacy are merely proxies for structural differences related to poverty, residential stability, and demographic features of the sampled neighborhoods. For example, it is possible that residents with a high percentage of youthful residents under the age of 25 are more likely to perceive that there is a lack of collective efficacy in their neighborhoods because youth are perceived as problematic and unsupervised.

To assess whether disorder and collective efficacy are proxies for systemic structural differences between neighborhoods or are themselves important covariates, we estimated an additional set of models that included neighborhood factors related to concentrated poverty,[27] residential stability (percentage of residents living in the neighborhood for five years or longer), age (percentage of males under 25 years old) and Latino or immigrant concentration (average of percentage of Latino and foreign-born residents), population density (residents per square mile), as well as the violent-crime rate per 100,000 residents (natural log of the average total 2004–2005 crime reports for murder, rape, robbery, and aggravated assault). Because these structural features of concentrated poverty, age and ethnic distributions, residential stability, and population density are highly correlated with each other (average $r > 0.60$; see Appendix A), we estimate separate models for each covariate.

The results from these models are displayed in Table 4. Models 1 to 5 show that the direct effects of collective efficacy and disorder remain statistically significant predictors of youth violence even after introduction of structural covariates of concentrated disadvantage, percentage of males under 25, percentage foreign born or Latino, level of residential stability, population density, and crime in each neighborhood. The direct effect of collective efficacy barely changes depending on the specification and is consistently a significant predictor of youth violence across all specifications. Similarly, perception of disorder in one's neighborhood is significantly associated with youth violence across all models and changes only slightly across specifications.

These findings indicate that, even when we include neighborhood-level covariates associated with concentrated poverty, residential stability, population density, Latino and immigrant concentration, males under age 25, and average level of violent crime reported in the previous two years, perceived neighborhood environments remain important predictors of youth violence. Importantly, these associations are not a reflection of underlying structural differences between neighborhoods sampled.

Table 5. Neighborhood-cluster estimates of youth violence.

Variable	OR	95% CI	P-Value
BID	1.15	0.73-1.82	0.532
Disorder	1.26	1.00–1.59	0.043
Collective efficacy	1.25	0.93–1.67	0.123
X^2	54.02*		

Notes:
Controlling for individual- and family-related variables shown in Table 3.
n = 5,240 item responses, 542 individual households, 71 neighborhood clusters.
X^2 = Likelihood ratio test comparing multilevel variance component to single variance logistic regression.
*$p < 0.01$

Neighborhood clusters

The neighborhood cluster (NC) estimates are presented in Table 5 in an attempt to investigate the potentially larger geographic grouping effects across areas. Individual/household attributes were also estimated but, for ease of exposition, are not included in this table. The results are consistent with those displayed in Table 3: Disorder and collective efficacy are associated with the odds of youth violence. The 95-percent confidence interval on these estimates, however, crosses zero and suggests that the relative association of these attributes diminishes in both strength and statistical inference when one includes a random-effect intercept that allows for between-NC variance. These findings suggest that estimating the effect of disorder and collective efficacy at larger geographic units results in a loss of precision when attempting to approximate the probability of experiencing youth violence. The estimates from the NC model indicate that BIDs have no significant direct association with youth violence at larger areas of aggregation.

Alternative tests

It is possible that the lack of BID effects on youth violence is symptomatic of the differences between BIDs, such that some BIDs are located in areas with youth-violence levels at different ends of the distribution of these outcomes. Thus, some BIDs may be directly associated with reduced rates of youth violence through their community-change efforts, while others are not actively engaged enough in the community to have an effect. To explore this potential heterogeneity in BID areas, we also estimated a fixed-effects model that included individual coefficients for each BID. The heterogeneity in BID areas precluded the ability to estimate random-effect specifications. In other words, there was not a large enough sample size in each BID area to assess BID effects separately from neighborhood grouping effects. As a result, the model estimated was a standard fixed-effect logistic regression that corrects for respondents being clustered in each BID area but not each census tract. The results from these models include 19 of the 30 BIDs that had sufficient sample size to estimate unique BID effects and indicate differences across BID catchment areas in the odds of a youth household member experiencing more-serious violent victimization. However, the sample sizes in these areas are sufficiently small that the point estimates vary substantially, suggesting that caution should be used in interpreting these estimates of BID areas. Ethnicity, social bonds, kinship networks, and collective efficacy remain significantly associated with serious youth violence.

These subsequent analyses suggest a consistent picture with the previous models in noting the importance of household features of immigrant origin, parental social control, and collective efficacy in explaining a significant amount of the incidence of more-serious forms of youth violence, suggesting that features of neighborhood life are important even when one includes statistical controls for specific BID areas. Again, we see no direct association between BIDs and a reduced likelihood of youth violence.

Limitations

BIDs are not randomly allocated to neighborhoods in Los Angeles. Despite our best effort to allocate our sample in such a way as to balance the exposure of household respondents in BID and non-BID neighborhoods to similar structural features of areas, it is reasonable to suspect that BID location is still not exogenous to the observational data collected in this study. A comparison of BID and matched area households indicated that the two groups differed only along a few observable features (e.g., SES, immigration status, percentage Latino). To remove the potentially confounding effects of these individual-level attributes, we estimated the series of multilevel models to effectively control for these between-group differences. A key assumption of this modeling approach is that of *ignorablity*. In other words, one has to assume that the features we observed effectively create a set of equivalent comparison groups, so that the only remaining difference is the assignment to a BID or non-BID neighborhood. It is quite possible that there are systematic differences between households in BID areas and non-BID comparison areas that we did not measure with our household survey or reliance on neighborhood census-tract data. Our sampling approach may have also matched residential areas at the wrong time period, by constructing a comparison group of areas in which residents are, on average, similarly situated to BID residents years after the positive benefits of established BIDs have transpired.

We explored whether we could effectively predict observable differences between living in a BID area and a comparison area along the attributes collected in this survey. As intended with our sampling design, the analysis indicated that the observed individual- and family-related attributes (e.g., SES, ethnicity, social bonds, religion) were not predictive of living in a BID area. Specifically, estimating the probability of living in a BID location by these observed features using logistic regression did not improve the predicted probability of living in a BID area over what one would get by using the intercept only, or the average case. These findings suggest that the sampling algorithm was effective in removing the majority of the observed between-group differences between respondents living in BID areas and those living in comparison areas.

CONCLUSION AND DISCUSSION

We set out to examine whether the formation of a BID in Los Angeles had an impact on youth violence outcomes after comparing youth in neighborhoods exposed to BIDs with those living in areas with similar exposure to structural features associated with crime, as well as controlling for family-related household features and neighborhood environments. We found no association between BID formation and youth violence outcomes. On average, neighborhood environments and youth-victimization outcomes are not related to living in or around a BID, suggesting that this form of community economic development does not translate into systemic neighborhood change that improves violence outcomes for youth in adjacent communities.

We did find a number of significant predictors of youth violence associated with household and neighborhood features. Youth living in immigrant households are protected from experiencing serious youth violence compared to youth living in similarly situated nonimmigrant households. In addition, our analysis indicates that the degree to which youth feel close bonds to family and school is consistently related to the odds of experiencing violence. These findings also provide a replication of seminal work on neighborhood effects in Chicago, Illinois, that found a significant association between neighborhood perceptions of collective efficacy and household victimization outcomes (Sampson et al., 1997). We extend this seminal study by finding similar effects of neighborhood-related processes on youth-violence outcomes in Los Angeles, in a different decade and with a heavier concentration of youth of Latin American ancestry. These findings are important because they indicate that, within the context of these Los Angeles neighborhoods, family-related social processes are not the only mechanisms that are important in explaining a youth's likely exposure to violence. Rather, it appears that neighborhood environments also influence the risk that a youth will experience more serious forms of violent victimization. Neighborhood mechanisms related to disorder and collective efficacy, or the willingness of neighbors to watch out for each other and share a sense of collective bonds, are important predictors of youth violence in both BID and non-BID neighborhoods.

Since we rely on longitudinal data these observations are not a result of a single cross-section – but take into account two years of youth violence exposure occurring sampled approximately 18 months apart. Because BIDs were already established in these neighborhoods we are limited in our ability to discuss the causal connection between establishing a BID and changes that occur in neighborhoods and youth violence outcomes. For example, it is possible that BID effects are observable only before and after their establishment when they initially implement private security and assist in the improvement of their local neighborhood environments. A more dynamic neighborhood-change process that effects youth may have occurred that we cannot capture in this longitudinal analysis when BID and comparison areas have few environmental differences (see Sampson, 2008, for a related discussion on the Moving to Opportunities experiments).

BID neighborhoods, compared to our matched control neighborhoods, are also not systematically correlated with differences in perceived neighborhood environments, such as collective efficacy or disorder. Including interactions between BIDs and these outcomes showed close to zero correlations. Because we designed the non–BID exposed neighborhoods to be similarly situated to BID-exposed neighborhoods in their population dynamics, our methodology provides a very conservative test of perceived between-group differences in neighborhood environments. Maybe it is not surprising to see that the mere presence of a BID is not systematically associated with reduced incidence of youth violence in neighborhoods.

The results from this study do, however, confirm other seminal work (see Skogan, 1990; Sampson et al., 2005) in noting that the perceptions of neighborhood environments, as measured by disorder and collective efficacy, are associated with crime-related outcomes. In both BID and non-BID comparison neighborhoods, a great perception of trust and shared responsibilities for civic life between neighbors was significantly associated with a reduced likelihood that youth experienced serious forms of violence. These findings are important because they suggest that increasing positive interactions among neighbors in BID and non-BID areas can serve as a protective factor from youth violence.

There are several limitations that are worth addressing. Because this study relied primarily on observational data without a pre-post intervention design, we cannot know the extent to which the correlations observed are causally related. We attempted to remove the potential selection effects of the adoption of BIDs to neighborhood areas by creating a matched comparison sample of residents living in non-BID areas but equally exposed to aggregate patterns of poverty, income, and ethnicity. In the absence of an experimental design, in which we could randomly assign neighborhoods to BIDs, we cannot know the extent to which self-selection of residents into communities surrounding BIDs affects our estimates. In addition, the associations between perceived neighborhood environments (e.g., collective efficacy and disorder) and youth violence are not necessarily causal mechanisms. It is likely that effects of perceived levels of neighborhood disorder and collective efficacy do not cause exposure to youth violence but may reflect an association that occurs through individuals selecting into specific neighborhoods with better or worse social and physical environments, which, in turn, are associated with violence outcomes. However, it is worth noting that the effects of collective efficacy remain even when we statistically control for neighborhood mechanisms related to poverty, population density, prior years of violent crime, and other covariates classically associated with youth-violence outcomes at the neighborhood level. The implications of this research are, therefore, important because they confirm prior work in Chicago and other cities in noting that perceived neighborhood environments matter and that the likelihood of exposure to violence in neighborhoods involves more than just differences in levels of social class and other household factors.

For policy discourse on citywide efforts to encourage the establishment of BIDs as catalysts of CED, our research suggests that understanding the broader neighborhood dynamics of the areas in which BIDs operate is more important for their role in creating change than the simple adoption of BIDs. While one of the main strengths of the BID model is its localized governance capability, in which local actors, knowledgeable about local problems, can tailor a strategic response to the problems of economic development and community problems, our analysis suggests that BID organizations cannot be expected to serve as agents of change for larger systemic social problems related to neighborhood environments and youth violence in surrounding communities. While research suggests that the adoption of BIDs leads to measurable reductions in crime within BID areas (see Cook & MacDonald, 2010; MacDonald et al., 2010), these crime reductions may not transcend to across to neighborhoods bordering BIDs or lives of youth and families living in them. At best, BIDs may result in an enhanced local community services and social control that yield direct crime control benefits in their immediate boundaries, but these social benefits do not transcend to the outer borders of the neighborhoods they touch. Creating sustainable community change that benefits families and youth in urban neighborhoods is difficult. Local CED models like BIDs do not appear to be the short-term panacea for improving neighborhood environments and adolescent well-being.

REFERENCES

Anderson, E. (1998). The social ecology of youth violence. In M. Tonry and M. Moore (Eds.), *Youth Violence* (pp. 65-104). Chicago, IL: University of Chicago Press.

Anderson, R. & Smith, B. (2009). Deaths: Leading causes for 2001. *National Vital Statistics Reports, 52*(9), 1–86. Retrieved January 2, 2009, from http://www.cdc.gov/nchs/data/nvsr/nvsr52/nvsr52_09.pdf

Blumstein, A., Rivara, F., & Rosenfeld, R. (2000). The rise and decline of homicide—and why. *Annual Review of Public Health, 21,* 505–541.

Bondonio, D. & Greenbaum, R. (2005). *Decomposing the impacts: Lessons from a multistate analysis of enterprise zone programs.* Retrieved April 2010, from https://kb.osu.edu/dspace/bitstream/1811/436/1/Bondonio_Green baum%20 Glenn%2 0working%2 0paper.pdf

Boston, T. & Ross, C. (Eds.). (1997). *The inner city: Urban poverty and economic developoment [sic] in the next century.* New Brunswick, NJ: Transaction Publishers.

Briffault, R. (1999). A government for our time? Business Improvement Districts and urban governance. *Columbia Law Review, 99,* 365–477.

Brooks, L. (2008). Volunteering to be taxed: Business Improvement Districts and the extra-governmental provision of public safety. *Journal of Public Economics, 92,* 388–406.

Bursik, Jr., R. (1988). Social disorganization and theories of crime and delinquency: Problems and prospects. *Criminology, 26,* 519–552.

Bursik, Jr., R. & Grasmick, H. (1993). *Neighborhoods and crime: The dimensions of effective community control.* New York, NY: Lexington Books.

Busso, M. & Kline, P. (2008). *Do local economic development programs work? Evidence from the Federal Empowerment Zone Program.* Retrieved April 2010, from http://www-personal.umich.edu/~matiasb/Busso-Kline%20EZ.pdf

Coleman, J. (1988). Social capital and the creation of human capital. *American Journal of Sociology, 94,* Supp.: *Organizations and Institutions: Sociological and Economic Approaches to the Analysis of Social Structure,* S95–S120.

Cook, P. & Laub, J. (2002). After the epidemic: Recent trends in youth violence in the United States. *Crime and Justice: A Review of Research, 29,* 1–37.

Cook, P. & MacDonald, J. (2010). Public safety through private action: An economic assessment of BIDs, locks, and citizen cooperation. NBER Working Paper No. 15877.

Cormen, T., Leiserson, C., Rivest, R., & Steine, C. (2001). *Introduction to algorithms.* Second Edition. Cambridge, MA: MIT Press.

CPC (Carolina Population Center), University of North Carolina. (undated home page). *Add Health*. Retrieved January 5, 2009, from http://www.cpc.unc.edu/projects/addhealth

DeFilippis, J. & Saegart, S. (2008). *The community development reader*. New York: NY: Routledge.

Elliott, D., Huizinga, D., & Menard, S. (1989). *Multiple problem youth: Delinquency, substance use, and mental health problems*, New York, NY: Springer-Verlag.

Elvery, J. (2009). The impact of Enterprise Zones on resident employment: An evaluation of the Enterprise Zone Programs of California and Florida. *Economic Development Quarterly, 23,* 44-59.

Fainstein, S. (1994). Government programs for commercial redevelopment in poor neighborhoods: The cases of Spitalfields in East London and Downtown Brooklyn, NY. *Environment and Planning A, 26,* 215–234.

Farrington, D. (1989). Early predictors of adolescent aggression and adult violence.
Violence and Victims, 4, 79–100.

Felson, M. (1995). Those who discourage crime. In J. Eck & D. Weisburg (Eds.) *Crime and place: Crime prevention studies, vol. 4* (pp. 53-66). Monsey, NY: Criminal Justice Press.

Finestone, H. (1976). *Victims of change: Juvenile delinquents in American society*. Westport, CT: Greenwood Press.

Glaeser, E. & Sacerdote, B. (1999). Why is there more crime in cities? *Journal of Political Economy, 107,* S225–S229.

Greenbaum, R. & Engberg, J. (2004). The impact of state Enterprise Zones on urban manufacturing establishments. *Journal of Policy Analysis and Management, 23,* 315-339.

Grunbaum, J., Kann, L., Kinchen, S., Ross, J., Hawkins, J., Lowry, R., Harris, W., McManus, T., Chyen, D., & Collins, J. (2004). Youth risk behavior surveillance: United States, 2003. *Morbidity and Mortality Weekly Report: Surveillance Summaries, 53,* 1–96. Retrieved January 2, 2009, from http://www.cdc.gov/mmwr/PDF/ss/ss5302.pdf

Hall, T. & Hubbard, P. (Eds.). (1998). *The entrepreneurial city: Geographies of politics, regime, and representation*. New York, NY: Wiley.

Harcourt, B. (2005). Policing L.A.'s skid row: Crime and real estate development in downtown Los Angeles (An experiment in real time). *University of Chicago Legal Forum*.

Hawkins, J., Herrenkohl, T., Farrington, D., Brewer, D., Catalano, R., & Harachi, T. (1998). A review of predictors of youth violence." In R. Loeber & D. Farrington (Eds.), *Serious and violent juvenile offenders: Risk factors and successful interventions* (pp. 106-146). Thousand Oaks, CA: Sage Publications.

Hebert, S., Vidal, A., Mills, G., James, F., & Gruenstein, D. (2001). Interim assessment of the Empowerment Zones and Enterprise Communities (EZ/EC) Program: A progress report. Washington, D.C.: U.S. Department of Housing and Urban Development, Office of Policy Development and Research.

Herrenkohl, T., Maguin, E., Hill, K., Hawkins, J., Abbott, R., & Catalano, R. (2000). Developmental risk factors for youth violence. *Journal of Adolescent Health, 26,* 176–186.

Hindelang, M., Hirschi, T., & Weis, J. (1981). *Measuring delinquency.* Beverly Hills, CA: Sage Publications.

Hoyt, L. (2004). Collecting private funds for safer public spaces: An empirical examination of the Business Improvement District concept. *Environment and Planning B: Planning and Design, 31,* 367–380.

Inter-University Consortium for Political and Social Research. (undated home page). *Project on human development in Chicago neighborhoods.* Retrieved January 5, 2009, from http://www.icpsr.umich.edu/PHDCN/

Janowitz, M. (1975). Sociological theory and social control. *American Journal of Sociology, 81,* 82–108.

Kawachi, I. & Berkman, L. (Eds.). (2003). *Neighborhoods and health.* New York, NY: Oxford University Press.

Kobrin, S. (1959). The Chicago Area Project: A 25-year assessment. *Annals of the American Academy of Political and Social Science, 322,* 19–29.

Kornhauser, R. (1978). *Social sources of delinquency: An appraisal of analytic models.* Chicago, IL: University of Chicago Press.

Krivo, L. & Peterson, R. (2000). The structural context of homicide: Accounting for racial differences in process. *American Sociological Review, 65,* 547–559.

Krupka, D. & Noonan, D. (2009). Empowerment Zones, neighborhood change and owner-occupied housing. *Regional Science and Urban Economics, 39,* 386-396.

Land, K., McCall, P., & Cohen, L. (1990). Structural covariates of homicide rates: Are there any invariances across time and social space? *American Journal of Sociology, 95,* 922–963.

Lipsey, M. & Derzon, J. (1998). Predictors of violent or serious delinquency in adolescence and early adulthood: A synthesis of longitudinal research. In R. Loeber & D. Farrington, *Serious and violent juvenile offenders* (pp. 86-105). Thousand Oaks, CA: Sage.

Loeber, R. & Farrington, D. (Eds.). (1998). *Serious and violent juvenile offenders: Risk factors and successful interventions.* Thousand Oaks, CA: Sage Publications.

MacDonald, J., Golinelli, D., Stokes, R., & Bluthenthal, R. (2010). The effect of Business Improvement Districts on the incidence of violent crimes. *Injury Prevention.*

Mallet, W. (1993). Private government formation in the DC Metropolitan Area. *Growth and Change, 24,* 385–415.

Mazerolle, L., Kadleck, C., & Roehl, J. (1998). Controlling drug and disorder problems: The role of place managers. *Criminology, 36,* 371-402.

McCord, J., Widom, C., & Crowell, N. (2001). *Juvenile crime, juvenile justice,* Washington, D.C.: National Academies Press.

McCulloch, C. & Searle, S. (2001). *Generalized, linear, and mixed models.* New York, NY: John Wiley and Sons.

MacDonald, J., Bluthenthal, R., Golinelli, D., Kofner, A., Stokes, R., Sehgal, A., Fain, T., & Beletsky, L. (2009). *Neighborhood effects on crime and youth violence: The role of business improvement districts in Los Angeles.* Santa Monica, CA: RAND Corporation.

McLaughlin, C., Yelon, J., Ivatury, R., & Sugerman, H. (2000). Youth violence: A tripartite examination of putative causes, consequences, and correlates. *Trauma, Violence, and Abuse, 1,* 115–127.

Messner, S., Raffalovich, L., & McMillan, R. (2001). Economic deprivation and changes in homicide arrest rates for white and black youths, 1967–1998: A national time-series analysis. *Criminology, 39,* 591–614.

Mitchell, J. (2001). Business Improvement Districts and the 'new' revitalization of downtown. *Economic Development Quarterly, 15,* 115–123.

Moore, M. & Tonry, M. (1998). Youth violence in America. In M. Tonry & M. Moore (Eds.), *Youth violence* (pp. 1-26). Chicago, IL: University of Chicago Press.

Morenoff, J., Sampson, R., & Raudenbush, S. (2001). Neighborhood inequality, collective efficacy, and the spatial dynamics of urban violence. *Criminology, 39,* 517–558.

Neumark, D. & Kolko, J. (2010). Do Enterprise Zones create jobs? Evidence from California's Enterprise Zone Program. *Journal of Urban Economics, 68*(1), 1-19. Retrieved April 13, 2010, from http://www.socsci.uci.edu/~dneumark/JUE%20Neumark%20and%20Kolko.pdf

Newman, O. (1995). Defensible space: A new physical planning tool for urban revitalization. *Journal of the American Planning Association, 61,* 149–155.

Oakley, D. & Tsao, H. (2006). A new way of revitalizing distressed urban communities? Assessing the impact of the federal Empowerment Zone Program. *Journal of Urban Affairs, 28,* 443-471.

Oakley, D. & Tsao, H. (2007). Socioeconomic gains and spillover effects of geographically targeted initiatives to combat economic distress: An examination of Chicago's Empowerment Zone. *Cities, 24,* 43-59.

Ousey, G. (2000). Deindustrialization, female-headed families, and black and white juvenile homicide rates, 1970–1990. *Sociological Inquiry, 70,* 391–419.

Park, R. (1915). The city: Suggestions for the investigation of human behavior in the city environment. *American Journal of Sociology, 20,* 577–612.

Peterson, C., Sastry, N., Pebley, A., Ghosh-Dastidar, B., Williamson, S., & Lara-Cinisomo, S. (2004). *The Los Angeles Family and Neighborhood Survey: Codebook.* Santa Monica, CA: RAND Corporation, DRU-2400/2-1-LAFANS. Retrieved January 5, 2009, from http://www.rand.org/pubs/drafts/DRU2400.2-1/

Porter, M. (1997). New strategies for inner-city economic development. *Economic Development Quarterly, 11,* 11–27.

Raudenbush, S. & Bryk, A. (2002). *Hierarchical linear models: Applications and data analysis methods*, 2nd ed. Thousand Oaks, CA: Sage Publications.

Riposa, G. (1996). From Enterprise Zones to Empowerment Zones: The community context of urban dconomic development. *American Behavioral Scientist, 39*, 536-551.

Sampson, R. (1987). Urban black violence: The effect of male joblessness and family disruption. *American Journal of Sociology, 93*, 348–382.

Sampson, R. (1995). The community. In J. Wilson & J. Petersilia (Eds.), *Crime* (pp. 193-216). San Francisco, CA: Institute for Contemporary Studies.

Sampson, R. (2008). Moving to inequality: Neighborhood effects and experiments meet social structure. *American Journal of Sociology, 114*, 189–231.

Sampson, R. & Groves, W. (1989). Community structure and crime: Testing social disorganization theory. *American Journal of Sociology, 94*, 744–802.

Sampson, R. & Lauritsen, J. (1994). Violent victimization and offending: Individual-, situational-, and community-level risk factors. In A. Reiss & J. Roth (Eds.), *Understanding and preventing violence, vol. 3: social influences* (pp. 1-114). Washington, D.C.: National Academies Press.

Sampson, R., Morenoff, J., & Gannon-Rowley, T. (2002). Assessing 'neighborhood effects': Social processes and new directions in research. *Annual Review of Sociology, 28*, 443–478.

Sampson, R., Morenoff , J., & Raudenbush, S. (2005). Social anatomy of racial and ethnic disparities in violence. *American Journal of Public Health, 95*, 224–232.

(1999). Systematic social observation of public spaces: A new look at disorder in urban neighborhoods. *American Journal of Sociology, 105*, 603–651.

Sampson, R. & Raudenbush, S. (2004). Seeing disorder: Neighborhood stigma and the social construction of 'broken windows.' *Social Psychology Quarterly, 67*, 319–342.

Sampson, R., Raudenbush, S., & Earls, F. (1997). Neighborhoods and violent crime: A multilevel study of collective efficacy. *Science, 277*, 918–924.

Sampson, R. & Wilson, W. (1995). Toward a theory of race, crime, and urban inequality. In J. Hagan & R. Peterson (Eds.), *Crime and Inequality* (pp. 37-54). Stanford, CA: Stanford University Press.

Shaw, C. & McKay, H. (1942). *Juvenile delinquency and urban areas: A study of rates of delinquents in relation to differential characteristics of local communities in American cities*. Chicago, IL: University of Chicago Press.

Shihadeh, E. & Steffensmeier, D. (1994). Economic inequality, family disruption, and urban black violence: Cities as units of stratification and social control. *Social Forces, 73*, 729–751.

Simon, W. (2001). *The community economic development movement: Law, business, and the new social policy*. Durham, NC: Duke University Press.

Skogan, W. (1990). *Disorder and decline: Crime and the spiral of decay in American neighborhoods*. Berkeley, CA: University of California Press.

St. Jean, P. (2007). *Pockets of crime: Broken windows, collective efficacy, and the criminal point of view.* Chicago, IL: University of Chicago Press.

Stata Corporation. (2005). STATA Version 10. College Station, TX.

Stokes, R. (2002). Place management in commercial areas: Customer service representatives in Philadelphia's central business district. *Security Journal, 15,*7–19.

Taub, R., Taylor, D., & Dunham, J. (1984). *Paths of neighborhood change: Race and crime in urban America.* Chicago, IL: University of Chicago Press.

Taylor, R. (2001). *Breaking away from broken windows: Baltimore neighborhoods and the nationwide fight against crime, grime, fear, and decline.* Boulder, CO: Westview Press.

Taylor, R., Gottfredson, S., & Brower, S. (1984). Block crime and fear, defensible space, local social ties, and territorial functioning. *Journal of Research in Crime and Delinquency, 21,* 303–331.

Thornberry, T. & Krohn, M. (2000). The self-report method for measuring delinquency and crime. in D. Duffee, R. Crutchfield, S. Mastrofski, L. Mazerolle, D. McDowall, & B. Ostrom (Eds.), *CJ 2000: Innovations in measurement and analysis* (pp. 33-83). Washington, D.C.: National Institute of Justice.

Thrasher, F. (1927). *The gang: A study of 1,313 gangs in Chicago.* Chicago, IL: University of Chicago Press.

U.S. Census Bureau. (2009). *American FactFinder.* Retrieved January 4, 2009, from http://factfinder.census.gov/servlet/DatasetMainPageServlet:

U.S. General Accounting Office. (1999). Community development: Businesses' use of Empowerment Zone tax incentives. Washington, D.C.

Welsh, B. & Hoshi, A. (2002). Communities and crime prevention. In L. Sherman, D. Farrington, B. Welsh, & D. MacKenzie (Eds.), *Evidence-based crime prevention* (pp. 165-197. New York, NY: Routledge.

Wiewel, W., Teitz, M., & Giloth, R. (1993). The economic development of neighborhoods and localities. In R. Bingham & R. Meir (Eds.), *Theories of local economic development.* Santa Monica, CA: Sage Publications.

Wilson, J. & Kelling, G. (1982). Broken windows: The police and neighborhood safety. *Atlantic Monthly, March,* 29–38.

Wilson, W. (1987). *The truly disadvantaged: The inner city, the underclass, and public policy.* Chicago, IL: University of Chicago Press.

ENDNOTES

[1] A detailed description of the demographic and income characteristics of household residents in census-tract neighborhoods exposed to the 30 BIDs in Los Angeles is available in MacDonald et al. (2009).

[2] *Householder* refers to the person (or one of the persons) in whose name the housing unit is owned or rented (maintained) or, if there is no such person, any adult member, excluding roomers, boarders, or paid employees. If a married couple owns or rents the house jointly, the householder may be

either the husband or the wife. The person designated as the householder is the reference person to whom the relationship of all other household members, if any, is recorded.

[3] *Shape files* are a set of files that contain a collection of points, arcs, or polygons that hold tabular data and associate it with a spatial location. This file format is used in ArcView® and other geographic information system (GIS) software.

[4] There are a total of 1,072 RDs and 837 census tracts that are located primarily within the city of Los Angeles.

[5] Had we chosen a smaller unit of analysis, such as the census-block group, we would not have enough variation within blocks to estimate area effects with sufficient statistical power or reliability.

[6] The sampling algorithm was developed by Greg Ridgeway, Senior Statistician, RAND Corporation.

[7] A shape file containing the 30 established BIDS was obtained from the City of Los Angeles Office of the City Clerk in December 2005 and overlaid with the shape files for the census tracts in the city of Los Angeles available from: http://www.census.gov/geo/www/cob/tr2000.html

[8] Calls were conducted between 9:00 a.m. and 9:00 p.m. pacific standard time (PST). Project staff also held regular quality-control meetings with telephone interviewers and supervisors. Human subject protection committees (HSPCs) from RAND, RTI, and the Centers for Disease Control and Prevention (CDC) approved the procedures for the survey.

[9] Conserving interviewer resources for the important work of obtaining cooperation and conducting interviews also led to the use of market-research firms that were capable of dialing all list-assisted cases within two business days and assigning codes of (1) disconnected, (2) business, (3) English-speaking household, (4) Spanish-speaking household, or (5) unknown, ring, or no answer. Of the 44,762 cases that used this approach, only 16,323 (36.5 percent) were confirmed as residential numbers. Lead letters were mailed to these confirmed residences, and RTI interviewers began conducting telephone follow-up of these numbers in December 2006.

[10] Inverse-probability weighting (IPW) of the BID and non-BID samples to their original allocations yielded effective sample sizes (n = 365 BID; n = 390 non-BID) that were statistically comparable to those actually achieved (n = 362 BID; n = 374 non-BID).

[11] A total of 96 households provided a parent interview but not a complete youth interview, and 15 households provided a youth interview but not a complete parent interview.

[12] The scalable measures of violence and neighborhood-level processes were adapted from publicly available instruments used in previous research, including the Project on Human Development in Chicago Neighborhoods, the National Longitudinal Study of Adolescent Health (Add Health), the Los Angeles Family and Neighborhood Survey, and other

sources (see Peterson et al., 2004; Inter-University Consortium for Political and Social Research, undated; and CPC, undated).

[13] Because of insufficient counts of African Americans and Asians across the sampled neighborhoods, we could not parse out the correlation between these ethnic groups from that of individual or family attributes and neighborhood factors that are the focus of this analysis.

[14] The average inter-item covariance for this summed index was 1.41 (alpha = 0.75) with an average correlation coefficient of 0.50.

[15] *Neighborhood* was defined to respondents to include the block or street on which they live and several blocks or streets in each direction.

[16] "Don't know" responses were recoded into the middle range for these items.

[17] These models are also referred to as hierarchical linear models in the field of education statistics (Raudenbush & Bryk, 2002) or variance components models in biostatistics and economics (McCulloch & Searle, 2001).

[18] These models were estimated using Stata 10.0, where the distribution of the random effects is assumed to be Gaussian and the conditional distribution of the response function (violence) is assumed to be Bernoulli, with probability of endorsing violence determined by the logistic cumulative distribution function (CDF). The log likelihood for this model has no closed form, so it is approximated in Stata by an adaptive Gaussian quadrature (see Stata Corporation 2005).

[19] Unlike those in Chicago and other older cities, L.A. neighborhoods are not presently defined by the city planning agency by small area locations. Instead, L.A. neighborhoods are defined by larger geographic areas (e.g., neighborhood council areas) that make up diverse demographic and economic compositions.

[20] It is also possible to extend this model and add a random intercept for individual respondents, thereby allowing the effects of household and neighborhood attributes to vary within individual respondents and neighborhood locations. Such a model, however, would have to be based on the theory that there are different effects of SES, social bonds, and such on the probability of endorsing different violent-victimization items within respondents that are not confounded with the observed variables. We found such a theory highly improbable. We did, however, specify this three-level error structure and estimated random intercept terms at the individual and neighborhood levels. The results were not substantively different from the coefficients reported in the following section using our more conservative specifications.

[21] Our sampling approach matches households in BID neighborhood to non-BID neighborhoods exposed to similar environmental attributes, but several years after the establishment of several BIDs. Therefore, it is possible that we have matched a set of BID neighborhoods to areas that are more similar after BIDs have fostered change than they were before.

[22] A more conservative Kolmogorov-Smirnov test for equality of distribution functions between the two groups found only a significant difference from 0 for SES.

[23] Non-response in this study occurred because respondents indicated that they were unwilling or did not know how to answer some questions. Analysis of non-response patterns, with and without mean/median imputation adjustments, yielded estimates comparable to those herein, but deflated.

[24] $= \text{Exp}(Bx_{SD})$.

[25] The estimated OR increases by 14 percent for disorder and 17 percent for collective efficacy when entered separately as opposed to together.

[26] We also estimated models allowing for a shared covariance between collective efficacy and disorder at the neighborhood census-tract level. The results were substantively the same as those reported here and yielded no improvement in model fit.

[27] Concentrated poverty represents an index of the percentage of female-headed households, percentage unemployed, percentage living below the poverty line, and percentage receiving welfare. A principal-component analysis indicated that 66 percent of the variation across all four measures could be explained by a single component (Eigenvalue = 2.63).

APPENDIX A.
CORRELATIONS AMONG NEIGHBORHOOD STRUCTURAL FACTORS

Factor	Correlation					
Concentrated disadvantage	1.00					
Percentage males under age 25	0.69	1.00				
Latino/immigrant concentration	0.75	0.83	1.00			
Residential stability	−0.72	−0.48	−0.65	1.00		
Population density	0.60	0.42	0.60	−0.71	1.00	
Average violent-crime rate (log)	0.56	0.50	0.54	−0.41	0.19	1.00

Do Business Improvement Districts Exert a Contextual Effect on Adolescent Well-Being?

Gina Penly Hall
Alan J. Lizotte

Policy research is essential in the social sciences—it provides insight into the viability of our theories and research in real-world settings. In particular, it is valuable for the evaluation of programs that are established to reduce crime and violence. These programs tackle crime and violence from a variety of theoretical standpoints and range from offender rehabilitation to community revitalization. The amount of money spent on these programs requires that they are research-based and effective. The paper by MacDonald, Bluthenthal, Stokes, and Grunwald provides such information. Taking a community-level perspective, it examines the effectiveness of business improvement districts (BID) in the reduction of youth violence within the city of Los Angeles, CA. It is a theoretically-driven, methodologically sophisticated analysis that not only evaluates the role that community economic development plays in reducing violent victimization among youth, but demonstrates the direction in which community-level research is headed.

MacDonald et al. examine BIDs within the social ecological framework, specifically that which is explicated in social disorganization theory (Shaw & McKay, 1942, 1969). They provide an excellent summary of this theoretical background and clearly state the theoretical model they plan to test. Ultimately, they hypothesize that BIDs can increase the level of residential social cohesion and foster neighborhood environments less conducive to criminal victimization by mediating the effects of structural sources of disadvantage that cause social disorganization. This hypothesis implies a causal relationship between measures. The authors admit they cannot test the relationship without pre- and post-BID data for the areas they are examining. They match BID areas to non-BID areas on a number of aggregate-level measures gathered from the census to manage this data issue so the effectiveness of BIDs can be assessed. However, they do not test the causal model that is theorized. Instead, all variables in the model, exogenous structural sources of disadvantage, endogenous measures of collective efficacy and disorder, and presence of a BID are tested simultaneously in Models 1 and 2, the results of which are illustrated in Table 3. A test of the causal model using the data they have from the two time periods would require that structural variables be measured at Time 1 and the endogenous variables and the outcome measure of violent victimization be measured at Time 2 (additional waves would be ideal so that the outcomes could be measured at a later time). Testing such a model would further require that the date of establishment for each BID precede the date at which the Time 2 data were collected. The front section of this paper is solid and such a causal analysis would strengthen it further.

Given the lack of pre- and post-BID data and the inability to test a causal model, the authors may have examined their hypothesis that BIDs influence levels of collective efficacy by estimating interaction models to provide a sense of the strength of the effect of collective efficacy on violent victimization in BID compared to non-BID areas. This could have been done in one of two ways. First, the variable for BID could have been interacted with the measure of collective efficacy in Models 1 and 2. They also could have created two samples, BID and non-BID, and examined whether the effect of collective efficacy on violent victimization is statistically different between the two groups. This method, which draws on the work of Paternoster, Brame, Mazerolle, and Piquero (1998), compares regression coefficients for a single variable between two independent samples. The authors would be able to conclude whether the strength of the effect of collective efficacy on violent victimization was larger or smaller in BID areas. If indeed they found that it was larger, they may have been able to conclude that levels of collective efficacy are indeed enhanced by the BID. While this does not provide a complete test of their hypothesis, it does provide insight as to the contextual influence of BIDs on collective efficacy.

The authors find no effect of BIDs on violent victimization. This is not surprising, especially when the ideas that comprise the backbone of social disorganization theory are considered. One of the basic tenets of contemporary ecological theory is that of the temporal stability of delinquency regardless of changes in the population (Bursik, 1984, 1986; Bursik & Webb, 1982; Byrne & Sampson, 1986). This was established in the early work of human ecologists (e.g., McKenzie, 1924; Park, 1936; Park & Burgess, 1921) and adopted by Shaw and McKay (1942, 1969). It states that regardless of changes in the population that occur over time, levels of delinquency will remain stable within geographical areas. This was built from the idea that the city is a "growth" (Park, 1915, p. 578), the organization of which is driven by biotic forces (e.g., invasion and succession). These forces control the interrelations among human beings, which results in the formation of relatively stable natural areas and natural social groups (McKenzie, 1924; Park, 1926; Zorbaugh, 1926). This theoretical idea leads us to question the ability of any community-based program to effect a change in a potentially deep-rooted problem like delinquency over a short period. The authors state that the 30 BIDs they examined were established between 1994 and the beginning of their study. While it is not totally clear when they started their study, their survey data are from 2006 and 2007. This means that, at the most, there is 13 years between the establishment of the BID and the collection of data on violent victimization. If indeed the areas around which BIDs were established were disorganized, it seems that 13 years is not long enough to reduce this disorganization to the point that levels of a temporally stable social problem like delinquency will show any statistically significant reduction. It would be interesting if the authors included a measure of length of time since the formation of each BID in a model predicting victimization for those cases in BID areas. They could look for direct effects of this measure or whether it interacts with any of the other independent variables. Regardless, whether BIDs were developed to specifically reduce crime through an increase in collective efficacy is not known, but if so, a subsequent evaluation made at a later date may show BIDs to be effective after all.

Community-level dynamics not only are important predictors of crime and violence, but also serve to mediate effects at other levels of analysis and provide a context within which such effects are better realized. MacDonald et al. do an excellent job in their examination of the effect of a community-level intervention, BIDs, on violent victimization among youth. It is argued, however, that an examination of the contextual effects of BIDs would improve this paper. In particular, an examination of how collective efficacy interacts with BID presence to influence victimization would provide a better picture of how BIDS influence the effect of this community level measure on victimization, as hypothesized in this paper. The interactions between BID and all other measures—the individual- and family-level variables, could also be estimated. It is possible that the effects of these measures are different for BID areas compared to non-BID areas. We think that these comparisons would provide insight as to the influence of BIDS on violent victimization that would supplement the interesting findings already provided by this paper.

REFERENCES

Bursik, Jr., R. (1984). Urban dynamics and ecological studies of delinquency. *Social Forces, 63*, 393-413.

Bursik, Jr., R. (1986). Ecological stability and the dynamics of delinquency. In A. Reiss & M. Tonry (Eds.), *Crime and justice: Vol. 8. Communities and crime* (pp.35-66). Chicago: University of Chicago Press.

Bursik, Jr., R., & Webb, J. (1982). Community change and patterns of delinquency. *American Journal of Sociology, 88*, 24-42.

Byrne, J. & Sampson, R. (1986). *The social ecology of crime*. New York: Springer-Verlag.

McKenzie, R. (1924). The ecological approach to the study of the human community. *American Journal of Sociology, 30*, 287-301.

Park, R. (1915). The city: Suggestions for the investigation of human behavior in the city environment. *American Journal of Sociology, 20*, 577-612.

Park, R. (1926). The concept of position in sociology. *Publications of the American Sociological Society, 20*, 1-14.

Park, R. (1936). Human ecology. *American Journal of Sociology, 42*, 1-15.

Park, R., & Burgess, E. (1921). *Introduction to the science of sociology*. Chicago: University of Chicago Press.

Paternoster, R., Brame, R., Mazerolle, P., & Piquero, A. (1998). Using the correct statistical test for the equality of regression coefficients. *Criminology, 36*, 859-866.

Shaw, C., &. McKay, H. (1942). *Juvenile delinquency and urban areas*. Chicago: University of Chicago Press, 1969.

Zorbaugh, H. (1926). The natural areas of the city. In E. Burgess (Ed.), *The urban community* (pp. 219-229). Chicago: University of Chicago Press.

Geographically Targeted Economic Development Policy and Youth Violence

Robert T. Greenbaum

The United States and many other countries have long experimented with programs targeted at particular distressed geographic areas to combat poverty, stimulate business activity, and restore neighborhoods. Some U.S. programs have been implemented at the federal level, such as the Model Cities Program from the late 1960s and early 1970s or the more recent Empowerment Zone program, and other programs, such as enterprise zones (EZs) or tax increment financing (TIF) districts have been administered at the state or municipal level. While many of these programs require planning and cooperation at the local level, they all provide the targeted area some sort of benefit from the larger government, including special programs, grants, subsidized loans, or tax incentives.

Business improvement districts (BIDs) are unique in that, while they share the goal of attempting to improve the economic conditions of a specific area, they represent the culmination of efforts of the local citizens to *increase* their tax burden to provide local public goods to the business district. Much like with EZs, BIDs are not a uniform program, but rather they can represent different sets of policies in different locations, even within the same city. Typical BID expenditures include enhanced security, business marketing, or more intensive cleaning and upkeep. Because of their focus on the physical environment and safety, most of the evaluations of BIDs have focused on their ability to reduce crime. Indeed, evaluations have shown some success at reducing economic crimes such as theft and robbery in Philadelphia (Hoyt, 2004) and Los Angeles (Brooks, 2008; Cook & MacDonald, 2010; MacDonald, Golinelli, Stokes, & Bluthenthal, 2010). There has not been a demonstrated impact on crimes less directly targeted by BID activities in the extant literature. For example, Brooks (2008) did not find similar reductions in crimes such as domestic abuse, forgery, fraud, or embezzlement attributable to the establishment of BIDs.

MacDonald, Bluthenthal, Stokes, and Grunwald take this research an important step forward by examining the more indirect outcome of youth violence. Because BIDs are not typically designed to directly reduce youth violence, for them to affect adolescent well-being they must ameliorate some of the correlates. That is, they examine whether BIDs can affect outcomes beyond the immediate policy goals. Establishing that BIDs can have such an indirect effect is a difficult methodological challenge, as one must demonstrate that the policy intervention rather than the underlying neighborhood characteristics have led to the outcomes. To do so, the authors carefully match households in BIDs to similar households in similar neighborhoods without BIDs. While they find neighborhood and household predictors of youth violence that are consistent with the literature, they do not find any impact of the BID intervention. These results are not particularly surprising given both that they are looking for an indirect effect and that previous research has found stronger ties between economic conditions and property crime than with violent crime.

In what follows, I address two possible mechanisms for BIDs to affect youth well-being discussed by MacDonald et al., that BIDs can affect youth violence by improving the economic and/or social conditions in targeted neighborhoods. I follow that with a brief discussion of the methodological challenges of tying the BID policies to the outcomes examined.

CAN BIDs AFFECT ECONOMIC OUTCOMES?

One of the ways in which BIDs could affect youth violence is by improving economic opportunities in the local economy, which would help to reduce concentrated poverty. As MacDonald et al. point out, the literature has linked both to youth violence. Further, Ihlanfeldt (2002; 2006) found relationships between job accessibility the criminality of young men.

For the most part, the BID literature has focused more on examining whether BIDs reduce crime rather than on whether BIDs have improved the local economy, with the belief that crime is an important component of businesses ability to succeed in particular neighborhoods (Brooks, 2008). Much more effort has gone into examining whether state EZs and federal Empowerment Zones have been successful at inducing businesses to move into or expand their operations in particular distressed locations. This makes sense, as unlike with BIDs, these other programs typically provide tax breaks and other incentives designed to directly lower the cost of doing business in the neighborhood. However, despite these enticements, the evidence on state EZs is mixed at best, and the evidence on the more generous federal Empowerment Zones is a bit more positive, although results also differ based on the specific outcomes examined, the locations studied, and the nature of the individual programs (Greenbaum & Landers, 2009).

While BIDs seek to improve the business climate by reducing disamenities such as crime, deterioration, and poor perceptions, it is important to note that there are aspects of BIDs that do not necessarily improve the business climate for all. For one, BIDs represent an increased tax burden for local businesses within the BID boundaries. Crime may have differential impacts across different types of businesses (Greenbaum & Tita, 2004), thus any associated drop in crime due to the BIDs may more beneficial to some businesses, such as those that have frequent interactions with customers, than others. However, once a BID has been agreed to by a majority and established, all businesses and property owners must contribute, even those who voted against formation. Further, Cook (2008) notes that critics of BIDs complain that they both privatize public spaces and that they may be undemocratic. Finally, all of the time and effort, including economic and political costs, spent trying to forge the political coalition needed to implement the BID are costs that should be weighed against BID benefits.

Even if BIDs are successful at improving the local economy, the link between the economy and violent crime is far from established. Cantor and Land (1985) highlight two primary influences of the economy on crime: motivation and opportunity. When the economy is poor, social strain increases and social control decreases. Both can increase the motivation to offend (Arvanites & Defina, 2006). Opportunity works in the opposite direction. When more people are unemployed, there are both fewer attractive targets for economic crimes and there is increased guardianship as people spend more time closer to home. Both factors likely serve to reduce crime.

There has been more support in the literature establishing relationships between the economy and property crimes than for violent crimes (Levitt, 2004). Cook and Zarkin (1985), for example, found a relationship between robbery and burglary and the business cycle between 1933 and 1981, but they did not find a correlation between homicide rates and the business cycle. Examining more recent data, Arvanites and Defina (2006) found support for the motivation argument and no support for the opportunity effect. That is, they attributed some of the reduction in property crimes and robbery during the 1990s to the robust economy. Bowes (2007), on the other hand, did find some support of the opportunity theory, finding that retail development may have attracted crime in Atlanta.

Larger macroeconomic forces, too, have been tied more closely to property crime than violent crime. White (1999) linked manufacturing job losses in the largest American cities to increases in poverty and unemployment that were correlated with increases in economic crimes such as robberies, burglaries, and drug crimes. Crimes such as larceny, murder, and aggravated assaults were found to be uncorrelated with the decline of the manufacturing sector and the accompanying unemployment.

Beyond attempting to affect outcomes through the mechanism of improving the local economy, BIDs may help improve the social structure within BID neighborhoods, thus leading to reduced youth violence. This is addressed next.

CAN BIDS IMPROVE SOCIAL CONDITIONS?

As MacDonald et al. describe, social disorganization theory hypotheses that breakdowns in neighborhood structural characteristics, including residential stability, concentrated poverty, and ethnic and racial heterogeneity can lead to less guardianship and residential cohesion, which ordinarily would work to reduce crime (Park & Burgess, 1921; Shaw & McKay, 1942). To address these correlates of crime, the BIDs work not through any particular policy feature but through the nurturing collaborative action to improve the neighborhood.

The process of creating a BID demands a great deal of local buy-in, including support of local businesses and property owners to tax themselves and the navigation of a non-trivial application processes (MacDonald, Golinelli, Stokes, & Bluthenthal, 2010). This galvanizing around the BID application and shared effort to improve the community may foster collective efficacy, which could lead to reductions in violence. Communities with stronger social ties may additionally take further action that could reduce violence. For example, Vittie (2010) found that communities with more social capital were more likely to implement neighborhood block watch programs.

There is also some evidence from the EZ and Empowerment Zone context to support this link between collective action and positive outcomes. For example, Cuomo (1995) claimed that even cities denied federal Empowerment Zones benefited by going through the arduous process of putting together an application and planning for the community's future. Further, in an evaluation of 11 state EZ programs, Bondonio and Greenbaum (2007) found that sales growth and zone-induced capital investment were larger in EZs that required a strategic economic development plan as part of the application process.

While there is some evidence to support the notion that formation of community economic development programs can lead to increased collective efficacy, it may also be the case that communities with greater social capital are more likely to successfully create opportunities for themselves. Thus, I lastly turn to some methodological issues.

TYING POLICY TO OUTCOMES

To address the concern that neighborhoods with BIDs are different than neighborhoods without BIDS, and that this might account for any observed outcomes attributed to the policy, MacDonald et al. used a clever design to draw households to survey from a carefully matched comparison group of neighborhoods that were very similar to the BID neighborhoods. The biggest drawback to their methodology, however, is the inability to go back in time to survey residents prior to BID formation, thus greatly limiting the ability to make causal claims. Particularly problematic is that the matching process relies on data subsequent to the establishment of the BIDs, thus eliminating the possibility of doing a pre-post evaluation. As the authors note, if, for example, the BIDs were successful at reducing youth violence and those positive program effects occurred prior to the period studied, these positive effects would be missed by the analysis.

It is interesting to consider the processes leading from BID formation to desired outcomes described above. In the first explanation, in which outcomes are tied to economic processes, it is important to distinguish among different BID policy features and treatment intensity. In the second explanation, the mere process of establishing the BID is more important, and policy variation is likely less of an issue. While the MacDonald et al. paper does not examine policy variation (they do, however, estimate an alternative fixed effects model that controls for the heterogeneity of the neighborhoods that adopted BIDs), some of the earlier did so with mixed findings. Brooks (2008) finds that her results of BIDs reducing economic crimes were not driven by the type of BID. This lends support to the idea that the social factors in neighborhoods that establish BIDs may be more important than the BID features. However, Cook and MacDonald (2010) do find a dosage effect in their analysis, with BIDs having greater security expenditures experiencing larger drops in both crime and arrests. Also, MacDonald, Golinelli, Stokes, and Bluthenthal (2010) look at the effect of BIDs on robbery, using a pre-post estimation strategy. They find a statistically significant decrease in robberies attributed to BIDs and also provide some anecdotal evidence that the efforts were more successful in neighborhoods that made larger anti-crime investments. Thus, future research should continue to move beyond dichotomous treatment variables in order to help policymakers better design policy interventions.

REFERENCES

Arvanites, T. & Defina, R. (2006). Business cycles and street crime. *Criminology, 44*(1), 139-164.

Bondonio, D. & Greenbaum, R. (2007). Do local Ttax incentives affect economic growth? What mean impacts miss in the analysis of Enterprise Zone policies. *Regional Science and Urban Economics, 37*, 121-136.

Bowes, D. (2007). A two-state model of the simultaneous relationship between retail development and crime. *Economic Development Quarterly, 21*(1), 79-90.

Brooks, L. (2008). Volunteering to be taxed: Business Improvement Districts and the extra-governmental provision of public safety. *Journal of Public Economics, 92*, 388-406.

Cantor, D. & Land, K. (1985). Unemployment and crime rates in the post-World War II United States: A theoretical and empirical analysis. *American Sociological Review, 50*(3), 317-332.

Cook, I. (2008). Mobilising urban policies: The policy transfer of US Business Improvement Districts to England and Wales. *Urban Studies, 45*(4), 773-795.

Cook, P., & MacDonald, J. (2010). *Public safety through private action: An economic assessment of BIDs,locks, and citizen cooperation.* Cambridge, MA: NBER Working Paper No. 15877.

Cook, P., & Zarkin, G. (1985). Crime and the business cycle. *The Journal of Legal Studies, 14*(1), 115-128.

Cuomo, A. (1995). U.S. seeks to rebuild battered inner cities. *Forum for Applied Research and Public Policy, 10*, 92-95.

Greenbaum, R. & Landers, J. (2009). Why are state policy makers still proponents of Enterprise Zones? What explains their action in the face of a Preponderance of the research? *International Regional Science Review, 32*(4), 466-479.

Greenbaum, R. & Tita, G. (2004). The impact of violence surges on neighborhood business activity. *Urban Studies, 41*(13), 2495-2514.

Hoyt, L. (2004). Collecting private funds for safer public spaces: An empirical examination of the Business Improvement District concept. *Environment and Planning B: Planning and Design, 31*, 367-380.

Ihlanfeldt, K. (2006). Neighborhood crime and young males' job opportunity. *The Journal of Law and Economics, 49*(1), 249-283.

Ihlanfeldt, K. (2002). Spatial mismatch in the labor market and racial differences in neighborhood crime. *Economic Letters, 76*(1), 73-76.

Levitt, S. (2004). Understanding why crime fell in the 1990s: Four factors that explain the decline and six that do not. *Journal of Economic Perspectives, 18*(1), 163-190.

MacDonald, J., Golinelli, D., Stokes, R., & Bluthenthal, R. (2010). The effect of Business Improvement Districts on the incidence of violent crimes. *Injury Prevention.*

Park, R. & Burgess, E. (1921). *Introduction to the science of sociology.* Chicago, IL: University of Chicago.

Shaw, C. & McKay, H. (1942). *Juvenile delinquency and urban areas.* Chicago, IL: University of Chicago Press.

Vittie, J. (2010). *A look at perceived efficacy of neighborhood watch programs in Franklin County, Ohio.* Columbus, OH: John Glenn School of Public Affairs, The Ohio State University.

White, G. (1999). Crime and the decline of manufacturing, 1970-1990. *Justice Quarterly, 16*(1), 81-97.

Fraud Vulnerabilities, The Financial Crisis, and the Business Cycle[*]

Michael Levi

Abstract

This paper examines the (in fact only partial) Global Financial Crisis (GFC) and its possible universal and differential direct impacts on frauds of various kinds, and on anti-fraud monitoring and responses which, as routine activities perspectives would suggest, should have an impact upon fraud. The paper examines the limited evidence about fraud reporting processes and argues that some frauds whose commission long preceded the crisis will be brought into victim and/or public consciousness as a result of the credit squeeze; some "organised criminals" may be drawn into greater confidence in making fraud participation offers to insiders or blackmailing them because of the latter's inability to repay debts and because they believe that people are more corruptible at times of economic stress; some fraud opportunities linked to workplaces will be reduced because if people motivated to defraud have lost their jobs, they can no longer commit internal frauds; but in other cases, temptations are greater because of the desire not to lose lifestyle and social status. It describes what is known about commercial, public sector, and criminal justice reactions to frauds, and what impact this plausibly has upon them. Using a fraud typology (drawn from Levi, 2008) of pre-planned fraud, intermediate fraud (starts off honest and consciously turns to fraud), and slippery-slope fraud (tells lies to continue trading in unrealistic hope that things will turn around), the study examines these extra and reduced risks of motivation, opportunity, and capable guardianship. The net effect of these changes in guardianship, motivations and opportunities is difficult to determine, and most fraud data – other than plastic card fraud – are too dependent on changing probabilities of recognition, reporting, and recording to enable confident inferences about trends to be drawn. It seems plausible that more slippery-slope insolvency frauds occur in times of recession, as some company directors and professionals seek to preserve income and wealth from the economic consequences of the downturn. However, there is no evidence that the GFC has had or is likely to have a major impact on increasing the cost of fraud or levels of fraud overall in the areas about which we have the best knowledge: Australia, the United Kingdom, and the United States.

TRENDS IN FRAUD

"You only find out who is swimming naked when the tide goes out."
Buffet (2001)

A key aim of this paper is to examine what the evidence is that would enable us to judge what has happened and what is plausibly likely to happen to frauds in the context of what is often referred to as the Global Financial Crisis (GFC) – though as it transpired, it has not dramatically affected Australia, China, Singapore, or much of South America - whether as a result of that crisis or of other factors that coincide with it. The Australian banking system has been less hard hit than elsewhere, to the extent that it has overtaken the United States to take second spot after the United Kingdom as a financial services heavyweight, with the only net positive score among the leading countries in the Financial Development Index (World Economic Forum, 2009). The primary focus will be in areas where at least some fraud data are available which, unfortunately, are mostly volume rather than management frauds, and care should be taken about generalisation elsewhere. Other kinds of corporate crime data – for example, health and safety and/or pollution – might be interesting to correlate with economic trends, but that will be left to others.

Normally, we would look to statistical data on recorded/surveyed crime and/or cost of crime trends to enable us to judge whether a problem is getting better or worse. However as will be seen, even in the best countries, fraud data are quite poor, and this is an area that requires some redress if empirical criminology is not to continue to neglect white-collar crimes (see, more generally, Simpson & Weisburd, 2009). Despite planned activities to improve fraud statistics in the United Kingdom (Levi & Burrows, 2008; NFA, 2010) and in Australia, but apparently not in the United States, these cannot be applied retrospectively to past data (especially since the last serious recession in Australia was almost two decades ago and the last comparable global financial crisis that affected it was in the 1930s); and other than in the case of payment card frauds, where annual U.K. and Australian data are published. The latter category has the advantage that there is little time lag from crime to discovery, but in higher value management frauds – which arguably are far more serious – there typically is a much longer time before detection and even longer for criminal justice outcomes, if any. Thus, any given year's data will be a mix of crimes occurring at very variable years. This is a particular problem for evaluating the impact of economic trends, and there has been no opportunity here for the individual case analysis that would be a desirable alternative to aggregate data. This paper could be seen as premature, but given the importance of the issues, and the wave of economic pain – intentionally criminal, recklessly criminal[1] or neither – that has flooded around Europe and the United States, and by domino effect elsewhere, it seemed important to pursue the issues.

In addition to numbers of frauds, another measure worth pursuing might be the impact of frauds—including both direct costs and indirect collateral damage. Reasonably comprehensive Australian cost of fraud data are currently available only for one year and for consumer frauds only (Smith & Bud, 2009) and therefore cannot be trended without unacceptable speculative leaps.[2] In the United States, very little effort has been made to generate better fraud and cost of fraud data outside the populist consumer area of identity fraud (Baum, 2007), and even the latter has not been updated since the GFC began (see also ACFE, 2008; Barnett, 2000; and international accounting surveys). The U.K. National Fraud Authority is seeking to make costs of fraud data annual or biennial, in the light of its follow up to the report to the Association of Chief Police Officers (Levi, Burrows, Fleming, & Hopkins, 2007; NFA, 2010). Currently, however, reliable time series cost data are available in the United Kingdom only for payment card and check frauds (U.K. Payments, 2009), some aspects of identity frauds (CIFAS), and for external frauds against government departments (U.K. Treasury, 2009). Intermittent or recent data only are available for other data such as social security fraud and error (Department of Work and Pensions, 2010) and fraud against local authorities and some national non-departmental bodies (Audit Commission, 2010), where serious statistical estimates have been made which are scrutinised by Parliament. No similar efforts have been conducted in other countries around the world, and fraud cost and incidence surveys carried out by accounting firms in many parts of the world are both intermittent and have been applied only to large corporate victims, who are their primary clients and target markets for awareness-raising (Levi et al., 2007; Levi & Burrows, 2008). Indirect costs have not been examined significantly in any of these studies. Finally, there are the usual problems of whether it is possible to place within the category of fraud acts and actors that have not yet been subject to any criminal justice verdict—the action for civil fraud against Goldman Sachs by the Securities and Exchange Commission in 2010 being a case in point. Such elite cases pose questions about the limitations of the relationship between crime and social harm and, if included as fraud, would have a dramatic effect on the composition of the dependent variable.

This may seem to be a rather roundabout way of stating that no reliable or valid data exist anywhere in the world that would enable us to tell with defensible confidence whether fraud or almost any subcomponent of it (other than plastic fraud) was being strongly affected by the GFC. However such warnings may be needed because otherwise opinions – however plausible – may be confused with evidence. If we take the effort to collect data as an indicator of what information the State considers important, as Jeremy Bentham intended criminal statistics to be in the 19th century, one inference is that fraud data are plainly considered unimportant by most governments most of the time, both to inform their resource allocation decisions and for public information about levels of crime.[3]

With these caveats, for the sake of completeness and for illustrative purposes, we include in Figure 1 the trend in recorded fraud data in

Australia. Australia has enjoyed a lengthy period of growth, during which time fraud conviction statistics have risen modestly but unevenly, rising dramatically during the high unemployment era of the mid-1980s and then falling significantly after the recession of 1991 until 1995, when they began to rise again. Unfortunately, data more recent than 2007 are unavailable.

Figure 1. Rate of fraud offences recorded by Australian police, 1953-2007, per 100,000 population.

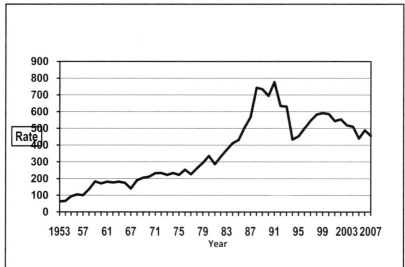

Source: Officially recorded fraud and dishonesty statistics derived from state and territory police services.

Quite apart from any confounding problems caused by statistical recording changes and resources/value changes that may affect the recording process itself (for example, in the United Kingdom), the criminal justice category of fraud is too broad to be helpful for examining the relationship between it and GFC. Criminal charges tell us little about the situational position or social background of offenders and (usually) almost nothing about who the victims are, and media reports are quite selective, focusing upon "widows and orphans" victims and celebrity offenders (Levi, 2006, 2008). The conventional wisdom attributes the rise of fraud to the impact of globalisation, but globalisation is insufficiently linear or specific to be useful as an explanatory variable.

TYPOLOGIES OF FRAUD

In terms of offender-victim combinations, fraud includes, for example:

- *Crimes by élites against consumers, clients, or other lower status businesspeople,* (e.g., the looting of a bank or building society;

misrepresentation of the quality of goods beyond mere inflation of the quality of what one is selling; price-fixing cartels that generate overpayment for contracts or corruption of the tendering process so that the public get poor services).

- *Crimes by small business people against consumers and employees*, (e.g., selling counterfeit goods as genuine ones; pocketing the pension/health contributions paid by staff who then are left benefitless—which is theft but usually with long-delayed recognition of loss).
- *Crimes by professional criminals against élites/large corporations*, (e.g., bankruptcy long firm fraud (Levi, 2008); major counterfeiting rings; mortgage frauds; some advance fee frauds such as fictitious prime banking scams targeted at high net worth—i.e., very rich—individuals).
- *Crimes by professional criminals against consumers/savers/people looking for work*, e.g., offering tickets for holiday and sports events that never materialise; lotteries and prize draws; offers of jobs in more prosperous countries or regions within their own country.
- *Crimes by blue-collar persistent offenders/opportunists against financial institutions*, e.g., using lost and stolen credit cards and (for e-commerce) card data; check frauds.
- *Crimes by individuals of various status against government*, e.g., tax evasion; social security frauds by landlords and claimants; frauds against foreign governments.

There are offenses that can occupy multiple categories. An example is mortgage frauds, which principally defraud grantors of credit such as banks; but they can also devastate mortgagees who – reasonably or not – have pinned their suburban dreams of home ownership and rising asset values onto "affordable" loans that they cannot repay, and then suffer long term credit blight when they are dispossessed or walk away from their devalued homes. The offenders can be professional fraudsters/racketeers or can be criminal professionals such as financial intermediaries/mortgage brokers.

We may also be interested in the broader category of financial crimes. Money laundering can include not just the proceeds of any or all of the above crimes, but also – now in most jurisdictions around the world – the proceeds of any other crime (Levi & Reuter, 2009). Clarity of terminology is important. The term consumer fraud – which might appear to encompass frauds in the consumption process, such as unknowing purchase of counterfeit goods, contamination of food and medicines – has been judged to include (Smith, 2007):

1. Advanced fee schemes
   - pretending to sell something you do not have while taking money in advance

2. Non-delivery and defective products and services
   - supplying goods or services of a lower quality than the goods or services paid for, or failing to supply the goods and services at all
3. Unsolicited and unwanted goods and services
   - persuading consumers to buy something they do not really want through oppressive or deceptive marketing techniques
4. Identity fraud.

ESTIMATING FINANCIAL CRIME COSTS

Many estimates of fraud and money laundering are based on very limited evidence, derive from institutional profile-raising, and take on a life of their own as "facts by repetition," seldom critiqued either by media always hungry for sensational headlines (Levi, 2006) or by pressure groups. On the other hand, if we rely on cases brought to conviction, the data may be absurdly low in both harm caused and case complexity, the most subtle cases of fraud and money laundering being hardest to prove beyond a reasonable doubt in the minds of juries or judges. We must be careful to avoid throwing the baby out with the bathwater by using only very low figures from convictions and treating them as "the figures" rather than just as validated minimum figures (see Levi & Burrows, 2008; Levi & Reuter, 2009).

The elapsed time from fraud to discovery and then from discovery to criminal justice action (if any) means that many of the larger frauds coming to light in 2008-10 will have been committed some years before. One classic notable example is the Madoff long-running Ponzi scheme (van de Bunt, 2010) though this was atypically long for this type of investment fraud. Although such schemes all come to an end eventually when incoming funds are insufficient to meet current payments, the link with the economy is that drops in confidence and increases in need for funds derail the criminal business model. In some other cases where fraud is alleged, for example, the near-collapse of insurers AIG,[4] only careful case-by-case examination can enable us to understand when the fraud began in relation to the business cycle, but one might expect the frauds to result from a combination of ambitious expansion plans with unexpected reductions in business opportunities and/or cash flow. This time attrition for frauds differs from volume crimes such as credit and debit card fraud, which usually come to light promptly (though seldom as promptly as burglaries and vehicle thefts).

PAYMENT CARD AND ALLIED CREDIT FRAUDS

In the United Kingdom, data collected by the nonprofit fraud prevention service CIFAS (2009a, 2009b)[5] indicate a rise in identity takeover frauds, as new credit becomes harder to get, generating displacement to impersonating existing account-holders. Such frauds emerge quite quickly. At the end of the third quarter of 2009, CIFAS data show an 11 percent increase in the level of fraudulent activity, and a 38 percent upturn in misuse of facility fraud (where an account, policy, or other facility is used fraudulently) when compared with the same period in 2008. No equivalent data are available for Australia or the United States, because no equivalent organisations exist there to integrate credit application data.

Since 2006, U.K. payment card fraud data have displayed a broad downwards trend in fraud on lost or stolen cards, due to the introduction of Chip and PIN in Europe; a more recent (2009) drop in counterfeit frauds on skimmed and cloned cards, which previously had risen substantially, mainly being used overseas to sidestep Chip and PIN controls; a slower, modest rise in cards obtained by identity theft; and a less obviously explained very recent drop in card-not-present frauds over the phone and internet (U.K. Payments, 2009). In concert with the fall in check usage, check fraud losses have fallen significantly, while online banking fraud losses rose 55 percent to £39 million in the first half of 2009 – perhaps due to improved awareness and reporting, but also reflecting increased phishing for passwords and sophisticated bank site-cloning.

In Australia, after falling to a low of 5.9 cents per $1,000 over the 12 months to June 2007, total payment card fraud increased to 8.2 cents per $1,000 in June 2009, driven largely by credit card fraud. The following trends are evident for financial institutions:

- Checks – the fraud rate per $1,000 dollars fell to a low in mid-2008. By mid-2009, it had risen but remains at a low level of 0.88 cents per $1,000. The number of checks written continues to fall.
- Debit card fraud shows a fall to 6.6 cents per $1,000 in mid-2009, and was then at a series low.
- Credit and charge cards showed a small decrease over the calendar year 2006. Since then, the rate of fraud per $1,000 has increased to 53 cents per $1000.

None of these Australian or U.K. changes has any obvious relationship to the GFC.

Canadian data for debit card fraud are set out in Table 1. These data show that debit card frauds have risen since the recession, though no breakdown is available beyond the total and, by deduction, the mean values, which fell somewhat in 2008-09.

Table 1. Canadian debit card fraud 2004-2009.

Year	Dollars Lost to Debit Card Fraud	Cardholders Reimbursed
2004	$60 million	49,000
2005	$70.4 million	72,000
2006	$94.6 million	119,000
2007	$106.8million	159,300
2008	$104.5 million	148,000
2009	$142.3 million	238,000

Source: Data retrieved June 1, 2010, from www.interac.ca/media/stats.php

Unfortunately, comparable U.S. data are unavailable, but there are some trend data in the report of the Federal Trade Commission (FTC) (2010), showing a continuing rise since 2007 (see Figure 2).

Figure 2. Consumer Sentinel Network complaint count, calendar years 2000-2009.

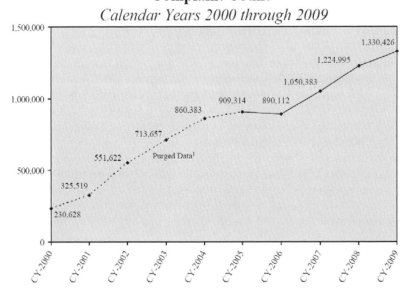

Source: FTC. (2010). *Consumer Sentinel Network data book January–December 2009.* Washington, DC: Federal Trade Commission.

INSURANCE FRAUDS

No comparable data are available for Australia or the United States, but a study by the U.K. ABI (2009) estimated that in 2006, £2.1 billion of fraud was committed and the insurance industry detected £0.5 billion (23 percent) of this (so £1.6 billion was undetected). In 2008, they estimated that £2.7 billion of fraud was committed and the insurance industry detected £0.7 billion (27 percent). So, between 2006 and 2008, while total fraud increased, the proportion of total fraud that the U.K. insurance industry detected increased by 16 percent.[6] The ABI (2009, p. 7) argues:

"To date (July 2009), our research finds that there are clear indications that the recession, which began in the third quarter of 2008, is leading to an increase in general insurance fraud. While these indications are clear, they are not conclusive. They include:

- An increase in "walk-aways" where the claimant drops the claim in response to enquiries from the insurer.[7]
- Significant increases in the proportion of 'suspect' claims and in applications for insurance where underwriting fraud to reduce the level of premiums is suspected.
- An increase in the proportion of claims referred for investigation that are proven to be fraudulent. This is in part due to improved processes for 'flagging' suspect claims. It is also thought this reflects an increase in the level of fraud. Estimates of the increase in fraud – in particular opportunistic fraud – are not available from all the insurers we interviewed but have been put in the range of a 15-25% increase in Q1 2009 compared to Q1 2008.
- An increase in very amateur attempts at claims fraud indicating that otherwise honest customers are attempting to make fraudulent claims for the first time.
- Interviews with loss adjustors indicating that detected fraud, while on an upward trend anyway, dramatically increased in 2008 suggesting an increase in the underlying level of total fraud. One loss adjustor had detected 41% more fraud in 2008 compared to 2007, another estimates a fraud increase of between 15% and 21%, varying by line of business. However, these estimates are likely to also pickup on improved flagging of suspect claims for passing to loss adjustors by insurers which would increase the success-rate of loss-adjustors.
- Research by RSA showing that the number of people in Britain who think insurance fraud is acceptable increased dramatically (from 3.6 to 4.6 million people) between March 2008 and January 2009.

- An increase in calls to the IFB's 'Cheatline'....Over the course of 2008 alone, the volume of calls more than doubled. This increase is in part due to higher public awareness of the Cheatline and the new facility allowing online reporting. It also appears that the public attitude towards fraudsters has hardened: many callers cite the fact that they are motivated to call as they have to pay increased premiums as a result of the activity of fraudsters. Subject to these caveats, the large increase in calls to Cheatline may be indicative of an increase in opportunistic claims fraud."

Insurers also reported that claims on LCD TVs, high-end watches and laptops had increased by as much as 35 percent between 2007 and 2008, though it is possible that much of this was the result of a rise in genuine crime rates for those items, which are attractive because of the resale opportunities and values. On the other hand, though overtime opportunities fell earlier, the U.K. unemployment rate did not begin to start increasing rapidly until the first quarter of 2009, and there is normally a lagged effect between unemployment and serious deprivation, depending on levels of savings and the capacity to defer obligations to repay.[8] Savings ratios have been declining as people shift to a credit mindset, and tightening of credit due to the LIBOR market and the liquidity capital ratios imposed under Basel II, so this lagged effect may diminish, subject to the willingness of people to walk away from their homes in negative equity and of mortgage holders to push for forced sales of properties in a poor market.

Figure 3. Unemployment rate vs fraud and forgery offences (1971 – 2007).

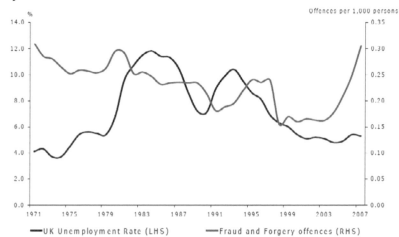

Note: Fraud and Forgery offences are for England and Wales only. Various definition changes occur throughout.

Source: Office For National Statistics (2009), Home Office (2009) and World Bank (2009).

The ABI study also (2009, p. 15, Figure 7) generated its Figure 7 (Figure 3 here), though changes in fraud recording procedures that might have affected this graph and might have driven recent recorded data upwards artificially are not discussed.

This suggests a slight inverse but lagged relationship between changes in the unemployment rate and recorded fraud and forgery statistics. However this evidence is not strong, since payment card and social security frauds constitute a large proportion of recorded fraud and forgery cases.

MORTGAGE FRAUDS

The Key Findings in a report by the FBI (2009) state that:

> "A decrease in loan originations and an increase in defaults and foreclosures continued to dominate the downward trend in the housing market in 2008. While the amount of mortgage fraud cannot be precisely determined, industry experts agree that there is a direct correlation between fraud and distressed real estate markets.... The downward trend in the housing market during 2008 provided a favorable climate for mortgage fraud schemes to proliferate. Several of these schemes have the potential to spread if the current economic downward trend, as expected, continues into 2009 and beyond. Increases in foreclosures, declining housing prices, and decreased demand place pressure on lenders, builders, and home sellers. These and other market participants are perpetuating and modifying old schemes, including property flipping, builder-bailouts, short sales, and foreclosure rescues. Additionally, they are facilitating new schemes, including reverse mortgage fraud, credit enhancements, condo conversion, loan modifications, and pump and pay in response to tighter lending practices."

However, whether this is a correct interpretation is open to question. It seems likely that it has failed to take sufficient account of the lagged effect of the fraud identification process, and that the frauds began typically before the financial crisis, though the general report usefully outlines the precipitating factors behind the mortgage fraud crisis and suggests that the rate of deception accelerated as brokers sought to retain their commission bonuses in a falling market. (Though the latter is plausible, the data are not available to demonstrate it.) Many of the situational opportunities to defraud are fairly widespread over time, so variation is likely to be accounted for in terms of the spread of techniques among the wider population, expectations of the corruptibility of others, and changes in motivation, including the fear of downward economic mobility.

A contrasting example of much longer elapsed time from fraudulent to business-detected awareness is "rogue trading" in the form of illicit (and –

perhaps more importantly – unsuccessful!) betting on market trends, for example by Nick Leeson at Barings in 1995 (http://www.nickleeson.com) and, allegedly, by Jérôme Kerviel at Société Générale in 2007–08 (Kerviel, 2010). In both cases the primary accused alleged that more senior managers turned a blind eye to the risk taking, because they were incompetent (Barings) or because they stood to gain if the risks paid off (both Barings and Société Générale). The popular explanation for this (and other excrescences of the financial sector) is that it is caused by greed. However, unless it is a tautology, greed is not a helpful discriminator between those who both see and take fraud opportunities and those who do not.[9] Nor is it obvious that the recession – local or global – had any impact at all on these sorts of alleged frauds, except indirectly, inasmuch as credit and controls tend to be tighter in recessionary times. In essence, they were cases in which ill-supervised traders found ways of breaching their dealing limits without detection and, having lost significant sums in early trading, carried on trading in the hope that they would be able to recoup those losses. Whether others behaved similarly but were more fortunate in their later dealings (or gambling) and remained forever undetected is unknown.

Finally, a typology of frauds based on victim categories developed by Levi et al. (2007) is set out in Table 2.

Table 2. A typology of fraud by victim category and form of activity.

Victim sector	Victim subsector	Examples of fraud
Private	**Financial Services**	Check fraud
		Counterfeit intellectual property and products sold as genuine
		Counterfeit money
		Data-compromise fraud
		Embezzlement
		Insider dealing/market abuse
		Insurance fraud
		Lending fraud
		Payment card fraud
		Procurement fraud

Victim sector	Victim subsector	Examples of fraud
	Non-financial services	Check fraud
		Counterfeit intellectual property and products sold as genuine
		Counterfeit money
		Data-compromise fraud
		Embezzlement
		Gaming fraud
		Lending fraud
		Payment card fraud
		Procurement fraud
	Individuals	Charity fraud
		Consumer fraud
		Counterfeit intellectual property and products sold as genuine
		Counterfeit money
		Investment fraud
		Pension-type fraud
Public	**National bodies**	Benefit fraud
		Embezzlement
		Procurement fraud
		Tax fraud
	Local bodies	Embezzlement
		Frauds on municipal and state taxes
		Procurement fraud
	International (but affecting public)	Procurement fraud [by national against other – mainly but not always foreign - companies to obtain foreign contracts]

Note: See Levi & Burrows (2008, Box 1) for a glossary of common fraud types. The counterfeiting of intellectual property counts as fraud only if the vendor represents it as being the genuine manufacturer's product (or, arguably, if the purchaser believes it to be genuine). Otherwise, it may be a loss of the manufacturer's property rights, but no one is defrauded. The manufacturer loses principally if the purchaser would have bought the legitimate product at the price offered for it, but also if there is collateral damage to the product's reputation.

THE GFC AND ITS ECONOMIC AND SOCIAL IMPACT

Australia was less affected by the GFC than were many other OECD countries such as the United Kingdom and the United States. Before looking at the implications for fraud, it might be helpful to see what the general financial crime-relevant effects might be expected to be. One plain effect (and cause) of the GFC is uncertainty in economic markets. A standard measure of uncertainty – the implied volatility of the S&P 100 of the U.S. stock market, commonly known as the index of financial fear – increased six-fold between the first emergence of the U.S. subprime crisis in August 2007 and October 2008, not long after the collapse of Lehman Brothers and at the height of the financial crisis. Indeed, the index reached levels far higher than after the 9/11 terrorist attacks, the Gulf wars, the Asian crisis of 1997, and the Russian default of 1998 (Vaitilingam, 2009). The lack of credit strangles firms' abilities to make investments, hire workers, and start new innovation projects. Second, even firms with access to credit postpone making investment and hiring decisions (Bloom, 2009): since many of Australia's and the United Kingdom's markets are international – a factor that is less important to the United States – this affects the rate of growth. As for consumers, when uncertainty is high, people avoid buying consumer durables. Uncertainty makes people cautious about buying a bigger house, and negative equity (price minus borrowings) in houses freezes geographic mobility. In the early stages of the recession, some commentators suggested that it might be a middle-class or white-collar recession, unlike anything seen in the past. Because the recession started in the financial sector (which also saw the first mass lay-offs), it was argued that university-educated workers would suffer more than their semi-skilled and manufacturing counterparts – in stark contrast to previous recessions, in which low-skilled, low-educated workers were hardest hit.

Institute for Fiscal Studies research indicates that these predictions are not borne out by the U.K. data (Muriel & Sibieta, 2009). Low-skilled elementary occupations have suffered most since 2008, followed by skilled trades and sales. In contrast, managers and senior officials have seen their unemployment increase by only one percent, and white-collar professional unemployment has increased by just 0.7 percent, about one-sixth of the increase in the other groups. This does not mean that the white-collar workers are not fearful, but the impact of these fears on their propensity to defraud or launder money remains unresolved. The rise in unemployment among those with housing commitments and negative equity constitutes a serious economic trap, and could lead to increased personal bankruptcies and/or crime to support living standards. However, social security fraud and payment card fraud are the two types most readily open to such persons.

A demonstration that increased unemployment – whether generally or in a particular sector from which fraudsters came – always tended to be followed by increased crime rates would provide more compelling evidence of a causal relationship than would mere cross-sectional data for a particular point in time. Most criminology is concerned with juvenile and young adult crime, and it is hardly surprising that fraud was not discussed in traditional studies of the relationship between economic factors and crime (e.g., Chiricos, 1987). Even if they had done so, they would not have been able to overcome unreported and unrecorded fraud data problems, some but not all of which are being resolved in the United Kingdom by the Action Fraud Reporting Centre, currently (May 2010) being trialled, which is based partly on the US and Canadian NWC3/RECOL reporting centres, though these latter are more web than telephone-based.

In a review of the evidence that was conducted in the wake of the previous Australian recession, Weatherburn (1992, p. 8) concluded that:

> "[T]here would appear to be no reason to expect the criminogenic effects of sustained economic deprivation to be any quicker to dissipate than they were to arrive.... In the final analysis, the effect of passing economic crises, even severe ones such as the current recession, would seem less important to the future course of crime trends, than the overall pattern of economic development. Uncontrolled and rapid economic development, chronically high levels of unemployment in certain sectors of the economy, and the existence of a marginalised under-class of individuals and families living in poverty are all conditions which can just as easily be found in booming as in contracting economies.... Nothing could be more inimical to law and order than an economy which generates rapidly rising living standards for some and an abundance of criminal opportunities for the remainder."

THE GFC AND MODELS OF FRAUD EXPLANATION

There has never been a simple link between recession, poverty, and crime. Barbara Wootton (1959) observed that if there were, then widows and elderly people would have the highest offending rates. Gary Becker's valuable contribution to the economic explanation of crime has been eroded over time by the understanding from behavioural economists that his individualistic focus on crime and rational choice is mistaken, since our beliefs about what other people are doing and will find acceptable significantly mediate our behaviour and even our desires. The reaction of people to often dramatic changes in their financial circumstances and their social prestige (and in their *expectations* of unbroken progress towards 'the good [consumer] life') is a good test of the adequacy of criminological theories. In the particular case of white-collar crimes (see Simpson & Weisburd, 2009), the anxieties among well-paid (and often highly wealth-oriented) professionals about the personal and corporate impact of the GFC gives plausible grounds for concern about what extra crime risks will be generated. These might take the form of greater willingness to trade off the risk of money-laundering prosecution against doing extra business.[10] There is also the possibility that lower paid white-collar workers – for example in call centres and banks – may be tempted to engage in fraud and money-laundering on behalf of organised crime groups. These phenomena are not new. What is being proposed is that there may be a significant escalation in take-up of such opportunities.

Clarity is important here. To the extent that crimes are *occupational*, one must have an occupation in order to commit them. To illustrate this, we might examine the extent to which fraudulent chief executives such as Lord Conrad Black, Alan Bond, Kenneth Lay (Enron), and dot.com bubble chiefs were able to allocate to the company expenditures that, in fact, were largely or wholly personal. (This also applies to kleptocratic dictators in developing countries, whose coffers may become larger because of the increased desperation of sales divisions of international corporations; though this may be counteracted by the increased activism of prosecutors noted recently in the United Kingdom as well as the United States). Accountants, bankers and lawyers cannot readily manipulate clients' accounts or set up trust and other corporate secrecy vehicles if they no longer work, though they (and anyone else) can make up *imaginary* firms and may have a pretext for corporate instructions to firms ("Starting a new phase in my life – wonderful opportunities for new investments in country or product x"). If others have confidence in them, such entrepreneurs can develop new businesses that may generate new manipulative possibilities, but this would usually take longer at times of recession. At a lower level, staff in call centres (whether physically located in the Western jurisdiction or in India/Bangladesh) cannot so easily copy and extract personal data of account-holders if they are no longer employed in the call centres. If still employed, they may be more tempted to defraud if they consider that they may shortly become unemployed and/or that the company will show no loyalty towards them. (Though their *ability to offend* may be reduced by physical opportunity controls such as the absence of USB and CD drives on computers and rapid integrity checks.) Under such circumstances, *voluntary* compliance via procedural legitimacy (Tyler, 2009) becomes much harder to achieve. (Financial and social pressures to offend may also be affected positively or negatively by fear of redundancy and peer group pressures, though threats from organised crime groups may not be GFC-related.)

Knowledge of criminal techniques should be differentiated from *opportunity and motivation to offend,* though offending may be inhibited if people do not believe that they have enough knowledge to commit any particular sort of fraud that they contemplate. *It is the expectation or fear that one may become unemployed, not post-employment status, that presents the extra risk here.* There may be some crimes – computer hacking for example – where employment status may be unimportant, though the importance of social engineering in getting passwords or other elements of crime (see Grabosky, 2006; Wozniak, Mitnick, & Simon, 2003, http://news.cnet.com/8301-1009_3-9995253-83.html, http://www.zdnet.co.UK/tsearch/kevin+mitnick+social+engineering.htm) may suggest that having a job in which one *knows* these current gateways is useful (past gateways may still be current if controls are not changed immediately when people are let go). Impacts of the GFC on professionals elsewhere may impact any country (even those like Australia that have suffered less) because, given international finance and trade – both for business and individuals – Americans, Australians, or British people may be the victims of frauds originating elsewhere, and expatriate professionals who lose their jobs may return home and exercise their skills illicitly. On the other hand, there are significant segments of technologically sophisticated people in Eastern Europe who have never had sufficient economic opportunities to meet their wants, so, except in reducing their future expectations, the downwards shift in economic status implied by the term GFC has not happened for them. The greater time available to the unemployed can give greater room for experimentation, and criminal attempts seldom are punished or even logged by targets or financial intermediaries.

The crime triangle of motivation, opportunity, and capable guardians can be applied to fraud, and it is here in human and technological changes to these parameters that one may search for an explanatory framework. *A priori*, it would appear that different skill sets, commercial/personal background and formal qualifications will be needed for different fraud offences, and the barriers to entry depend on the starting point of any given individual or network *in relation to the practical opportunity and criminal justice obstacles that confront them.* The longer and more intensive an investigation, the more likely it is that surveillance will generate an accurate model of interactions between players in the network. In most countries of the world, a distinction is made between laissez-faire opportunities to set up and work in commerce and some restrictions applied to people who want to open or work in the financial services sector, largely on the grounds that the latter can directly steal funds from the public. It is important to understand such restrictions in a global context rather than the traditional nation-state perspective of regulation and criminal justice.

Sometimes what is needed for the accomplishment of fraud is compliant colleagues – both inferiors and superiors – who do not ask critical questions. This was the case with Nick Leeson and Barings Bank, where as a leading trader, Leeson was surrounded with Singaporean subordinates and colleagues who were passive, and with British superiors who understood little about trading and were content to take the results he fed them that inflated their own large bonuses (Leeson, 1997).

Many of the larger cases in which corporate vehicles are used as a vehicle for fraud begin in good economic times, when there is an atmosphere of optimism among lenders, and large bonuses for corporate takeover activity (though recent bonuses have been much larger than in earlier eras). Some corporate fraudsters – such as the chiefs of Enron, Alan Bond and other Australian entrepreneurs of the 1980s, and the late British pension fund fraudster Robert Maxwell – appointed staff on much higher than normal market salaries to ensure their loyalty or wilful blindness when facing alternative employment on much lower salaries. Alternatively, as in the recent U.S.-regulated Madoff and Stanford scandals, they may employ small firms of accountants who are dependent on them, whether or not they were active participants in the frauds. Such alleged scams are facilitated by trust combined with pressure on investors to get higher than average returns (and by greed). By contrast with credit card skimmers who may need to be helped by an army of people to use the card numbers they have skimmed before the breach of identity is realised and reported, there may be no need for conscious co-conspirators in other frauds, depending on the chain of authority within large corporate or governmental settings and their competence. What some offenders are able to do is simply to deploy the range of global corporate mechanisms available in a free enterprise society where there are insufficient capable guardians to stop them misusing the disguises offered by the corporate form or the authority and power of a corporate role. Barry (2001) highlights the role played by Bond's ingenuity and the (skillfully manipulated) delays of law in enabling him to exploit the rule whereby gifts "not for value" could be set aside only if they preceded bankruptcy by two years. The lawyers who enabled that delay were paid by generous international benefactor friends and by a Swiss who was alleged to have acted as a nominee for Bond, using a variety of foreign trust companies. Enron offered a dazzling array of Special Purpose Vehicles to hide transactions. This was long before the GFC, and it is moot whether the impact on fraud of the crisis was affected by the Sarbanes-Oxley and other supervision measures introduced in the aftermath (see Tillman, 2009, for some insights).

LEVELS OF INDEPTEDNESS AND REGULATION

Corporate indebtedness is a major trigger for the revelation of fraud, as it becomes impossible to hide large-scale fraud (or at least to hide great loss, since it may be possible to misrepresent fraud as legitimate commercial failure amongst all the other corporate collapses, especially if creditors can be strung out long enough to risk throwing good money after bad). At the individual level, levels of indebtedness and illiquidity are major components that make some aspects of the current GFC different, and the reduction in lending capacity has affected the depth of the economic crisis. One would not want to overstress this – the great scammers of the 1980s were highly leveraged on their corporate assets and gave personal guarantees that turned out to be worthless (Barry, 2001). However, not only are wealthy entrepreneurs of the current era (e.g., Russian oligarchs) highly mortgaged on their assets and therefore more pressured to lie to stay afloat long enough to avoid a forced sale; but also a broad range of people in many walks of life are hugely indebted compared with the 1980s (see Keen, 2007, for an Australian dataset). The long period of prosperity is one reason for this, alongside the rising housing market that tempted many to borrow for current optional expenditure beyond their capacity to repay. Business, consumers and regulators fell victim to the convenient myth that the boom and bust cycle had been abolished.[11]

The rise in visible mortgage frauds (Carswell & Bachtel, 2009) and consumer/investment scams has energised the regulatory process, assisted by forensic linking software developments which make it easier proactively to search out connections between banking and insurance fraud networks. Since Ponzi investment pyramids rely on a high rate of incoming investments to sustain pay-outs, a fall in the rate of *increase* of investments or a *reduction* in the rate of re-investment of imaginary profits causes them to collapse earlier.

JUDGMENTS ABOUT THE IMPACT OF THE GFC ON FRAUD

Even professional judgments about trends in fraud should be treated with care, because unless there is plausible argument and some data/case studies, this can be the product of group-think rather than of rigorous review of evidence. Conventional wisdom is not always correct. However given these caveats, it seems plain that professionals are not at all unanimous that fraud will go up. Interviews with business people and fraud managers conducted for the U.K. National Fraud Authority (Gill & Goldstraw-White, unpublished), plus a fraud professional networking request for evidence and for views conducted by this author in the United Kingdom in June 2009 for this study, support the proposition argued here that some frauds are expected to go down while others are expected to go up. This is a function of impact on both motivation and opportunities, the latter rising as a result of declining staffing numbers in fraud and compliance departments.

A pan-European study of 2,246 employees by Ernst & Young (2009) found that 55 percent of respondents expected corporate fraud to increase over the next few years, one-third because changes to their business opened up new areas of risk, 31 percent because management were not focused on anti-fraud measures, 29 percent because they did not trust management, and an equal number because pressures to protect the future of the company will be greater. East Europeans were particularly sceptical about their own management. Over one-third of respondents mentioned that normal controls were likely to be forgotten or overlooked during cycles of redundancies, especially when linked to merger activity which could easily lead to disorganisation and low morale. When asked whether activities would be justified if they help a business survive the economic downturn (a form of noble cause corruption), one-quarter found it justifiable to make cash payments or give personal presents to win or retain business, one-fifth to provide entertainment to win or retain business, and one-twelfth to misstate the company's performance. Only two-fifths said that it was unjustifiable to commit corruption or fraud under such circumstances. Stock-exchange listed companies differed little from others. The extent to which there is a read-across from this to the United States, Australia, or any other country is open at present.

As regards the impact of the financial crisis on consumer frauds, as with other scams, any "current idea" generates scam possibilities, and eligibility for an economic stimulus payment may appear to come from a rebate company or from the Internal Revenue Service. A key is often an incorrect web address, but this sometimes is not obvious to viewers. As with 419 scams generally, there follows a request to send a small processing fee, which then escalates; or a bank account number so they can "deposit" your check, which leads to the cleaning out of an account or opening of new credit lines. Some stimulus scams encourage targets to click on links, open attached forms, or call phony toll-free numbers, installing malware. Such frauds, like adverts offering employment opportunities, usually overseas, are a product of economic stress and downturn, but are basically tuned into some desired goal of potential victims and could as well happen (perhaps in a different form) in an economic boom.

CONCLUSIONS

The impact of the Global Financial Crisis upon fraud depends upon what one includes within the latter category. The damning verdict of the Valukas (2010) report into Lehman Brothers and the civil charges of fraud against Goldman Sachs by the SEC (and the media treatment thereof which signalled this in a quasi-criminal mode) make the fluctuating boundaries of fraud even more apparent. Frauds and white-collar crimes need to be broken down in conformity with the purposes for which one wants to use the typology, especially if a link to the business cycle is to be established. Opportunity, culture and the expectations about others' behaviour are so central to the propensity to defraud that one must be wary of automatic assumptions about transferability. If that were not the case, there would be more uniformity in fraud levels between countries than appears to be the case, though analytically, the vulnerability criteria that underlie comparative risks rates remain to be explored.

In their powerful analysis of animal spirits, Akerlof and Shiller (2010) identify confidence, fairness, corruption and bad faith, money illusion, and stories as the key drivers of economic change, both positive and negative. As they acknowledge, their work is of a high level of generality, and to turn them into operationalizable models capable of correlating with financial crimes of various kinds is too major a task for this study. What seems plain is that generalizations about the correlation between economic crises and fraud (or other types of financial crime) are far too glib to be sustainable in the round. More limited evidence exists of some subsets of fraud but even here, the recession serves to mask the complexity of trends and, once the lagged awareness, reporting and investigation of larger frauds is taken into account, the relationship is shown to be less strong than it initially appeared. In short, we are only a little way along this empirical journey, but I hope that readers have found it an interesting road to travel.

REFERENCES

ABI. (2009). *General insurance claims fraud.* London: Association of British Insurers.
http://www.abi.org.U.K./Media/Releases/2009/07/40569.pdf

ABS. (2008). *Personal fraud.* Canberra: Australian Bureau of Statistics.

ACFE. (2008). *2008 ACFE report to the nation: On occupational fraud and abuse.* Austin, TX: AFCE. http://www.acfe.com/documents/2008-rttn.pdf

Akerlof, B. & Shiller, R. (2010). *Animal spirits: How human psychology drives the economy, and why it matters for global capitalism,* Princeton, NJ: Princeton University Press.

Attorney General's Department. (forthcoming). *Annual report to the government: Fraud against the Commonwealth.* Canberra: Australian Institute of Criminology.

Audit Commission. (2010). *National Fraud Initiative report 2008/09.* London: Audit Commission.

Barnett, C. (2000). *The measurement of white-collar crime using Uniform Crime Reporting (UCR) data.* Washington, DC: U.S. Department of Justice.

Barry, P. (2001). *Going for broke.* Melbourne: Bantam.

Baum, K. (2007). *Identity theft 2005.* Washington, DC: Bureau of Justice Statistics. http://www.ojp.usdoj.gov/bjs/pub/pdf/it05.pdf

Bloom, N. (2009). The impact of uncertainty shocks. *Econometrica, 77*(3), 623-85.

Buffet, W. (2001). *Berkshire Hathaway 2001 Chairman's Letter.* http://www.berkshirehathaway.com/2001ar/2001letter.html

Carswell, A. & Bachtel, D. (2009). Mortgage fraud: A risk factor analysis of affected communities. *Crime Law and Social Change, 52,* 347–364.

Chiricos, T. (1987). Rates of crime and unemployment: An analysis of Aggregate Research Evidence. *Social Problems, 34*(2), 187-212.

CIFAS. (2009a). *CIFAS fraud threat assessment 2009-2010.* Unpublished.

CIFAS. (2009b). *The anonymous attacker.* London: CIFAS.

Coates, J. & Herbert, J. (2008). Endogenous steroids and financial risk taking on a London trading floor. *Proceedings of the National Academy of Science, 105*(16), 6167-6172.

Department of Work and Pensions. (2010). *Fraud and error in the benefit system: October 2008 to September 2009.* London, UK: DWP.

Ernst & Young. (2009). *European fraud 2009: Is integrity a casualty of the downturn?*
http://www2.eycom.ch/publications/items/fraud_eu_2009/200904_EY_European_Fraud_Survey.pdf

FBI. (2009). *2008 mortgage fraud report "Year in Review".* http://www.fbi.gov/publications/fraud/mortgage_fraud08.htm

FTC. (2010). *Consumer Sentinel Network data book January – December 2009* Washington, DC: Federal Trade Commission.

Gill, M. & Goldstraw-White, J. (unpublished). *The impact of the economic climate on the behaviour of fraudsters,* Leicester: Perpetuity Research and Consultancy.

Grabosky, P. (2006). *Electronic crime,* New York, NY: Prentice-Hall.

Keen, S. (2007). *Deeper in debt.* http://cpd.org.au/deeper-debt

Kerviel, J. (2010). *L'engrenage: Mémoires d'un trader.* Paris: Flammarion.

Leeson, N. (1997). *Rogue trader.* London, UK: Sphere.

Levi, M. (1994). Masculinities and white-collar crime. In T. Newburn & B. Stanko (Eds.), *Just boys doing business* (pp. 234-252). London: Routledge.

Levi, M. (2006). The media construction of financial white-collar crimes. *British Journal of Criminology, Special Issue on Markets, Risk and Crime*(46), 1037-1057.

Levi, M. (2008). *The phantom capitalists: the organisation and control of long-firm fraud,* 2nd edition. Andover: Ashgate.

Levi, M. (2010, August). Serious tax fraud and noncompliance: A review of evidence on the differential impact of criminal and noncriminal proceedings. *Criminology and Public Policy, 9*(2), 493-513.

Levi, M. & Burrows, J. (2008). Measuring the impact of fraud: a conceptual and empirical journey. *British Journal of Criminology, 48*(3), 293-318.

Levi, M., Burrows, J., Fleming, M. & Hopkins, M. (with the assistance of Matthews, K.). (2007). *The nature, extent and economic impact of fraud in the UK. London: Association of Chief Police Officers.* Accessed August 3, 2010 from
http://www.cardiff.ac.uk/socsi/contactsandpeople/academicstaff/I-L/professor-michael-levi-publication.html

Levi, M. & Reuter, P. (2009). Money laundering. In M. Tonry (Ed.), *The Oxford handbook on crime and public policy* (pp. 356-380). New York: Oxford University Press.

Minsky, H. (2003). The financial instability hypothesis. In F. Stilwell & G. Argyrous (Eds.), *Economics as a social science: Readings in political economy* (pp. 201-203). North Melbourne: Pluto Press.

Muriel, A. & Sibieta, L. (2009). *Living standards during previous recessions.* IFS Briefing Notes No. 85. London: Institute for Fiscal Studies. http://www.ifs.org.U.K./publications/4525

NFA. (2010). *Annual fraud indicator.* London: National Fraud Authority.

Simpson, S. & Weisburd, D. (Eds.). (2009). *The criminology of white-collar crime.* New York, NY: Springer.

Smith, R. & Budd, C. (2009). Consumer fraud in Australia: costs, rates and awareness of the risks in 2008. *Trends & issues in crime and criminal justice No.382.* Canberra: Australian Institute of Criminology.

Tillman, R. (2009). Reputations and corporate malfeasance: Collusive networks in financial statement fraud. *Crime Law and Social Change, 51,* 365–382.

Treasury Committee. (2009). *Banking crisis: Regulation and supervision.* http://www.publications.parliament.U.K./pa/cm200809/cmselect/cmt reasy/767/767.pdf

Tyler, T. (2009). Self-regulatory approaches to white-collar crime: The importance of legitimacy and procedural justice. In S. Simpson & D. Weisburd (Eds.), *The criminology of white-collar crime* (pp. 195-216). New York, NY: Springer.

The UK Cards Association. (2009). *Fraud: the facts.* London, UK: The UK Cards Association. http://www.apacs.org.uk/resources_publications/documents/Fraudth eFacts2009.pdf

U.K. Payments. (2009). *Financial fraud action: U.K. announces latest fraud figures.* http://www.U.K.payments.org.U.K./media_centre/press_releases/- /page/732/

U.K. Treasury. (2009) *2008-2009 fraud report: An analysis of reported fraud in government departments.* London, UK: U.K. Treasury.

Vaitilingam, R. (2009). *Recession Britain.* Swindon: ESRC.

Valukas, A. (2010). *Lehman Brothers Holdings Inc. Chapter 11 Proceedings Examiner's Report.* http://lehmanreport.jenner.com/

van de Bunt, H. (2010). Walls of secrecy and silence: The Madoff case and cartels in the construction industry. *Criminology and Public Policy, 9*(3), 435-453.

Weatherburn, D. (1992). Economic adversity and crime. *Trends and Issues in Criminal Justice, 40.* Canberra: Australian Institute of Criminology.

Wootton, B. (1959). *Social Science and Social Pathology.* London: Allen and Unwin.

World Economic Forum. (2009). *The financial development report 2009.* Davos: World Economic Forum.

Wozniak, S., Mitnick, K. & Simon, W. (2003). *The art of deception: Controlling the human element of security.* Chichester: Wiley.

ENDNOTES

* The author expresses thanks to the UK Economic and Social Research Council Professorial Fellowship RES-051-27-0208, and to the Australian Institute of Criminology who granted me a Visiting Fellowship in 2009 to conduct some of this work.

[1] Jurisdictions vary in their legislation, but broadly, criminal recklessness is seeing that there is a risk of harm to others and ignoring it.

[2] Though the Australian Bureau of Statistics has surveyed the cost of personal fraud to individuals, totalling almost A$1 billion in 2007 (ABS, 2008), it is not known how regularly this will be updated.

[3] Some skeptics may believe that this is a conspiracy to keep white-collar crimes out of the public eye, but there is no evidence for this proposition.

[4] Though in May 2010, it was disclosed that the U.S. authorities had notified principal senior executive suspects at AIG that they would not be prosecuted.

[5] CIFAS (2009b) data reveal that over 59,000 victims of impersonation were recorded by them in the first 9 months of 2009 - a 36 percent increase from

the same period in 2008. The overall number of identity frauds has increased by one-third in the first 9 months of 2009 from 2008. Account takeovers have risen by 23 percent in 2009 when compared with the same period in 2008; and by 238 percent in the last 24 months. More than 1 in 2 account takeovers have targeted victims' plastic card (i.e., credit card) accounts. Mobile phone account takeovers have already more than doubled in 2009, from 2008 levels.

[6] The improved detection performance is plausible in the light of changes in the forensic analysis of insurance claims by voice stress and data linkage software.

[7] Though some or all of this may be the result of enquiries by more risk-aware insurers.

[8] Home Office statistical model predictions of general crime rises in the United Kingdom have not hitherto been realized.

[9] Some might argue that offenders and non-offenders are equally greedy but that the latter are more risk-averse by temperament/social training/testosterone levels (Levi, 1994, Coates & Herbert, 2008). This is too big a question for this paper and, arguably, for our existing knowledge.

[10] Though a wider range of professionals are subject to money-laundering regulations in Europe than in Australia or the United States, which have resisted the encroachment of suspicious transaction reporting of their clients as part of the "responsibilization" process (see Levi et al., 2007; Levi, 2010).

[11] Minsky (2003) suggests that periods of stability lull market players (and regulators) into thinking that the stability is an inherent and defining aspect of the financial system. In such a situation, more risky financial tactics are adopted, as investors believe that they can have high profits without risk. More speculative patterns emerge and, as this way of thinking spreads from the professional investment world to the whole population, Ponzi styles of investment become generalized. Regulators and politicians, too, became absorbed into this group-think, and by no means solely in the United Kingdom (Treasury Committee, 2009).

THE EFFECT OF ECONOMIC CONDITIONS ON FRAUD ARREST RATES: A COMMENT ON LEVI

PHILIP J. COOK[*]

Michael Levi's interesting essay introduces us to the complex of crimes that could be classified as "fraud," and provides some speculations on why the volume of such crimes might be affected, up or down, by the business cycle, and in particular by what he calls the Great Financial Crisis (GFC). Data to test these speculations are generally lacking. As he notes at the beginning, "fraud data are quite poor," and then, more definitively, "...no reliable or valid data exist anywhere in the world that would enable us to tell with defensible confidence whether fraud or almost any sub-component of it (other than plastic fraud) was being strongly affected by the GFC." He does offer dollops of evidence, including expert opinion and a few statistics, but neither the evidence nor the speculation leads him to an answer he can endorse with respect to the "up or down" question.

The lack of data is inherent to this crime category, since by definition crimes of fraud involve deception and concealment. While a new owner of the Brooklyn Bridge will eventually find out that he has been swindled, much fraudulent activity may never come to light. Consider, for example, counterfeit scientific claims, tax evasion, identity theft, accounting irregularities designed to inflate corporate earnings, and embezzlement. And as Levi emphasizes, when and if frauds are discovered, it can be long after they were perpetrated. Of course, some types of fraud are more routine and routinely detected by private or public authorities, including payment card fraud and bad checks. Note that the data on these volume frauds are generated by financial institutions and unlikely to be reported to law enforcement, but could be collected and used to estimate the overall financial losses due to such crimes. The UK National Fraud Authority generates such estimates annually in the *Annual Fraud Indicator* (http://www.attorneygeneral.gov.uk/nfa/GuidetoInformation/Documents/NFA fraud indicator.pdf).

Even when some data are available, what should be the unit of account for estimating the aggregate volume? The FBI's Uniform Crime Reports Index Crime data are based on incident counts (except for murder, where it is the number of victims that is counted), and while there has been much concern about problems of aggregation, there is at least some sense in summing up a city's known robbery incidents over the year and comparing that count with other cities or with previous years. But it is not so clear how Bernard Madoff's fraudulent investment scheme should be represented, even in principle. When it comes to quantifying his crimes, is there some equivalent to a robbery incident? Perhaps we could count each investor, or each deposit by an investor, or each deceptive communication by Madoff's operation, but none of those possibilities illuminate the magnitude of the problem. Another possibility would be to count the *number* of victims. It is surely meaningful that in Madoff's scheme there were thousands of investors over twenty years or more who were technically defrauded (although by no means all of them lost money).

More obvious, however, is to estimate the financial value of the loss to his investors, so that instead of an incident count or a victim count, the estimate of the "amount" of fraud would be in dollars. If we agree that the fraud should be measured in monetary terms, then there remains a difficult question of which financial accounting best captures the magnitude of the crime. A wide range of relevant numbers can be cited in the Madoff case. For example, when his Ponzi scheme was finally revealed, "the amount missing from client accounts, including fabricated gains, was almost $65 billion. The court appointed trustee estimated actual losses to investors of $18 billion" (en.wikipedia.org/wiki/Bernard_Madoff). Do either of these numbers usefully represent the scope or volume of the crime? And if so, how should they be apportioned in time? The fraudulent misrepresentations had occurred over decades, but in a sense there were no losers until 2009, when for the first time Madoff could not make good on his inflated promises. So here is a case where the GFC was a direct cause of losses due to fraud, rather than to the fraud itself. Perhaps the ideal measure for this type of fraud would be an annual estimate of the extent to which Madoff misrepresented the value of his assets, either implicitly or explicitly. By that measure the fraud would appear on the crime books every year the scheme was in operation, and not just when the tide went out.

It is not just the Madoff-type of investor fraud, developing meaningful measures of each of the many types of fraud has similar problems of conceptualization and data availability. In the absence of any agreement on how the volume of fraud should be measured, even in principle, we cannot get a handle on the question of how the business cycle influences fraud. Still, in the interest of saying *something*, it is intriguing that the FBI's Uniform Crime Reports include statistics on the arrest rate for fraud, and given these data, it is certainly possible to investigate the relationship of this indicator to the business cycle. I now turn to this task, with the caveat that the appropriate interpretation for the results is somewhat obscure.

In reporting the number of arrests for fraud, police agencies are instructed by the FBI to apply the following definition (FBI, 2007):

> **"Fraud**—The intentional perversion of the truth for the purpose of inducing another person or other entity in reliance upon it to part with something of value or to surrender a legal right. Fraudulent conversion and obtaining of money or property by false pretenses. Confidence games and bad checks, except forgeries and counterfeiting, are included."

In 2008, there were 234 thousand arrests reported under this category through the Uniform Crime Reports compared, say, with 1.3 million larceny arrests and just 129 thousand robbery arrests. I have not seen an analysis of the types of crimes that contribute to the fraud arrest statistics, but it is reasonable to expect that bad checks and use of stolen payment cards form a substantial portion of the total. Are fraud arrests related to overall business conditions?

One simple procedure for estimating the strength of the relationship between short-term movements in economic conditions and resulting short-term movements in crime rates was developed by Cook and Zarkin (1985), and replicated by Bushway, Cook, and Phillips (2010). This procedure generates estimates that are free from the possible biases introduced by secular movement in the underlying causes of crime.

A simple method for eliminating secular movements in the crime rate and the economic measures is to write each of them as a ratio of the contemporaneous value to a moving average. The actual specification used in our analysis is as follows:

$$(1) \qquad \ln (C_t / \overline{C}_t) = a + b \ln (Q_t / \overline{Q}_t) + e_t,$$

where C_t = crime rate in year t; Q_t = employment ratio or unemployment rate in year t; e_t= residual "error" term, assumed to be generated by a first-order autocorrelation process with $Ee_t = 0$; $\overline{C}_t, \overline{Q}_t$ = moving geometric means centered on year t.

This specification eliminates secular movements in crime rates caused by trends in crime reporting, demographic structure, "culture," public policy, and so forth. It also eliminates secular trends in the business conditions indicators, which in recent years have been caused by changes in demographic structure, earlier retirement, the changing role of women in the labor force, and so forth. Cook and Zarkin demonstrate that b can be estimated by a time-series regression, and can be interpreted as the causal effect of Q on C under reasonable assumptions. In particular, the coefficient is properly interpreted as the elasticity of the fraud arrest rate with respect to changes in the indicator.

Following Cook and Zarkin, I experiment with two indicators of economic conditions, the *employment/population ratio* (employed population divided by the adult population), and the *unemployment rate* (the number who are not employed but looking for work, divided by the labor force). The data are for the 61-year period 1948-2008.

The effect of business conditions on fraud arrest rates
(standard error in parentheses)

	Employment ratio	Unemployment Rate
Fraud arrest rate/100,000	-1.614 (.781)	0.199 (.060)

Note: The regression specification is given by equation 1. The Prais-Winston correction for serial correlation in the error term is employed.

Both coefficient estimates are highly significant, and both indicate that fraud (by this measure) is counter-cyclical – it is positively related to the unemployment rate and negatively related to the employment ratio. A bit of arithmetic suggests that a 1 percentage point increase in the unemployment rate (from, say, 6 percent to 7 percent) has, according to these results, a similar effect as a 1 percentage reduction in the employment ratio (from 60 percent to 59 percent). The increase in unemployment would increase the fraud arrests rate by 3.3 percent, and the reduction in the employment ratio would increase the fraud arrest rate by 2.8 percent.

This result helps confirm our intuition about property crime generally, namely that it tends to go up during hard times – although that does not appear to be the case for motor vehicle theft (Bushway et al., 2010). Still, the proper interpretation of these results will have to await a better understanding of how the fraud arrest statistics relate to the underlying concept of fraud. That problem is just another illustration of Professor Levi's conclusion that "we are only a little way along the empirical journey to link frauds to economic factors...."

REFERENCES

Bushway, S., Philip J., & Phillips, M. (2010). *The net effect of the business cycle on crime and violence.* Working paper. Durham, NC: Duke University.

Cook, P. & Zarkin, G. (1985, January). Crime and the business cycle. *Journal of Legal Studies, 14,* 115-128.

FBI, (2007). *Offense definitions.* Retrieved August 3, 2010, from http://www.fbi.gov/ucr/cius2007/about/offense_definitions.html

National Fraud Authority. (2010, January). *Annual fraud indicator.* Retrieved June 15, 2010, from http://www.attorneygeneral.gov.uk/nfa/GuidetoInformation/Documents/NFA_fraud_indicator.pdf

Wikipedia. (n.d.). Retrieved June 15, 2010, from en.wikipedia.org/wiki/Bernard_Madoff

ENDNOTE

* Acknowledgements: Thanks to Matthew Phillips for computing the regression results.

Evolutionary Ecology, Fraud, and the Global Financial Crisis

Michael L. Benson

In this insightful piece, Michael Levi reminds us of an important fact about crime that is often overlooked by politicians, the news media, the general public, and occasionally by criminologists. To wit, crime does not always come from bad things. It is a mistake to assume that seemingly negative and unwanted social events or conditions always precipitate or are somehow associated with increases in crime. The assumption that such associations always exist appears to be built into the modern psyche. Crime is a "bad thing." It must somehow be caused by other bad things, such as poverty or child abuse, or some other individual or social pathology. Therefore, in searching for the causes of crime one should look for bad things. Or, starting from the other side of the coin, if some bad thing happens, such as the global financial crisis, then obviously it is going to lead to more crime. This approach ignores important insights from Durkheim (1964, 1938) and Sutherland (1940, 1949) as well as other important theorists. Durkheim argued that a certain amount of crime and deviance is normal in naturally functioning societies. Sutherland famously ridiculed the idea that white-collar crime could be explained by poverty or feeblemindedness or the oedipal complexes of executives. Although most criminologists are aware of these dictums, their implications are often not seriously considered or appreciated. One of the important contributions of Levi's piece is to show how this way of thinking is sloppy, lazy, and likely often to be wrong.

In this short reaction piece, I attempt to examine some of the potential implications that can be drawn from the idea of crime as normal and to suggest that criminologists need occasionally to forego the standard practice of focusing on variation in criminal behavior across individuals and to think instead of variation in a different way; that is, as variation in behavior patterns. I will suggest that it might be useful to adopt a more ecological approach and to focus on how social contexts may influence the availability of different types of behavior patterns.

Before turning to my main topic, however, I must first make clear that I do not wish to appear to be denying that poverty, discrimination, child abuse, economic recessions, or any of the host of other harmful social and individual conditions studied by criminologists are unimportant. They are serious social problems in their own right, and they can have criminogenic effects. People exposed to these stressful and destructive experiences and circumstances sometimes do respond by resorting to criminal behavior of one sort or another. But when we think about the causal connections between these factors and crime, we often make the mistake of focusing only on how they might potentially affect the motivations of actors. We ignore or downplay how they may simultaneously affect the suitability of targets and the availability of guardianship. We ignore, that is, the other two sides of the crime triangle, that is the opportunity side of offending. This is a mistake because it leads us into a linear one-dimensional view of crime and criminal behavior.

One simple example may suffice here. It seems relatively clear that the global financial crisis was sparked in part by massive fraud and unconscionable risk-taking in the mortgage and finance industries during the 1990s and early 2000s (Financial Crimes Enforcement Network, 2006; Partnoy, 2003). How many of these frauds and risky activities are still continuing today? It seems likely to me that the answer is considerably less than before. So-called "liar loans" must be a thing of the past, and one would suspect that the now infamous credit default swap instruments based on toxic assets are now viewed with much greater skepticism than before. I would be willing to speculate that they are much harder to foist off on unsuspecting buyers. So, while hedge fund managers, mortgage brokers, real estate agents, appraisers, and all of the other players in the mortgage and investment fraud games may still be motivated to commit fraud (Indeed, their motivations may be stronger than ever given the tremendous slow down in the housing market that has followed the financial crisis in the United States.), their opportunities to do so may have been drastically reduced. Yet, on the other hand, now that there are millions of families facing foreclosure and the prospect of losing their homes, opportunities for fraudsters have opened up in other areas, such as scams that purport to help people avoid foreclosure or scams designed to cheat the various government programs established to help people hold on to their homes (Federal Bureau of Investigation, 2010). In short, even though the advent of the global financial crisis or, as Levi calls it, the partial global financial crisis, is obviously a bad thing, it probably reduced some types of fraud while increasing opportunities for others. Of course, as Levi is at pains to point out, we do not really know for sure what has gone up and what has gone down because of the general lack of good data on most types of fraud.

As I see it, one of the main themes in Levi's analysis is that we need to think about the connections between crime and historical events, such as the global financial crisis, in more multi-faceted and subtle ways. For example, the possibility must be recognized that while the global financial crisis may have stimulated criminal motivations among some people, which would in theory drive crime up, paradoxically at the same time it may have reduced criminal opportunities among those very same people, which would in theory drive crime down. The net result, obviously, would be a wash. Yet, even this way of thinking is too simplistic because it presents crime as a single unitary phenomenon, which it is not. Financial crises may increase motivations and opportunities for some types of crimes but reduce them for others. Again, the point here is that we need to recognize the possibility that social events may have multi-faceted and differential effects on criminal opportunities as well as criminal motivations.

The advent of the current global financial crisis has raised the salience of the connection between economic cycles and crime, and it provides us with an opportunity to reconsider this connection in a new light. With few exceptions, theorizing about crime and the economy historically has focused on the effects of poor economic conditions or negative economic events on crime. The other end of the economic boom and bust cycle has typically been ignored. At the aggregate level, criminologists have investigated the effects of economic depressions or recessions on crime rates, as well as the relationship between unemployment rates and crimes rates (Chiricos, 1987). Recently, there has been an explosion of interest in the effects of economic disadvantage on neighborhood crime rates (Sampson, Raudenbush, & Earls, 1997). At the individual level, poverty is considered an important risk factor in individual involvement in crime (Freeman, 1987; Hagan, 1993). The implicit and unexamined assumption of many of these analyses is that when economic conditions are good at either the aggregate or individual level crime will be less of a problem. But is this really true? Or is it possible that economic growth may actually create more opportunities and even more motivation for crime, at least for certain types of crime? Over three decades ago, Cohen and Felson (1979, p. 605) argued just this point with respect to ordinary street crime. Recall the stunning conclusion to their groundbreaking article on routine activities theory:

> "Rather than assuming that predatory crime is simply an indicator of social breakdown, one might take it as a byproduct of freedom and prosperity as they manifest themselves in the routine activities of everyday life."

While Cohen and Felson were focusing on direct contact predatory crimes, I suspect that their conclusion may apply even better to white-collar crimes, such as fraud. To return again to the mortgage industry and mortgage fraud, one wonders if one of the reasons why fraud and risk-taking became so pervasive is precisely because in the 1990s and early 2000s the economy looked so strong. As this period was unfolding, people made the mistake of assuming that growth and stability in the market would last indefinitely. In other words, they assumed that stability was going to last, when in reality markets are always inherently unstable. When the market appears stable and profits appear to be reliable, then some players seek ways to innovate and speculate so as to do better than average. The success of some of these players attracts attention and their strategies start to diffuse and generalize throughout the market (Cassidy, 2009). Indeed, we need to recognize also the possibility that types of fraud may increase not because motivations or even opportunities have increased, but rather because knowledge of the necessary techniques has diffused through some population. This is a possibility that criminologists have paid little attention to. How does knowledge of criminal opportunities and techniques spread through a population? Are there fads in fraud? Perhaps we can learn something from those who study fads in music and fashion.

During boom times new types of fraud or double-dealing may explode in popularity for reasons involving both victims and offenders. One of my colleagues, John Eck, notes that booms may increase the pool of potential victims because people receive signals from friends, expert analysts, and the news media that there is money to be made. So, when the proverbial offer that is "too good to be true" comes along, potential victims are more likely to interpret it as "too good *not* to be true." People abandon their normal skepticism and financial prudence in a desire to get in on all of the windfall profits. The risk of losing money to fraud is considered not that important when weighed against all of the seemingly legitimate profits there are to be made. From the offender's point of view, the level of guardianship that has to be overcome is reduced. As Levi notes, fraud in certain organizational settings may also be enabled by the very people who should be in control, the higher executives. They turn a blind eye to their subordinates' gambles because they hope to benefit indirectly in terms of bonuses based on growth in the organization's bottom line. Something akin to this appears certainly to have been going on at Enron (McLean & Elkind, 2003). These changes in the market then start pushing it toward instability. The familiar boom and bust cycle starts once again.

Indeed, as Levi notes at one point in his paper, economic downturns may be more important in exposing certain types of fraud, such as Ponzi schemes, than they are in motivating fraud. When the economy is growing and everybody is looking for the next big thing to invest in, the Ponzi schemer has little trouble attracting new investors. But when the economy starts to contract, new investors become few and far between. Current investors become more cautious. People start asking for their money back, and ongoing schemes begin to unravel. This is apparently what happened in the case of Mr. Madoff (Lenzner, 2008). Similarly, the downturn in real estate in 2007 and 2008 may have brought to light growing numbers of mortgage industry related frauds. Thus, it might be a mistake to conclude that the downturn in the housing market caused the frauds. It is perhaps more likely that they had been ongoing and only came to light at that point in time. For example, liar loans only become evident when housing prices stop rising and fraudsters cannot refinance their way out of their indebtedness.

Of course, the idea that economic growth leads to crime should not be pushed too far even in regards to white-collar crime. There are many examples where the reverse is true, where white-collar offenders resort to crime because of financial difficulties. Antitrust offenses, for example, appear often to be motivated by economic troubles in industries (Geis, 1977). Likewise, the fight for economic survival also clearly motivates other types of white-collar crime by small business owners (Barlow, 1993; Benson, 1985; Leonard & Weber, 1977). But this simply proves the more general point that the relationship between economic cycles and white-collar crime is complex and multifaceted. It is not one-dimensional.

Because the relationship between economic conditions and white-collar crime is not one-dimensional, it may be helpful to consider approaching its analysis using ecological and evolutionary metaphors rather than the mechanical, linear, push and pull images that dominate contemporary criminological theorizing. Cohen and Machalek (1988) attempted such an analysis for what they called "expropriative" crime over two decades ago. Although the main focus of their discussion seemed to be on ordinary street type offenders and offenses, it seems to me that such an approach might fit even better in regards to white-collar type offenses. Fraud and other forms of white-collar crime are always dependent on legitimate activities. They either mimic or feed off legitimate activities. They depend on what I have elsewhere called the "superficial appearance of legitimacy" (Benson & Simpson, 2009). Hence, thinking in terms of symbiotic or parasitic relationships and alternative behavioral strategies as ecologists do may lead to some profitable insights (Felson, 2006; Cohen & Machalek, 1988). In taking an ecological approach, the first step is to substitute the term "behavioral strategy" for the term "crime." Thinking in terms of behavioral strategies as opposed to crimes helps one avoid the mistake of slipping into the "bad things cause bad things" mindset. For an ecologist, a strategy refers to a behavioral pattern for attaining an end, such as food, finding a mate, or avoiding predators. When a strategy increases fitness, reproductive success, ecologists call it an evolutionary strategy. Whether fraud is a behavioral strategy that leads to fitness in the ecological sense is an intriguing question, but well beyond the scope of this essay. I think, instead that following Cohen and Machalek (1988) we should consider strategies that convey what ecologists call "advantages" – an advantage is a trait that contributes to the survival and well-being of an individual organism. Expropriative strategies often convey advantages. An expropriative strategy is one in which an individual or group takes something of material, symbolic, or social value from another individual or group to the benefit of the individual or group employing the strategy. In regards to human behavior, fraud and many forms of white-collar crimes can be considered expropriative strategies that convey advantages.

One of the few examples of this kind of thinking, though not expressed using the terminology of ecological theory, can be found in Malcolm Sparrow's work on health care fraud. He describes the relationship between fraud and fraud control in health care as being like an arms race (Sparrow, 1996, 1998). New forms of fraud, that is new expropriative strategies, evolve in response to new developments in control strategies.

Returning to the global financial crisis and the relationship between economic cycles and crime, I would suggest that economic cycles are important because they create contexts in which the availability of different types of alternative behavioral strategies varies. So, what I am getting at here is that when we think about the relationship between the global financial crisis and crime, or more generally, economic cycles and crime, we should think about them as contexts which influence the availability of alternative behavioral strategies, especially expropriative strategies, rather than as events that affect motivations. At this point, the next question asked by many criminologists would be "Well, who adopts these strategies and what determines adopters from non-adopters? What are the variables that influence adoption?" These are of course good questions, but I wonder if there is a deeper question we could ask, a question that harkens back to Durkheim and the normality of crime. To wit, does the overall level of the rate of adoption of expropriative behavioral strategies remain constant over time or vary within some limited range in modern human societies? In other words, is the level of crime, especially white-collar and fraud type crimes, as a behavioral strategy, stable? According to ecologists, the stability of behavioral strategies is common in many animal populations, where, for example, 70 percent of a population pursues one strategy and 30 percent pursues another strategy, or where individuals in a population pursue one strategy 70 percent of the time and another strategy 30 percent of the time (Cohen & Machalek, 1988). One wonders if something roughly similar happens in human societies in regards to white-collar crime. When housing prices are rising we get liar loans; when they are falling we get bankruptcy scams.

REFERENCES

Barlow, H. (1993). From fiddle factors to networks of collusion: Charting the Waters of small business Crime. *Crime, Law and Social Change, 20,* 319-37.

Benson, M. (1985). Denying the guilty mind: Accounting for involvement in a white-collar crime. *Criminology, 23,* 583-608.

Benson, M. & Simpson, S. (2009). *White-collar crime: An opportunity perspective.* New York, NY: Routledge.

Cassidy, J. (2009). *How markets fail : The logic of economic calamities.* New York, NY: Farrar, Straus and Giroux.

Chiricos, T. (1987). Rates of crime and unemployment: An analysis of aggregate research evidence. *Social Problems, 34,* 187-212.

Cohen, L. & Felson, M. (1970). Social change and crime rate trends: A routine activities approach. *American Sociological Review, 44,* 588-605.

Cohen, L. & Machalek, R. (1988). A general theory of expropriative crime: An evolutionary ecological approach. *The American Journal of Sociology, 94,* 465-501.

Durkheim, E. (1964, 1938). *The rules of sociological method.* New York, NY: Free Press of Glencoe.

Federal Bureau of Investigation. (2010). *2009 mortgage fraud report "year in review".* Retrieved June 18, 2010, from http://www.fbi.gov/publications/fraud/mortgage_fraud09.htm

Felson, M. (2006). *Crime and nature.* Thousand Oaks, CA: Sage.

Financial Crimes Enforcement Network. (2006). *Mortgage loan fraud: An industry assessment based on suspicious activity report analysis.* Retrieved June 18, 2010, from http://www.fincen.gov/news_room/rp/reports/pdf/MortgageLoanFraud.pdf

Freeman, R. (1987). The relation of criminal activity to black youth unemployment. *The Review of Black Political Economy, 16,* 99-107.

Geis, G. (1977). The heavy electrical equipment antitrust cases of 1961. In G. Geis & R. Meier (Eds.), *White-collar crime: Offenses in business, politics, and the professions* (pp. 117-132). New York, NY: The Free Press.

Hagan, J. (1993). The social embeddedness of crime and unemployment. *Criminology, 31,* 465-92.

Lenzner, R. (2008). *Bernie Madoff's $50 billion Ponzi scheme.* Forbes.com. Retrieved June 18, 2010, from http://www.forbes.com/2008/12/12/madoff-ponzi-hedge-pf-ii-in_rl_1212croesus_inl.html

Leonard, W. & Weber, M. (1977). Automakers and dealers: A study of criminogenic market forces. In G. Geis & R. Meier (Eds.), *White-collar crime: Offenses in business, politics, and the professions* (pp. 133-148). New York, NY: The Free Press.

McLean, B. & Elkind, P. (2003). *The smartest guys in the room: The amazing rise and scandalous fall of Enron.* New York, NY: Penguin Books.

Partnoy, F. (2003). *Infectious greed : How deceit and risk corrupted the financial markets.* New York, NY: Times Books.

Sampson, R., Raudenbush, S., & Earls, F. (1997). Neighborhoods and violent crime: A multilevel study of collective efficacy. *Science, 277,* 918-24.

Sparrow, M. (1996). *License to steal: Why fraud plagues America's health care system.* Boulder, CO.: Westview Press.

Sparrow, M. (1998, December). *Fraud control in the health care industry: Assessing the state of the art.* Washington, DC: National Institute of Justice.

Sutherland, E. (1940). White-collar criminality. *American Sociological Review, 5,* 1-12.

Sutherland, E. (1949). *White-collar crime.* New York, NY: Holt, Rinehart and Winston.

POLITY

Imprisonment and Crime Control: Building Evidence-Based Policy

Daniel S. Nagin

Abstract

In this essay I summarize the three primary conclusions of recent reviews on sanctions effects on crime and discuss their implications for public policy and research. These reviews conclude that: (1) Compared to non-custodial sanctions, the experience of incarceration has a null or mildly criminogenic impact on future criminal involvement. (2) There is little evidence that increases in the severity of punishment yield large general deterrent effects. (3) By contrast, there is substantial evidence that certainty-enhancing effects such as the strategic deployment of police can deter crime. Thus, sensible sanction policy must balance the deterrent effect of the threat of punishment with the potentially criminogenic effect of the experience of punishment. Existing research suggests that that balance is best achieved by certainty-based deterrence policies that prevent crime in the first place and not by severity-based policies. Delineating the specific form of such policies, however, requires a concerted research effort on the deterrent effects of alternative sanctions policies. I urge criminologists to play an active role in doing this research.

Imprisonment may prevent crime by three distinct mechanisms: incapacitation, specific deterrence, and general deterrence. The focus of this essay is deterrence. Specific deterrence refers to the reduction in reoffending that is presumed to follow from the *experience* of actually being punished whereas general deterrence refers to preventive effects stemming from the *threat* of punishment. Thus, specific deterrence is about the effect of past experience of punishment on present and future criminal behavior whereas general deterrence concerns the effect of the prospect of punishment on crime commission in the present or future.

It is important to distinguish these two effects because they may be very different. Specifically, the experience of punishment may be criminogenic, even as the threat of punishment is preventive. This indeed is the conclusion of recent literature reviews that I have coauthored. Nagin, Cullen, and Jonson (2009) in a review titled *Imprisonment and Reoffending* examine the evidence on specific deterrence. Apel and Nagin (forthcoming) and Durlauf and Nagin (forthcoming a&b) review the general deterrence literature with a special emphasis on the deterrent effect of the threat of imprisonment.

In this essay I summarize the three primary conclusions of these reviews and their implications for public policy and research. As preface to these remarks, I emphasize that the conclusions are not novel. They echo arguments that have recently been advanced by Kleiman (2009) in *When Brute Force Fails How to Have Less Crime and Less Punishment* and by Kennedy (2009) in *Deterrence and Crime Prevention Reconsidering the Prospect of Sanction*. These conclusions are:

1. Compared to non-custodial sanctions, the experience of incarceration has a null or somewhat criminogenic impact on future criminal involvement. This assessment is not sufficiently firm to guide policy, with the exception that it calls into question wild claims that imprisonment has a strong specific deterrent effect.

2. There is little evidence that increases in the severity of punishment yield large general deterrent effects. By contrast, there is substantial evidence that certainty enhancing effects such as the strategic deployment of police can deter crime.

3. Sensible sanction policy must balance the deterrent effect of the threat of punishment with the potentially criminogenic effect of the experience of punishment. Existing research suggests that that balance is best achieved by certainty-based deterrence policies that prevent crime in the first place and not by severity-based policies.

I turn now to summarizing the basis for these conclusions. Dating back to the Enlightenment, deterrence theorists have drawn a distinction between the severity of punishment, as measured, for example, by the length of incarceration or the type of sanction received, prison versus probation; and the certainty of punishment. For sanctions to deter they must be unpleasant. This is the logical basis for the severity dimension of deterrence theory. However, severity alone cannot deter. There must be some possibility that the sanction will be incurred. For that to happen, offenders must be apprehended, usually by the police. They must next be charged and successfully prosecuted, and finally sentenced by the judiciary. In this chain of events the most important set of actors are the police—absent detection and apprehension, there is no possibility of punishment. For this reason the deterrence review papers co-authored with Apel and Durlauf focused specifically on what is known about the deterrent effect of the police.

Going back to the deterrence literature of the 1960s and 1970s, deterrence studies rather consistently found evidence of a deterrent effect of certainty but not of severity. As developed in the National Research Council report, *Deterrence and Incapacitation: Estimating the Effects of Criminal Sanctions on Crime Rates* (Blumstein, Cohen, & Nagin, 1978), the statistical basis for this conclusion was deeply flawed. Notwithstanding, more recent evidence not only supports this conclusion but also helps us better understand its basis.

Since the1980s, a solid literature has developed testing the deterrent effect of severity. Most of these studies test for deterrent effects in specialized yet diverse topic settings such as sentence enhancements for firearms use in the commission of another crime, mandatory minimum statutes for various sorts of crime, and three-strikes type laws. Most find no evidence of a deterrent effect. Scientific conclusions, however, should be based on the quality of the studies on either side of an issue not on the number. My own evaluation of this literature as reflected in Apel and Nagin (forthcoming) and Durlauf and Nagin (forthcoming a & b) is that there are well-conducted null effect studies and well conducted studies that do find an effect. Indeed one of the best conducted severity studies does find a deterrent effect. I briefly summarize it because of its high quality and because it is an exemplar of how I believe deterrence studies should be conducted to make them useful in making evidence-based policy recommendations.

Helland and Tabarrok (2007) examine whether California's *Three Strikes* law deters offending among individuals previously convicted of strike-eligible offenses. The future offending of individuals convicted of two strikeable offenses was compared with that of individuals who had been convicted of only one strikeable offense, but who in addition had been tried for a second strikeable offense but were ultimately convicted of a non-strike eligible offense. The study demonstrates that these two groups of individuals were comparable on many characteristics such as age, race, and prior time in prison. Even so, it finds that arrest rates were about 20 percent lower for the group with convictions for two strikeable offenses. The authors attribute this reduction to the greatly enhanced sentence that would have accompanied conviction on a third strikeable offense.

Helland and Tabarrok, however, do not stop at this conclusion. They conduct a cost-benefit analysis of whether the social benefits of the crimes averted are sufficient to justify the social cost of incarcerating individuals for an additional 20 years or more. This analysis clearly shows the benefits fall far short of the costs.

As noted, I believe that the Helland and Tabarrok analysis was an exemplar of how scientific evidence should be used in making evidence-based policy recommendations. For too long deterrence research has been conducted in the form of two warring camps—one mostly composed of economists arguing that deterrence works and the other composed mostly of criminologists arguing that deterrence does not work. This is not a constructive way of accumulating evidence about deterrence because it is built on the faulty premise that deterrence either works or does not work.

In my view something closer to the medical model for accumulating evidence on effectiveness is the appropriate way to proceed. Medical research builds from the premise that not all treatments are effective and among those that are effective the degree of effectiveness varies. Deterrence research should consciously adopt this same premise. Specifically, evidenced-based research on deterrence should be framed in terms of estimating the magnitude of the effect and if an effect is statistically identifiable assessing whether its size warrants implementation based on a sensible weighing of costs and benefits. In my judgment the severity literature shows that it is difficult to justify severity-based crime preventions policies by a cost-benefit criterion. Either no effect is identifiable or if an effect is identified it has not been shown to be large enough to justify the costs.

I turn now to the policing literature and what it tells us about the deterrent effect of certainty. The police may prevent crime through several mechanisms. Apprehension of active offenders is a necessary first step for their conviction and punishment. If the sanction involves imprisonment, crime may be prevented by the incapacitation of the apprehended offender. The apprehension of active offenders may also deter would-be criminals by increasing their perception of the risk of apprehension and thereby the certainty of punishment. Even more importantly the very presence of police may prevent crime before it even happens. As a result, there is no apprehension because there is no crime.

A knowledgeable long-time observer of the deterrence literature, Michael Tonry, has pointed out to me that the affirmative conclusion about the deterrent effect of police in Apel and Nagin (forthcoming) and Durlauf and Nagin (forthcoming a & b) would have been greeted with considerable skepticism 20 years ago. While I am sure that there will still be skeptics, the evidentiary base for an affirmative conclusion that the police can deter crime is now far stronger. Further, components of that evidentiary base are actually consistent with earlier arguments about the ineffectiveness of police in deterring crime. I say this because the newer literature makes clear that the deterrent effect depends how the police are utilized—some deployment strategies are effective in preventing crime and others are not effective.

Research on the deterrent effect of police has evolved in two distinct literatures. One has focused on the deterrent effect of the aggregate police presence. The other has focused on the crime prevention effectiveness of different strategies for deploying police. The aggregate police presence literature is mostly the work of economists. Using various econometric methods, the studies analyze the relationship between the crime rates in metropolitan areas and aggregate police presence in those areas, measured, for example, by police expenditures per capita. These studies consistently find evidence of a greater police presence reducing crime. As emphasized in Durlauf and Nagin (forthcoming a &b), it is a challenge to infer cause and effect relationships from these analyses. Thus, it is important that the conclusions from this literature are consistently supported by the lesser known but actually more important targeted studies. These studies, for example, have examined the effect of heightened police presence in the Washington, DC, Mall area due to terror alerts, and consistently find evidence that police presence or lack thereof affects crime rates.

This brings me to the second part of the literature that focuses on the effect of police deployment strategies on crime. For the most part, deployment strategies affect the certainty of punishment through its impact on the probability of apprehension. There are, however, notable examples where severity may also be affected. This literature which has been largely constructed by criminologists such as Braga, Mazerolle, Mastrofski, Sherman, and Weisburd, to name just a few, forms the evidentiary basis for two key points that may seem obvious once stated but are often neglected in policy discussions.

The first point is that deterrent effects are not of uniform magnitude. On the one hand, the police deployment literature clearly demonstrates that certain types of police tactics, such as rapid response to calls for service and improved investigative services, are not effective in preventing crime, probably because they do not affect apprehension risk (Weisburd & Eck, 2004). By contrast, a series of experiments conducted by Sherman, Weisburd and colleagues provide convincing evidence that hotspots policing is effective in deterring crime rather than displacing it (Sherman & Weisburd, 1995; Weisburd & Green, 1995; Weisburd et al., 2006)

My point that there is not one deterrent effect is obvious once stated but, as I earlier indicated, discourse about deterrence often lapses into deterrence works-deterrence doesn't work type rhetoric. Such rhetoric gets in the way of the right issue from both a scientific and policy perspective. Research should be focusing on identifying the factors and circumstances which moderate the size of deterrent effects.

The second point I want to make is that the police deployment literature makes clear that the most effective deterrence strategies are those that make the threat of apprehension tangible and direct. This conclusion is entirely consistent with a key finding from the developmental criminology literature on the present orientation and impulsivity of most offenders (Jolliffe & Farrington, 2009; White et al., 1994). Because of long delays between apprehension and sentencing, their presentation orientation helps to explain the ineffectiveness of severity-based policies in getting their attention. Hot spots policing is probably effective because it tangibly and directly increases apprehension risk at the hot spot by substantially increasing police presence. I am not the only one to draw this conclusion. Both Kleiman (2009) and Kennedy (2009) emphasize the need for tangible and direct sanction consequences in their two fine books.

I close this discussion of deterrence by connecting it with my review article with Cullen and Jonson (2009) on the effect of imprisonment on reoffending. According to a 2006 Bureau of Justice Statistic study of felony defendants in the 75 largest counties, at the time of arrest 32 percent of defendants had an active criminal justice status and 76 percent of all defendants had been arrested previously, with 50 percent having at least five prior arrest charges (Cohen & Reaves, 2006). There are two very different interpretations of these statistics. One is that the high concentration of recidivists in the criminal justice system represents the ongoing failure of deterrence to suppress the criminal behavior of a small minority of the population. The other is that the experience of contact with the criminal justice system, most specifically in the form of imprisonment, is criminogenic. These two diametrically opposing interpretations of the data lay at the core of much academic and public policy debate about the role of imprisonment in crime control.

As I indicated at the outset, discussions of the effect of imprisonment on crime often fail to distinguish between the potentially very different behavioral responses to the *threat* of imprisonment versus the *experience* of imprisonment. In the economic model of crime, deterrence is the behavioral response to the threat of punishment. In criminology, the term "specific deterrence" is used to describe the behavioral response to the experience of punishment. The findings of Nagin et al. (2009) suggest that there is no evidence of a specific deterrent effect of imprisonment. To the contrary, if anything the prison experience is criminogenic. What this means is that sensible sanction policy must balance the deterrent effect of the threat of punishment with the potentially criminogenic effect of the experience of punishment. Existing research suggests that that balance is best achieved by certainty-based deterrence policies that prevent crime in the first place and not with severity-based policies. In an article titled *Imprisonment and Crime: Can we have less of both?* (Forthcoming b), Durlauf and I lay out the evidentiary and theoretical basis for why certainty-based sanction policies have the potential for resulting in less crime and less imprisonment. Delineating the specific form of such policies, however, requires a concerted research effort on the deterrent effects of alternative sanctions policies. I urge my fellow criminologists to play a far more active role in doing this research.

REFERENCES

Apel, R. & Nagin, C. (Forthcoming). Deterrence. In J. Wilson & J. Petersilia (Eds.), *Crime* (4th ed.). Oxford, UK: Oxford University Press. Also, in M. Tonry, (Ed.), *The Oxford handbook on crime and criminal justice* (forthcoming). Oxford, UK: Oxford University Press.

Blumstein, A., Cohen, J., & Nagin, D. (1978). *Deterrence and incapacitation: Estimating the effects of criminal sanctions on crime rates.* Washington, DC: National Academies Press.

Cohen, T & Reaves, B. (2006). *Felony defendants in large urban counties, 2002.* Washington, DC: Bureau of Justice Statistics.

Durlauf, S. & Nagin, D. (Forthcoming a). The deterrent effect of imprisonment. In P.Cook, J. Ludwig, & J. McCrary (Eds), *Making crime control pay: Cost-effective alternatives to incarceration.* Chicago, IL: University of Chicago Press.

Durlauf, S. & Nagin, D. (Forthcoming b). Imprisonment and crime: Can we have less of both? *Criminology and Public Policy.*

Helland, E. & Tabarrok, A. (2007). Does three strikes deter? A nonparametric estimation. *Journal of Human Resources, 42,* 309-330.

Jolliffe, D. & Farrington, D. (2009). A systematic review of the relationship between childhood impulsiveness and later violence. In M. McMurran & R. Howard (Eds.), *Personality, personality disorder, and violence* (pp. 40-61). New York, NY: John Wiley and Sons.

Kennedy, D. (2009). *Deterrence and crime prevention reconsidering the prospect of sanction.* New York, NY: Routledge.

Kleiman, M. (2009). *When brute force fails how to have less crime and less punishment.* Princeton, NJ: Princeton University Press.

Nagin, D., Cullen, F., & Jonson, C. (2009). Imprisonment and re-offending. In M. Tonry (Ed.), *Crime and justice: A review of research, 38,* pp. 115-200. Chicago: University of Chicago Press.

Sherman, L. & Weisburd, D. (1995). General deterrent effects of police patrol in crime 'hot spots': A randomized study. *Justice Quarterly, 12,* 625-648.

Weisburd, D. & Eck, J. (2004). What can police do to reduce crime, disorder, and fear? *Annals of the American Academy of Political and Social Science, 593,* 42-65.

Weisburd, D. & Green, L. (1995). Policing drug hot spots: The Jersey City drug market analysis experiment. *Justice Quarterly, 12,* 711-735.

Weisburd, D, Wyckoff, L., Ready, J., Eck, J., Hinkle, J., & Gajewski, F. (2006). Does crime just move around the corner? A controlled study of spatial displacement and diffusion of crime control benefits. *Criminology, 44,* 249-591.

White, J., Moffitt, T., Caspi, A., Bartusch, D. Needles, D., & Stoutheimer-Loeber, M. (1994). Measuring impulsivity and examining its relationship to delinquency. *Journal of Abnormal Psychology, 103,* 192-205.

LESS IMPRISONMENT, LESS CRIME: A REPLY TO NAGIN

MICHAEL TONRY

Were policy makers to take account of evidence, Nagin argues, American criminal justice policies could look very different. Here is how and why. Lengthy prison sentences have few general deterrent effects, if any. People sent to prison come out worse, more likely to reoffend than if they had received a lesser punishment. Some things police do can reduce crime rates. American jurisdictions should reduce their use of imprisonment and increase their investment in policing, thereby lowering crime and imprisonment rates and saving money, all at the same time. Everybody—offenders, prospective victims, taxpayers—wins.

Nagin's proposal is a product of his extraordinary range.[1] He has recently completed comprehensive reviews of the literatures on general deterrence (Apel & Nagin, forthcoming), the effects of imprisonment on released inmates' subsequent offending (Nagin, Cullen, & Jonson, 2009), and the effects of variations in police numbers, per capita spending, and crackdowns on crime (Durlauf & Nagin, forthcoming). The deterrence survey concludes that there is credible evidence that changes in sentencing laws sometimes produce deterrent effects, but that the effects are highly contingent, depending on threat communication and patterns of implementation, are not easily replicable, and provide an insufficient basis on which to build sentencing policies. The prison effects survey concludes that there is no credible evidence that imprisonment reduces reoffending by released offenders. To the contrary, there is tentative but not yet conclusive evidence that imprisonment is criminogenic, and increases released inmates' rates of reoffending. The police effectiveness survey presents evidence that increases in police numbers and per capita spending reduce crime rates and that police crackdowns reduce crime rates net of displacement effects.

Drawing on classic works by Cesare Beccaria and Jeremy Bentham, Nagin proposes a theoretical framework that links his findings. Beccaria famously distinguished among the severity, certainty, and celerity (speed) of sanctions, and argued that severity was the least important. Certainty and celerity are what matters. Court and prosecution systems are notoriously uncertain and slow and likely always will be. Police, however, can by means of their increased presence and changed tactics deter crime by increasing the certainty of observation and the speed of apprehension. If certainty and celerity are what matters, investments in police are much likelier than investments in prisons to affect crime rates.

This commentary offers three sets of observations concerning Nagin's proposals. The first section discusses their policy implications, the second

317

the solidity of the underlying research, and the third the theoretical framework. In a nutshell, my conclusions are that Nagin's proposals and logic are likelier to resonate in relation to policing than to imprisonment: politicians probably care about police effectiveness; with punishment, effectiveness is seldom a matter of significant concern. Nagin's research summaries seem to me reasonable, though I believe the evidence in favor of general and marginal deterrence is less strong than he suggests and the evidence concerning police effectiveness is less convincing than he suggests. His theoretical framework is plausible and useful.

POLICY

The inelegantly named "research utilization" literature instructs that evidence some times on some subjects in some places influences policy choices.[2] For a positive example, findings from developmental research have formed the basis for greatly increased public investment in early childhood prevention programs. The critical question confronting Nagin's proposals is whether, in the United States in the second decade of the twenty-first century, policy makers are likely to be influenced by research findings concerning severity of sanctions, adverse effects of imprisonment on offenders, and police effectiveness. My best guesses are no, no, and yes. Legislators like and trust police and prosecutors, and seldom worry that they are unduly lenient or coddle criminals. Proposals to increase public investment in the police to enhance their crime-fighting effectiveness are likely to be well received. Sentencing and punishment polices have in the past 30 years been impermeable to influence by evidence. There are no significant signs that things will soon be different.

Nagin acknowledges that the novelty of his overall policy proposal lies in the blending of the findings on which it is based, and not in the findings themselves. Two of the main findings are not new. Many reviews of deterrence research over the past 35 years, several by him (e.g., Nagin, 1998) have reached similarly or more skeptical conclusions. The criminogenic effects of imprisonment have been widely recognized in many countries for many years; only in the United States could policy makers with straight faces claim to be surprised by that finding. The findings on police effectiveness can plausibly be described as new, at least compared with 20 or 30 years ago.

Sentencing

The core difficulty for Nagin's proposal is that policy makers are moved by many considerations other than evidence of effectiveness and cost. Many of the sentencing and corrections policies that would be suspect if Nagin's proposals were taken seriously have long been known to be ineffective. Practitioners, for example, have known for two centuries that mandatory penalties seldom operate as their proponents claim and, partly as a result, that they are not effective deterrents. Successive cycles of empirical research in the United States in the 1950s, 1970s, 1980s, and 1990s confirmed what practitioners have long known.[3] Or, another example, no one claims that the federal 100-to-1 law for crack and powder cocaine sentencing deters sales of crack cocaine. It has been widely recognized for 20 years that it is unjust, a primary cause of racial disparities in federal prisons, and based on drastic distinctions between two substances that are pharmacologically indistinguishable. Former president Bill Clinton in 2008 referred to it as a "cancer," but, when he was President, signed legislation overruling a proposed U.S. Sentencing Commission proposal to eliminate the distinction (Wickham, 2008).

Clinton stalemated Republicans in the game of law-and-order politics by announcing he would never let them get to his right on crime issues, he stuck to it. As a result, federal law contains a three-strikes law and 50-plus more crimes punishable by death than before he became President. Crime has not been a major issue in an American presidential election since 1988 (remember Willie Horton?), and is seldom one in state or local elections.

However, the stalemate continues. Neither party, particularly the Democrats, seems willing to break out of it for fear of being labeled as soft on crime. Despite two decades of declining crime rates and rising imprisonment rates, neither the federal government nor any state has enacted legislation substantially amending or repealing harsh sentencing laws or creating mechanisms likely to substantially reduce prison populations. The federal government slightly altered the 100-to-1 law.[4] A few states have slightly altered mandatory minimum sentence laws or released a few thousand inmates under new release programs, but those changes have only nibbled at the outermost edges of modern American prison populations and sentencing policies. Research can influence policy when "windows of opportunity" open through which evidence can pass. Concerning imprisonment and sentencing, the windows remain almost completely closed.

Criminogenic Prisons

That prisons make people worse has been a commonplace observation for two centuries. As long as there have been prisons people have known they are criminogenic. More than two centuries ago the English prison reformer John Howard called prisons "schools for crime." More than 40 years ago, the German parliament for that reason enacted the most effective sentencing law change in a Western country in the last century (Weigend, 2001). The law created a strong legal presumption against imposition of prison sentences of six months or less.[5] Short prison sentences fell by 80 percent, from an average 120,000 such sentences per year in the 1960s to under 20,000 per year thereafter, a level which continues to this day.

The underlying logic was that six months is too short a time for a prison sentence to do an offender any good as, for example, through participation in treatment programs. Six months, however, is plenty of time to cause an offender to lose a job, a family, and a home, and to damage his or her children. In addition, the stigma associated with being an ex-prisoner is greater than that associated with a conviction, and may diminish an offender's prospects for the rest of his or her life. Those are among the reasons why most continental European countries worked hard to restrain the growth of their prison populations from the 1960s to 1990s in the face of doubling and trebling crime rates. That is also a reason why successive Finnish governments worked for 30 years to drive the prison population down even though crime rates trebled between 1965 and 1990. They succeeded, lowering the imprisonment rate by 60 percent, from 165 per 100,000 in 1965 to 60 in 1990 (Lappi-Seppälä, 2001).

The one major exception in continental Europe was England and Wales from 1993 to the present. New Labour patterned its approach to crime on Bill Clinton's. In my view, Labour's criminal justice policies were the most repressive of any Western country's since World War II. The only competitor for that distinction, the United States, enacted harsher policies and retains capital punishment. Even right-wing Republican governments, however, did not enact Anti-Social Behaviour Order laws, threaten parents of wayward children with criminal convictions, maintain DNA from innocent people in police databases, or authorize or carry out routine surveillance of people not suspected of being criminals (or terrorists). Nor did any attempt to eliminate the double jeopardy rule, restrict jury rights, or weaken rules of evidence in order to make convictions easier to obtain. Nor have conservative American governments made powerful rhetorical arguments impugning defense counsel who represent their clients' interests as best they can or systematically urging that the policy interests of victims and offenders are irreconcilably opposed (Tonry, 2010*b*). Even in the United States, such arguments and proposals are made by cranks and crackpots, not by government ministers speaking in their official capacities.

That period in English history appears to have ended with the 2010 election of a Conservative-Liberal Democrat coalition government. Kenneth Clarke, the new English Minister of Justice, in a July 1, 2010 speech at King's College London signalled a change of direction (Travis & Sparrow, 2010). Clarke attacked the "Victorian bang 'em up" prison culture of the preceding 20 years. He warned that simply "banging up more and more people for longer" makes some criminals worse without protecting the public. "In our worst prisons," he said, "it produces tougher criminals. Many a man has gone into prison without a drug problem and come out drug dependent. And petty prisoners can meet up with some new hardened criminal friends."

Clarke was previously in charge of prisons as Home Secretary in 1992-1993, when the prison population in England and Wales stood at 44,628. He observed that the June 2010 population of 85,000 is "an astonishing number which I would have dismissed as an impossible and ridiculous prediction if it had been put to me in a forecast in 1992." He said that "for as long as I can remember" the political debate on law and order has been reduced to a competition over whether a government has spent more public money and locked up more people for longer than its predecessor.

He also said that "The consequence is that more and more offenders have been warehoused in outdated facilities and we spend vast amounts of public money on prison. But no proper thought has been given to whether this is really the best and most effective way of protecting the public against crime."

Finally, he noted that reoffending rates among prisoners given short sentences has reached 60 percent but observed "This does not surprise me. It is virtually impossible to do anything productive with offenders on short sentences. And many of them end up losing their jobs, their homes and their families during their short time inside."

Such a transformation is unlikely any time soon in the United States, no matter what the research evidence shows.

Police

Proposals to spend money to improve police effectiveness are an entirely different matter. Under current economic conditions, police may not win budget increases. They may suffer cuts. In neither case will that be because legislators are hostile to the police, or committed for ideological, partisan, or self-interested reasons to policies that have long been shown to be ineffective or counter-productive.

It is not entirely obvious to me, however, that increased expenditures to enable more intensive policing would be a good thing. Zero-tolerance, public-order, and misdemeanor policing have notoriously increased the extent of racial profiling and compromised traditional civil liberties restraints on police interactions with citizens. In principle, police should stop citizens only when individualized bases exist—that satisfy legal requirements of proof—to believe they have been involved in a crime. In practice, especially in minority areas of cities, those restraints are honored only in the breach.

I have similar concerns about crackdowns on drug markets. As a legal matter, police should make arrests only when they believe there are individualized bases to hold and prosecute each person arrested. In many crackdowns, most prominently concerning political demonstrations at controversial events such as WTO or G8 meetings, or recent Republican National Conventions in New York City and St Paul, Minnesota, police have routinely apprehended, or restricted the movement of, large numbers of people as to whom individualized bases for the actions could not be shown. As a result, huge numbers of arrests resulted in almost-inevitable dismissals at probable cause hearings. Drug crackdowns raise similar issues. It is possible in police sweeps to arrest many people in the environs of large open-air drug markets. Making large numbers of near-simultaneous arrests almost inevitably means that many will not satisfy individualized basis requirements of proof. It is to me not an obviously good idea to encourage police to increase their use of crackdowns.

RESEARCH

Others more qualified than I am will no doubt express their disagreements, if any, with Nagin concerning his analyses of the three literatures. I do no more than explain why I think his conclusions concerning deterrence are a mite strong and why I am more skeptical than he is about the research on police effectiveness. I have little to say about criminogenic prisons so I start with them.

Criminogenic prisons

My observations about John Howard, Kenneth Clarke, and German sentencing reform probably say all that need be said. Especially in the United States (and England), it would be remarkable if prisons were not criminogenic. Most people sent to prison are socially and economically disadvantaged, majorities are or have been alcohol or drug dependent, and most lack strong private systems of familial or social support. Most offenders, following release, are stigmatized, and often are explicitly handicapped by laws precluding many kinds of employment. Neither in the United States nor in England are there strong systems of state support to provide adequate housing or income to ex-prisoners. In lawyer talk, a judge could take "judicial notice" (that is, form a conclusion without needing to hear evidence) that already disadvantaged ex-prisoners facing additional handicaps and lacking systems of support are more likely than other people to engage in crime. Duhh!

Deterrence

Nagin notes that many economists claim to find general deterrent effects from penalty increases or from severe punishments, but that other social scientists almost always reach the opposite conclusion. He mentions a couple of economists' studies he finds particularly persuasive, but concludes that the findings are not generalizable, and accordingly that the best conclusion is that available evidence does not justify assumptions that severe punishments or punishment increases are effective general deterrents.

Fair enough, but I dissent. I agree with the policy inferences Nagin draws but believe he gives the economists' findings too much credit. To show why, I rehearse the findings of a sizable number of other surveys of the deterrence literature that reach stronger negative conclusions about deterrence effects[6] and then explain why the economists' occasional contrary findings should generally be disregarded.

Social scientists. A continuous series of reviews of deterrence research by social scientists other than economists (and a few by economists) over 30 years has concluded that general deterrent effects of severe punishments or of increases in punishment cannot be shown, setting aside the very different situations of parking and traffic law enforcement, tax laws, and penalties for administrative offenses. Here is a sampling of the more recent and widely-cited reviews.

Nagin himself in 1998 observed that he "was convinced that a number of studies have credibly demonstrated marginal deterrent effects," but concluded that it was "difficult to generalize from the findings of a specific study because knowledge about the factors that affect the efficacy of policy is so limited" (1998, p. 4). He highlighted four major factors: the relation between short- and long-term effects, the relation between risk perceptions and sanctions policies, the methods of implementation, and the extent of implementation.

Von Hirsch, Bottoms, Burney, and Wikström (1999), in a report commissioned by the English Home Office, conclude that "there is as yet no firm evidence regarding the extent to which raising the severity of punishment would enhance deterrence of crime" (1999, p. 52).

Doob and Webster in 2003 noted some inconclusive or weak evidence of marginal deterrence but concluded: "There is no plausible body of evidence that supports policies based on this premise [that increased penalties reduce crime]. On the contrary, standard social scientific norms governing the acceptance of the null hypothesis justify the present (always rebuttable) conclusion that sentence severity does not affect levels of crime" (2003, p. 146).

All of those reviews discuss works of economists and non-economists. A meta-analysis by Pratt, Cullen, Blevins, Daigle, and Madensen (2006), by contrast citing no economists, produced a main finding, one "noted by previous narrative reviews of the deterrence literature," that "the effects of severity estimates and deterrence/sanctions composites, even when statistically significant, are too weak to be of substantive significance (consistently below -.1)" (Pratt et al., 2006, p. 379).

Nagin's conclusions are not vastly different but nonetheless are more positive about deterrence effects than the earlier reviews. Mostly, it appears, this is because of a couple of recent articles by economists he holds in high regard (Helland & Tabarrok, 2007; Drago, Galbiati, & Vertova, 2009).

Economists. Economists discussing deterrence research tend to write only about the work of other economists.[7] Three major literature surveys by economists, summarizing work principally by economists, find that increases in punishment achieve general or marginal deterrent effects. Lewis describes "a substantial body of evidence which is largely consistent with the existence of a deterrent effect from longer sentences" (1986, p. 60). Levitt, relying principally on data from two of his own analyses, describes them as evidence "for a deterrent effect of increases in expected punishment" (2002, p. 445).

Levitt and Miles (2007) conclude: "The new empirical evidence [produced exclusively by economists] generally supports the deterrence model. . . . Evidence of the crime reducing effects of the scale of policing and incarceration is consistent across different methodological approaches" (p.

456). Much of their discussion focuses on whether capital punishment, recent increases in the scale of imprisonment, and changes in use of police manpower have reduced crime rates; the marginal deterrence hypothesis receives little attention except concerning a study by Kessler and Levitt (1999) of the effects of a change in California law.

There are two reasons why the economists' conclusions are so strong. First, they ignore work by other social scientists and accordingly make no effort to explain why others' conclusions are wrong. Second, notwithstanding the increased influence of behavioral economics, the economists who write on this subject mostly seem wedded to the price model.

Ronald Coase (1960), one of the law-and-economics movement's founders, long ago observed that many economists "rarely shrink from applying in every context the model of rational, self-interested, human behavior that they borrow from economics proper" (p. 7). Elsewhere, concerning deterrent effects, he wrote, "Punishment, for example, can be regarded as the price of crime. <u>An economist will not debate whether increased punishment will reduce crime</u>; he will merely try to answer the question, by how much?" (1978, p. 210; emphasis added). This may explain why economists, especially politically conservative ones, tend to conclude that increased penalties must in the nature of things have marginal deterrent effects and that capital punishment must deter homicide better than other penalties do. Economists assume penalties deter and begin with that prediction. That is why Doob and Webster (2003) propose that future deterrence research start from the tougher null hypothesis that penalty severity or increased severity has no deterrent effects.

Here is an example. Shawn Bushway and Peter Reuter (2008), celebrating the contributions of economists to studies of sentencing, discuss an "important" article by William Landes (<u>1971</u>). Landes, in modeling sentencing and bail decisions, assumed that prosecutors behave rationally in pursuit of the goal of maximizing aggregate punishment: "The prosecutor's objective function is such that he attempts to maximize the expected number of convictions weighted by the expected sentence given at trial, subject to a budget constraint on his resources." Put more simply, Landes assumes that prosecutors seek to maximize sentencing severity. Anyone who works with courts or prosecutors knows that is nonsense. Prosecutors do not generally seek the harshest possible sentence but one which they consider just or appropriate in the individual case. Numerous studies, and the conventional wisdom of courts, demonstrate that prosecutors are central figures in circumventing three-strikes laws, mandatory minimum sentence laws, and rigid sentencing guidelines in cases in which they believe the prescribed sentence would be unjustly severe.

Two influential and widely cited articles by economists illustrate the difficulties. Kessler and Levitt (1999) sought to identify deterrent effects from passage in 1982 of a California referendum that increased penalties for certain crimes.[8] They examined crime data at two-year intervals and thereby missed a downward trend that began in 1980 and continued after passage of the referendum. This made the post-1982 decline as likely to be the extension of a preexisting trend as a deterrent effect (Webster, Doob, & Zimring, 2006). Findings like this recur throughout the non-economic social science literature on the effects of sentencing law changes. Initial evaluations of California's 1976 Uniform Determinate Sentencing Law, using one-year pre-post comparisons, concluded that it caused prison admission rates to increase and average sentence lengths to decrease. Subsequent analyses showed that both changes began several years before passage of the 1976 law and that the best explanation of the post-implementation changes is that they extended pre-existing trends (Blumstein, Cohen, Martin, & Tonry, 1983). Even an economist as celebrated as Steve Levitt missed this sentencing evaluation 101 point.

Drago et al. (2009) analyzed the deterrent effects of a broad Italian prison amnesty program in 2006 that reduced the prison population by 40 percent. One amnesty condition was that people who re-offended would be sentenced for the new crime plus an additional amount equal to the period by which the amnesty reduced the previous sentence. Recidivism rates were compared with those of offenders released in an earlier year and the analysis found a deterrence effect for 2006 releasees serving short sentences but not for those serving long sentences. Lots of data quality issues can be raised concerning Italy's chaotic systems of official statistics, but there is a bigger problem: people who work in or study the Italian court system find the findings unbelievable. Italian courts are famously slow and inefficient, cases often are not concluded for years (appealed cases are completely retried), convictions are not final until the final appeal dates have expired, and Italian magistrates are famously independent. Even were it realistic to impute knowledge of the amnesty penalty increment to people released from prison, it is completely unrealistic to assume they believe it would be imposed (or that it would consistently be imposed).

POLICE

Here I have less to say except to offer two cautionary notes. First, since 1991 in the United States everything works. After California enacted its three-strikes law in 1994, and New York City implemented zero-tolerance policing, crime rates and violent crime rates fell in both places. However, we also know that crime rates in both places began to fall before the policy changes were adopted, and that they fell in every other populous state and every other large American city. Mayor Giuliani and Governor Wilson both benefitted from the happy timing and were able to claim their policies worked. Fifteen years later the clear weight of opinion concerning those policies is that they do not deserve major credit for the crime rate declines in those places (see, e.g., Tonry, 2004 [California and New York]; Harcourt & Ludwig, 2006 [New York]).

Most of the research showing that increases in police numbers of expenditure have crime-reductive effects has been carried out and published during the two decades of crime rate declines. It is striking, and ought to make us think a bit, that during the quarter-century of crime rate increases, most research on police numbers and expenditure concluded that no crime-reductive effect could be shown. I sat in many meetings in the 1980s in which senior police officials cautioned that the police could not be expected to overcome the influence of deep social and economic forces which cause crime rates to rise and fall.

Second, I am skeptical about the generalizability of the findings of research on drug market and hot-spots crackdowns. Of course it is a good thing that drug markets are occasionally shaken up and that for a time other related forms of crime (market-related assaults, muggings) occur less often, net of displacement effects (Sherman, 1990). The important questions, though, are whether drug use, sales, or prices fall other than in the short term, whether dealers are driven out of the market and not replaced, and whether the crackdown is a viable strategy for addressing other crimes. If crackdowns have no aggregate long-term effects, they are little different from constructions of sand built on ocean beaches; the waves will wash them away as if they never existed.

THEORY

Nagin and Beccaria are surely right about severity, certainty, and celerity. Formal criminal sanctions are so uncertain and variable in their severity that there are no good reasons to believe that they do much if anything to influence crime rates and trends. Increased police presence and visibility can make some response to criminal and antisocial behavior more likely, so it is not implausible to hypothesize that shifting emphasis and money from prisons to police may have some crime-reducing effects.

Nagin's is an ingenious effort to combine the findings of diverse research literatures to draw general strategic conclusions about criminal justice policy. Were he to write this paper, and act as an advisor to governments in Finland, Germany, or most continental European countries, the effects could be salutary. By confirming that there is little to be gained but much harm to be caused by means of repressive sentencing policies and heavy use of imprisonment, he would provide bases for continuing to place primary emphasis on policing and crime prevention approaches.

The United States is another matter. The inferences he draws about general deterrence and criminogenic prisons do not support the prevailing political conventional wisdom. The police findings do. My prediction is that policy makers will heed only those findings which they find congenial.

REFERENCES

Apel, R. & Nagin, D. (forthcoming). Deterrence. In M. Tonry (Ed.), *The Oxford handbook on crime and criminal justice.* New York, NY: Oxford University Press.

Blumstein, A., Cohen, J. Martin, S., & Tonry, M. (Eds.). (1983). *Research on sentencing: The search for reform.* Washington, DC: National Academy of Sciences.

Bushway, S. & Reuter, P. (2008). Economists' contribution to the study of crime and the criminal justice system. In M. Tonry (Ed.), *Crime and justice: A review of research*, volume 37, 389-451. Chicago, IL: University of Chicago Press.

Coase, R. (1960). The problem of social cost. *Journal of Law and Economics, 3*, 1-44.

Coase, R. (1978). Economics and contiguous disciplines. *Journal of Legal Studies, 7*, 210-11.

Donohue, J. (2006). The death penalty: No evidence for deterrence. *Economists' Voice, April*, 1-6.

Donohue, J. & Wolfers, J. (2005). Uses and abuses of empirical evidence in the death penalty debate. *Stanford Law Review, 58*, 791-846.

Doob, A. & Webster, C. (2003). Sentence severity and crime: Accepting the null hypothesis." In M. Tonry (Ed.), *Crime and justice: A review of research*, volume 30, 143-195. Chicago, IL: University of Chicago Press.

Drago, F., Galbiati, R., & Vertova, P. (2009). The deterrent effects of prison: Evidence from a natural experiment. *Journal of Political Economy, 117*(2), 257–80.

Durlauf, S. & Nagin, D. (forthcoming). Imprisonment and crime: Can we have less of both? *Criminology and Public Policy.*

Harcourt, B. & Ludwig, J. (2006). Broken windows: New evidence from New York City and a five-city social experiment. *University of Chicago Law Review, 73*, 271-320.

Helland, E. & Tabarrok, A. (2007). Does three strikes deter? A nonparametric estimation. *Journal of Human Resources, 42*, 309-330.

Kessler, D. & Levitt, S. (1999). Using sentence enhancements to distinguish between deterrence and incapacitation. *Journal of Law and Economics, 42*, 343–63.

Landes, W. (1971). An economic analysis of the courts. *Journal of Labor Economics, 14*(1), 61–107.

Lappi-Seppälä, T. (2001). Sentencing in Finland: The decline of the repressive ideal. In M. Tonry & R. Frase (Eds.), *Sentencing and sanctions in western countries*, 92-150. New York, NY: Oxford University Press.

Levitt, S. (2002). Deterrence. In J. Wilson & J. Petersilia (Eds.), *Crime: Public policies for crime control*, 435-450. Oakland, CA: Institute for Contemporary Studies Press.

Levitt, S. & Miles, T. (2007). Empirical study of criminal punishment. In A. Polinsky & S. Shavell, (Eds.), *Handbook of law and economics*, vol. 1, 453-495. Amsterdam: Elsevier.

Lewis, D. (1986). The general deterrent effect of longer sentences. *British Journal of Criminology, 26,* 47-62.

Nagin, D. (1998). Criminal deterrence research at the outset of the twenty-first century. In M. Tonry (Ed.), *Crime and justice: A review of research*, volume 23. Chicago: University of Chicago Press.

Nagin, D., Cullen, F., & Jonson, C. (2009). Imprisonment and re-offending. In M. Tonry (Ed.), *Crime and justice: A review of research*, volume 38. Chicago: University of Chicago Press.

Pratt, T., Cullen, F., Blevins, K., Daigle, L., & Madensen, T. (2006). The empirical status of deterrence theory: A meta-analysis. In F. Cullen, J. Wright, & K. Blevins (Eds.), *Taking stock: The status of criminological theory*, 367-397. New Brunswick, NJ: Transaction.

Shepherd, J. (2004). Testimony printed in Terrorist Penalties Enhancement Act of 2003: Hearing on H.R. 2934 Before the Subcommittee on Crime, Terrorism, and Homeland Security of the House Committee on the judiciary, 108th Congress, pp. 10-11.
http://judiciary.house.gov/media/pdfs/printers/108th/93224.pdf

Sherman, L. (1990). Police crackdowns: Initial and residual deterrence. In M. Tonry (Ed.), *Crime and justice: A review of Research*, volume 12. Chicago, IL: University of Chicago Press.

Tonry, M. (2004). *Thinking about crime: Sense and sensibility in American penal culture.* New York, NY: Oxford University Press.

Tonry, M. (2008). Learning from the limitations of deterrence research. In M. Tonry (Ed.), *Crime and justice: A review of research,* volume 37. Chicago, IL: University of Chicago Press.

Tonry, M. (2009). The mostly unintended effects of mandatory penalties: Two centuries of consistent findings. In M. Tonry (Ed.), *Crime and justice: A review of research,* volume 38. Chicago, IL: University of Chicago Press.

Tonry, M. (2010*a*). 'Public criminology' and evidence-based policy. *Criminology and Public Policy* (forthcoming).

Tonry, M. (2010*b*). The costly consequences of populist posturing: ASBOs, victims, 'rebalancing', and diminution of support for civil liberties. *Punishment & Society* (forthcoming).

Tonry, M. & Green, D. (2003). Criminology and public policy in the US and the UK. In A. Ashworth & L. Zedner (Eds.), *The criminological foundations of penal policy*, 485-524. Oxford: Oxford University Press.

Travis, A. & Sparrow, A. (2010, July 1). Kenneth Clarke hints at prison sentencing reform with attack on 'bang 'em' up culture; Justice secretary launches major assault on 'prison works' orthodoxy espoused by former Tory home secretary Michael Howard. *The Guardian.* Retrieved July 1, 2010, from
http://www.guardian.co.uk/society/2010/jun/30/kenneth-clarke-prison...

von Hirsch, A., Bottoms, A., Burney, E., & Wikström, P-O. (1999). *Criminal deterrence and sentence severity: An analysis of recent research.* Oxford: Hart.

Webster, C., Doob, A., & Zimring, F. (2006). Proposition 8 and crime rates in California: The case for the disappearing deterrent. *Criminology and Public Policy, 5,* 417–48.

Weigend, T. (2001). Sentencing in Germany. In M. Tonry & R. Frase (Eds.), *Sentencing and sanctions in western countries,* 188-221. New York, NY: Oxford University Press.

Wickham, D. (2008, March 4). Bill Clinton expresses 'regret' on crack cocaine sentencing." *USA Today.*

Zimring, F., Hawkins, G., & Kamin, S. (2001). *Punishment and democracy: Three strikes and you're out in California.* New York, NY: Oxford University Press.

ENDNOTES

[1] Extraordinary because the deterrence literatures by economists and social scientists are almost completely separate, as are the scholarly worlds of corrections and police research. Few people bridge either of those gaps; Nagin bridges both.

[2] I do not discuss that literature in any detail here. I discuss it at length in a forthcoming article in *Criminology and Public Policy* (Tonry, 2010a). David Green and I discuss it exhaustively in Tonry and Green (2003).

[3] By coincidence, I surveyed the historical and modern literatures on mandatory penalties in a recent article (Tonry, 2009).

[4] After this article was written Congress enacted and President Obama on August 3, 2010, signed the Fair Sentencing Act of 2010, which slightly modified the 100-to-1 law. The crack/powder sentencing difference was reduced to 18-to-1. People convicted of selling 28 grams of crack or 500 grams of powder are subject to mandatory minimum 5-year sentences. The change was not retroactive and, though it will help a few sellers of small quantities of crack, does not begin to address the fundamental problems with the original law.

[5] German law then and now provides in most cases for remission of one-third of a prison term. The law thus discouraged imposition of nominal sentences of nine months or less.

[6] I also recently surveyed the several deterrence literatures, but in this article rely on other peoples' work (Tonry, 2008).

[7] In a classic instance, Joanna Shepherd, author of several economic studies finding a deterrent effect of capital punishment, in 2004 testified before the U.S. Congress that there was a "strong consensus among economists that capital punishment deters crime" and that "the studies are unanimous" (2004, pp. 10–11), without mentioning the equally strong consensus among non-economists (with agreement of many economists [Donohue & Wolfers, 2005; Donohue, 2006] that capital punishment cannot be shown to deter homicide).

[8] I don't discuss Helland and Tabarrok (2007), which found deterrent effects of California's three-strikes laws, other than to point out that of 18 quantitative analyses of the deterrent effects of California's three-strikes laws, 15 (many by economists) find no deterrent effects. The three that find effects are all by economists. Just about every imaginable basis for comparison has been used (minors compared with adults; people meeting two-strikes criteria compared with those meeting three-strikes criteria; crime rates in counties in which the three-strikes law was aggressively enforced compared with counties in which it was barely enforced at all; crime trends in California compared with those in other populous states without three-strikes laws; crime trends in large California cities compared with those in large cities in states without three-strikes laws) (Zimring et al., 2001; Tonry, 2008, table 3).

Deterrence, Economics, and the Context of Drug Markets

Shawn Bushway
Peter Reuter

Part I: An Argument for a Nuanced Discussion of Deterrence by Criminologists using Key "Economic" Concepts

Nagin (2010), drawing on work with Durlauf and others, has again reviewed the evidence for general deterrence. This is a touchy subject, and one that often leads to contentious arguments that pit criminologists and fellow travelers against economists (e.g., Zimring, 2008; Levitt & Dubner, 2005). Economists, committed to general deterrence by their belief in rationality (Bushway & Reuter, 2008), discuss deterrence without citing work by criminologists (Levitt, 2002; Levitt & Miles, 2007), and criminologists return the favor (Pratt, Cullen, Blevins, Daigle, & Madensen, 2006). Nagin's paper attempts to talk about deterrence research in more nuanced terms, with equal reference to research by economists and criminologists.

However, it is important to note that this nuance is executed with direct reference to three principal concepts from economics –the rational choice framework itself, marginal effects, and elasticity. Too often tests of deterrence are viewed by both criminologists and economists as a referendum on the rational choice model, or more broadly, the ability of economists to productively comment on crime-related topics.

But, Michael Tonry, decidedly not an economist, has called for just this kind of nuance in research on deterrence, based directly on the observation that there are "differences in individuals' susceptibility to changes in legal threats" (Tonry, 2008, p. 281). This observation is not a refutation of rational choice, but simply a call to recognize that there are different preference functions in the population (see also Cook, 1980), or alternatively, there are heterogenous treatment effects, a common observation now in the economics evaluation literature.

Although the rational choice framework itself is clearly not perfect, it has considerable power to predict and explain – and it can easily handle differences between individuals in the population. Productive conversations about policy can be had while staying within the confines of the model – a valuable constraint given the absence of other formal theories with comparable predictive power. A great example of this power comes from political scientist Bernard Harcourt's critique of statistical discrimination, which is made using the rational choice model itself (Harcourt, 2007).

Nagin's critique of policies that increase sentencing severity is an excellent example of a critique of deterrence policies that is rooted in rational choice theory. If criminals are rational, the fact that punishment (or money) 10 years from now is worth less than the same amount of punishment (or money) this year means, by definition, that a rational criminal will be less deterred from an extra year of punishment in a world where he already faces a threat of 10 years, versus a world where he currently faces only 6 months of incarceration. One year of punishment 10 years from now is simply not as "costly" as one year of punishment 6 months from now. This is especially true, if as we believe is the case, crime prone individuals are likely to be impulsive (likely to discount the future heavily). Staying within the simple rational choice model, as we advocate, this can be made explicit using simple calculations—calculations that Nagin and Durlauf complete in a clear and compelling manner in the full version of their article.

The concept of marginality, so central to the economic approach, is also relevant here, and again, Michael Tonry takes the lead here in his 2008 article with his consistent reference to marginal deterrence. The question is not, as it is often phrased, does deterrence work, but, can the deterrence threat be heightened, given the current level of threat. The United States already has a fairly severe system of punishment in the United States; sentence lengths are severe both by historical and international standards. The policy question is whether those who are not already deterred (by evidence of their continued commission of crime) can be deterred by additional punishment threats. This is a fundamentally different question than "does deterrence work."

The concept of elasticity, which is central to Nagin's approach, is linked directly to the issue of marginality. Elasticity as a concept is well developed in economics, but is not often used in criminology, which tends to focus on effect size. That is unfortunate, because elasticity, unlike effect size, has inherent in its definition a relative assessment of returns. To be precise, an elasticity refers to the percent change in Y "caused by" the percent change in X. Percents can only be calculated if we know the current level of an activity. The same effect size can have a large elasticity if the initial investment in X was low, and a low elasticity if the initial investment in X is high (or vice versa). Responsivity, in a world of elasticity, depends on the location with respect to current efforts. The current discussion about incarceration depends crucially on the understanding of where we are in the margin. Additional expenditures on incarceration now occur on top of substantial sums already devoted to that effort; effects will be smaller because of declining elasticity compared to additional expenditures in a world where incarceration is relatively low (Donohue, 2009). The power of Nagin's suggestion for a focus on certainty comes from the recognition that certainty of punishment has not been increased as much, and therefore, changes at the margin are likely to be more elastic.

Nagin's discussion, with its explicit use of rational choice theory, marginality, and elasticity, naturally moves the discussion away from an all or nothing debate about the use of punishment threat to create deterrence. This is a productive movement in the debate about deterrence. It mirrors the discussion about rehabilitation programs, which moved from a "nothing works" mentality, to a more nuanced "what works for whom" approach" (Cullen, 2005). Although skeptical that the medical model with the discretionary doctor choosing from the available treatment options presents the right framework for this discussion, we do not see why discussions of deterrent effects are any different from the discussion of job training or rehabilitation programs. In all cases, it is useful to adopt a nuanced perspective where the search is for different treatment effects for different types of programs aimed at different populations, with special awareness of the context in which the programs are being implemented (Bushway & Smith, 2007).

Economists have demonstrated an ability to think about these issues with nuance, most clearly with respect to the topic of death penalty, where prominent economists have clearly and explicitly made the case against a deterrent impact for the death penalty on both theoretical and empirical grounds (Levitt, 2004; Donohue, 2006; Donohue & Wolfers, 2005). The fact that not all economists agree should hardly be reason to tar all economists with the same brush.

PART II: ECONOMICS IS ABOUT MARKETS TOO

Part I contended that a productive and nuanced discussion about the relative merits of the punishment threat can be carried out within the context of the economic model of rational choice. Within this discussion, we pointed out that the model can predict, *a priori*, cases where particular deterrence strategies will be ineffective (e.g., severity-based strategies in a world where current punishments are already severe). But, this use of the rational choice model is inherently limited, because it fails to exploit the "market" part of the basic rational choice model. This is particularly true when speaking about deterrence strategies in a world where much of the punishment is being directed at drug markets, and drug dealers, either directly or indirectly. This observation is true for severity or certainty-based strategies.

Specifically, Nagin's analysis about the potential for deterrence strategies needs modification to deal with enforcement against drug markets, particularly drug sellers. The distinctive feature of such enforcement is that price serves as a mediating factor; higher risk can be compensated for by higher returns to sellers, in the form of higher prices. The result is that the decline in drug selling may only be slight; drug selling may in fact only decline with more incarceration. Moreover, it is possible, indeed likely, that the higher price results in higher levels of property crimes by drug users.

A theory

A principal goal of drug enforcement is reduction in the number of drug users and the amount of crime that it causes; the dealers are essentially instruments for the adverse consequences of drug use with which we are concerned. The dealers themselves are thus not the ultimate object of enforcement, a contrast with robbery or crimes of violence where the perpetrator is the sole object of the enforcement. Raising dealer risks and costs by increasing sentence severity or certainty is simply a method for making drugs less available and more expensive and thus inducing users to cut back or desist altogether. Quantity serves as a summary measure of the two dimensions of harm, the number of users and the average quantity consumed; quantity also captures health harms (Reuter & Caulkins, 1995). Expenditures is of separate interest as it provides a measure of the potential income generating crime (both property and market) arising from drug use.[1]

The question then is whether Nagin's analysis and conclusion generalize to this situation. Assuming the market equivalent of general deterrence, is it possible, by raising the risk of apprehension of drug dealers, to simultaneously reduce the number of dealers incarcerated, the quantity of drugs consumed, and the total expenditures?

This is not a minor matter for those interested in reducing the population in prisons and jails. Caulkins and Chandler (2006) estimate that the number of individuals incarcerated for drug offenses rose approximately 10 fold over the period 1980 to 2005; the total in 2005 was close to 500,000, about 22 percent of the incarcerated population in the United States. As with other crime, the rise in drug incarcerations is remarkable since it has continued long after the indicators of the size of drug markets have shrunk (ONDCP, 2001).

As articulated by Reuter and Kleiman (1986) and more recently updated by Caulkins and Reuter (forthcoming), the "risks and prices" theory of price formation for an illegal drug posits that it is determined largely by the intensity of enforcement, that is, the probability that a dealer will be punished. Punishment affects two risks faced by drug dealers; directly it increases the risk of incarceration and other criminal justice penalties (including seizures of drugs and assets) and indirectly the risks of violence from other participants. The indirect effect comes through concerns about informants and through prices.[2] The model does not distinguish between the probability and severity of punishment.

Nagin has introduced the concept of an elasticity, the percentage response of one outcome variable on a 1 percent change in some other variable. As noted in part I, this is an important concept, and it plays a central role in any discussion of market dynamics. There are two critical elasticities here; the elasticity of the supply of risky labor to expected punishment, which we will designate $e(L)$ and the elasticity of the demand for the drug with respect to its price $e(D)$. Assume that $e(L)$ is very high, that is, that there are many other individuals willing to sell the drug for a slightly higher reward than that generated by current prices. Assume also that the $e(D)$ is low, so that the quantity consumed is not much reduced by the higher price needed to bring in the marginal seller; the parameter is set at -0.3.[3]

Now assume that police are able to increase the probability of arrest for a cocaine selling offense from 2 percent to 3 percent; post-arrest risks stay unchanged. This has two kinds of effects on the supply side. First, some current dealers are removed from the population; for simplification assume that the system was in steady state before, with an equal number of dealers exiting (through incarceration) and returning to the market each year. The higher arrest rate means that there will now be a shortage of sellers and buyers will bid up the price as a consequence. That will attract some new sellers, who were not willing to deal drugs at the previous price. The higher price will also lower the amount that users are willing to buy so that the total number of dealers will decrease.[4] Whether the total number of dealers incarcerated in the new equilibrium decreases along with the decrease in drug sales depends on $e(L)$. If this parameter is high enough then the price rise will be small enough that the total number of incarcerations (apprehension probability times number of dealers) will rise.

This is only the first part of the analysis. There is also the effect on drug users; does total expenditure, a surrogate for related crime, go down? There is a standard exposition for this, as shown in Figure 1. The higher arrest rate lowers the amount that will be offered at each price. That is indicated by the shift in the supply curve. The shift of the supply curve moves the equilibrium along the demand curve: since the elasticity of demand is less than one in absolute value, the result is that consumption declines but total expenditures increases.[5]

Figure 1. Inelastic demand curve.

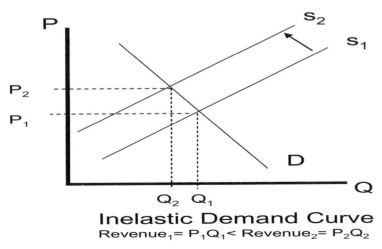

Inelastic Demand Curve
$Revenue_1 = P_1Q_1 < Revenue_2 = P_2Q_2$

In this simple model, only the elasticity of demand matters. We will observe an increase in expenditures on the illegal drug, whether the shift in the supply curve is large (i.e., the price has increased a lot to attract in the marginal dealers to replace those who are being incarcerated now) or small, so long as it leads to a shift along the demand curve characterized by inelastic demand. Since there are few estimates of price elasticity for cocaine or heroin that are greater than one in absolute value, it seems that even increased police efficiency does not save us from the opposite of Nagin's conclusion; better policing that increases a dealer's risk of arrest and punishment generates both more incarceration and more crime.

There are numerous assumptions built into this analysis and hence a number of avenues for chipping away at this. We consider just two here:

1. Markets may become less efficient as they become smaller. At some stage the higher incarceration rates may make dealers few enough in number that the costs of users and sellers finding each other become high. This in effect shifts the demand curve down, since the non-monetary costs have risen.
2. Dealers are also users; indeed many of them are very frequent users (Pollack, Reuter, & Sevigny, forthcoming). Thus incarcerating dealers also reduces demand. A much higher incarceration rate shifts the demand curve down at the same time as it shifts the supply curve out. The consequence may be a reduction in quantity consumed and in price.

Policy implications

Critiques of the war on drugs abound (e.g., Tonry, 1995); it is essentially impossible to find academic defenders of the U.S. campaign to suppress drug markets through extensive incarceration. The arguments against the current campaign are empirically strong but analytically casual. Does the above analysis help?

The empirical case is straightforward enough. Apart from the extraordinary racial disparity in incarceration, even greater than for crime generally, the mass incarceration of drug dealers has not managed to make drugs more expensive or harder to obtain. The failure with respect to price of cocaine and heroin is captured in Figure 2.

Figure 2. U.S. drug-related incarceration and retail heroin and cocaine prices.

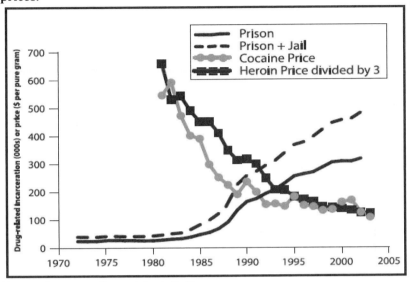

Note: prices are adjusted for inflation

The explanations offered for this failure generally focus on the ease of replacement. Locking up one dealer simply provides an opening for another is a standard commentary. What we offer here is a more theoretically grounded basis for that claim. There may well be a limited supply of individuals willing to take the specific risks prevailing at the current prices and earnings, so that the removal of a dealer now creates not a niche but a gap. However, the supply of risk-taking labor is upward sloping, so that for higher incomes (associated with higher prices), there will indeed be another individual willing to take the place of the incarcerated dealer. As described above, that higher price will reduce consumption but probably will increase total expenditures on drugs and thus other crime.

Would less incarceration improve matters? That raises a difficult question about the optimal price of an illegal drug. The assumption has always been that society's interest is served by high drug prices, since they serve to discourage initiation and encourage desistance. There has been acknowledgement of the problem created by an inelastic demand but the tension has not been made explicit, with one exception. Moore (1973) argued that society wanted drugs to be cheap for addicts and expensive to new users. He suggested that targeting enforcement against sales to new users was a way to accomplish this; dealers would then presumably be willing to offer lower prices to known addicts. That has never been put into practice, though it is possible to imagine undercover officers simulating new rather than experienced customers. However the aging of the cocaine and methamphetamine populations suggests that there are limits to this tactic; there simply aren't many new users of these drugs in contemporary

America. One would hope though to aspire to policy recommendations that are not so contingent as that.

One way out is again to note that many drug sellers are frequent users of the drugs they sell. If prison or community supervision can reduce their drug use, it may lead to lower aggregate demand for drug and thus to fewer drug deals. That would permit higher apprehension to generate lower incarceration in the long-run. This is the insight of Kleiman's (2009) mandated desistance; as Nagin notes, Kleiman presents a whole range of approaches aimed at lowering both prison and crime. There is some evidence, notably Hawken and Kleiman (2009), that close supervision with frequent drug testing followed, most importantly, by immediate graduated sanctions can generate much lower recidivism. Thus one may be able to attain Nagin's goal but general deterrence is not the mechanism.

PART III: CONCLUDING COMMENTS

The s analysis in Part II does not disturb either the findings or policy recommendations that Nagin offers. It does, however, point to a limited domain of generalization. Enforcement against drug sellers involves price mechanisms that complicate the analysis both directly (whether the number of drug dealers in prison falls) and indirectly (whether there will be more incarceration of drug users as a result of their income generating crime).

This analysis covers enforcement against sellers. What about deterring drug users through arrest? Here the price mechanism works in favor of deterrence. A higher risk of arrest for users increases the "full price" of the drug, which includes both money cost and time and risks of acquisition (Moore, 1973). Thus, tougher enforcement will reduce the demand for drugs; there will be a shift down the supply curve, to lower price and lower quantity; fewer drug deals at lower prices and thus lower revenue.

Is this an important insight? Though many inmates of state prison are there for possession offenses, the self-report of the inmates themselves indicate that most of them have pled to possession charges to avoid being convicted of more serious offenses of distribution (Sevigny & Caulkins, 2004) The incarceration of users is not a major tool of drug control; the incarceration of dealers for possession offenses is important but our analysis does not apply there.

Finding ways of reducing both the numbers imprisoned because of their drug selling and the amount of drug distribution is an important policy objective. Deterrence does not seem likely to help in this case because of the nature of the market, and the inelasticity of demand in the drug market.

REFERENCES

Bushway, S. & Reuter, P. (2008). Economists' contribution to the study of crime and the criminal justice system. In M. Tonry (Ed.), *Crime and justice: An annual review of research, Vol. 37* (pp. 389-452). Chicago, IL: University of Chicago Press.

Bushway, S. & Smith, J. (2007). Sentencing using statistical treatment rules: What we don't know can hurt us. *Journal of Quantitative Criminology, 23*(4), 377-387.

Caulkins, J. & Chandler, S. (2006). Long-run trends in incarceration of drug offenders in the US. *Crime and Delinquency, 52*(4), 619-641.

Caulkins, J. & Reuter, P. (forthcoming). How drug enforcement affects drug prices. In M. Tonry (Ed.), *Crime and justice: A review of research.* Chicago, IL: University of Chicago Press.

Cook, P. (1980). Research in criminal deterrence: Laying the groundwork for the second decade. In N. Morris & M. Tonry (Eds.), *Crime and justice: An annual review of research* (pp. 211-268). Chicago, IL: University of Chicago.

Cullen, F. (2005). The twelve people who saved rehabilitation: How the science of criminology made a difference – The American Society of Criminology 2004 Presidential Address. *Criminology, 43,* 1-42.

Donohue, J. (2006). The death penalty: No evidence for deterrence. *Economists' Voice, April,* 1-6.

Donohue, J. (2009). Assessing the relative benefits of incarceration: Overall changes and the benefits on the margin. In S. Raphael & M. Stoll (Eds.), *Do prisons make us safer? The benefits and costs of the prison boom* (pp. 369-342). New York, NY: Russell Sage Foundation.

Donohue, J. & Wolfers, J. (2005). Uses and abuses of empirical evidence in the death penalty debate. *Stanford Law Review, 58,* 791- 846.

Durlauf, S. & Nagin, D. (Forthcoming). Imprisonment and crime: Can both be reduced? *Criminology and Public Policy.*

Durlauf, S. & Nagin, D. (Forthcoming). The deterrent effect of imprisonment. In P.Cook, J. Ludwig, & J. McCrary (Eds). *Making crime control pay: Cost-effective alternatives to incarceration.* Chicago, IL: University of Chicago Press.

Grossman, M. (2005). Individual behaviors and substance use: The role of price. In B. Lindgren & M. Grossman (Eds.), *Substance use: Individual behaviors, social interactions, markets and politics,* Advances in Health Economics and Health Services Research Vol. 16 (pp. 15-39). Amsterdam: Elsevier. http://ideas.repec.org/p/nbr/nberwo/10948.html

Harcourt, B. (2007). *Against prediction: Profiling, policing, and punishing in an actuarial age.* Chicago, IL: University of Chicago Press.

Hawken, A. & Kleiman, M. (2009). *Managing drug involved probationers with swift and certain sanctions: Evaluating Hawaii's HOPE.* Washington, DC: National Institute of Justice.

Kleiman, M. (2009). *When brute force fails.* Princeton, NJ: Princeton University Press.

Levitt, S. (2002). Deterrence. In J. Wilson & J. Petersilia (Eds.), *Crime: Public policies for crime control*, 435-450. Oakland, CA: Institute for Contemporary Studies Press.

Levitt, S. (2004). Understanding why crime fell in the 1990s: Four factors that explain the decline and six that do not. *Journal of Economic Perspectives, 18*(1) (Winter 2004), 163-90.

Levitt, S. & Dubner, S. (2005). *Freakonomics: A rogue economist explores the hidden side of everything.* New York, NY: William Morrow/HarperCollins.

Levitt, S. & Miles, T. (2007). Empirical study of criminal punishment. In A. Polinsky & S. Shavell, (Eds.), *Handbook of law and economics*, vol. 1, 453-495. Amsterdam: Elsevier.

MacCoun, R., Kilmer, B., & Reuter, P. (2003). Research on crime-drugs linkage: The next generation of research. In H. Brounstein & C. Crossland (Eds.), *Toward a drugs and crime research agenda for the 21ˢᵗ Century* (pp. 65-95). Washington, DC: National Institute of Justice.

Moore, M. (1973). Achieving discrimination in the effective price of heroin. *American Economic Review, 63*(2), 270-77

Office of National Drug Control Policy. (2001). *What America's users spend on drugs: 1988-2000* Washington, DC; Executive Office of the President.

Pollack, H., Reuter, P., & Sevigny, E. (forthcoming). If drug treatment works so well, why are so many drug users in prison?

Pratt, T., Cullen, F., Blevins, K., Daigle, L., & Madensen, T. (2006). The empirical status of deterrence theory: A meta-analysis. In F. Cullen, J. Wright, & K. Blevins (Eds.), *Taking stock: The status of criminological theory*, 367-397. New Brunswick, NJ: Transaction.

Reuter, P. & Caulkins, J. (1995). Redefining the goals of national drug policy: Report of a working group. *American Journal of Public Health, 85*(8), 1059-1063.

Reuter, P. & Kleiman, M. (1986.) Risks and Prices: An economic analysis of drug enforcement. *Crime and justice: An annual review, 9*, 128-179.

Sevigny, E. & Caulkins, J. (2004). Kingpins or mules? An analysis of drug offenders incarcerated in federal and state prisons. *Criminology and Public Policy, 3*(3), 401-434.

Stevens, A. (in press, 2010). *Drugs, crime and public health: The political economy of drug policy.* London: Routledge.

Tonry, M. (1995). *Malign neglect.* New York, NY: Oxford University Press.

Zimring, F. (2008). Criminology and its discontents: The American Society of Criminology 2007 Sutherland Address. *Criminology, 46*, 301.

ENDNOTES

[1] There is a substantial literature on the positive relationship between crime and drug use. See MacCoun, Kilmer and Reuter (2003) for a review; a more skeptical assessment of the strength of the relationship is given in Stevens (in press).

[2] The use of violence against informants is a common source of injury and death in these markets. The higher the risk to which an informant can expose a dealer, the greater the incentive to retaliate against him. Higher prices increase the incentives for theft of drugs.

[3] That is within the ranges reported by Grossman (2004) in his review of the elasticity of demand for addictive substances.

[4] We assume here that the optimal amount for a drug dealer to sell per unit time does not change.

[5] For example, If price rises by 10 percent and the result is a decline in demand of 3 percent, then revenue will be $1.10*0.97 = 1.067$.

THE GREAT RECESSION AND THE GREAT CONFINEMENT: THE ECONOMIC CRISIS AND THE FUTURE OF PENAL REFORM

MARIE GOTTSCHALK

ABSTRACT

The Great Recession coupled with the election of Barack Obama has raised expectations that the United States will begin emptying its jails and prisons because it can no longer afford to keep so many people locked up. Although the current economic crisis provides an opening to rethink the direction of U.S. penal policies, if history is any guide, rising public anxiety in the face of persistent economic distress and growing economic inequalities might actually ignite more hard-line penal policies. Economic crises create enormous societal anxieties and insecurities that could fortify the "culture of control" that David Garland identified as the lifeblood of the prison boom that took off three decades ago. In times of political and social unrest, public officials and prominent commentators often conflate crime and social protest, providing an opening to build up the law-and-order apparatus. Also, as evidenced by the New Deal, economic crises provide an opportunity to legitimize the expansion of all sorts of federal and state powers, from control of the economy to law enforcement. Certain economic development arguments in favor of prisons have more sway in economic hard times, and the vested interests in maintaining an expansive penal system in the United States remain considerable. A brief analysis of the protracted process of the deinstitutionalization of the mentally ill in the United States provides a cautionary tale.

The financial crisis, coupled with the election of Barack Obama, has raised expectations that the United States will begin to empty its jails and prisons because it can no longer afford to keep so many people behind bars (Pew Center on the States, 2009, p. 2; Robinson, 2009). As Attorney General Eric Holder told the American Bar Association in August 2009, the country's extraordinary incarceration rate is "unsustainable economically" (Pallasch, 2009).

Some evidence suggests that the Great Recession has prompted a major shift in penal policy that will reduce the country's incarceration rate, which for years has been the highest in the world. States have enacted a slew of penal reforms aimed at shrinking their prison populations, including expanding the use of alternative sentences and drug courts, loosening restrictions on parole eligibility, and reducing revocations of parole and probation for minor infractions (King, 2009). Dozens of states have cut their corrections budgets the last couple of years, and many have proposed closing penal facilities to save money (Reutter, 2009; Gramlich, 2009b). Four states—New Jersey, New York, Michigan, and Kansas—have reduced their prison populations by 5 to 20 percent since 1999 (Greene & Mauer, 2010, p. 2). Last year the total state-prison population in the country dipped for the first time since 1972 (Pew Center on the States, 2010).

Enthusiasm for the "war on drugs" appears to be waning at the federal and state level. Congress and the Obama administration have been working to reduce the sentencing disparity between crack and power cocaine and to soften other drug laws. Several states and municipalities have designated enforcement of marijuana laws their lowest priority, and a number of states are debating marijuana decriminalization. Last fall Minneapolis became the first major U.S. city without a narcotics squad when it disbanded its special drug unit to save money. The U.S. Sentencing Commission, the panel that sets guidelines for the federal courts, has begun to investigate alternatives to incarceration, and in October 2009, Congress ordered the Commission to review mandatory minimum sentencing.

Although the current economic distress is providing an opportunity to rethink the direction of U.S. penal policies, we should not assume that the crushing economic burden will single-handedly unhinge the carceral state. While the prison population declined in 26 states between 2008 and 2009, it continued to grow in 24 others. Meanwhile, the federal prison population increased by 3.4 percent (Pew Center on the States, 2010).

Mounting fiscal pressures will not be enough on their own to spur communities, states, and the federal government to make deep and lasting cuts in their prison and jail populations. It was mistakenly assumed four decades ago that shared disillusionment on the right and the left with indeterminate sentences and prison rehabilitation programs would shrink the inmate population. Instead, it exploded. The race to incarcerate began in the 1970s at a time when states faced dire financial straits. It persisted over the next four decades despite wide fluctuations in the crime rate, public opinion, and the economy.

The previous recession in 2001 raised expectations that the prison boom would end as severe budget deficits forced states to close prisons and lay off guards (King & Mauer, 2002). At the time, fiscally conservative Republicans previously known for being penal hard-liners championed some of the sentencing and drug-law reforms (Bennett & Kuttner, 2003, p. 36). But the penal reforms enacted in the wake of that recession did not make a dent in the U.S. incarceration rate, which continued to march upward.

If history is any guide, rising public anxiety in the face of persistent economic distress and growing economic inequalities might, in fact, spur more punitiveness. This essay examines several reasons why. It then turns to the decades-long project to shut down state mental asylums to see what parallels there might be between deinstitutionalization of the mentally ill and recent efforts to reduce the penal population.

THE CULTURE OF CONTROL, REVISITED

Economic crises may foster public punitiveness for several reasons. Rising economic despair, spreading poverty, unprecedented foreclosure rates, escalating unemployment, growing uncertainty about the country's economic future, and massive dislocations in the labor, real estate, and financial markets may effectively fortify the "culture of control" that David Garland (2001) identified as the lifeblood of the prison boom launched nearly four decades ago. In Garland's account, societal angst stemming from deep structural changes in the U.S. economy and society in the immediate postwar decades, including suburbanization, the flow of women into the workforce, rapid advances in technology, transportation, and communications, the democratization of social and cultural life, and the rise of the electronic media, ushered in a new culture of control premised on harsh punishment and extensive surveillance. Widespread perceptions of state impotency in addressing the economic upheavals of the 1970s further bolstered the shift in policies.

The U.S. government's inability to tame the economic demons in the current financial crisis (and its alleged culpability in releasing those demons) casts doubt on the efficacy, legitimacy, and raison d'etre of the state. While the government struggles to restore economic health, some public officials may be tempted to act out in impulsive, unreflective ways, promoting highly punitive measures for their immediate symbolic and expressive value (Garland, 2001, p. 132-33). The apparent surge in firearm purchases in early 2009 (Blow, 2009) and the brazen display of weapons in public venues like Starbucks stores and at public events (most notably at the health care reform town meetings in summer 2009) are ominous indicators of growing public anxiety that may have important implications for penal policy and law enforcement. The not-too-subtle message appears to be that if the state is not prepared to protect the public, individuals are locked and loaded to do so.

Furthermore, there is a well established "relationship between economic insecurity and scapegoating behavior" (Matravers & Maruna, 2005, p. 128). Claims that immigrants are stealing jobs from citizens have more salience in a weak economy, justifying harsher attacks on them. In April 2009, Arizona enacted a stringent and highly controversial immigration bill that requires the police to arrest people who cannot immediately prove they are in the country legally. High-profile raids of workplaces that employ large numbers of immigrants have become more commonplace, and local police are collaborating more closely with the federal authorities to detain and deport immigrants.

As a consequence, immigration detention has become a growth industry. A whole new penal apparatus to apprehend immigrants—documented and undocumented—has been quietly under construction for decades. It operates under the auspices of the U.S. Immigration and Customs Enforcement (formerly the Immigration and Naturalization

Service), but has been largely shielded from public and legal scrutiny. Changes in immigration policy over the past 25 years or so have become new drivers of the U.S. penal system (Bohrman & Murakawa, 2005). Two landmark pieces of legislation in 1996—the Antiterrorism and Effective Death Penalty Act and the Illegal Immigration Reform and Immigrant Responsibility Act—dramatically expanded the categories of crimes for which legal residents could be deported and eliminated many opportunities for waivers. A conviction for simple battery or shoplifting with a one-year suspended sentence can trigger mandatory detention and deportation (Dow, 2004, p. 173-74). The number of people held by Immigration and Customs Enforcement on any given day has increased more than eleven-fold since the early 1970s as the immigration service has become a miniature Bureau of Prisons.[1] In a striking development, Latinos now represent the largest ethnic group in the federal prison system (Gorman, 2009).

CRIME RATES AND ECONOMIC DISTRESS

Studies of the United States and other advanced industrialized countries indicate that the imprisonment rate tends to rise with the unemployment rate, regardless of whether the crime rate is rising or falling (De Giorgi, 2006, p. 3-33). Studies that use unemployment as a proxy for economic distress have not settled the question of whether rising unemployment causes spikes in crime. Certain crimes tend to rise in recessions and recede in good times, but this relationship is not ironclad. For example, crime rose during the boom years of the 1960s; it fell during the Reagan recession of the early 1980s and rose during the recession of the late 1980s and early 1990s (due in part, most likely, to the destabilization of established drug markets with the introduction of the crack trade). Some evidence suggests that the crime rate for certain offenses drops during tough economic times as people go out less, shop less, carry less money, and have less to spend on alcohol. This correlation may explain why crime spiked in the Roaring 20s but plummeted after the 1929 stock market crash.

Alternate measures of macroeconomic distress appear to have found a more nuanced relationship between economic distress and crime (Reiner, 2006, p. 33-34). Unemployment per se may not be the key factor in driving crime rates but rather the deterioration in labor market conditions for young, unskilled men, particularly an erosion of their wages (Gould, Weinberg, & Mustard, 2002). The crime rate may also be inversely related to changes in consumer confidence about the economy. When people feel less confident about their own financial situation and the economic future of the country, the crime rate rises (Rosenfeld & Fornango, 2007; Rosenfeld & Messner, 2009).

While there is no consensus about the underlying causal relationship between the unemployment rate and the incarceration rate, experts generally agree that public opinion about crime and punishment is highly susceptible to political manipulation. Some suggest that during hard economic times, it is easier—and more tempting—for government officials and politicians to exploit the popular stereotype of a marauding underclass, which helps explain the correlation between the unemployment rate and the incarceration rate. Judges, prosecutors, legislators, the media, and the public end up supporting more punitive measures out of the often unfounded fear that crime inevitably rises as the economy falls. Recent public opinion data support this conclusion. A vast and growing number of Americans thought crime worsened in the country in 2009 even though the crime rate fell to lows not seen since the early 1960s (Keohane, 2010). In short, deteriorating economic conditions do not necessarily cause the crime rate to spike—but the public often believes they do. And as the sociologist W. I. Thomas once remarked, if people define situations as real, they are real in their consequences.

THE CRIMINALIZATION OF CIVIL UNREST

Although crime does not necessarily rise during periods of economic distress, protests, strikes, and civil unrest often do as the unemployed, unions, the elderly, veterans, the poor, the sliding middle class, and other groups take to the streets. When that happens, government officials, politicians, and prominent commentators often conflate crime and social protest and, by doing so, provide an opening to strengthen the law-and-order apparatus. The imposing armories that dot American cities, for instance, were built as part of the late-19th century response to the widescale urban unrest of the Gilded Age, including the infamous strike wave in 1877 and the 1886 Haymarket riot. These massive structures were home to National Guard units that were thought to be more willing than local police to fire at strikers. The armories were "designed to intimidate the 'dangerous classes,'" according to Robert Fogelson (1989), their leading historian (quoted in Bowles & Jayadev, 2007, p. 1).

Labeling demonstrations and other acts of protest as crimes is an age-old strategy to justify expansions of law enforcement and delegitimize challenges to the prevailing political and economic order. The response to the civil rights movement is a good case in point. When Sen. Barry Goldwater (R-Ariz.) denounced the "growing menace" to personal safety in his electrifying speech before the 1964 Republican convention, he was appealing not only to fears of crime but also to fears of racial integration and the burgeoning civil rights movement. A full decade earlier, conservative Congressional Democrats were already strategically using the street crime issue to delegitimize the civil rights movement, even though the crime rate remained stable in the mid-1950s (Murakawa, 2005, p. 81-82). Southern conservatives initially cast their opposition to major civil rights legislation in criminological terms, arguing that "integration breeds crime" (Murakawa, 2005, p. 82). To push this point, conservative Democrats even proposed in 1960 to make the new Civil Rights Commission responsible for collecting criminal data (Murakawa, 2005, p. 88). In the 1960s, conservatives reformulated the connection between civil rights and crime so as to make it more palatable in a rapidly changing political environment in which overt racial appeals were increasingly discredited. As riots broke out in major cities across the country in the mid-to-late 1960s, they exploited growing fears of crime. The new conservative doctrine in the 1960s "worked vociferously to conflate crime and disobedience, with its obvious extensions to civil rights" (Weaver, 2006, p. 29).

This was a doctrine not just of words but also of deeds. Conservative southern Democrats shrewdly used civil rights bills as a vehicle to stiffen and broaden criminal penalties. For example, they added an anti-riot measure onto the liberal open housing law of 1968. The measure was nicknamed the "Rap Brown bill" after the Black Power leader (Weaver, 2006, p. 27). These add-ons to civil rights legislation experimented with certain sanctions that later became central features of the major federal and state-level crime bills of the 1980s and 1990s, including stiff mandatory minimum sentences, denial of federal benefits to people convicted of certain felonies, and sentencing enhancements for vaguely and capaciously defined violations, like rioting (Weaver, 2006, p. 27-28). As Weaver observes, "the graveyard of civil rights legislation was the same place where the crime bills were born" (p. 57).

One notable feature of the current economic crisis in the United States is the political quiescence thus far in the face of rapid economic deterioration and far-reaching irresponsibility, trickery, and corruption in the financial sector. Except for the electoral mobilization to turn a vote for Barack Obama into a no-confidence vote for the Bush administration and the Republican Party, public angst and anger have not been channeled into major collective actions. While the Tea Party has begun to stir, we have yet to see many large street demonstrations, sit-ins, or other major acts of protest that fundamentally challenge the economic and political order, as we saw during the Gilded Age, the Progressive era, the Great Depression, and the civil rights era. It is still too early to tell whether the United States will ride out the sharpest economic downturn in 80 years with widespread anger resting alongside collective passivity (Venkatesh, 2009). Remember that widespread civil unrest did not erupt immediately after the 1929 stock market crash but rather a few years later as the Great Depression dragged on. Should large-scale civil unrest break out in the next couple of years, calls to bolster law enforcement will likely increase, as will efforts to portray ensuing protests as criminal behavior.

THE GREAT DEPRESSION AND PENAL POLICY

The Great Depression and the New Deal offer a cautionary tale to those who claim that mounting fiscal pressures will automatically soften U.S. penal policies and ultimately reverse the prison boom. During the Great

Depression, huge numbers of Americans took to the streets, fueling fears that the social and economic fabric of the United States was coming apart. The 1930s "represented a high-water mark for labor insurgency, broad social movements, and radical organization" (Goldfield, 1989, p. 1257). Armed soldiers stood guard at government buildings in Washington, and "[c]ommentators talked casually of the need for dictatorship" (Badger, 2009). This political unrest sparked calls for greater policing powers to regain control.

The Depression provided an opportunity to legitimize the expansion of a number of federal and state powers, ranging from government control of the economy to law enforcement (Gottschalk, 2006, p. 65-70). The profound social anxiety associated with massive economic distress made the public susceptible to calls from President Franklin D. Roosevelt and J. Edgar Hoover, director of the Federal Bureau of Investigation (FBI), to get tough on criminals—whatever the cost—even as crime rates fell in the 1930s. Furthermore, the construction of prisons and the expansion of law enforcement were touted as public works programs that promised to boost the flailing economy.

Elected in a landslide just a few months after the notorious Lindbergh kidnapping and murder, Roosevelt had less compunction than Herbert Hoover about exploiting sensational crimes to expand federal powers and sell his relief programs. FDR and members of his administration regularly appealed to the public for greater coercive powers to tackle crime, which they presented as a dire issue (O'Reilly, 1982, p. 642). Roosevelt directly linked the fight against crime with the struggle for economic recovery and identified crime prevention as an important byproduct of his broader economic and social agenda. He argued that his social welfare programs would strike at "the very roots of crime" by providing subsistence income to needy families who might otherwise be forced to turn to illegal activities (Roosevelt, 1939, quoted in Johnson, Kantor, & Fishback, 2007, p. 3).

Under Homer Cummings, FDR's first attorney general, the federal government began aggressively using the new powers granted in the 1932 crime package enacted under Herbert Hoover. Meanwhile the Roosevelt administration developed a crime package of its own. In May 1934, Congress—without even making a record of its vote—approved six major crime bills requested by Cummings and drafted by his Justice Department. A handful of legislators regarded these bills as an alarming usurpation of states' rights. F.D.R. heralded the enactment of the legislation "an event of the first importance," and his signing of the six bills was front-page news (*New York Times,* 1934).

The country's dire economic straits in the 1930s did not preclude investing heavily in prisons and other tough sanctions. Shortly after Cummings took office, the federal Bureau of Prisons took over the military prison at Alcatraz in northern California and announced plans to turn it into the nation's toughest civilian prison. Funding from key New Deal programs like the Works Progress Administration was used to conduct the first comprehensive national survey of parole practices, repair local jails and build new ones, and construct new federal penal facilities (Keve, 1991, p. 155-63; McKelvey, 1977, p. 307).

Upon assuming office, Roosevelt and Cummings encouraged J. Edgar Hoover, the director of the F.B.I., which was then a small and obscure division in the Justice Department, to develop and mobilize the bureau's investigative resources and publicity department. Hoover was behind a grandiose public relations campaign to turn the G-men into public heroes. Beginning in the 1930s, the public relations department of the F.B.I. under Hoover's direction convinced newspapers to portray criminals like John Dillinger, Bonnie and Clyde, Pretty Boy Floyd, and Ma Barker as major threats to society. As legislators in Washington debated F.D.R.'s crime package in early 1934, the country was riveted by the exploits of Dillinger, who had escaped from an "escape-proof" jail in Indiana and managed to stop for a haircut, buy several cars, and have Sunday dinner with his family while 5,000 law enforcement officers were reportedly in hot pursuit. Hoover's G-men became the heroes of the day as they killed or apprehended outsized criminals. Hoover controlled the image of crime and crime fighters not just by cajoling editors, journalists, movie producers, radio executives, and novelists, but also by manipulating the national crime statistics to stoke the public's fear of crime and polish the image of the G-men (Leuchtenburg, 1963, p. 334; O'Reilly, 1982, p. 645; and Woodiwiss, 1988, p. 35-36).

The 1930s were a wildly successful period for the FBI, despite the economic hard times. The 1934 crime package vastly expanded the FBI's authority. In 1935, the bureau opened the National Police Academy, and top FBI officials began organizing and participating in dozens of state and local law enforcement conventions. In the mid-1930s, the bureau fomented a national obsession with universal fingerprinting, imploring communities to take up the civic cause to fingerprint all their residents and turn the prints over to the F.B.I. (Walker, 1977, p. 157-58).

STIMULATING THE ECONOMY AND LAW ENFORCEMENT

The recent economic downturn may spur a comparable expansion of law enforcement and the penal apparatus. As Congress began putting together the economic stimulus package in late 2008, the U.S. Conference of Mayors promulgated a $5.5 billion public safety wish list. The mayors said they wanted to use stimulus money to purchase all kinds of S.W.A.T. equipment, including helicopters, armored vehicles, and military grade rifles. Unmanned drones were an especially popular item (Stimulus Watch, n.d.).

The American Recovery and Reinvestment Act enacted in February 2009, resuscitated two controversial law enforcement programs that Congress and the Bush administration had begun to phase out. The stimulus bill pumped $1 billion into Community Oriented Policing Systems, or COPS, which provides federal grants to local police forces. COPS was one of the signature programs of the Clinton administration's draconian 1994 crime bill. COPS was created to reduce crime by promoting community policing tactics whereby police officers would walk (or bicycle) their beat and act more like members of the community than aggressive outside enforcers. But COPS also fostered more confrontational styles of policing by funding SWAT teams and encouraging the wider use of paramilitary tactics and equipment (Balko, 2008). Over the years, COPS has had a minimal effect on reducing the crime rate (Worrall & Kovandzic, 2007; Eisler & Johnson, 2005). Nonetheless, the Democrats have persistently defended COPS while many conservatives and Republicans have called for phasing it out. In the stimulus package debate, Sen. Patrick Leahy (D-Vt.), chairman of the Senate Judiciary Committee, defended resurrecting COPS on grounds that it would aid the economy "as fast, or faster than, other spending." In pushing for COPS Leahy, joined by police chiefs and law enforcement organizations, played on public fears of rising crime during economic downturns (Lewis, 2009).

The stimulus package also threw a lifeline to the controversial Byrne Justice Assistance Grants program, which was established under the Anti-Drug Abuse Act of 1988 and became a cornerstone of the war on drugs. Over the years Byrne money has supported a wide range of activities, including after-school programs, victims' assistance, and substance abuse programs. But the bulk of these grants have been used to fund law enforcement programs, most notably special drug enforcement units and anti-gang initiatives. The drug units, which are largely unaccountable to local police chiefs and sheriffs, have proliferated across the country (thanks to Byrne money) in spite of their contested efficacy. These grants encourage law enforcement officials to focus on low-level drug arrests rather than pursuing big dealers because the funds are typically awarded based on the number of arrests—not the significance of the arrests (Balko, 2008). The American Civil Liberties Union (ACLU) has documented numerous abuses by Byrne drug task forces. A Byrne-funded drug unit was responsible for the debacle a decade ago in Tulia, Texas, in which dozens of African Americans received lengthy sentences for drug dealing based on the uncorroborated testimony of a single undercover police officer.

Though championed by police unions and other law enforcement organizations, the Byrne program has come under withering attack from the right and the left over the years, including critics at the Heritage Foundation, the National Taxpayers Union, the ACLU, the National Black Police Association, and the Drug Policy Alliance (Balko, 2008). In December 2007, Congress unexpectedly slashed Byrne grants by two-thirds to a record-low allocation of $170 million. Dozens of states responded by participating in a major drug sweep in March 2008 nicknamed "Operation Byrne Blitz" that resulted in over 4,000 drug-related arrests and seizures of millions of dollars of cash and drugs. On the campaign trail in fall 2008, Obama promised to restore the Byrne grant program, arguing it is "critical to creating the anti-drug task forces our communities need" (quoted in Hunt, 2008, in Alexander, 2010, p. 82-83). State and local officials pushed hard to restore the Byrne grants in the stimulus package, promoting it as a key crime-stopping measure and a way to generate jobs (Gramlich, 2009a). The Economic Recovery Act of 2009 included more than $2 billion in new Byrne funding (more than double the amount provided in any single year up until then) and an additional $600 million to increase state and local law enforcement across the country (*Drug War Chronicle*, 2009a).

A stated goal of the Obama administration's stimulus package was to favor projects that were "shovel ready." As a result of the unprecedented prison boom of the last three decades, many states now have the experience and capacity to build prisons fast. Some states and communities planned to use stimulus money from Washington to expand or maintain their penal capacity (Calmes, 2009; Seaton, 2009; Reutter, 2010b).

In his address to the ABA in summer 2009, Attorney General Holder lamented that spending on incarceration has continued to increase even as crime rates have flattened. "We will not focus exclusively on incarceration as the most effective means of protecting public safety," he promised (Pallasch, 2009). But the proposed 2010 budget for the Department of Justice (DOJ) slashed spending for juvenile justice programs and increased allocations for law enforcement, including $512 million for the Byrne program and $761 million for COPS. Research shows that communities that spend more on law enforcement have higher drug imprisonment rates than those that spend less (Beatty, Petteruti, & Ziedenberg, 2007). The proposed DOJ budget for 2010 also boosted the allocation of the Bureau of Prisons, including money to build two new federal penitentiaries—with a total of 4,800 beds—and to contract out 1,000 beds to private providers (Justice Policy Institute, 2009). The DOJ's $100 million allocation for the Second Chance Act, to provide services to people reentering the community after prison, is a drop in the department's $27 billon budget and comprises barely .14 percent of the nearly $70 billion spent nationwide on corrections each year. In short, as many states grapple with how to reduce their budget deficits by closing prisons and diverting offenders to probation and other community-based programs, the federal government continues to bolster its law enforcement and penal apparatus.

PENAL KEYNESIANISM

New scholarship is providing a more nuanced understanding of who benefits economically from the penal system and who does not. For anti-prison activists, growing evidence of the limited contribution that prisons make to local economies has provided important ammunition to resist pressure from state officials to build new prisons in their backyards in the name of economic development. Evidence increasingly shows that prisons provide few economic benefits to local communities, notably the rural areas that have been the primary sites for new prison construction since the 1980s. Residents of rural counties with prisons are no less likely to be unemployed than people living in counties without prisons nor do they have higher per capita incomes (Gilmore, 2007; King, Mauer, & Huling, 2003). We now know that many of the new jobs created by prisons go to people living outside the county where the prison is built. Prisons also fail to generate significant linkages to the local economy, because local businesses often are unable to provide the goods and services needed to operate penal facilities.

Nevertheless the economic development arguments in favor of prisons can be compelling and persuasive, especially during hard economic times. First, the huge incarcerated population in the United States artificially lowers the official unemployment rate for males by at least 2 percent, making the U.S. economy appear more successful than it actually is (Beckett & Western, 1999, p. 1040). It also masks the huge and deteriorating unemployment rates among young African-American men, many of who are incarcerated but not included in standard measures of unemployment (Western, 2006).

In an economic downturn, mass incarceration may "exert a Keynesian, stabilizing effect, to be sustained for economic reasons" (Downes, 2001, p. 74). Corrections and law enforcement have become major sources of employment on a national level, even if individual prisons do not necessarily buoy the local labor market. The country spends some $70 billion on corrections, which employs an estimated 750,000 prison guards and other personnel. It spent another $100 billon on police and $47 billion on the judiciary (U.S. Department of Justice, 2008). As Cavadino and Dignan explain, "In a perverse variation of Keynes's hypothetical cure for recession—get the state to hire large numbers of people to dig holes and then fill them in again—the USA has hired one lot of people to keep another lot locked up" (2006, p. 58).

Public officials who attempt to close penal facilities face fierce local resistance, even when they promise not to eliminate anyone's job or release any offenders early (Reutter, 2009). Notably, overall prison expenditures in New York State have increased markedly despite a decade-long decline in the prison population. Until 2009, the state was unable to shutter any prisons despite thousands of empty beds in upstate correctional facilities (Greene & Mauer, 2010, p. 60). Prison guards' unions, private prison companies, public bond dealers, and the suppliers of everything from telephone services to Taser stun guns compose a "motley group of perversely motivated interests" that has coalesced "to sustain and profit from mass imprisonment" (Herivel, 2007, p. ix). Moreover, cash-starved towns do not want to give up the inmate work crews that provide cherished services they have come to depend on, everything from road maintenance to landscaping to painting the local church.

Anti-prison activists are developing fresh economic arguments and strategies to challenge these vested interests. They have seeded growing doubts that prisons necessarily bring economic development to rural communities (Mosher, Hooks, & Wood, 2007; Gilmore, 2007, p. 149) and have tried to make the financial burden of penal facilities more visible. For example, some groups have begun to educate the public about lease-revenue bonds (LRBs)—a popular backdoor way to finance new prison construction that skirts states' balanced budget rules and voter-ratification requirements for new government-bond projects.

The prison boom coincided not only with rising conservatism on law-and-order issues but also growing fiscal conservatism with the 1978 passage of California's Proposition 13, which became a beacon for fiscal conservatives nationwide. Lease-revenue bonds ended up providing legislators, corrections officials, and underwriting firms in California and elsewhere a creative way to maneuver around anti-tax sentiment. LRBs skirted states' balanced budget rules and the requirements that voters must ratify new government bond projects. They were originally designed to provide financing for projects that could generate enough revenue over time to pay for themselves. LRBs typically had been used to finance items like mortgages for veterans and farmers and construction loans for hospitals, colleges, and universities. In a creative sleight of public financing, money that corrections departments would use to "pay back" the LRBs was considered "revenue" even though it came from general fund appropriations authorized to corrections by the legislature in the annual operating budget.

Revenue bonds became a popular backdoor way to finance new prison construction in California and elsewhere beginning in the mid-1980s. Prior to that, new prisons had to be funded either on a pay-as-you-go basis out of general revenue funds or by borrowing money through the sale of government bonds sanctioned by taxpayers through bond referendums (Pranis, 2007, p. 37). By 1996, more than half of all new prison debt was in the form of LRBs, which tend to be more expensive than straightforward state bond sales (Pranis, 2007, p. 38).

The new-fangled LRBs allowed the huge costs of the prison build-up and the budgetary trade-offs they necessitated (notably the conspicuous drop in public funding for higher education) to stay out of public view. And LRBs could be quickly organized and issued. In less than a decade, California's state debt for prison construction expanded from about $763 million to nearly $5 billion, or a proportional increase from about 4 percent to over 16 percent of the state's total debt for all purposes (Gilmore, 2007, p. 101). Anti-prison activists have begun to highlight how LRBs are "overpriced, fiscally unsound, and undemocratic," so as to spur "a public debate over what was previously an invisible issue" (Pranis, 2007, p. 51).

In other ways, opponents of mass incarceration are attempting to make the real costs of the expansive penal system more visible. The identification of nearly three dozen "million-dollar blocks" in Brooklyn, where so many residents have been sent to prison that the total annual cost of incarcerating them exceeds $1 million per block, helped build support for penal reform in New York State to reduce the incarcerated population (Gonnerman, 2004, p. 28). Coded maps showing how much Connecticut and Texas spend on prison, probation, and parole for people living in certain urban neighborhoods were powerful visual aids that helped build momentum for major penal reforms in these states (Jacobson, 2005, p. 198;

Kurgan, 2009). Connecticut, which had one of the fastest growing prison populations, experienced one of the steepest declines (JFA Institute, 2007; Jacobson, 2005, pp. 198-204).

THE CRIMINALIZATION OF POVERTY

Most prison costs are fixed and are not easily cut. The only way to substantially reduce spending on corrections is to send fewer people to jail or prison and shut down penal facilities. Confronted with powerful interests that profit politically and economically from mass imprisonment, public officials have been making largely symbolic cuts that do little to reduce the incarcerated population--or save much money. Rather, these cuts render life in prison and life after prison leaner and meaner.

As the federal prison population grows and staff positions go unfilled, homicides, assaults, and other acts of violence appear to be on the rise in federal penitentiaries (Sample, 2009). There also has been a spate of reports about major riots and disturbances in severely overcrowded and mismanged state prisons (Hoberock, 2010). Some states are considering copying Georgia, where three days a week inmates receive only two meals. Reports of inmates being fed spoiled or inedible food are rising nationwide, as are reports of riots sparked by poor or insuffient food (Reutter, Hunter, & Sample, 2010; Reutter, 2010a). Budget cutters have targeted so-called nonessential prison services like educational, substance abuse, and vocational programs that help reduce recidivism and were already grossly underfunded. Despite a three-fold increase in the number of prisoners and correctional officers, the number of educators employed in state prisons actually fell slightly between the late 1970s and the mid-1990s (Western, 2006, p. 175).

Charging prisoners fees for services like meals, lodging, and visits to the doctor is becoming more common. Politicians in Des Moines, Iowa, even considered charging inmates for toilet paper to save $2,300 a year (Hastings, 2009). In some cases, former prisoners and family members of juvenile offenders have been sent to prison because they could not pay fees charged by corrections.

As judicial budgets contract, judges in some states have become exceptionally aggressive about collecting fines and fees. In some instances, people are serving more jail time for failing to pay court costs than they served under their original sentence (Hunter, 2010). Sending poor people to jail if they cannot pay corrections fees or court-imposed fines is a practice of dubious constitutionality. Justice delayed is increasingly justice denied as judges and courthouses go on furloughs, judgeships remain vacant to save money, and trials are postponed. The quality of justice is also deteriorating because of cuts in legal services for the indigent. As the budget crisis dragged on in Pennsylvania in 2009, Philadelphia was forced to suspend payments for court-appointed attorneys who represent the poor, and the mayor's "doomsday" budget called for eliminating all funding for the courts.

These developments are part of what some are calling a new war on the poor, as poverty is increasingly criminalized (Ehrenreich, 2009; Beckett & Herbert, 2009). A recent study by the National Law Center on Homelessness and Poverty found that the number of ordinances against the poor for acts of vagrancy, panhandling, and sleeping on the street has been rising since 2006. With the economic downturn, "zero tolerance" policing appears to have been ramped up as officers issue more tickets and make more arrests for minor infractions like jaywalking, littering, truancy, and carrying an open container of alcohol. More and more petty defendants cannot afford in this bad economy to post even minimal bonds, so many are staying in local jails longer, boosting the incarceration rate. Faced with an overflowing jail, Wichita Falls, Texas, was still arresting and booking people who failed to return library materials (Langdon, 2009). Legislators in at least six states have introduced bills of questionable constitutionality that would require people seeking unemployment benefits and/or public assistance like welfare or food stamps to submit to random drug testing, with their benefits at stake (*Drug War Chronicle,* 2009b).[2]

At the same time that poverty is being criminalized, states and the federal government are slashing social services for the poor, which may result in more people ending up in prison. For decades conservatives have brazenly dismissed the claim that social welfare spending reduces crime. Although the relationship between crime and spending on social welfare has been a hotly debated topic, research in this area is surprisingly sparse (Johnson, Kantor, & Fishback, 2007, p. 4). The limited research available suggests that certain types of social welfare spending reduce crime (Johnson, Kantor, & Fishback, 2007, pp. 20-21, note 4). For example, relief spending targeted at the unemployed and low-income groups during the Great Depression has been credited with a drop in property crime (Johnson, Kantor, & Fishback, 2007, p. 5). What we do know conclusively is that states and countries that spend more on social welfare tend to have lower incarceration rates, while high rates of inequality are associated with higher rates of imprisonment.

LESSONS FROM THE DEINSTITUTIONALIZATION OF THE MENTALLY ILL

The vested interests in maintaining the vast U.S. penal system are considerable. A sea of red ink may be a necessary, but not sufficient, condition to force the closing of prisons and jails and spur a sharp drop in the imprisoned population. The most telling precedent for such a shift is the deinstitutionalization of the mentally ill in the latter half of the 20th century. Deinstitutionalization was a rare instance of the government eventually shutting down a vast archipelago of asylums that states had invested in heavily for many years. But the shutdown involved a protracted political drama that played out for decades.

In 1955, the state asylum population was 559,000, nearly as large on a per capita basis as the prison population today. By 2000, it had fallen to below 100,000, a drop of more than 90 percent (Spelman ,2009). The development of new drugs like Reserprine and chlorpromazine to combat mental illness helps explain some of this drop. But decades of political agitation around this issue that finally prodded the federal government into action were the primary catalyst.

The deinstitutionalization case illustrates that the politics of constructing certain state institutions may be quite different from the politics of mothballing them. A complex set of economic, political, sociological, cultural, and medical factors explain why state mental institutions proliferated in the late 19th and early 20th centuries (Grob, 1994; Rothman, 1990). The federal government was largely inconsequential in the growth of state mental hospitals, but federal policy was a decisive factor in their demise. With passage of the Community Mental Health Act in 1963, local governments (but not states) became eligible for grants to create alternatives to state asylums. This spurred the establishment of hundreds of new community mental health centers in a few short years. Another major development was the creation of Medicare and Medicaid in 1965. Medicaid regulations stipulated that the federal government would pay for inpatient care of the mentally ill in local hospitals and nursing homes but not in state mental institutions. As a result, some of the residents of state mental hospitals were transferred to other facilities but most were released to the community.

The powerful psychiatric profession was a key player in this development. In the mid-19th century, psychiatrists effectively thwarted the development of non-institutional alternatives that would have threatened their power base in state mental institutions. They thus succeeded in marginalizing the embryonic community mental health movement. It took nearly a century for the psychiatric profession to become disenchanted with state mental hospitals. As the aged population began to grow, and families were less able to provide care at home due to the strains of industrialization and urbanization, mental hospitals became de facto almshouses for the elderly. These facilities became increasingly identified as providers of custodial care at a time when a new generation of psychiatrists coming of age in the early-to-mid 20th century was attempting to identify more closely with the rest of the medical profession and with cutting edge advances in acute care. The experience of treating soldiers traumatized by combat in World War II bolstered the belief that providing short-term psychological care early on in a noninstitutional setting could obviate the need for long-term institutionalization later on (Grob, 1994; Gillon, 2000).

These developments fueled the psychiatric profession's growing disenchantment with state mental hospitals and undermined the symbiotic relationship that psychiatrists and state mental asylums had enjoyed for more than a century, whereby each reinforced and conferred legitimacy on the other (Grob, 1994). As the once inseparable bonds between psychiatrists and state mental hospitals began to dissolve, so did a central pillar of political support for state mental hospitals. Increased popular and journalistic attention to the warehousing of the elderly and mentally ill in dirty, overcrowded, unhealthy facilities further undercut the legitimacy of the state hospitals. Conscientious objectors assigned to state mental institutions during World War II were critical muckrakers in exposing these conditions and leaders in the community mental health movement (Gillon, 2000; Torrey, 1997), which attracted vital public support from luminaries like Pearl S. Buck, Eleanor Roosevelt, and J. Robert Oppenheimer (Torrey, 1997).

These political developments provided an opening for federal intervention but did not make federal action inevitable. Political leadership was crucial. Robert Felix, director of the Division of Mental Health of the U.S. Public Health Service, seized on the political opening and shrewdly maneuvered to end federal passivity on mental health. He was an indispensable catalyst for the development of a succession of pieces of federal legislation that helped empty the state mental hospitals. The 1946 National Mental Health Act created the National Institute of Mental Health, which provided critical research and analysis for the development of community mental health centers. It also established the National Mental Health Advisory Council, which became a nerve center to promote community alternatives among politicians, policymakers, and the wider public (Grob, 1994). The 1946 act spurred development of a mental health lobby that was so critical years later in pushing for the Community Mental Health Act of 1963 and other landmark federal legislation. Felix and other public health professionals also gave mental illness an image makeover. Mental disorders were no longer seen primarily as individual diseases to be treated by individual practitioners but rather as public health problems that affected the entire health of the community, thus warranting a community-wide response.

The community mental health movement did not act in isolation. It was buoyed by important connections with and advances in other burgeoning social movements, including the civil rights movement and the senior citizens movement. Philanthropic support was also vital to passage of the Community Mental Health Act (Gillon, 2000). Community mental health advocates also forged vital alliances with fiscal conservatives by promising to improve the condition of the mentally ill while saving vast sums of government money (Gillon, 2000). The expected financial savings from deinstitutionalization were oversold to politicians and the wider public, thus undermining the case for adequate funding of services for the mentally ill. States were able to reduce their mental health tab by getting someone else to pick up the bill. Under the landmark Medicare and Medicaid legislation enacted in 1965, the federal government would not reimburse states for the cost of care for indigent and senile elderly people residing in state asylums. As a result, the elderly, who comprised a large proportion of the state mental hospital population, were transferred to nursing homes, where the federal government would pick up the cost.

Due to a variety of exceptional institutional and political factors, including the absence of an insulated, highly-skilled, widely-respected professional civil service, deinstitutionalization, like other major public policy shifts in the United States, was highly vulnerable to the vagaries of partisan politics at the federal level (Gottschalk, 2006; Brodeur, 2007). Richard Nixon waged a high-profile battle with Congress to impound money authorized for mental health. Jimmy Carter attempted to address the problem of inadequate funding for mental health with passage of the 1980 Mental Services Act, which the Reagan administration repealed the following year. Reagan slashed federal money for mental health and made wide use of block grants to the states, quickly reversing three decades of federal involvement and leadership on mental health (Grob, 1994).

Despite the groundswell of support for community mental health, politicians and policymakers faced enormous bureaucratic resistance to closing state asylums. Mental institutions were a huge and growing drain on state budgets for years, yet deinstitutionalization progressed very slowly (Koyanagi, 2007). Unions and communities where mental hospitals were the primary employer bitterly opposed closing the facilities. Only after many contentious years did unions win recognition that workers in psychiatric hospitals needed retraining to move into community programs. Even though many of the psychiatrists moved on and many residents of state mental hospitals were eventually transferred to other facilities or released, these largely empty hulks remained open for decades. It was not until the 1990s—three decades after deinstitutionalization began—that whole institutions began to close in significant numbers. It took just as long for political leaders and the public to acknowledge that successful integration requires more than adequate medical treatment; the mentally ill need access to housing and jobs as well (Koyanagi, 2007). Remarkably, it was not until 1993 that state funding for community mental health surpassed state funding for mental institutions (Koyanagi, 2007).

The deinstitutionalization case demonstrates the enormous importance of the political context for the development and implementation of successful federal and state policies to dramatically shrink public institutions. Rising anxiety among state officials about the escalating costs of state mental institutions in the late 1940s did not on its own empty state asylums. Leadership at the federal level was critical to enacting change. Another vital component was the shift in the training, worldview, and identity of the psychiatric profession as the American Psychiatric Association split over the question of institutional care versus the community mental health model. Furthermore, the emergence of major new and inter-connected social movements (including the civil rights movement and the senior citizens movement), as well as journalistic and popular attention to the dire conditions in state mental hospitals were pivotal in pushing policy makers to embrace change. Moreover, the issue had to be reconceived. No longer was mental health concerned only with individuals and their individual diseases. Rather mental health became a barometer for the health of the whole community.

Cutbacks in mental health funds together with cuts in federal money for public housing and other services led to streams of apparently deranged people living on the streets. This outcome fueled a backlash against deinstitutionalization and community mental health and overshadowed the fact that many mentally ill people made successful transitions to community life (Grob, 1994). With the closing of state mental hospitals and the contraction of federal money for treatment, services, and housing, jails and prisons unfortunately became the mental institutions of last resort for many seriously ill people (Gillon, 2000; Torrey, 1997; Harcourt, 2006).

PARTISAN POLITICS AND PUBLIC OPINION

Although important parallels exist between the deinstitutionalization case and efforts to end mass incarceration, there also are major differences. Successfully reducing the country's incarcerated population is likely to be an even greater challenge. Debates about crime, punishment, and law and order have been deeply entangled in wider political battles and electoral strategies in ways that the mental health issue never was. Mental health policy has been a controversial subject from time to time. For example, an enormous fuss erupted in Congress in 1955 when legislation was introduced to permit Alaska, which was still a territory, to build a psychiatric hospital for residents. Conservative groups circulated thousands of letters and petitions claiming that psychiatrists would use the new facility to involuntarily hospitalize conservatives and other political dissidents. They even charged that the mental health movement was a communist plot (Torrey, 1997). The conservative movement denounced mental health practitioners for purportedly encouraging immorality and for deemphasizing personal responsibility. They also attacked state mental institutions as symbols of out-of-control government spending. Despite these controversies, mental health policy has never been a lightning rod in American politics in the way that penal policy and law and order have been since the 1960s.

Republicans waged the rebirth of the modern Republican Party on the "southern strategy." They used the rhetoric of law and order as code words to stoke racial anxieties and animosities. The aim was to undermine the new Democratic majority resting on the civil rights movement and to build a new coalition of white voters anchored in the South and West. Bill Clinton staked his campaign for the White House on a kinder, gentler version of the southern strategy to woo the so-called Reagan Democrats back to the party. Given the high profile of crime and punishment at the federal level and how this issue has been a pillar for repositioning the major political parties, political openings to shift penal policy in a less punitive direction are fraught with risk and are hard to sustain. The opportunity for the penal equivalent of a Robert Felix to emerge and put into motion from a federal perch a major decarceration of state prisons is less likely.

Another significant difference is that the mentally ill and their legal advocates had considerable access to the courts in the 1960s and 1970s to press their civil rights claims and to expose the dire conditions in state mental hospitals. By contrast, with passage of the Prison Litigation Reform Act and the Antiterrorism and Effective Death Penalty Act in 1996 and a string of unfavorable court decisions, prisoners and their legal advocates have had increased difficulty using the courts to pursue civil rights claims and to document and expose the conditions in U.S. jails and prisons. Likewise, the media no longer serve as vehicles to prod reform. Due to cutbacks and restructuring in the news business, investigative pieces documenting abuses in all kinds of institutions (prisons, nursing homes, hospitals) are increasingly rare. Furthermore, prison and state officials have been erecting ever-higher barriers for journalists attempting to cover what happens behind prison walls, including, in some states, complete bans on face-to-face interviews with inmates (Bergman, 2006; Prendergast, 2007). Moreover, the once vibrant in-house penal press is nearly extinct. Award-winning prison newspapers and underground prison publications that once reached thousands inside and out no longer exist (Caldwell, 2006).

Public opinion poses an additional hurdle to penal reform. Policymakers seriously misperceive public opinion on penal matters, mistakenly seeing the public as more punitive than it actually is (Gottfredson & Taylor, 1987). This may explain their persistent reticence to make bold moves that would significantly cut the incarceration rate, and why politicians across the political spectrum respond to increases in the crime rate by reflexively calling for more prisons and for keeping more people locked up for longer periods.

Penal policy is particularly vulnerable to moral panics—often fueled by politicians—in the wake of certain high-profile crimes or events. Some suggest that moral panics are more likely to occur during periods of broad uncertainty and insecurity in society (Erikson, 1966). Two horrific crimes in Connecticut in 2007 jeopardized a promising set of penal reforms to lower the state's incarceration rate. In their wake, the state tightened up parole eligibility and considered new get-tough measures, including three-strikes legislation (*New York Times,* 2008). In fall 2008, Democratic Governor Ed Rendell of Pennsylvania suspended all parole in the state after a parolee reportedly killed a police officer during a traffic stop. This occurred at the very time that the Pennsylvania legislature was finalizing approval of a wide range of bills designed to soften some of the state's get-tough policies and to reduce the state prison population. The governor eventually lifted the moratorium on parole. Nonetheless, in his first official act for 2009, Rendell called on the Pennsylvania legislature to end parole for certain violent and gun-related offenders and enact stiffer and fixed sentences for such violations (Reuters, 2009). Mired in a budget standoff to close a $3 billion deficit in 2009, Pennsylvania nonetheless continued full steam ahead on breaking ground for four new penal facilities, estimated to cost over $800 million. The state's prison population is projected to grow 4 percent annually through 2012—and more if the legislature enacts Rendell's proposals (Phucas, 2009). As the budget negotiations dragged on and Pennsylvania became the last state to hammer out a 2010 budget, corrections remained off the budget chopping block.

Faced with a particularly heinous high-profile violent crime, many public officials believe that they need to respond with bold law-and-order gestures to address what they perceive to be the public's anger and moral outrage. Yet policy-makers grossly misperceive public opinion on penal matters, mistakenly seeing the public as more supportive of punitive measures than it actually is. This judgment error may explain policy-makers' persistent reticence to make bold moves that would slash the incarceration rate, and why politicians across the political spectrum respond to increases in the crime rate by reflexively calling for more prisons and tougher sentences.

In reality, public opinion research indicates that Americans have a much more nuanced view of spending on criminal justice than the popular media or public policy debates suggest. The public overwhelmingly favors spending more on policing, crime prevention programs for young people, and drug treatment for nonviolent offenders. But it strongly opposes additional funding for prisons (Cohen, Rust, & Steen, 2006). Participants in focus groups organized by the city of Philadelphia in spring 2009 to get public feedback on how to close the city's projected $2 billion budget gap were "strongly supportive" of the idea of closing one prison to save money. But most participants "were horrified at the thought" of closing the budget gap by trimming funds for education, job training, or re-entry counseling for former offenders (Sokoloff & Satullo, 2009). Recent surveys of public opinion in California found similar results (DiCamillo & Field, 2008; Marelius, 2010).

Differences in the structure of state institutions, the quality of civic life, and the power and organization of various interest groups, especially prison guards' unions, victims' groups, and law enforcement associations, may help to explain why redirecting penal policy from the law-and-order path, however costly it has become, will be more difficult in some states than in others (Barker, 2009; Page, forthcoming 2011). The case of California is a stark reminder that political and institutional logic can matter as much as or more than economic logic in determining the future course of penal policy. California has been teetering on the brink of fiscal and social disaster for several years. Commentators have even begun to refer to it as a "failed state," a term usually associated with countries like Congo or Afghanistan. The Golden State has been unable or unwilling to soften its Three Strikes law, the toughest in the nation. Third-strike offenders in California—some with modest third offenses like petty theft—languish in its overcrowded prison system at an average cost of $49,000 a year (Kristof, 2009).

The state's voter initiative and referendum process continues to warp penal policies, making California highly vulnerable to penal populism and well-funded single-issue groups. Facing fiscal Armageddon, the state's voters nonetheless narrowly approved Proposition 9 in November 2008, which toughens up requirements for granting parole and calls for amending the state's constitution to give crime victims unprecedented influence on criminal cases (*Prison Legal News,* 2009). Voters soundly rejected Proposition 5. This ballot initiative would have expanded alternative sentences for nonviolent drug offenders and saved billions of dollars (Legislative Analyst's Office, 2008). Governor Arnold Schwarzenegger and four former governors opposed the measure, including Attorney General Jerry Brown, who hopes to succeed the Guvinator in the November 2010 election by living down his Governor Moonbeam reputation from the 1970s. For Brown, this means courting the state's powerful prison guards' union and taking a hard line on penal policy.[3]

California faced a $24 billion budget shortfall in 2009 at the same time that a federal court was demanding that the state spend billions more on prison health care or else release about 40,000 offenders to relieve gross overcrowding. A proposal to release some nonviolent offenders created a political firestorm. A watered-down compromise was nearly scuttled in the eleventh hour in the State Assembly after the sensational story of Phillip Garrido became front-page news worldwide in summer 2009. Garrido was accused of kidnapping an 11-year-old girl and confining her to an undiscovered backyard encampment for nearly two decades while he was on parole for rape and kidnapping offenses dating back to 1976. The significantly weaker Assembly bill eventually passed in late August without a vote to spare. The measure unleashed over-the-top rhetoric. One Republican assemblyman warned: "We might as well set off a nuclear bomb in California with what we are doing with this bill" (Rothfeld, 2009). Law enforcement groups, led by the California Correctional Peace Officers Association, successfully pressed Democrats to strip the bill of provisions to reduce sentences for some nonviolent offenders and establish a commission to revise sentencing guidelines (Moore, 2009a; Page, forthcoming 2011). The final bill projected to reduce the prison population by 16,000 inmates, far fewer than originally proposed (Moore, 2009b).

END OF THE BEGINNING

The current economic crisis presents an opportunity to redirect U.S. penal policy that opponents of the prison boom should exploit. But framing this issue as primarily an economic one will not sustain the political momentum needed over the long haul to drastically reduce the prison population. Economic justifications also ignore the fact that a successful decarceration will cost money. The people re-entering society after prison need significant educational, vocational, housing, health, and economic support. We need to make considerable reinvestments in re-entry to ensure that the communities these people are returning to are not further destabilized by waves of former prisoners whose time inside has greatly impaired their economic, educational, and social opportunities.

In addition, while we need to make re-entry a priority, we cannot focus only on those who are being released. We need to reduce the number of people who are sent to jail or prison and the length of their sentences. Prisons and jails exacerbate many social ills that contribute to crime and poverty and are unlikely to significantly rehabilitate anyone. Roughly half the people in U.S. prisons are serving time for nonviolent offenses (many of them property or petty drug offenses that would not warrant a sentence in many other countries), while sentences for violent offenses have lengthened considerably.

Criminal justice is fundamentally a political problem, not a crime-and-punishment problem. A vast penal system is well on its way to becoming the new normal and a key governing institution in the United States. Like the vast military-industrial complex that quickly insinuated itself into the political and economic fabric in the postwar decades, the penal system has become so large and so integral to the U.S. polity and the economy that we barely see it anymore.

Framing the carceral state primarily as an economic issue may yield some short-term benefits. However, focusing too heavily on the economic burden may draw attention away from how the vast penal system has begun to fundamentally alter how key social and political institutions operate and to pervert what it means to be a citizen in the United States.[4] A single-minded focus on the economic costs of incarceration also undercuts the compelling civil- and human- rights arguments that the carceral state raises as it removes wide swaths of African Americans, Latinos, and poor Americans from their neighborhoods. Mass incarceration devastates the families and communities the imprisoned leave behind and raises troubling questions about the fairness and legitimacy, not only of the criminal justice system, but also of the political system more broadly (Alexander, 2010). In the absence of more compelling arguments against the prison buildup and of a durable movement to propel these arguments, it becomes that much easier to revert to funding a vast carceral state, no questions asked, once the economy picks up.

A durable reform movement to weather the backlash that efforts to substantially reduce the incarceration rate will inevitably spark has yet to coalesce. The economic crisis does not spell the beginning of the end of mass incarceration in the United States. To borrow from Winston Churchill, "It is not even the beginning of the end. But it is, perhaps, the end of the beginning" (quoted in *Drug War Chronicle*, 2009c).

REFERENCES

Alexander, M. (2010). *The new Jim Crow: Mass incarceration in the age of colorblindness*. New York, NY: The New Press.

Badger, T. (2009, January 7). FDR: A model for Obama? *The Nation*.

Balko, R. (2008, October 6). Bad cop: Why Obama Is getting criminal justice wrong. Retrieved March 11, 2009, from http://www.slate.com/id/2201632/

Barker, V. (2009). *The politics of imprisonment: How the democratic process shapes the way America punishes offenders*. Oxford: Oxford University Press.

Beatty, P., Petteruti, A., & Ziedenberg, J. (2007). *The vortex: The concentrated racial impact of drug imprisonment and the characteristics of punitive countries*. Washington, DC: Justice Policy Institute.

Beckett, K. & Herbert, S. (2009). *Banished: The new social control in urban America*. New York, NY: Oxford University Press.

Beckett, K. & Western, B. (1999). How unregulated Is the U.S. labor market? The dynamics of jobs and jails, 1980-1995. *American Journal of Sociology, 104*(4), 1030-60.

Bennett, D. & Kuttner, R. (2003). Crime and redemption. *The American Prospect, December*.

Bergman, H. (2006, April 4). Barring journalists. *The News Media & the Law, 30*(4), 18.

Blow, C. (2009). Pitchforks and pistols. *New York Times*, p. A-17.

Bohrman, R. & Murakawa, N. (2005). Remaking big government: Immigration and crime control in the United States. In J. Sudbury (Ed.), *Global lockdown: Race, gender, and the prison-industrial complex* (pp. 109-26). New York, NY: Routledge.

Bowles, S. & Jayadev, A. (2007, March). Garrison America. *Economist's Voice*, The Berkeley Electronic Press. Retrieved March 11, 2009, from http://www.bepress.com/ev/vol4/iss2/art3/

Brodeur, J. (2007). Comparative penology in perspective." In M. Tonry (Ed.), *Crime, punishment, and politics in comparative perspective—Crime and justice: A review of research*, vol. 36 (pp. 49-91). Chicago, IL: University of Chicago Press.

Caldwell, L. (2006). The decline and fall of the prison press. *Prison Legal News, June*, 20.

Calmes, J. (2009, February 17). Obama gains support from G.O.P. governors. *New York Times*, p. A1.

Cavadino, M. & Dignan, J. (2006). *Penal systems: A comparative approach*. London: Sage.

Cohen, M., Rust, R., & Steen, S. (2006). Prevention, crime control or cash? Public preferences towards criminal justice spending priorities. *Justice Quarterly, 23*, 317-35.

De Girorgi, A. (2006). *Re-thinking the political economy of punishment: Perspectives on post-Fordism and penal politics*. Aldershot, U.K.: Ashgate.

DiCamillo, M. & Field, M. (2008, June 10). Paradoxical views about the state deficit. Press release no. 2275. San Francisco, CA: Field Research Corporation.

Dow, M. (2004). *American gulag: Inside U.S. immigration prisons.* Berkeley, CA: University of California Press.

Downes, D. (2001). The *macho* penal economy: Mass incarceration in the United States—A European perspective. *Punishment and Society, 3* (1), 61-80.

Drug War Chronicle. (2010, February 5). *Drug testing. Missouri Senate Committee passes bill to drug test welfare recipients,* No. 619.

Drug War Chronicle. (2009a, February 20). *Federal budget: Economic stimulus bill stimulates drug war, too,* No. 573.

Drug War Chronicle. (2009b, March 20). *Bills to require drug testing for welfare, unemployment pop up around the country,* No. 577.

Drug War Chronicle. (2009c, May 1). *Editorial: What's with all the good news lately?* No. 583.

Ehrenreich, B. (2009, August 9). Is it now a crime to be poor? *New York Times,* p. wk9.

Eisler, P. & Johnson, K. (2005, April 10). 10 years and $10B later, COPS drawing scrutiny. *USA Today.* Retrieved March 21, 2009, from http://www.usatoday.com/news/washington/2005-04-10-cops-cover_x.htm

Erikson, K. (1966). *Wayward Puritans: A study in the sociology of deviance.* New York, NY: John Wiley & Sons.

Fogelson, R. (1989). *America's armories: Architecture, society, and public order.* Cambridge, MA: Harvard University Press.

Garland, D. (2001). *The culture of control: Crime and social order in contemporary society.* Chicago, IL: University of Chicago Press.

Gillon, S. (2000). *That's not what we meant to do: Reform and Its unintended consequences in twentieth century America.* New York, NY: W.W. Norton & Co.

Gilmore, R. (2007). *Golden gulag: Prisons, surplus, crisis, and opposition in globalizing California.* Berkeley, CA: University of California Press.

Goldfield, M. (1989). Worker insurgency, radical organization, and new deal labor legislation. *American Political Science Review, 83*(4), 1257-1282.

Gonnerman, J. (2004, November 9). Million-dollar blocks. *Village Voice.*

Gorman, A. (2009, February 19). Latinos make up a growing bloc of federal offenders. *Los Angeles Times,* p. A10.

Gottfredson, S. & Taylor, R. (1987). Attitudes of correctional policymakers and the public. In S. Gottfredson & S. Mcconville (Eds.), *America's correctional crisis: Prison populations and public policy* (pp. 57-75). New York, NY: Greenwood Press.

Gottschalk, M. (2006). *The prison and the gallows: The politics of mass incarceration in America.* New York, NY: Cambridge University Press.

Gottschalk, M. (2009). City on a hill, city behind bars: Criminal justice, social justice, and American exceptionalism. *Nanzan Review of American Studies,* 31.

Gould, E., Weinberg, B., & Mustard, D. (2002). Crime rates and local labor market opportunities in the United States: 1979-1997. *The Review of Economics and Statistics, 84*(1), 45-61.

Gramlich, J. (2009a, February 11). *Stimulus prompts debate over police.* Stateline.org. Retrieved March 6, 2009, from http://www.stateline.org/live/details/story?contentId=375802

Gramlich, J. (2009b, August 11, updated 2009, August 14). *At least 26 states spend less on prisons.* Stateline.org. Retrieved October 16, 2009, from http://www.stateline.org/live/details/story?contentId=418338

Greene, J. & Mauer, M. (2010). *Downscaling prisons: Lessons from four states.* Washington, DC: The Sentencing Project.

Grob, G. (1994). *The mad among us: A history of the care of America's mentally ill.* New York, NY: The Free Press.

Harcourt, B. (2006). From the asylum to the prison: Rethinking the incarceration revolution. *Texas Law Review, 84*(7), 1751-1786.

Hastings, D. (2009, August 16). *Some states are charging inmates for prison stay.* Associated Press.

Herivel, T. (2007). Introduction. In T. Herivel & P. Wright (Eds.), *Prison profiteers: Who makes money from mass incarceration* (pp. ix-xviii). New York, NY: New Press.

Hoberock, B. (2010, April 16). State corrections officer staffing historically low. *Tulsa World.*

Hunt, D. (2008, September 22). Obama fields questions on Jacksonville crime. *Florida Times-Union.*

Hunter, G. (2010). Washington jail a modern-day debtor's prison. *Prison Legal News, 21*(4), 8-9.

Jacobson, M. (2005). *Downsizing prisons: How to reduce crime and end mass incarceration.* New York, NY: New York University Press.

JFA Institute. (2007). *Public safety, public spending: Forecasting America's prison population 2007-2011.* Philadelphia, PA: Public Safety Performance Project of the Pew Charitable Trusts.

Johnson, R., Kantor, S., & Fishback, P. (2007, January). *Striking at the roots of crime: The impact of social welfare spending on crime during the Great Depression.* Working Paper No. 12825. Washington, DC: National Bureau of Economic Research.

Justice Policy Institute. (2009). More of the same. Press release.

Keohane, J. (2010, February 14). Imaginary fiends: Crime in America keeps going down. Why does the public refuse to believe it? *Boston Globe.*

Keve, P. (1991). *Prisons and the American conscience: A history of U.S. federal corrections.* Carbondale and Edwardsville, IL: Southern Illinois University.

King, R. (2009). *The state of sentencing 2008: Developments in policy and practice.* Washington, DC: The Sentencing Project.

King, R. & Mauer, M. (2002, February). *State sentencing and corrections policy in an era of fiscal restraint.* Washington, DC: The Sentencing Project.

King, R., Mauer, M., & Huling, T. (2003, February). *Big prisons, small towns: Prison economics in rural America.* Washington, DC: The Sentencing Project.

Kolodner, M. (2006, July 19). Private prisons expect a boom: Immigration enforcement to benefit detention companies. *New York Times*, p. C1.

Koyanagi, C. (2007, August). *Learning from history: Deinstitutionalization of people with mental illness as precursor to long-term care reform.* Menlo Park, CA: The Henry J. Kaiser Family Foundation, Kaiser Commission on Medicaid and the Uninsured.

Kristof, N. (2009, August 19). Priority test: Health care or prison? *New York Times.*

Kurgan, L. (2009, March). Prison blocks: The toll of incarceration on one New Orleans neighborhood. *The Atlantic*, p. 70.

Langdon, J. (2009, July 13). Room scarce at jail. *Times Record News.*

Legislative Analyst's Office. (2008, September 28). Proposition 5: Nonviolent drug offenses. Sentencing. Parole and rehabilitation. Initiative statute. Sacramento, CA: Legislative Analyst's Office.

Leuchtenburg, W. (1963). *Franklin D. Roosevelt and the New Deal, 1932-1940.* New York, NY: Harper & Row.

Lewis, N. (2009, February 6). Recovery bill has $1 billion to hire more local police. *New York Times.*

Marelius, J. (2010, March 24). Poll: Voters political will flags on cuts. *San Diego Union-Tribune.*

Matravers, A. & Maruna, S. (2005). Modern penalty and ssychoanalysis. In M. Matravers (Ed.), *Managing modernity: Politics and the culture of control* (pp. 128-44). London: Routledge.

McKelvey, B. (1977). *American prisons: A history of good intentions.* Montclair, N.J.: Patterson Smith.

Moore, S. (2009a, September 1). California State Assembly approves prison legislation. *New York Times.*

Moore, S. (2009b, September 13). California passes bill addressing prisons." *New York Times.*

Mosher, C., Hooks, G., & Wood, P. (2007). Don't build it here: The hype versus the reality of prisons and local employment. In T. Herivel & P. Wright (Eds.), *Prison profiteers: Who makes money from mass incarceration* (pp. 90-97). New York, NY: The New Press.

Murakawa, N. (2005). *Electing to punish: Congress, race, and the American criminal justice state.* (Doctoral dissertation, Yale University). New Haven, CT: Yale University.

The National Law Center on Homelessness & Poverty and the National Coalition for the Homeless. (2009, July). *Homes not handcuffs: The criminalization of homelessness in U.S. cities.* Washington, DC: The National Law Center on Homelessness & Poverty.

New York Times. (1934, May 19). Roosevelt opens attack on crime, signing six bills as 'challenge.'

New York Times. (2008, October 10). Fiscal disaster in California. P. A32.

O'Reilly, K. (1982, December). A new deal for the F.B.I.: The Roosevelt Administration, crime control, and national security. *The Journal of American History, 69*(3), 438-68.

Page, J. (forthcoming 2011). *The toughest beat.* New York, NY: Oxford.

Pallasch, A. (2009, August 3). Prisons not the answer to crime problems: Attorney general. *Chicago Sun-Times.*

Pew Center on the States. (2010, March). *Prison count 2010.* Washington, DC: Pew Center on the States.

Pew Center on the States. (2009). *One in 31: The long reach of American corrections.* Washington, DC: Pew Center on the States.

Phucas, K. (2009, February 19). New state prison planned. *Times Herald.*

Pranis, K. (2007). Doing borrowed time: The high cost of backdoor prison finance. In T. Herivel & P. Wright (Eds.), *Prison profiteers: Who makes money from mass incarceration* (pp. 36-51). New York, NY: The New Press.

Prendergast, A. (2007, October). Fortress of solitude: The Bureau of Prisons Is as good at keeping prisoners in as it is at keeping reporters out. *Prison Legal News*, p. 27.

Prison Legal News. (2009, May 12-13). *Billionaire-funded California initiative triples lifer parole denial intervals, imposes restrictions on parole violators.*

Reiner, R. (2006). Beyond risk: A lament for Social Democratic criminology. In T. Newburn & P. Rock (Eds.), *The politics of crime control: Essays in honour of David Downes* (pp. 7-49). Oxford: Oxford University Press.

Reuters. (2009, January 4). *PA Gov. Rendell to legislature: End paroles for repeat violent offenders to keep communities safe.*

Reutter, D. (2009). Economic crisis prompts prison closures nationwide, but savings (and reforms) are elusive. *Prison Legal News, 20*(4), 1, 3-10.

Reutter, D. (2010a). Food problems contribute to riot at Kentucky prison. *Prison Legal News, 21*(4), 10-11.

Reutter, D. (2010b). Indian country gets sStimulus money...to build more jails. *Prison Legal News, 21*(4), 28.

Reutter, D., Hunter, G., & Sample, B. (2010). Appalling prison and jail food leaves prisoners hungry for justice. *Prison Legal News, 21*(4), 1-7.

Robinson, S. (2009, February 4). *Five big ideas we should be talking about.* OurFuture.org. Retrieved March 24, 2009, from http://www.ourfuture.org/blog-entry/2009020604/five-big-ideas-we-should-be-talking-about

Roosevelt, F. (1939, April 17). Address at the National Parole Conference. Washington, D.C. Accessible at The American Presidency Project, http://www.presidency.uscb.edu

(2007). The impact of economic conditions on robbery and property crime: The role of consumer sentiment. *Criminology, 45*(4), 735-69.

Rosenfeld, R., Fornango, R., & Messner, S. (2009). The crime drop in comparative perspective: The impact of the economy and imprisonment on American and European burglary rates. *The British Journal of Sociology, 60*(3), 445-71.

Rothfeld, M. (2009, September 1). California Assembly passes a slimmed-down prison measure. latimes.com. Retrieved September 9, 2009, from latimes.com/news/local/la-me-prisons1-2009sep01,0,2193725.story

Rothman, D. (1990). *The discovery of the asylum: Social order and disorder in the New Republic.* Boston, MA: Little, Brown, and Co.

Sample, B. (2009). Violence on the rise in BOP facilities. *Prison Legal News, 20*(8), 10-12.

Seaton, D. (2009, February 28). Stimulus money could save local prison. *Winfield Daily Courier.* http://realcostofprisons.org/blog/archives/2009/02/ks_stimulus_mon.html

Sokoloff, H. & Satullo, C. (2009, March 2). *The city budget: Tight times, tough choices.* Philadelphia, PA: Penn Project for Civic Engagement.

Spelman, W. (2009). Cash, crime, and limited options: Explaining the prison boom. *Criminology and Public Policy,* 8(1 April), 29-77.

Stimulus Watch. (n.d.). Retrieved March 24, 2009 from http://www.stimuluswatch.org/project/search/public+safety

Torrey, E. (1997). *Out of the shadows: Confronting America's mental illness crisis.* New York, NY: John Wiley & Sons, Inc.

U.S. Department of Justice, Bureau of Justice Statistics. (2008, December 18). Direct expenditures by criminal justice function, 1982-2006. Retrieved March 24, 2009, from http://www.ojp.usdoj.gov/bjs/glance/tables/exptyptab.htm

Venkatesh, S. (2009, March 29). Feeling too down to rise up. *New York Times.*

Walker, S. (1977). *A critical history of police reform.* Lexington, MA: Lexington Books.

Worrall, J. & Kovandzic, T. (2007). COPS grants and crime revisited. *Criminology, 45*(1), 159-90.

Weaver, V. (2006). Dark prison: Race, rights, and the politics of punishment. Presented at the 102nd Annual Meeting of the American Political Science Association, Philadelphia, PA.

Western, B. (2006). *Punishment and Inequality in America.* New York, NY: Russell Sage Foundation.

Woodiwiss, M. (1988). *Crime, crusades, and corruption: Prohibition in the United States, 1900-1987.* Totowa, N.J.: Barnes and Noble.

ENDNOTES

[1] Calculated from Dow (2004) and Kolodner (2006).

[2] Some of these bills try to circumvent constitutional obstacles to mandatory drug testing by limiting it to instances when caseworkers have "a reasonable suspicion" that someone is using drugs (*Drug War Chronicle,* 2010).

[3] In a thoroughly mixed result, voters also overwhelmingly rejected Proposition 6, which would have increased spending on law enforcement, ratcheted up the penalties for "gang-related" activities, and toughened up the criminal justice system in dozens of other ways (*New York Times,* 2008).

[4] For a development of this point, see Gottschalk (2009).

MASS INCARCERATION AND THE GREAT RECESSION: A COMMENT ON GOTTSCHALK

JONATHAN SIMON

More than a decade ago, the late Stuart Scheingold (1998) called for a new "political criminology" to confront the growth of what was not yet called mass incarceration. For Scheingold this new political criminology had to meet three criteria. First, it had to be grounded in a concern with street crime. For many, a political criminology should critique the popular obsession with street crime and instead educate the public as to the far more consequential crimes of business and political elites. But Scheingold recognized that, whatever its empirical distortions, the public concern with street crime was rooted deeply in American culture and powerfully shaped American politics. Treating it as a case of "false consciousness" would not do. Second, it had to be political in the sense of concerned with crime control strategies as both a reflection of and a determinate of the distribution of power in the polity. That is, it could not take crime control strategies as the given products of a democratic process of policy formation.

Third, it had to be post-liberal (he actually used the term postmodern as well, but I'll focus on the liberal bit), by which he meant anchored in a "disillusionment" with the liberal state. Disillusionment means not a disaffection or desertion (Scheingold remained a liberal in both the 19th and 20th century senses to the end of his life), but a recognition of the limits of liberalism. Most importantly this third point was a call for criminology to recognize its important role in the project of liberalism, a role that goes back to the very founding of scientific criminology. Cesare Lombroso had conceived of the project of criminology as a necessary bridge between the legal fiction of the equality of all citizens (central to the liberal state in the 1860s as much as the 1960s), and the reality of tremendous variegation in natural and social attributes of the actual population. Without abandoning this historic mission to diagnose and address the causes of crime in free societies, the new political criminology must also confront the excesses of crime control that inhere in the very nature of the liberal state.

With this Presidential Session of the American Society of Criminology, and Marie Gottschalk's lecture (and larger work, Gottschalk 2006), I think we can say with confidence that Scheingold's call has been heard. While nothing can compensate us for the loss of Stuart Scheingold—who died this June after a lifetime of contributions to political science, socio-legal studies, and criminology—this is a moment to pause and recognize how much has changed about the political awareness of American criminology, as well as to reflect on how much remains to be done if we are to disable mass incarceration and begin to remediate the tremendous damage it has done to American society and democracy.

In this light, I take Gottschalk's lecture to be a sober assessment of where we stand in that project; as she puts it, at the "end of the beginning." While there are those in this Society and indeed high up in the ministries of government criminology who would continue to reject political criminology (and indeed the very concept of mass incarceration) as inherently unscientific, we no longer need to argue seriously that mass incarceration is a social problem at least as serious as street crime itself. But establishing mass incarceration as a social problem does not mean that it is on the endangered species list (after all street crime has been a class A social problem for more than a century).

Gottschalk draws on American history and institutions, especially the lessons of the Great Depression of the 1930s, to highlight just how difficult it may be for the current economic crises to produce a sustained downturn in the practices of imprisonment. Overall, I agree with Gottschalk's sober assessment, and her main point that the Great Recession will not reverse mass incarceration by itself. We would do well to follow her advice and not trade in our only recently abandoned criminological positivism, for an equally illusory budgetary positivism. If we start where Scheingold did, with the cultural hold of street crime in the American risk imaginary, it is clear that cost alone will not compel Americans or their elected official to rethink the rituals of security to which they have become habituated. Yet, it is to that imaginary, and its relationship to the economy that we must turn if we are to make the most of the current moment. Toward that end, I will offer three reasons why, not withstanding Gottschalk's lessons, I believe the Great Recession is an opportunity of considerable importance.

BEEN THERE, DONE THAT

As Gottschalk discusses in great detail in her book (2006), the Great Depression produced more than the revolution in political-economy we call the New Deal, it also produced a vigorous federal "war on crime," one whose consequences for American institutions and society were profound and which pales only in comparison with the second "war on crime," whose consequences we are now trying to unwind. From the start, under the leadership of Attorney General Homer Cummings (our first crime-centered Attorney General), the Roosevelt administration took unprecedented steps to increase the visibility and power of federal law enforcement.

As Gottschalk notes in her lecture, a major White House conference on crime in 1934 showcased FBI Director J. Edgar Hoover, and laid out a wide agenda for national action against crime. Eventually the urgency and political success of the New Deal economic program largely eclipsed this embryonic war on crime (which remained heavily focused on a limited number of notorious bank robbers), but had the Supreme Court continued to obstruct FDR's economic program and political success failed to materialize, it is not hard to imagine a Roosevelt 2nd term dominated by efforts to demonize a wider class of criminals (or even worst an effort to supplant FDR with Hoover himself).[1]

The major reason why the Great Recession, whatever the success of President Obama's current economic policies, is unlikely to produce a new "war on crime," is that we already have one, albeit somewhat recast as a "war on terror," that has been going on nearly 40 years now (Simon, 2007). While the 1920s saw some expansion of crime control in response to the high homicide rate unleashed by Prohibition, the space for a war on crime, especially at the national level, remained largely unoccupied.[2] Given the continuing scale and visibility of our current war on crime/terror, it is hard to imagine that declaring a major effort to ramp up the effort against crime/drugs/terror would provide a significant advantage to any particular politician today (one that would not be quickly checked by comparable stances among a well prepared generation of politician crime fighters). That is not to say that politicians will not continue to swear fealty to that war (as Obama has done repeatedly) or that a new front in the war, like an active intervention against Mexican drug cartels, is unimaginable; only that it is likely to be marginal and episodic.

THE CRIME DECLINE

The second reason for my cautious optimism is the crime decline of the 1990s, especially the steep drops in homicides, has by and large not been reversed, and in some areas is continuing (Zimring, 2007). The two previous wars on crime, 1933-1941, and 1968-2001, were preceded by dramatic increases in homicides. One need not believe that periods of increased punitiveness are simply a rational response to the increased risk of homicide to believe that homicide increases provide a crucial precondition for an escalation in crime control policies. Almost invariably, real risks of homicide vary more between groups of people than they do over time. The crime decline in New York, for example, has probably changed the odds of being murdered on the Upper West Side only very marginally. Yet, homicide has a capacity to influence the risk imaginary far beyond its actuarial significance (especially given the media's historic embrace of homicide as news). America is not the only nation to experience serious problems with homicide, but our culture, with its intense emphasis on life as an individual opportunity for consumption and pleasure, seems to isolate homicide (a "game over" event when it comes to consumption and earthly pleasure) as a unique and defining risk which demands priority and defies rational cost/benefit assessment (Simon, forthcoming).

Based on the two previous crime wars, we can identify several interacting factors that seem to be crucial to activating support for intensive governmental responses like mass incarceration.

First, a surge in homicides helps define the present as a time of lawlessness and violence regardless of who the actual victims are. Second, even a few atypical killings, where the victims fall outside the normal range of expected victims, helps to define homicide as a risk to everyone (even if actuarial odds have not changed to a calculable degree). In the 1960s and 1970s, serial killers like the Manson family, helped define homicide as a risk that could show up on anyone's doorstep, without warning or some risky lifestyle choice. Finally, even drops in homicide may not reverse this logic, unless they are sustained and dramatic. A dropping homicide rate may indicate to observers that tough crime control measures are working, not that the basic threat is gone. Only a widespread drop in homicide that clearly goes beyond any particular policies, and seems to indicate a basic change in underlying social behavior, can hope to undermine support for a war on crime.

The crime decline that has occurred since 1994 meets these final criteria. The drop has been dramatic, sustained, and has occurred all over the country. While some policy choices, especially New York City's emphasis on tying police deployments to crime mapping patterns, may in fact deserve credit for deeper than average declines, the very fact that significant drops have occurred across the country, regardless of which policies have been favored, has helped redefine the risk imaginary of the present. That does not mean that atrocious murders will not happen or that when they do, politicians will not use them to declare the public at risk.[3] But what a decline in homicide can do is make room for other risks. So long as people see homicide as a real threat, larger scale systemic risks like global warming or the failure of our underinvested infrastructure to protect us in the face of predictable threats like earthquakes and hurricanes, are unlikely to expand their hold in our risk imaginary.

HOUSING AND THE AMERICAN RISK IMAGINARY

In recent work (Simon, forthcoming) I have been exploring the changes in American society that made the second war on crime so much bigger and more consequential than the first. As has been noted, Americans witnessed homicide increases in the 1920s that were even more dramatic than those of the 1960s or 1980s, but the resulting war on crime was shallower and shorter. There are many institutional reasons for this (see Gottschalk, 2006) including the scope of federal power and state capacity, but I also believe that molecular changes in American families and communities contributed to this by making Americans more sensitive to crime and more prone to being governed through crime. As David Garland (2001) argued in *The Culture of Control*, the rise of the suburbs and the increased role of women in the labor market, made American communities seem more vulnerable to crime. Related to both these trends (suburbanization and women's labor) was the spectacular rise of home ownership in America. By the 1950 census, slightly more than half of all American dwelling units were owned by their residents. By 1980 more than 60 percent were owned, a number that surged to close to 70 percent with the housing boom of the 1990s and 2000s.

While renters and homeowners may be equally vulnerable to being the victim of a crime (once we control for other socioeconomic correlates of both ownership and crime victimization), homeowners are uniquely vulnerable to loss of their equity through fear-induced declines in the prices that buyers are willing to pay for their homes. While many kinds of fear can reduce prices (pollution sent the value of homes near Love Canal, New York, to near zero in the 1970s after it became publicized, forcing a government buy-out), crime has been one of the most powerful and feared drivers of housing value declines in recent decades.

This alone means that, all other things being equal, homeowners are likely to be more sensitive to crime threats, and more ready to demand protective action from government, than comparably based renters. However, built into this relationship is an escalating logic. Once this crime-price equation is well known (and it was a highly publicized feature of the first wave of suburbanization in the 1960s as urban home prices dropped rapidly in response to perceived crime threats) security becomes a "built-in" feature of home building and marketing. This logic helps to explain a number of distinctive features of the American housing pattern including the relentless quest to build on the edges of the metropolitan areas (farm fields are rarely linked to crime fear) and the rise of the ubiquitous gated community. But as the home becomes marketed in part as a security product, it becomes ever more sensitive to information that would undercut that security. It need not be a real crime, the simple appearance of graffiti, or the threat of a bus line being extended to the subdivision, may be enough to raise the shadow of fear based price declines. Thus, over time, all other things being equal, homeowners should become more and more sensitive to crime.

Finally, for homeowners in the "hot" housing markets of the sunbelt (where the housing bubble reached its most dizzying heights in the middle of this decade), states like California, Florida, Arizona, and Nevada, the dramatic increases in homeowner equity began to reshape the very way Americans understood their economic security as the home became a source of wealth even without selling through the rise of the home-equity loan industry. For some Americans, their home may have effectively replaced their job as the source of their sense of economic security (of course this is a very dangerous illusion since once you lose your job it may be impossible to hold onto your home).

My hypothesis is that these changes in American housing tenure made Americans more sensitive to crime and more prone to being governed through crime, including mass incarceration. At this social and cultural level, even marginal shifts in degree of sensitivity may yield dramatic results at the political and institutional level (at least once politicians figure it out). Putting my last two points together we can see how the homicide waves of the 1960s and 1980s would have found and activated a far more crime sensitive American public than that of the 1920s.

It is in light of this potential relationship that the current Great Recession may mark an important turning point. Far more than past recessions, the current crisis has emerged from and devastated the housing market. The very areas of the country that experienced the apparent miracle of housing-based wealth over the past two decades, now find themselves reeling with foreclosures and homes priced at as little as half of their bubble peak price. It may be that this will only be a temporary halt to the relentless growth in the scale of homeownership and the prices of homes, in which case we can expect this housing based recession to produce only a short term break in the crime sensitivity (or no break at all). However, if combined with new restrictions on lending, and market pressures in favor of renting (primarily job mobility which makes homeownership an increasingly problematic choice for young families) it could mark a more profound shift away from the pattern of crime sensitivity that we have observed since the 1950s. Combined with the decline in homicides, this re-spatializing of the American risk imaginary could produce a public more sensitive to other kinds of risk (especially risk to the environment and to employment) and far less ready to support mass incarceration.

Asylums

The dramatic decarceration of American asylums during the period 1960-1980 offers important lessons for understanding mass incarceration (see, Caplow & Simon, 1999) and Marie Gottschalk has turned to it in just the right way. It is tempting to view that decarceration and prison mass incarceration as two parts of one process, with asylums closing and prisons opening to contain the same population; but there are good reasons to doubt that anything a simple as such a transfer has taken place.[4] What asylum decarceration reveals is how complex and multifaceted are the causes of any profound change in the shape of custodial institutions. The circumstances that permitted politicians of the left and right to agree on a major reform of the laws governing asylums in the 1960s and 1970s, were so unique it is difficult to imagine them ever repeating themselves. Still, the model is a useful one in suggesting on how many fronts we need to proceed if we are to reverse mass incarceration including: reforming laws, closing institutions, recruiting political allies on the right and left, and seeking new futures for professions sustained by mass incarceration (like correctional officers).

To just take up the first one, the great asylum decarceration was facilitated (and any reversal blocked) by changes in state law that made it much more difficult for a court to involuntarily commit someone. Up through the 1960s, a court could authorize the involuntary commitment of a person to an asylum based on little more than the testimony of one or sometimes two doctors that the person suffered from a mental illness and could benefit from treatment in an asylum. After 1970, most state laws required that a court also find that the person posed an imminent threat of physical harm to self or others.[5] This imminent harm standard is generally tied to tight time periods that require a court to revisit the harm question repeatedly and with fresh evidence. These time standards make it very hard to sustain the warehousing of someone who is not showing evidence of violent potential.

We need to consider building risk-based standards into state prison sentences that prevent warehousing offenders years after there has ceased to be any evidence that they pose a serious risk of violence. This is especially true of sentences for violent crime, which through a variety of laws that enhance penalties for weapons use, or repeated felonies, can produce what amount to "death in prison" sentences. In many states life sentences for murder which were intended to result in parole for those with good records after as little as 15 years, have become permanent imprisonment sentences because of political fear of parole. We need legal reform that demands repeated risk assessment based on fresh evidence. In California, courts are finally beginning to overturn parole rejection decisions when they are based on no new evidence beyond the original crime of commitment.[6] After several decades of increasingly tough parole policies, the public may also be ready for a more risk-based approach.

CONCLUSION

I agree with Marie Gottschalk that the fiscal pressures produced by our current economic crisis are unlikely by themselves to undermine the political and social logics that have supported mass incarceration so powerfully over the last four decades. Those of us engaged in trying to lead our fellow citizens away from these policies are well-advised not to pretend that it is simply an objective question of budget logic. Fear drives these policies, and fears rooted in culture are not terribly elastic with regard to price pressures. However, a number of features of our present conjuncture, including the proximity of our most recent crime war, the significant and sustained drop in homicides, and the weakening of housing market, all suggest that this is a good time to contest mass incarceration where it lives, in America's risk imaginary.

References

Caplow, T. & Simon, J. (1999). Understanding prison policy and population trends, *Crime and Justice, 26*, 66-103.

Garland, D. (2001). *The culture of control: Crime and social order in contemporary society*. Chicago, IL: University of Chicago Press.

Gottschalk, M. (2006). *The prison and the gallows: The politics of mass incarceration in America*. New York, NY: Cambridge University Press.

Lagos, M. (2010, April 13). Bill would increase sex crime penalties. *San Francisco Chronicle*, p. A1. Retrieved August 3, 2010, from http://www.sfgate.com/cgi-bin/article.cgi?f=/c/a/2010/04/13/MNVE1CTHUB.DTL

Roth, P. (2004). *The plot against America*. New York, NY: Houghton, Mifflin, Harcourt.

Scheingold, S. (1998). Constructing the new political criminology: Power, authority, and the post liberal state. *Law & Social Inquiry, 23*, 857-895.

Simon, J. (2007). *Governing through crime: How the war on crime transformed American society and created a culture of fear*. New York, NY: Oxford University Press.

Simon, J. (forthcoming 2010). Consuming obsessions: Housing, homicide, and mass incarceration since the 1950s. *University of Chicago Legal Forum*.

Zimring, F. (2007). *The great American crime decline*. New York, NY: Oxford University Press.

Endnotes

[1] Philip Roth's remarkable novel, *The Plot Against America* (2004) imagines a somewhat different counter-history with populist hero, and Nazi sympathizer, Charles Lindberg defeating Roosevelt in the 1940 election. Ironically, as Gottschalk pointed out, the kidnapping and murder of Lindberg's infant son just before the 1932 election provided some of the elements for a national moral panic about crime which Roosevelt seized upon.

[2] As Gottschalk notes, President Herbert Hoover, an engineer much enamored of statistics, was quite cautious in pursuing major changes in the national approach to crime control, preferring to launch a major national commission to study the issue instead.

[3] The speed of the politicization cycle was demonstrated recently in California where in February 2010, 19-year-old Chelsea King was murdered by a sex offender on parole and by April 2010, a law bearing her name was already making its way through the legislature (see Lagos, 2010).

[4] The demography does not fit. The asylum population in the 1950s was disproportionately older, white, and female, while prison population today is disproportionately younger, non-white, and male. This is not to say that had the asylum system survived it might not have found a way to claim this younger, non-white, male population.

[5] In several cases in the 1970s, the Supreme Court seemed to endorse this standard, see, for example, O'Connor v. Donaldson, 422 U.S. 563 (1973), but a careful reading of these cases suggests that "imminent harm to self or others" is not a constitutional requirement, at least where the asylum offers treatment.

[6] See In re Lawrence, 44 Cal. 4th 1181 (Cal. 2008).